T0299316

Continuous Delivery 2.0

Continuous Delivery 2.0

Business-leading DevOps Essentials

Qiao Liang

CRC Press
Taylor & Francis Group
Boca Raton London New York

CRC Press is an imprint of the
Taylor & Francis Group, an **informa** business

First edition published 2022
by CRC Press
6000 Broken Sound Parkway NW, Suite 300, Boca Raton, FL 33487-2742

and by CRC Press
2 Park Square, Milton Park, Abingdon, Oxon, OX14 4RN.

Published with arrangement with the original publisher, Posts & Telecom Press.

ISBN: 9780367490478 (hbk)
ISBN: 9781032117997 (pbk)
ISBN: 9781003221579 (ebk)

DOI: 10.1201/9781003221579

Typeset in Times LT Std
by KnowledgeWorks Global Ltd.

Contents

Foreword

Since the term "software engineering" was coined, "quality" and "efficiency" have been its goals. Most information technology (IT) institutions have been making explorations along this path, they first came up with the waterfall model and then Capability Maturity Model Integration (CMMI) which has been worshiped as the "Bible" by many IT groups. When the "agile movement" arose, they decided to "do" Agile; when they heard about "Continuous Delivery", they changed their mind to "do" Continuous Delivery. Now DevOps has come out and swept around the IT industry, becoming topic of salons and conferences and even hit the headline of various media. Not surprisingly, many companies cast their eyes at DevOps...

Of course, there are successful "stories", but they seem to have nothing to do with us. Even the people by our side cannot agree on these ideas or practices. It is so perplexing, just like walking in a fog, we can hear beautiful sound around us and lights flickering in the distance, but we cannot see clearly the road beneath our feet.

Years of working experience has enabled me to have a new understanding of this field, and summarize and reflect on it. "Continuous Delivery" sounds attractive and catches people's imagination. Business people seem to see a glimmer of hope that "all the requirements presented in the morning can be developed in the afternoon". Yet too many companies underestimate the difficulties they face. Some of these difficulties are explicit: no automation test or automation deployment, let alone Trunk-based Development. Some difficulties are implicit, such as the long-standing "wall" between functional departments. Business people are unhappy about developers' slow delivery, while developers are complaining about the unreliable requirements presented by business people. This is probably due to their different modes of value thinking.

The goal of this book is to help all roles in a company change their way of value thinking, improve the end-to-end business value delivery in software services, raise the teamwork efficiency, so as to achieve fast verification in a safe and reliable way, and shorten the time to realize genuine business value. In other words, the book not only elaborates on the process "from product backlog to workable software", but also proposes a double closed loop as "value discovery-fast verification" (see Figure 0.1), which implies the origin of "Continuous Delivery 2.0" – title of this book.

As it turns out, there is no one-size-fits-all business management solution that will be perfect for every business problem. However, only when managers start from the overall perspective and resist the

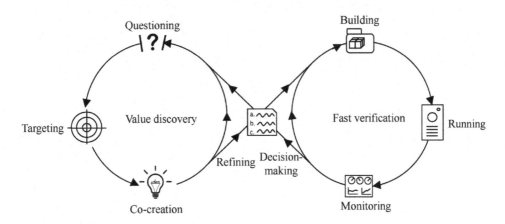

FIGURE 0.1 Double-flywheels of Continuous Delivery.

temptation of local optimization can they lead their companies to create greater value despite of limited resources. The book provides an overall framework, showing the principles and practices involved in each node of the framework, as well as their strengths and constraints.

If you apply the Double-flywheels of Continuous Delivery 2.0 across a company, it is an organizational transformation at the enterprise level. If you introduce it to a team, it will be path for it to improve it work mode. Since Continuous Delivery 2.0 is a management framework, companies are bound to tailor it to their own circumstances. For this reason, the book contains many practical examples showing how other businesses or teams achieved their goals by implementing these practices. These cases also show that solutions and implementation paths are unlikely to be replicated between companies, so they must follow the principles in the book in combination with their specific situations (product forms, stage of business competition, size of team, personnel skills, software system architecture, as well as corporate management mechanism and culture), and explore their own path step by step.

Target Readers

The book is intended for front-line managers of IT corporations or key technicians who are about to become front-line managers, as well as those who are dedicated to software project management and software process improvement. It is also valuable for founders of startups or technology executives in fast-growing companies. It is not available for the senior managers of large and sophisticated software companies. Of course, I'd be happy if they could take an interest in this book.

For product owners, development managers, test managers, and operations managers, this book will give them a more comprehensive perspective on how to work, discover more information beyond of their scope of work, and learn how to collaborate with other roles.

For process improvers or change makers, they can learn from successes or failures from other teams or companies in the real cases discussed in this book.

For founders of startups and executives of fast-growing companies, I hope they could find some effective ways to manage and expand their businesses from the beginning at the lowest possible cost.

The real cases listed in the book will help readers fully understand the double-flywheels of Continuous Delivery 2.0 and all necessary practices at each stage.

Content

Before getting into the main content of this book, let's talk about the structure of this book. It consists of three parts: Part 1 introduces the double-flywheels of Continuous Delivery 2.0. Part 2 focuses on the issues you may encounter while using the Continuous Delivery 2.0 framework and the principles you need to follow for making improvement. Part 3 shares typical cases about certain companies and teams for readers to learn about varied implementation priorities and solutions. The content of this book is briefly introduced as follows:

Part 1 describes the double-flywheels of Continuous Delivery 2.0 and the four working principles of Continuous Delivery 2.0. It also introduces the implementation steps and related principles of the two closed loops as Value Discovery Loop and Fast Verification Loop.

- Chapter 1 explains the inevitability of Continuous Delivery, and introduces the "Double-flywheels of Continuous Delivery 2.0" and its four basic principles.
- Chapter 2 lists the four key steps of the Value Discovery Loop ("Discovery Loop" for short), as well as the guiding principles and practices at each step. Continuous Delivery will be more powerful if business problems could be subject to "lean" thinking; otherwise, it is likely to retreat into the single-loop Continuous Delivery 1.0 with only the "Fast Verification loop".
- Chapter 3 briefly describes the main activities and working methods at each link in the Fast Verification loop ("Verification Loop" for short).

Part 2 expounds the working principles and implementation methods of the three plates in Continuous Delivery 2.0 Tangram. These three plates are made up of organizational mechanism, software architecture, and infrastructure. Since organizational mechanism is a complex subject, this book only discusses the culture needed for Continuous Delivery and the four steps in creating such culture. Such contents as organizational structure, talent structure, and incentive mechanism are about to be analyzed in the sequel of this book. Infrastructure is the most fundamental part in the product development process. Part 2 first introduces the deployment pipeline and tool design principles in Continuous Delivery, and then highlights the five areas for constructing and optimizing the deployment pipeline, that is, business requirements management, branch and configuration management, build and environment management, automation test management, and deployment and monitoring management.

- Chapter 4 argues that the improvement of Continuous Delivery capability requires an organizational culture which is safe, credible, and constantly improvable; and introduces the four steps implemented by Toyota and Google to improve organizational culture.
- Chapter 5 talks about the importance of software architecture in achieving fast verification of Continuous Delivery, the characteristics of software architecture favorable for Continuous Delivery, and three ways of software architecture transformation, namely, "demolition", "strangling", and "decoration".
- Chapter 6 explains how to use constraint theory and lean thinking to find bottlenecks in the process, make team members smoothly collaborate in handling business requirements, and increase the flow of requirements.
- Chapter 7 introduces the design principles and toolchain construction drafts for the deployment pipeline that Fast Verification Loop relies on.

- Chapter 8 discusses the significant impact of branch strategy of codebase on Continuous Delivery and how to implement deployment pipelines in different branching approaches. And finally, you will see how the number of code branches affects the release strategy.
- Chapter 9 reviews the history of continuous integration, explains how to determine if a team is practicing continuous integration, and presents five steps for a company to implement continuous integration.
- Chapter 10 discusses the factors to be considered for developing an automation test strategy prior to software release, and describes the requirements for writing and running automation testcases in continuous integration. Finally, it teaches the team how to write and add automation testcases for legacy systems in order to improve the return on investment (ROI) of automation test.
- Chapter 11 focuses on software configuration management, which is the foundation for the Fast Verification Ring in Continuous Delivery. To do a good job in the configuration management of code, configuration items, environment, and data, and finally realize one-click deployment and one-click testing, so that all stages in the collaboration process are fully automation and free from affecting each other. In this way, each role is able to more valuable things, and let machine do what it is good at – constant repetition.
- Chapter 12 introduces the techniques and approaches for reducing the risks in production deployment and release.
- Chapter 13 describes the importance of data collection and analysis while software is running, as well as metrics to measure data monitoring, including correctness, completeness, and timeliness of data. This chapter also introduces the test flattening trend, quality inspections, and drills in production environment.

Part 3 introduces and analyzes typical cases to readers. They occurred in companies of different types or teams of different sizes, with software products carrying varied features. All of these cases were of my personal experience. Their background, difficulties, and solutions are introduced in detail to inspire readers.

- Chapter 14 introduces a case happened in an Internet product team made up of 100 engineers. This team spent a year in building the fast-running double-flywheels of Continuous Delivery 2.0, and managed to have it operated continuously.
- Chapter 15 describes how a small team working on a large project transformed the teamwork model from "Death March" to "zero-defect delivery" under the condition of impossible "shift-right testing".
- Chapter 16 shows how a microservice-oriented team transformed into a "DevOps team" in the process of project implementation by gradually transforming infrastructure modules, improving quality and frequency of delivery, and motivating operations staff to make changes as well.

How to Read This book?

How to read this book? It depends on what do you want to get from this book. You can read it through to learn all the knowledge applicable to my work, the reason why Continuous Delivery 2.0 is an organizational capability, how to measure this capability, and how to apply principles in real scenarios to solve specific problems.

Of course, you can read any chapter as you like to learn to improve your work. Chapters 14~16 enumerate some cases happened in small and large teams, as well as in a large corporation, introducing their work methods and improvement tools in detail. You may get enlightened to find a way out of a stalemate.

Anyway, I appreciate for your feedback on this book. How do you like it? What else do you want to know? Do you have any suggestions? You can scan the QR code below, subscribe the WeChat official account of *Continuous Delivery 2.0*, or visit http://www.continuousdelivery20.com/ for extended reading.

How to Read This book?

Preface 1

I first met Qiao Liang in Beijing in 2007 when we worked together on go.cd, the first CI/CD tool to support deployment pipelines. What we learned from building that product was crucial to the development of the material in the Continuous Delivery book.

Over the last ten years, these ideas have gone from being bleeding edge to accepted wisdom. Every serious tech company aspires to the idea of being able to release at any time, on demand, without workers having to spend evenings or weekends doing deployments. Being able to release software quickly, frequently, and safely in turn enables delivering in small batches, which means we can get fast feedback on our ideas. We can build prototypes and test them with real users, and avoid building features that deliver no value to users. This, in turn, means better products, happier customers, and happier employees. These capabilities are important for every organization that uses technology.

But it's hard to get there. Organizations need to evolve an architecture that supports fast, effective testing and rapid deployment, and deploy a culture of experimentation. The cultural element is essential both for successful implementation, and to put in place the product management practices enabled by Continuous Delivery.

Qiao Liang has worked with all kinds of organizations in China to help them implement Continuous Delivery and realize its benefits. I can't think of anybody better to write a book on how to implement these ideas based on real-life experiences. I wish you every success as you experiment with getting better at software delivery, and using that capability to build better products and services and happier, more productive teams.

Jez Humble
Author of Continuous Delivery, co-founder and CTO of DORA

Preface 2

We are in the second half of the mobile Internet era. This means that, for the mainstream population, the basic needs of the head may have been met or "saturated", and the future direction may be the subversion of the existing model, or the full satisfaction of the long-tail personalized needs, or better serving the needs of China's ethnically diverse communities. In any case, I believe there is a good chance that the cost of innovation and the likelihood of failed innovation will continue to rise in the future.

In this context, it becomes particularly important to find new opportunities quickly and reduce innovation costs through extreme product development and operation efficiency. Mr. Qiao Liang is a master in the field of software engineering. As an agile consultant of Tencent, he has worked with us for years and experienced the whole process of the development of mobile Internet. Mr. Qiao has a thorough understanding of various problems in the product development and operation system, and he is tireless in the pursuit of efficiency.

"In this rapidly changing Internet environment, how can software development teams balance quality with speed? How to deliver software to users as quickly as possible so as to get their fastest feedback?" Mr. Qiao and I had an in-depth discussion on these issues many years ago. "There is no balance between quality and speed. Only product quality is ensured to certain extent, the pursuit of delivery speed is meaningful", said Mr. Qiao sharply. Unlike most consultants who like to say "It depends", Mr. Qiao pointed out an immutable law throughout the product life cycle. Although different product stages have different requirements for product quality, such requirements are almost constant at the same stage. "How to deliver product value quickly while meeting quality requirements?" The contents of this book are mainly unfolded to answer this question.

In order to quickly identify new opportunities, the product iteration must be accelerated, but it may increase the fixed costs in each iteration, such as the cost for product quality test and for product release. This transactional cost greatly hinders the iteration rate of product. In this book, Mr. Qiao breaks downs the steps for operating the Value Discovery Loop and Fast Verification Loop in Continuous Delivery. On the one hand, it brings you new dimensions and perspectives to probe into business problems; and on the other hand, it enlightens you to pay attention to the details in daily work to seek for optimization, which helps to reduce the fixed costs in iteration and innovate products more efficiently. At the same time, you will learn how to enhance the overall combat capability of your team.

This book *Continuous Delivery 2.0* exhibits the theoretical framework summed up by Mr. Qiao from a large number of practical projects; it is theoretical achievement based on solid realistic foundation. Instead of piling up empty theories, this book introduces plenty of positive and negative examples to support the principles and methodologies in software industry. This book is a pragmatic guide, just like its author who is a low-profile and down-to-earth person. It is especially recommended to the readers, either researchers in software industry or practitioners dedicated to R&D of operation system with efficient software applications. As I believe, in Internet industry, efficiency is the key to success in the future.

Zeng Yu
Vice President of Tencent

Acknowledgement

The publication of this book is attributed to many people's hard work. First of all, I'd like to thank the editorial team for their strong support, particularly Yang Hailing, Chief Editor of Posts & Telecom Press. Thanks to her encouragement, I finally got up the courage to write down my consulting practices and experiences in software development to share with more people. Though this book is not perfect, it's a retrospect of my years' endeavor and a summary of industrial achievements, including theories, methods, and practical tools. Second, I'll thank my friend Ren Fake for his proofreading of many chapters of this book and for his valuable suggestions. Thirdly, I'd like to thank CRC Press for publishing the English version.

Of course, I'm grateful to my former colleagues at ThoughtWorks, especially the GoCD team and my partner Jez Humble. I learned agile development and lean thinking from them. It was this work experience that made me proficient in Continuous Delivery practices, thereby guiding my clients solve practical problems in recent years. Wang Pengchao, another friend of mine, ushered me into the wonderland of Extreme Programming. He is now working in Facebook responsible for the development of Cassandra.

Finally, I must thank my wife and my son – the loves of my life. I once intended to giving up writing this book, it was their encouragement and accompany that helped me regain confidence. My wife is the first reader of this book, she helped me streamline and refine the language, and made the book in a more reasonable layout.

Author's Note

In 2002, I happened to get the book *Extreme Programming Explained: Embrace Change* written by Kent Beck, and couldn't help reading it through. The software development methods introduced in the book are utterly different from those in our actual work. The practices, such as test-driven development (TDD), continuous integration, pair programming, and user story, seem novel and unrealistic. I kept wondering how can a team do all of these things? So I tried some of them, but not thorough enough since I was still a little "skeptical". For example, I skipped over TDD, and only added some unit tests; I left out pair programming, but insisted on code review; and I preferred daily build to continuous integration. Certain effects started to show after a period of time, but not so significant.

Until 2005, a friend of mine showed me how did his team deliver a software project with the agile development method and how did they write code. Each time the code was modified, a series of automation testcases were written and executed; each submission was accompanied with continuous integration. It was a brand-new coding experience to me: developers rarely need to start the program, but detect the problems in the code through single-step debugging. I finally came to believe agile teams at not fictitious, they are real and not far away from me.

I joined ThoughtWorks in 2007, hoping to experience the agile development method. As a requirements analyst and delivery manager, I took part in the development of GoCD – an advanced CI and release management system. My partner was Jez Humble, product owner of this project and later co-author of the book *Continuous Delivery: Reliable Software Releases through Build, Test, and Deployment Automation*. Many practices described in his book come from our GoCD development process. From bringing forth the product idea to its official launch, I went through a complete product development process where I got access to the agile development method and learned how to do Continuous Delivery.

After 2009, as an external consultant or internal coach, I started to provide consultations on transition to Agile Development and Lean Production to domestic and foreign companies. Among my clients, there are leading PC Internet companies, traditional IT firms, powerful domestic corporations, and fast-growing mobile Internet startups. In the process of working with my clients, I've gained an in-depth understanding of "Continuous Delivery" and greater confidence in helping them realize the value of Continuous Delivery.

Back to 2007, I was believing that many agile development practices including Extreme Programming (XP) were a magic key for fast and high-quality software delivery. After 2010, I came to realize that although practice itself is important, it must be supported by organizational management, and work ideas and concepts. So I got a new pet phrase as "Don't talk about 'Agile', just solve problems!". After 2012, more software development methods and agile genres began to prevail in China, but the core concepts and main working principles behind them have not fundamentally changed. Regardless of the method, we should start from "solving problems", and an important prerequisite for doing so is to "correctly define problems and reach a consensus".

I'm certainly not a supporter of such absurd argument as "thought is useless". On the contrary, I believe that thought is essential to everyone's cognition and understanding of things. But years' consulting experiences tell me that a correct understanding of things cannot ensure implementation of correct ideas and concepts, nor can it provide direct and substantial assistance to companies. The goal of promoting correct thoughts is to guide project teams or their customers to address difficult problems.

Just like business management, the development process of software engineering is also a process where various methodologies emerge and develop endlessly. After the term "software engineering" was coined in the 1960s and the waterfall software development model was proposed in the 1970s, the iterative incremental development came out in 1985, Barry Boehm brought forth the Fountain Model in article *A Spiral Model of Software Development and Enhancement* published in 1986, the Capability Maturity Model Integration (CMMI) and various lightweight software development methods emerged in the 1990s, the Agile Manifesto was officially released in the early 21st century, and then Lean software development method, Kanban method, Continuous Delivery, and the DevOps movement sprang up successively in recent years. All these changes not only reflect the rapid evolution in IT industry but also prove that no single theory or method can solve all the problems in this industry on its own.

I do hope that this book could show a whole picture of "Continuous Delivery" to readers. When encountering problems related to the effectiveness of IT groups, readers will be able to deal with them reasonably based on background knowledge learned from this book. Or at least they can get inspired from the real cases included in this book so that they can take fewer detours when facing similar problems.

Continuous Delivery 2.0

1

The classic book *Continuous Delivery: Reliable Software Releases through Build, Test, and Deployment Automation*, since its publication almost a decade ago, is widely recognized by software technicians for its brilliant exposition of the principles and practices for software development. It is even taken as a bible by the practitioners in software industry in recent years when the business environment is increasingly characterized by "VUCA".

VUCA, an acronym of volatility, uncertainty, complexity and ambiguity, was initially a hot military word in the 1990s for describing the post-Cold War multipolar world, which was volatile, uncertain, complex, and ambiguous. This acronym had been little known before 2001, especially the 9/11 terrorist attack. But nowadays, business leaders with strategic vision like to characterize the "new normal" business environment, which is out of order and fast changing with VUCA.

However, when we are going to apply those principles and practices in our daily work to achieve Continuous Delivery, we will encounter all sorts of obstacles. For example, the mounting business pressure has drained us of energy for making further improvement, a tight schedule for development and testing forces us to work in the old way, and the risk is too high to ensure high-quality delivery by now if we work in a new way. These problems arise from the development inertia of software engineering, and now it is time for revamping the model.

1.1 OVERVIEW OF SOFTWARE ENGINEERING DEVELOPMENT

The discipline of "software engineering" was born in 1968 at the time of the first software crisis. The reason for this crisis was that the backward mode of software production no longer met the rapidly increasing demand for software applications, thereby giving rise to a series of grave problems in software development and maintenance. So people have made attempts, such as adopting the engineering approach applied in the field of construction engineering, to solve these problems and fulfill the expectations for "delivering software applications with required features on time and within budget".

1.1.1 Waterfall Model

The Waterfall Model (see Figure 1.1) was first proposed by Dr. Winston W. Royce in the article *Managing the Development of Large Software Systems* published in 1970[1]. It divides the software development process into multiple stages, and each stage has strict input and output criteria. Project managers hope to solve the software crisis with such development model that is heavy on plan, heavy on process, and heavy

---

[1] Dr. Royce also mentioned in the article that he believes in this concept, but the implementation described above is risky and invites failure and recommended to do it twice.

DOI: 10.1201/9781003221579-1

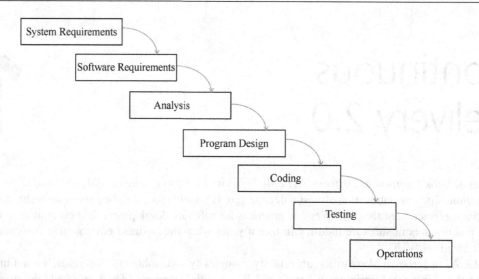

FIGURE 1.1 Waterfall Model.

on document. All the software development methods that have the three "heavy" traits are collectively referred to as the "Heavyweight Software Development Method".

In the 20th century, each stage of the Waterfall Development Model took months. Before the first line of product code was written out, Party A and Party B had already made significant efforts to determine the scope of requirements, and review the software requirements specifications as long as hundreds of pages. In spite of this, the two parties might still argue about "whether the scope of requirements has changed", "whether the software is delivered on time", or "whether the delivered software meets the pre-set business requirements".

1.1.2 Agile Method

Since the 1980s, microcomputers started to popularize rapidly. Then in the 1990s, there had been a robust demand for software applications. However, the *Chaos Report 1994* produced by the Standish Group shows that the proportion of failed software delivery or difficult delivery remained high (only 16.2% of software projects were successfully delivered, 52.7% of them confronted challenges, and 31.1% came to nothing). In this context, lots of ambitious software practitioners who were dissatisfied with the deliverables of Waterfall Model came up with several new development methods based on their own experiences. The well-known methods of Scrum and Extreme Programming (XP) were typical creations of that time.

At the February 2001 meeting at Snowbird Utah, 17 software masters, including Martin Fowler and Jim Highsmith, discussed the lightweight software development methods that emerged in those years, and coined the term "Agile" on this occasion. They came up with the Agile Manifesto and set out "Twelve Principles" for guiding the agile software methods (see Appendix A). All of them agreed that any software development method that conforms to the values advocated by the Manifesto and follows the Twelve Principles can be classified as the "Agile Method". It can be seen that "Agile" is in fact a synonym for a cluster of software development methods since its inception, rather than any specific method.

The Agile Method gives weight to individual initiative, face-to-face communication, changes, and early delivery of valuable software through iterative and incremental development. Because of it, many project teams have realized that software development is actually a process of continuous iteration and learning, that is, software engineers need to learn and understand domain knowledge rapidly, translate into the expressions of the digital world, and then keep iterating this process after discussions with business

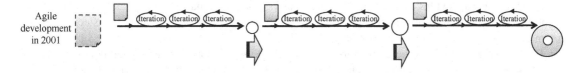

FIGURE 1.2 Iterative development, multi-deployment, and release.

domain specialists. A software delivery plan involves multiple iterations, with each iteration giving rise to a runnable software in the end (see Figure 1.2).

Since the Waterfall Model cannot bring forth a runnable software until the later stage of the project, the Agile Method seems to be more superior in this regard. "Continuous Integration" – an engineering practice while employing the Agile Method – was first adopted by a wider information technology (IT) sector, including the teams that had not tried any Agile Method, because it stresses frequent automation builds and testing, which prevent quality assurance (QA) team from doing repetitive work and smoothen its communication with development team.

The most requests for IT at that time were those enterprise-level customized software applications. Although the iterative model was employed for Agile Method, the interval between two software releases was often as long as months or even more than a year. Therefore, the contradiction between business personnel and the delivery team regarding requirements changes and delivery efficiency remained as the principal contradiction. The deployment and release of an application took less costs of time and money in the entire delivery cycle, so the deployment activities did not have any prominent contradiction with the work of operation and maintenance. Besides, the deployment was usually performed by a dedicated technical operation team, and free from bothering the research and development (R&D) team.

In this period, the top concern of software industry was neither the Waterfall nor the Agile Method, but the deliverable software assemblies themselves. To be specific, what it concerned about was how to quickly turn business requirements into deliverable software assemblies.

1.1.3 The DevOps Movement

The term "DevOps" sprouted on an impromptu topic "Agile Infrastructure" proposed by Andrew Shafer at the Agile Conference 2008 held in Toronto. The independent Belgian IT consultant Patrick Debois was so excited to learn of a like-minded person that he hunted him down at the conference and had that talk in the hallway. At his initiative, the "DevOpsDays" community conference was held in Ghent, Belgium in 2009 when the term "DevOps" was coined and officially made public.

In 2010, the website The Agile Admin published an article *What is DevOps*, pointing out that "DevOps is a term for a group of concepts that, while not all new, have catalyzed into a movement and are rapidly spreading throughout the technical community". This article also gave a practical definition: "DevOps is the practice of operations and development engineers participating together in the entire service lifecycle, from design through the development process to production support". It further proposed that "DevOps is also characterized by operations staff making use many of the same techniques as developers for their systems work".

The definition of DevOps on Wikipedia has kept been updated. As of 2017, it was defined as follows:

DevOps (a clipped compound of "development" and "operations") is a software development process that emphasizes communication and collaboration between product management, software development, and operations professionals. DevOps also automates the process of software integration, testing, deployment, and infrastructure changes. It aims to establish a culture and environment where building, testing, and releasing software can happen rapidly, frequently, and more reliably.

In fact, at the time of writing this book, a uniform definition of DevOps was not yet available. Just like every practitioner or every firm has their own view of "Agile", they may look at DevOps in different ways.

Some people regard DevOps as a subset of Agile, some people argue that "if Agile was done correctly, it would be DevOps", while some people go so far as to say that DevOps is a set of practices centering on automation and it is more or less associated with Agile.

DevOps originated from the application of Agile thinking and practice in development and operations, however the guidance on how to achieve the goal of DevOps was little at that time. Fortunately, the book *Continuous Delivery: Reliable Software Releases through Build, Test, and Deployment Automation*, which came out almost in the same period, has made DevOps more concrete and more actionable in daily work. It sets out a series of principles, methodologies, and practices for participants in the DevOps movement to follow, such as the strongly advocated principles of "everything is code, automating everything, and early feedback by deployment pipeline".

From my view, DevOps is not a criterion, a pattern or a set of fixed methods, but a trend for management of IT organizations. That is to say, it is able to break the barriers between the functional departments of an IT organization in various ways, transform their original cooperation model and make them better integrated, so as to further expedite their business iteration. This trend is sure to change the existing roles and division of labor within an IT organization, and even affect relevant business structure. In the case of Internet companies, software plays an extremely critical role in their business development; in other words, their business performance is closely bound up with IT efficiency, that's why they are more motivated and anxious to conform to this trend.

As a trend for management of IT organizations, DevOps is universally applicable in the domain of IT. But for IT organizations in different industries and enterprises, their management should be customized according to industry characteristics and specific situations of enterprises.

1.1.4 Continuous Delivery 1.0

In 2006, Jez Humble, Chris Read, and Dan North co-published a paper titled *The Deployment Production Line* to discuss the production efficiency brought along by software deployment, and put forward the "deployment production line" for the first time:

> *Testing and deployment can be a difficult and time-consuming process in complex environments comprising application servers, messaging infrastructure and interfaces to external systems. We have seen deployments take several days, even in cases where teams have used automation builds to ensure their code is fully tested.*
>
> *In this paper we describe principles and practices which allow new environments to be created, configured and deployed to at the click of a button. We show how to fully automate your testing and deployment process using a multi-stage automation workflow. Using this "deployment production line", it is possible to deploy fully tested code into production environments quickly and with full confidence that you can fall back to a previous version easily should a problem occur.*

The above three authors were all working at ThoughtWorks – an initiator, practitioner, and promoter of the Agile Method. The software development methods adopted by this company are also derived from XP. These authors not only introduced the prototype of the "deployment production line" in combination of their own practices, but also presented four basic principles to address the most common challenges facing automation of the build and deployment process.

These principles are:

1. Each build stage should deliver working software – don't have separate stages for intermediate artifacts such as frameworks.
2. Deploy the same artifacts in every environment – manage your runtime configuration separately.
3. Automate testing and deployment – use several independent testing stages.
4. Evolve your production line along with the application it assembles.

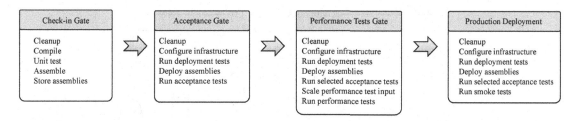

FIGURE 1.3   The deployment pipeline defined by David Farley in 2007.

In 2007, David Farley, also from ThoughtWorks, published a paper titled *The Deployment Pipeline – Extending the Range of Continuous Integration*, explaining that the "deployment pipeline"[2] is to tie together multiple quality verification levels and their validation content in an automation way, as shown in Figure 1.3.

In December of the same year, ThoughtWorks formed a team in Beijing to build a tool for management of software continuous release by adopting the concept of "deployment pipeline". Jez Humble was the product manager, and I was responsible for the product delivery and business analysis. The first version of this product was released in July 2008 by the name of "Cruise" (now known as "GoCD"[3]). Its most important feature is "deployment pipeline", and the design of most features (including built-in artifact repository and reference to multi-stage artifacts) embodies the "Build once, Run anywhere" principle.

While being busy with the R&D of GoCD, Jez Humble and David Farley coauthored a book *Continuous Delivery: Reliable Software Releases through Build, Test, and Deployment Automation*, with its English version published in 2010, and Chinese version coming out in 2011 and winning the Jolt Award in the same year, marking an official debut of the term "Continuous Delivery". According to Jez Humble, "Continuous Delivery is the ability to get changes of all types – including new features, configuration changes, bug fixes and experiments – into production, or into the hands of users, safely and quickly in a sustainable way". It should be noted that Continuous Delivery defined like this is written as "Continuous Delivery 1.0" in this book for distinguishing from "Continuous Delivery 2.0" (see Section 1.2).

In their book, Jez Humble and David Farley have discussed the philosophies, principles, methods, and practices of Continuous Delivery 1.0, and emphasized in the final chapter of the book that "Continuous delivery is more than just a new delivery methodology. It is a whole new paradigm for running a business that depends on software"[4].

Lots of the principles and methods of Continuous Delivery 1.0 are concrete operational guidelines for the DevOps movement, meaning that they can guide companies' IT teams to carry out the spirit of the DevOps movement (see Figure 1.4).

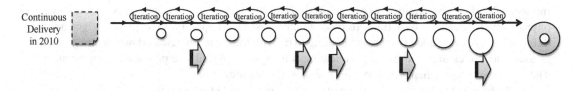

FIGURE 1.4   Continuous delivery 1.0 puts the release button back to the business side.

---

[2] https://continuousdelivery.com/wp-content/uploads/2010/01/The-Deployment-Pipeline-by-Dave-Farley-2007.pdf
[3] https://github.com/gocd
[4] "Paradigm" is a philosophical and theoretical framework of a scientific school or discipline within which theories, laws, and generalizations and the experiments performed in support of them are formulated. To put it simply, "paradigm = philosophies + methods".

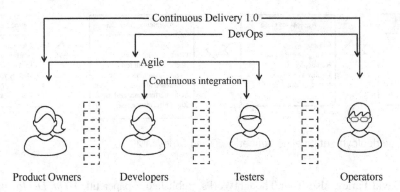

FIGURE 1.5   Different roles in agile development.

The collaborators involved in Agile method are mostly product managers, software developers and testers, and DevOps is more related to delivery teams (including developers and testers) and DevOps engineers, while Continuous Delivery 1.0 involves product demand side, software R&D teams, and DevOps engineers (see Figure 1.5).

CONTINUOUS DEPLOYMENT AND CONTINUOUS DELIVERY

Many people regard Continuous Deployment as an advanced state of Continuous Delivery, in which code change is automatically deployed into a production environment as soon as it has successfully passed all quality verification, and exempted from any approval. But in fact, the two words of "Deployment" and "Delivery" have different meanings.

"Deployment" is a technical operation, that is, it first acquires a software artifact from somewhere and then installs it on a compute node by following the pre-designed scheme, and ensures the normal start of the system; but it is not necessary to "release or deliver any part containing business function". In contrast, "Delivery", which is often referred to as "release", is a business decision, meaning that newly-built features can play a role in creating business value after they are delivered to them, for example, they are seen and used by customers (users).

The fact that "Deployment" and "Delivery" have become almost equivalent words is caused by historical reasons. In the past, there had been a long software release cycle, thus making it released immediately after new features were deployed. Then "Deployment" had gradually become synonymous with "Release" over time. In order to ensure software quality, IT department generally didn't allow irrelevant code (which had nothing to do with the currently released new features, such as undeveloped features and incomplete feature sets) to be deployed to a production environment. Therefore, each deployment must be a release of major features.

With the advent of Internet services, it is common to see "Deployment" and "Delivery" have different content and frequency. The code changes can be deployed to production for multiple times, but not released to users unless they are about to address business needs (see what the arrows indicate in Figure 1.4). For example, at Facebook's 2011 tech talk, the company's release engineer Chuck Rossi pointed that "right now on Facebook.com there is already the code for every major thing Facebook is going to launch in the next six months and beyond! It's the Gatekeeper which stops us from seeing it".

1.2 CONTINUOUS DELIVERY 2.0

Continuous Delivery 1.0 focuses on the process "from code change submission to product release" (see Figure 1.6), and provides a set of working principles and good practices that can raise the efficiency of development activities.

But while doing my consultation work, I've found that some software features, after being completed, didn't have any influence on customers or users, and some features were not used at all, regardless of their painstaking development. What a huge waste! And more features stand "idle", more waste will be produced. How can we make sure our hard work is fruitful? Or how can we verify the futile features at a small cost?

1.2.1 Lean Thinking

The book *The Lean Startup* (2011) of Eric Ries, co-founder and CTO of IMUV, has given me some inspirations. Its core idea is that when we develop a new product, we'd better first make a simple prototype – a minimum viable product (MVP). It is not to prelude a perfect final product, but to verify our business hypothesis. After receiving the real user feedback on each experiment, we should sum up the merits and demerits of the product features, then iterate quickly and fix bugs continuously to find the way to success before running out of our resources, so as to cater to the market demand in the end.

Eric Ries emphasized in his book that the lean startup is a "Build-Measure-Learn" process for verification and learning (see Figure 1.7), meaning that in this process we will rapidly convert our ideas into products, measure user feedback, and then decide to pivot or stick to our original intention.

In his book, which focuses on the initial stage of start-up, the Lean Thinking runs through the process where the product is "from zero to one". In fact, this thinking also applies to the process where the product is "from one to *n*".

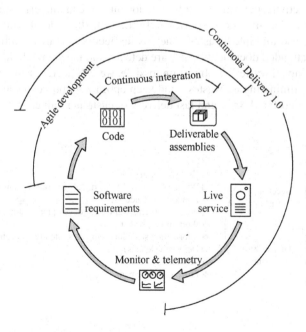

FIGURE 1.6 Concerns of Continuous Delivery 1.0.

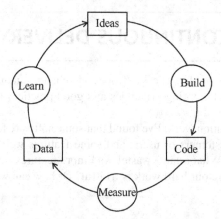

FIGURE 1.7 "Build-measure-learn" feedback loop.

In their coauthored book *Lean Thinking* (1996), James P. Womack and Daniel T. Jones pointed out that the Lean Thinking is to guide enterprises to define their production value according to user requirements, organize all production activities based on the value stream, draw the value flow between production activities and provide on-demand products, so as to identify the wastes inadvertently arise from the productive process and then have them eliminated.

According to the theory of Lean Thinking, "wastes" refer to the production activities or management processes that do not add value to quality products or services from the perspective of customers. This theory has summed up two types of production activities: value-added and non-value-added activities, with the latter identified as "wastes". Those activities labelled as "wastes" are further divided into necessary and unnecessary non-value-added activities, with the latter synonymous with pure wastes. From the customers' point of view, necessary non-value-added activities, although create no value, can help to avoid (potentially) greater wastes or reduce systemic risks (see Figure 1.8).

For example, assembly on a production line is a value-added activity, and quality inspection is a necessary non-value-added activity, but waiting for production due to scant material supply and rework due to quality defects are regarded as unnecessary wastes. In the full life cycle of SaaS, short for "Software-as-a-Service", there are also multiple "wastes", such as ineffective features, waiting in each production link (see Figure 1.9), unattended documents, software defects, and mechanical duplication of work.

Although "eliminating all wastes" is almost impossible, we still need to fully implement the philosophy of "identifying and eliminating all wastes", and keep optimizing processes and working methods to achieve high-quality, low-cost, risk-free, and fast delivery of customer value.

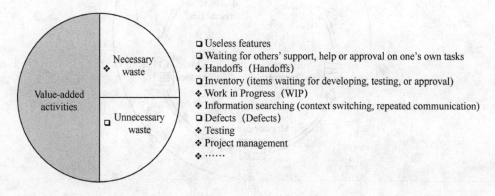

FIGURE 1.8 Example of wastes in software development.

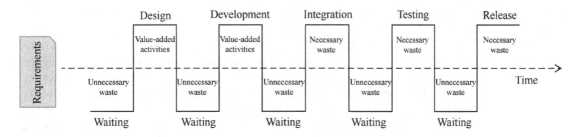

FIGURE 1.9 Value-added activities and wastes from user perspective.

1.2.2 Double-Flywheels Model

Since 2009 when Flickr – one of the most popular photo sharing sites – claimed to have ten times of deployment every day, "trunk-based development + CI + continuous release" has become a mainstream software R&D and management model for renowned Dot-com companies in Silicon Valley to cope with the VUCA environment. This change was not brought forth by the technical teams, but provoked by the demands from both business side and product side. In order to better understand massive users in the VUCA environment, and quickly validate business hypotheses and solutions, the business and product sides have adopted a new business exploration model, which stimulated the transformation of the software R&D and management model; then these two models began to promote each other and give rise to a "Double-flywheels Model" for internet-based software R&D and management, namely, "Continuous Delivery 2.0" (see Figure 1.10).

Continuous Delivery 2.0 is a thinking framework for product R&D. It combines lean startup with Continuous Delivery 1.0, stresses rapid closed-loop control between business and IT, sticks to the guideline of "Lean Thinking", and fully implements the philosophy of "identifying and eliminating all wastes", in an aim to help enterprises achieve high-quality, low-cost, risk-free, and fast delivery of customer value in a sustainable manner.

For companies undertaking software delivery, the goal of developing software is to create customer value. To this end, they should not only focus on rapid development of software features but also on the business correctness of the deliverable software and the ways for quick verification and resolution of business problems with limited resources. It means that they must constantly explore and discover the real business problem to be solved, propose scientific goals, and then come up with a minimum viable solution. After that, they should verify whether this problem could be addressed through fast implementation of this solution and collection of data from real user feedback. This is an intact business

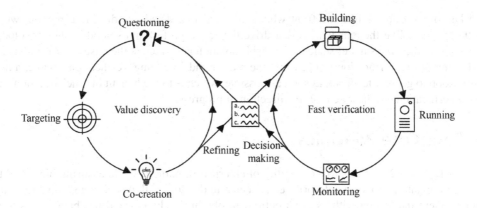

FIGURE 1.10 Double-flywheels Model of Continuous Delivery 2.0.

closed-loop starting from raising problems to solving problems, which is known as the "double-fly-wheels" of Continuous Delivery 2.0.

It consists of two connected loops: The first one is the "Discovery Loop", mainly aiming at identifying and defining the business problems and working out a minimum viable solution for entering the second loop, namely, the "Verification Loop". The main objective of the second loop is to deliver the minimum viable solution at the top speed, collect real feedback in a reliable manner, analyze and verify the effect of this solution so as to determine the next action, as shown in Figure 1.10.

The Discovery Loop consists of four steps in a sustainable cycle: questioning, targeting, co-creation, and refining.

1. "Questioning" is to define problems. By raising targeted questions to customers, we can find out their specific requirements, and the underlying reasons for these requirements, that is, the fundamental problems to be addressed after satisfying these requirements. In this way, the project team can know well about what goals they will achieve or what problems they will solve. Any problems in vague definition will lead to biased solutions. So we must clearly define problems before searching for their solutions.
2. "Targeting" is to define the target designator. After defining the business problems, we should collect and analyze the relevant data, remove interference information, identify assumptions, obtain the appropriate measurable metrics, and use them to describe the current situation, and at the same time discuss and define the desired outcome of our next action.
3. "Co-creation" is to jointly discover a variety of viable solutions to a problem, solve this problem together in a creative manner, or have these solutions to be verified.
4. "Refining" is to select the minimum viable solution from all viable solutions. It may be a single solution or a combination of multiple solutions.

The Verification Loop also consists of four steps in a sustainable cycle: building, running, monitoring, and decision-making.

1. "Building" is to accurately convert the minimum viable solution into a software package that meets the quality requirements according to the non-digital description.
2. "Running" is to deploy the software package that meets the quality requirements in a production environment or pass it on to users and make it at their service.
3. "Monitoring" is to collect the data generated in the production system and monitor the system to ensure its normal operation. At the same time, it presents the business data in an appropriate form and in a timely manner.
4. "Decision-making" is to analyze the collected data and compare them with the corresponding target obtained at the Discovery Loop, so as to decide the direction of the next step.

The Discovery Loop is like the front wheels of a car that decide its driving direction, while the Verification Loop is like the rear wheels that drive the car to go fast and smoothly. The two loops are supporting each other: the smaller scale of the viable solution generated at the Discovery Loop can speed up the running of the Verification Loop; while the more rapidly running Verification Loop can help the Discovery Loop to get real feedback as soon as possible, which is to the benefit of quick decision-making and timely verification or adjustment of the direction of progress.

1.2.3 Four Core Principles

"Continuous Delivery 2.0" refers to a capability of enterprises, namely, while ensuring high quality and low cost and mitigating risks, an enterprise can accelerate the double-flywheel in a sustainable way, and maintain frequent interaction with external entities to obtain timely and real feedback, so as to create more customer value in the end.

The four essential principles for accelerating the double-flywheels of Continuous Delivery 2.0 are introduced as follows:

1.2.3.1 Doing less

"Our biggest problem is lack of human resource" – a common complaint from my customers when I worked with them. No matter their firm is big or small sized, it seems that their ambition always exceeds their delivery capacity and they have endless requirements to deal with. Is that really good to do more? Definitely not. In fact, we should resist the temptation to "build the best features through a fair amount of planning", and insist on doing less and finding ways to verify new ideas as early as possible.

As Mike Moran has commented in his book *Do It Wrong Quickly*, Netflix believes that 90% of the things they want to do are probably wrong. In a paper *Online Experimentation at Microsoft*, Ron Kohavi and others[5] pointed out that Microsoft has elaborately designed and developed a host of functional features to improve key metrics, but only about a third of them can make it.

When asked how can five engineers support 40 million users? Mike Krieger, co-founder and CTO of Instagram, succinctly put it: "Do less, and do the simple thing first".

1.2.3.2 Continuous decomposition of problems

Complex business problems are bound to contain many uncertainties that affect the speed and effect of problem-solving. By decomposing the problems layer by layer before implementing the solution, the team can have a better understanding of the business and identify risks more rapidly. Enterprises should believe that even a big problem or a wide range of changes can be broken down into a number of small changes that are available for quick resolution and feedback, thereby eliminating risks as early as possible. Compared with designing a bunch of features and planning a one-time release that lasts for months, a far better approach is to keep trying out new ideas and delivering them to users separately.

1.2.3.3 Insistence on fast feedback (FFB)

After breaking down the problems, we should not immerse ourselves in our work and ignore the feedback on the results of each completed task, otherwise we may lose the other half of the benefits from problem decomposition, that is, we may fail to confirm that the risks are mitigated or eliminated. Only in the way of FFB can we get an early idea of the quality and effect of the accomplished work.

1.2.3.4 Continuous improvement and measurement

No matter what improvement is made, if we fail to measure its results in some way, how can we prove that it is really done? Before we start to tackle a problem, we need to find an appropriate measurement and put it on an equal footing with the corresponding functional requirements, and then fulfill these requirements together with problem-solving.

For example, a data company once failed to put forward a correct direction for improvement due to lack of metric data. It had developed a software platform for recruiting data labeling volunteers. The product was divided into multiple iterations, and each iteration would have several features released, but no features were available for data collection and statistical analysis, which were major concerns of product staff. As a result, the team knew that this platform could help people complete their work, but they had no idea whether they could work efficiently, nor could they determine the direction for next-step optimization of the platform.

---

[5] See https://ai.stanford.edu/~ronnyk/ExPThinkWeek2009Public.pdf

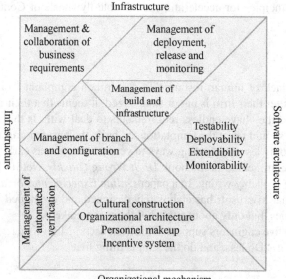

FIGURE 1.11   Tangram of Continuous Delivery.

1.2.4 Tangram of Continuous Delivery

The above subsections have discussed the guiding ideology, work philosophy and core principles of Continuous Delivery 2.0. It impresses people that it is fairly effective in adapting to the rapidly changing market environment and fierce market competition. So, how can companies make Continuous Delivery 2.0 an organizational capability and their DNA, as well as their own competitive edge that gets ahead of their rivals.

The implementation and improvement of the Double-flywheels Model for Continuous Delivery involve multiple departments and different roles within an enterprise, rather than accomplished independently by a single department. The idea, philosophy and principles of Continuous Delivery 2.0 must be implemented across the entire enterprise. Therefore, an enterprise has to take actions in three aspects: organizational management mechanism, infrastructure, and software architecture, each of which contains multiple elements, as shown in Figure 1.11.

All roads lead to Rome, and Rome wasn't built in a day. In terms of Continuous Delivery, each enterprise may have a different implementation path, different length of required period, and different requirements for various aspects of capacity. Just like playing the "tangram", a traditional Chinese intelligence-exploit toy with which each kid can make his own designed shape, each enterprise should draw an exclusive blueprint for continuous delivery practice according to its own will and demands.

1.3 SUMMARY

Continuous Delivery 2.0 is based on the two philosophies of Continuous Delivery 1.0: "quick software release in a sustainable way" and "MVP" for lean startup. It stresses to be business-oriented, decompose business problems from the beginning, and find the correct direction of progress quickly through continuous scientific discovery and rapid verification while reducing waste, which is referred to as the "Double-flywheels Model". Therefore, Continuous Delivery 2.0 involves multiple teams in an organization, and requires their close cooperation to shorten the cycle of the double-flywheels, as shown in Figure 1.12.

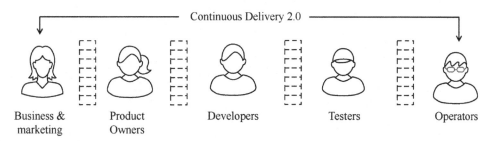

FIGURE 1.12   Different roles in Continuous Delivery 2.0.

Continuous Delivery 2.0 follows four essential working principles: doing less, continuous decomposition of problems, insistence on FBB, and continuous improvement and measurement. Only in this way can we keep accelerating double-flywheels of continuous delivery and speed up user feedback, and thereby improving business agility. This requires leadership to overcome the "fear of failure", replace the original thinking model of software delivery management with the one of "scientific discovery – fast delivery", attempt quick trial and error, improve continuous delivery capability, and then develop existing businesses and look for new business opportunities.

Value Discovery Loop

2

There are 12 principles in Agile development, the first one of which goes like this: "Our priority is to satisfy our customers by delivering valuable software as early as possible and continuously". However, as to the question "What is value?", everyone in the company may have his/her own point of view. The late management guru Peter Drucker had pointed out that value can only be defined by customers outside the company. A new product may be born on a whim or through a lot of market surveys, but its market acceptance is totally up to users. For example, today's customers are no longer satisfied with the basic functions such as "a good printing effect" for a printer, they prefer the printer equipped with more advanced features, such as downloading files by network.

How to discover and identify the real needs of users is a difficult problem facing all software companies. This chapter, which mainly discusses the principles and methods applicable to the Discovery Loop (see the box in Figure 2.1) in the double-flywheels of continuous delivery, will guide readers to solve this problem.

2.1 SIGNIFICANCE OF DISCOVERY LOOP

When companies design and develop a new product, they tend to adopt the method of "Proof of Concept" (POC) or "Product Prototype" early in the project to collect feedback from potential users, so as to prevent the development from going the wrong direction. Once the POC or product prototype is accepted, companies will start a long process for developing full product functions. But the final product will be more or less deviated from the POC and product prototype since they are incomplete in themselves.

The market in recent years changes almost daily, the final product based on the original design may no longer cater to the market demand, either because potential users' deviated understanding of the product prototype or because user requirements have changed, despite of a large amount of time spent on its development. In fact, this proposes three types of risk hypotheses that are common during the development of a new product. The first is the hypothesis about the target user group: whom you are going to serve. The second is the hypothesis about the problem: what is the pain that your target users are facing and you want to address. The third is the hypothesis about the solution: is the solution you are going to provide could solve those pains? Is it more effectively and efficiently than other existing solutions?

If any of those hypotheses is invalid, we will get half the results with twice the effort, or even come to naught. So the goal of Discovery Loop is to continuously identify and define the value hypotheses, find out the ones that are the riskiest or the easiest to be verified, and get real feedback in virtue of the Value Verification Loop, so as to better understand user requirements and determine a correct direction to press forward in business.

For example, at the inception of GoCD, a release management tool for software continuous delivery, and its target customers were defined as the small and medium-sized software companies or teams that expected to deliver software in the way of Agile development and improve the delivery speed with high quality. Such definition prevails to this day: the main purpose of GoCD is to help target customers to manage integration and release during the software research and development (R&D) process. Although GoCD was designed to have approximately 200 features when it was initiated in 2007, almost half of them

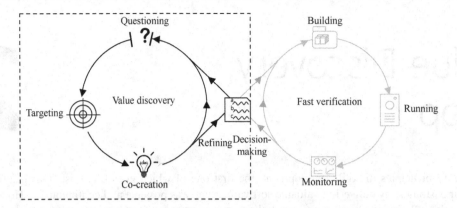

FIGURE 2.1   Discovery Loop in the double-flywheels of continuous delivery.

have been on hold or scrapped so far, because those unimplemented features are not the proper solutions for SMEs nor real demands from them to manage the problems in software integration and release at that time. In other words, some of the hypotheses for GoCD have proved to be invalid.

The GoCD's development was guided by the philosophy of Continuous Delivery 2.0, that is, decompose a big feature into several small functions, release these functions continuously and rapidly (the R&D team used the latest version of functions every week, and released them to the external customer every two weeks), get the real feedback from users, and then adjust the product function strategy, thereby laying a solid foundation for the success of this product.

Therefore, in the Discovery Loop, the team shall start from the business problems and work with its customer to put forward the three hypotheses. After that, through analysis and evaluation, the team should identify the maximum risk points, develop relevant measurable metrics, and work out the corresponding Minimum Viable Solution. Then, by the fast-running Verification Loop, they get feedback as early as possible and validate the risk points against the measurable metrics, and learn.

2.2 FOUR KEY STEPS IN DISCOVERY LOOP

The Discovery Loop is a process where a team, by going through a series of workflows, identifies and defines business problems, develops corresponding measurable metrics, and determines a low-cost and fast-verifiable Minimum Viable Solution. This process, which is for the team to comprehend real requirements from business and then have them prioritized and reevaluated, is made up of the following four steps:

1. Questioning: By raising targeted questions and initiating discussions, the team shall set its business objectives or identify the essential business problems it needs to solve.
2. Targeting: After identifying the business problems, the team shall collect relevant data, then remove those interference ones through data analysis so as to obtain appropriate metrics, and finally use them to describe the present circumstance, as well as the outcome or state that the team desires.
3. Co-creation: This step is for the team to thoroughly understand and verify the business problems, and then find all possible solutions through discussions.
4. Refining: The team shall evaluate all possible solutions in combination of the actual situation, screen out the Minimum Viable Solution or a set of solutions as the input of the Verification Loop, and then wait for its real feedback before making a value judgment.

The ways to perform the above four steps are specified in the following subsections:

2.2.1 Questioning

As the starting point for the double-flywheels of continuous delivery, the step of questioning is to identify the real objectives behind the customer requirements by raising questions without pause, for the sake of finding more ways to develop solutions, and also help team members to thoroughly understand the problems.

Agile practice has become increasingly popular for software development, and "user story" is now widely used as a way of describing requirements; however, engineers are more interested in the question of "what are the requirements", and they usually discuss requirements with business personnel in the following manner:

Business personnel: You just follow the business process and interface examples in this document to implement.
Engineer: If the implementation is based on the process and comes across... how many options should be filled in this field? And what are they?
Business personnel: Here it is. Follow this list...
Engineer: So what should to be done after that? Is it multiple-choice or single-one?

This conversation is not what we expected in the stage. It aims to identify the immediate requirements of users, that is, the solutions proposed by business personnel. Given the service philosophy of "satisfying business personnel's requirements", there is nothing wrong with this way of working. But how can we make sure that the implementation based on the document written by business personnel is able to meet the real user requirements?

Questioning is not only to learn "what to achieve" and "how to achieve" but also to figure out "why to achieve" – the essential problem about customer requirements, so as to come up with a faster and more convenient solution or verification scheme.

Because of occupational habit, from the moment the above conversation starts, developers are prone to skip over the most important problem, that is, how to solve the real concern of customers in a better way, which is exactly what we should do. In view of this, we must dig deep into the problems through nonstop questioning.

Imagine we are organizing an offline salon event with the theme of "DevOps and Continuous Delivery 2.0" – a paid Meetup. During the lunch break, a guest tells us he wants a cup of Starbucks coffee in the afternoon. In order to show him our hospitality, we ask him "What kind of coffee would you like?" "Hot or iced?" "Large or medium?" "What time do you want it?"

However, all of these questions are only about "what" and "how", and having nothing to do with the underlying reason. What if the guest only needs a cup of coffee to refresh himself? He doesn't want to miss the afternoon lecture because of falling sleepy. In this case, we could have multiple ways to address his concern. For example, we can record all activities for guests to review after the salon is over. More ways are listed below to guarantee that guests will not miss any important content:

1. Organizers of the Meetup shall increase interactive activities, and reduce monotonous speeches or lectures.
2. Demarcate a standing area for guests to walk around and stop to talk.
3. Speechmakers shall deliver substantive and constructive speeches.
4. Make hot and cold drinks available at the corner of the venue.

This fictional case may be not that accurate, but you must have grasped its full significance. We may come up with multiple solutions to address a customer's concern, but the core is to to identify the "real requirement" – the problem that the customer really wants to solve, which might not be the solution proposed by themselves.

Therefore, when we are assigned a task, we should find out the real problem to be solved and probe into the motives behind it. We should focus on the problem itself instead of rushing into discussion of its solutions. Only in this way can we better solve this problem, not just the implementation of software features.

In the "questioning" part, organizers need to pay attention to the following four points:

1. Those who propose the problem domain and those who provide solutions shall, to the best of their abilities, send representatives to join in the discussions on the scene.
2. Ask a few more "whys". It's too early to give up exploration even if you are familiar with the problem domain.
3. When conditions permit, collect data and information as much as possible to serve as basis for understanding and analyzing problems.
4. Empathize with or feel empathy for customers. Put yourself in the position of the customer to think about his concern, and restore the scenario where the customer concern is brought forward.

2.2.2 Targeting

After identifying the problem to be solved, we should determine the specific goals and results we must achieve. "Targeting" is a course of discussion for setting and decomposing goals, with an aim to determine the roadmap for achieving our goals and the corresponding measurable metrics, and to guide subsequent steps of co-creation and refining.

We should try to avoid ambiguous goals which will affect the communication between team members. All goals must be described articulately to let us know how many results we have achieved and how much work we still have to do. Only in this way can we move forward in the right direction, and work out reasonable solutions in combination of the actual situation. A definite goal is usually concrete, measurable, and time-bound. Without time limit, a goal is likely to become a vision, which is unable to directly guide companies to carry out daily production management and other specific activities, as shown in Figure 2.2.

The best way is to make the goals objectively measurable. Although sometimes it is difficult for us to develop a measurable metric immediately, we can look for objectively measurable goals and results by describing the target state and referring to the possible outcome of this target state. But how to find measurable metrics? Let's think about it this way: if a product satisfies the user demand, then user satisfaction will lead to repurchase and promote the brand awareness of this product, which will ultimately draw more and more users. Given this, we can set the number of users and operating income as the metric dimension of this product, as shown in Figure 2.3. These two metrics are characterized as "easy to collect" and "easy to measure", which helps reduce the cost of collecting the measurable metrics.

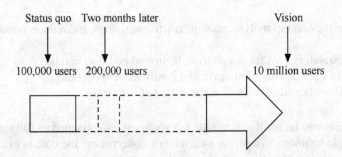

FIGURE 2.2 Vision and goal.

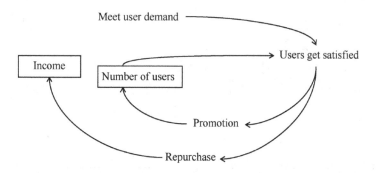

FIGURE 2.3   Goals that are easy to collect and measure.

For example, for a company that develops a News Feed mobile app, it wants "users to like the News Feed released by this app". However, "to like something" is a goal that is hard to measure and demonstrate, thus requiring further targeting. As shown in Figure 2.4, if users do like this product, they will:

1. Read more content and spend more time on it.
2. Recommend this product to their friends who may transform into its users.

The above hypotheses have revealed three easy-to-collect and easy-to-measure metrics: number of recommendations, number of active users in unit time, and average use time per user. These metrics can serve as the metric dimensions of business goals. But which metrics can be chosen as business goals? It is determined through a comprehensive evaluation of company's current situation and product's stage in the life cycle, as well as external market environment.

In addition, goals need to be set for different organizational levels. An overall goal is set for a company as a whole, not for individual teams in the company. Once an overall goal is established, all teams in the company must take it as their direction and set their subgoals based on their own duties and roles, and then draw on the wisdom of all team members to achieve their goals. For example, individual teams can try to further smooth user operation, quicken the response to application programming interface (API) requests, recommend more contents that interest users, and improve the stability of backstage services, as shown in Figure 2.5.

The selection of goals shall follow two principles: one is to identify value metrics, rather than vanity metrics; the other is to make sure that metrics should be measurable and accessible, and easy to be objectively compared. The concept of vanity metrics is expounded in the book *The Lean Startup*. It refers to things you can measure that don't matter. They're easily changed or manipulated, and they don't bear a direct correlation with numbers that speak to business success, such as the total number of registered users and the signal maximum page views. Although these metrics can reflect the state of products to a certain extent, they are not the most valuable metrics. Comparably speaking, daily active users (DAU),

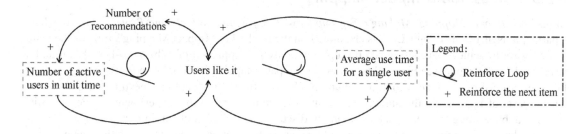

FIGURE 2.4   Example for choosing metrics of News Feed.

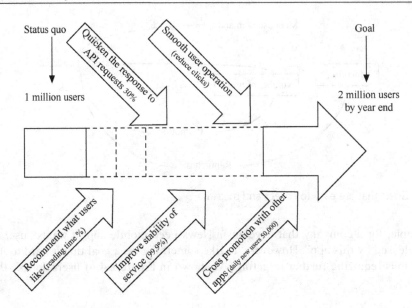

FIGURE 2.5 Overall goal and subgoals.

monthly active users (MAU), daily and monthly user retention rate (URR), and effective purchase rate are better value metrics.

Of course, for more specific problem domains or product stages, we can also find more appropriate value metrics than active users and retention rate. But this requires the team to explore and define by itself according to the business characteristics and the stages of the products or services.

2.2.3 Co-creation

Co-creation refers to the process where a team looks for viable solutions for verification or for achieving the goals after it has determined what it wants to fulfill. Co-creation should be carried out after understanding the problems and establishing the goals, otherwise the solutions may be too divergent due to lack of goal constraints. The output of the step of co-creation is ought to be multiple solutions with measurable metrics. In fact, every solution is based on certain hypotheses or conjectures, and every hypothesis is equivalent to a risk. Therefore, each solution is just an "experiment" that attempts to solve a particular problem in the problem domain.

Several analytical methods are available for this step. Among them, two typical methods of "Measurable Impact Mapping" and "User Journey Mapping" are introduced below:

2.2.3.1 Measurable Impact Mapping

In his book *Impact Mapping: Making a Big Impact with Software Products and Projects*, Gojko Adzic, a partner at Neuri Consulting LLP, has elaborated on the method of "Impact Mapping". It helps the team to find ways to achieve business goals through the analytical approach of Why-Who-How-What and a structured display mode (see Figure 2.6a). However, Impact Mapping is incomplete for scientific verification, because we not only need to know "doing XXX can affect YYY" but also need to learn about the current level of impact and the anticipated results after implementing this experiment. In view of this, we should, by starting from the problem domain, discuss a particular problem in the sequence of "role-impact-solution-measurement" (see Figure 2.6b), so as to discover as many viable solutions as possible. This method is known as "Measurable Impact Mapping".

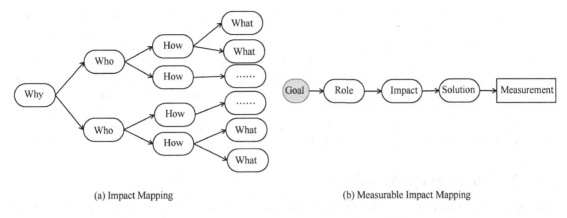

(a) Impact Mapping   (b) Measurable Impact Mapping

FIGURE 2.6   Measurable Impact Mapping.

The steps for drawing a Measurable Impact Map are shown below:

1. Role: List out the people or roles involved in the problem domain.
2. Impact: Regarding each type of person or role, think about the ways in which they can impact the solution of the problem (either positive or negative impact).
3. Solution: List out all possible solutions to each problem and discuss their viability.
4. Measurement: If possible, try to define a measurable metric for each solution.

Let's take the user growth goal of a mobile app (200,000 users in two months) as an example. The internal and external personnel that may be involved include: (1) app users; (2) promotion team; (3) customer service team; (4) product R&D and operation team; and (5) content provider and other roles. A variety of solutions can be listed out according to the four steps given above (see Figure 2.7).

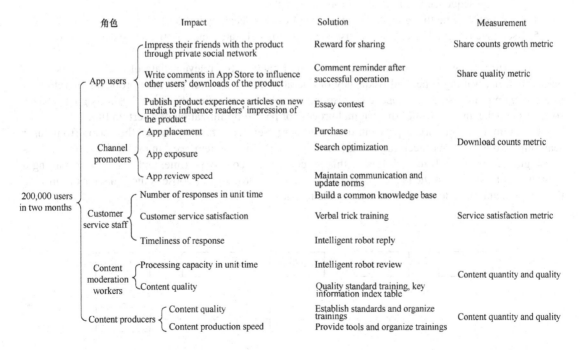

FIGURE 2.7   An exemplary Measurable Impact Map.

Sometimes, we cannot measure all metrics right away. When we haven't collected and counted the data related to metrics, we may collect a part of data provisionally, make corresponding inference on this basis, and then calibrate the metric measurement after a period of operation. For example, a company wanted to increase R&D efficiency by 10% (goal), one solution was to improve the efficiency of deployment process. However, no data about the deployment duration had been collected before. So, we could spend one week to collect data on the twice deployment during the week, made inference on this basis, and then jointly defined the required deployment time with the customer. Sometimes, certain indictors were hard to be measured directly, some relevant indictors were used instead. Since there are deviations introduced by using relevant indictors, special attention should be paid to the data.

2.2.3.2 User Journey Mapping

The User Journey Mapping is a method that presents the interaction between users and products or services in stages based on operation flow by means of visualization. A User Journey Map usually includes the following four parts:

1. Touch point: The critical moments in the journey such as an SMS and software interface.
2. Contact stage: Divide the entire journey into different stages in sequence such as product query, order placement, and payment.
3. Pain point: Something that makes users feel inadequate when they are receiving system service.
4. User emotion: All the emotion changes of users at different stage of the journey.

The steps for drawing a User Journey Map are shown below:

1. Define users: Define the User Journey Map for a specified type of users.
2. Define tasks or stages: Preconceive different events that may occur in these stages or when working on these tasks.
3. Interaction between users and service touch points: How users operate and how about their operation sequence when different events take place?
4. User motive: The thoughts and pain points of users in each operation.
5. User psychology: The changes of users' psychological states and emotions in each operation.

After visualizing users' operation flow, we shall capture the relevant data of each stage (such as operation time, waiting time, and frequency of operation), and discover potential problems by referring to users' pain points, so as to propose corresponding solutions to refine the initial business goals. These solutions may be an overhaul of the original process or partial optimization of a certain link.

For example, an important problem for e-commerce service is how to shorten the period from "user searching goods" to "user receiving goods". In response to this problem, we can model the entire process (see Figure 2.8) and analyze each link of this process (roles, consumed time, and cost). After making a hypothesis of the crux of the problem, we can build a new process or choose some links for optimizing the solution, and then determine the measurable metrics.

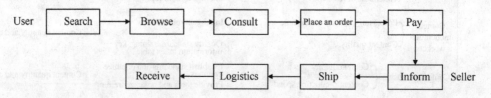

FIGURE 2.8 Business process diagram of e-commerce platform.

For merchants on the e-commerce platform, if the goal of the platform is to "improve merchant satisfaction", then it is likely to shorten the account period, thus making merchants more satisfied with the platform; but it may require the original financial settlement system and merchant management system to be upgraded.

We need to be alert to two "pitfalls" in the part of "co-creation": analysis paralysis and intuitive decision-making. Analysis paralysis refers to a state where decisions or actions cannot be taken due to excessive analysis or overthinking, which ultimately affects the output of results. It is usually because of too many detailed options or obsession with the best or "perfect" solution, and fear of making any decisions that may cause wrong results. Intuitive decision-making refers to an action that is prone to make fatal decisions based on hasty judgment or intuitive response without analysis; it is at the opposite extreme from analysis paralysis.

At the same time, it is worth noting that the results produced by multiple solutions are interactional and interrelated, and one solution may affect more than one result metric.

2.2.4 Refining

Refining is a process where the team evaluates the multiple solutions proposed during co-creation and then selects the Minimum Viable Solution. The evaluation factors are made up of the implementation cost (including time and manpower) of all alternative solutions, their effect feedback cycle, and impact on business goals.

In the volatility, uncertainty, complexity, and ambiguity (VUCA) environment, time is the biggest implicit cost. If too much time is spent carrying out a solution, lots of opportunities may be missed. Moreover, an additional period of time is required to observe the real effect of some solutions upon their implementation. But we still like to have as many experimental solutions as possible, because each of them may help to solve the problems and achieve the goals.

The search navigation bar of Etsy – an e-commerce website – designed in 2007 is shown in Figure 2.9. Although this design was not permanent, it had been free from any notable change before 2012. However, most buyers had no idea how to use this search navigation bar. For example, hardly anyone had ticked the search term "Shops" in the drop-down box.

In the five years by 2012, lots of contents had been added to the drop-down box, even if not all items were directly interrelated, thus making it bear too many responsibilities. Therefore, Etsy planned a makeover

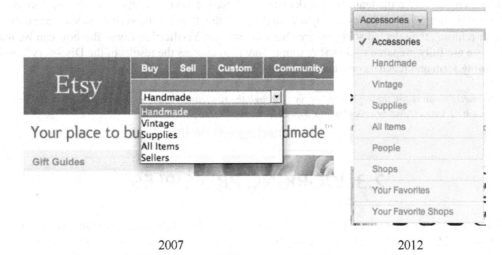

2007   2012

FIGURE 2.9   The search navigation bar of Etsy.

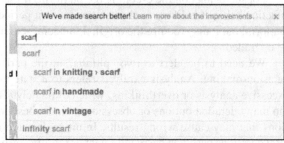

(a) Newly-added commodity classification area   (b) More newly-added auto-prompts in search terms

FIGURE 2.10   Two optimized items on the search page of Etsy.

of this search navigation bar and set up a special project for this purpose. The project team members had come up with plenty of ideas and solutions for this makeover, and finally made the following to-do list:

1. Redesign the search box.
2. Default settings of "All Items".
3. Remind richer automation recommendations.
4. Shown recommended shops in the search result list.
5. Add common filters to the search favorite.
6. Put the search bar on the product page and shop page, respectively.
7. Remove the original search drop-down box.

Each of the above tasks was relatively independent and developed in a short period of time, and all of their effects were subject to evaluation. During the makeover, each task was evaluated after its completion, and the evaluation result might lead to revision of the original solution, which was beneficial to achieve the business goals.

In the above to-do list, some refining tasks were successful, and some were not. As shown in Figure 2.10, after Task 1 (adding a commodity classification area on the search page) was done, user data showed that almost no users had noticed it, but the effect of Task 3 (adding automation recommendations) was fairly remarkable.

So far, it is not difficult for us to see that even for a huge revamp project, its solution can be a set of mini-solutions. The goal of refining is not to delete the solutions proposed during co-creation but to prioritize them, and have the team further decompose these solutions, select the widely recognized and most important improvement items one by one, and ensure that they can be verified as soon as possible.

After refining, the selected solutions are about to enter the Verification Loop. But how can we make sure that we are fully prepared to do so? A simple way is to express the results of the Discovery Loop in the following form and reach a consensus within the team:

If our metrics can reach the degree of "yyyyy" through the realization of the minimum function combination such as "xxxxx", we believe that our hypotheses about "zzzzz" are valid.

2.3 WORKING PRINCIPLES

In order to quicken the operation of the Verification Loop – which helps to shorten the entire operation cycle of the double-flywheels, and avoid falling into "analysis paralysis", the work in the Discovery Loop should follow the principles of "decomposition and quick trial and error", "verify only one point at a time", and "allow failure".

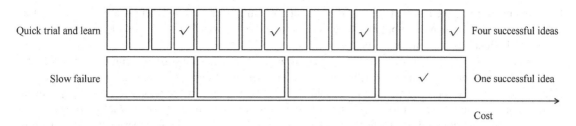

FIGURE 2.11 Slow failure versus quick trial and learn.

2.3.1 Decomposition and Quick Trial and Error

An "once-for-all" solution usually requires higher implementation costs, yet its actual effect is greatly uncertain. Due to a large upfront investment (i.e., sunk cost), even if the solution fails to bring the desired effect, the team is reluctant to give it up; decision makers tend to keep it or continue to optimize it, and wait for it to "scrap" gradually, but it will result in unnecessary complexity and maintenance costs of products.

If we can change our way of thinking and adopt more low-cost quick experimental methods, then we can try more ideas in more times at the same cost, meaning that we are likely to obtain more benefits. As shown in Figure 2.11, under the premise of the same cost, despite of many times of failures from quick trial and error, we may think up more ideas for making a hit.

2.3.2 Verify Only One Point at a Time

Only one requirement hypothesis is verified at a time. In the process of implementing the experiments, we need to keep an open mind to have them continuously optimized, and remind ourselves all the time that our goal is to verify the hypotheses, and these experiments are merely tools to achieve this goal.

Etsy once built a team to thoroughly revamp the commodity search page, so as to display its commodity list in the waterfall layout, which is similar to the infinite drop-down effect of Baidu's[1] image search results page. To be more specific, when returning more than one page of product results, all products will form a waterfall according to a certain sorting rule; users only need to swipe down the page, then the commodities will appear one by one until all search results are displayed.

After the team had immersed themselves in this makeover for a long time, a new commodity search page was ready to come out. To make sure of no risk at all, the team did an A/B Testing of the "waterfall layout", however hit hard by the result: only 40 people in the Experimental Group had continuous browsing behavior, while this number in the Control Group was 80 (see Figure 2.12). Moreover, in the

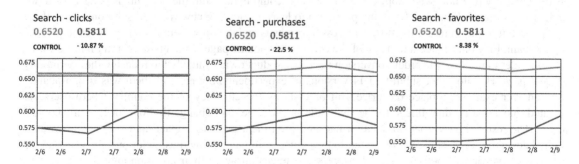

FIGURE 2.12 A/B Testing result of the search page in the waterfall layout.

---

[1] Baidu (www.baidu.com) is China's biggest search engine.

Experimental Group, the click rate dropped by about 10%, the purchase rate fell by about 22.5%, and the collection rate went down by about 8%. It turned out that the "waterfall layout" was of no use achieving the desired effect, but only made it worse.

After seeing this result, they believed that it was attributed to certain software bugs. So, they started troubleshooting at once, not only segmented users by browser and geographic location but also designated someone to log in to the Etsy website on an old-fashioned computer in the public library. They indeed found some bugs and had them fixed, but it made no notable difference to the unsatisfactory result.

Then, the team doubted that different browsers might bring users different experiences, so they optimized all sorts of browsers, although the same optimization yielded inconsistent effect on different browsers. However, no improvement was seen after all available optimizations were made. In the end, the team had to accept the reality that the "waterfall layout" would only worsen the display effect of the search page. In this process, the team had made so many changes at a time, thus making it unlikely to find any clues to identify the "culprit".

Through careful analysis, we can find that there is a hypothesis for the "waterfall layout", that is, "showing more commodities to users as fast as possible will bring them better shopping experience and trigger them to buy more commodities". This hypothesis consists of two parts: by displaying more search results to users, the page will have a higher conversion rate; and by displaying search results to users more quickly, the page will have a higher conversion rate.

In fact, we could figure out faster way to verify these two sub-hypotheses:

1. To verify the first sub-hypothesis, we can display twice the number of commodities to see if it improves the conversion rate of the detail page. The implementation cost of this verification method should be much lower than the original infinite waterfall design. But it turns out that the number of users browsing the commodity landing page has only increased a little, and this increment is unstable, resulting no change in the conversion rate.
2. Intuitively, it may be slightly difficult to verify the second sub-hypothesis, because someone would think that it requires a technical breakthrough to further speed up the current product display. However, we can take the opposite approach to deliberately extend the latency time (e.g., 200 ms) on the page to see if user purchase rate will drop. Although it is not a perfect method to verify the hypothesis that "delay time affects user purchasing behavior", it is still acceptable as long as a small traffic test is done to confirm that this method will not significantly affect the revenue of the entire website. However, the result of this verification shows that this hypothesis is of "no effect on the data".

2.3.3 Allow Failure

Although every product owner hopes that all solutions could make a hit, the outcome is not always desirable. Even so, we still need to keep an open mind to learn something new from all solutions, since these gains are fairly important for the future success of products and the improvement of personal competence of the team. Etsy once made a revision of the commodity details page, which is shown in Figure 2.13.

In order to improve the order conversion rate, the product owner intended to redesign the commodity details page. He altogether submitted 14 versions of experiments, but each of them was insignificantly revised. For example, replace the price unit of USD by the currency of the country where users are located, move the product image to the right side of the page, and change the font (or button) size and color. The result showed that no solution had any prominent positive impact, and some of them even pulled down the conversion rate. However, in the course of implementing these solutions, the team gained some new knowledge about users, such as which elements attracted their attention and which elements were not intriguing. In the end, by drawing lessons from these experiments, the commodity details page was gone through a full revision, so the final version of this page significantly increased the conversion rate, and the makeover project itself became Etsy's most successful project that year.

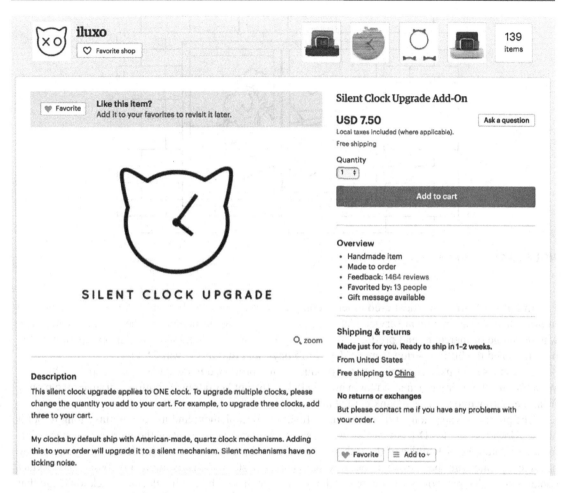

FIGURE 2.13   A commodity details page of Etsy.

2.4 COMMON METHODS FOR CO-CREATION AND REFINING

The premise for us to use the Value Discovery Loop is to adopt the way of thinking of "hypothesis before implementation" and identify the three types of hypotheses mentioned in Section 2.1 (user hypothesis, problem hypothesis, and solution hypothesis). In addition to these hypotheses, we still need some methods to design and implement quickly. Only in this way can we complete the closed Value Verification Loop at the fastest speed. Some practical methods are introduced as follows:

2.4.1 Decorative Window

The so-called "Decorative Window" method is to reserve an "entrance" for a new function so that users can notice it, however, it is not actually implemented, thus making it seem like a Decorative Window (see Figure 2.14). This is a way to learn about user preference, and verify whether users like a function and whether it is urgent at the minimum cost, so as to provide data support for developing a more comprehensive solution in the future.

FIGURE 2.14 Decorative Window.

In 2013, a Chinese vertical e-commerce company (let's call it EC hereinafter) made an experience improvement of the merchant service platform. When interviewing merchants, the product owner, who was in charge of merchant-end products, heard many interviewees mentioned that the competitor of EC had shortened the billing period from 45 days to 15 days, and that of EC was 21 days.

In response to this user complaint, the product owner promised to design a new function of "Instant Withdrawal", that is, merchants can login and click the "Instant Withdrawal" button to transfer the money from the platform to their own bank card at any time.

The product owner thought it was a simple function to implement and it wouldn't take long to put it online. However, the R&D team, which was assigned to the development of the merchant service platform, evaluated the difficulties of the task and said it would take six weeks to implement it, because they had to cooperate with the team that develops the financial system to change more. Of course, the product owner was not happy about such a long development cycle, but he had to intellectually acknowledge that this job was not easy at all for the following reasons:

1. At that time, the R&D team was busy with development of other functions, they couldn't start working on this merchant-end product until they had finished all the jobs at hand.
2. They had to work with the financial system developers to modify the existing financial process.
3. Even if the new feature was implemented, it should first go through joint debugging and then testing before its official launch.

Would merchants like this feature? Was it like "more flowers on the brocade" or "fuel in snowy weather"? These questions couldn't be answered before receiving users' real feedback. In order to find those answers as soon as possible, the product owner and the engineers decided to use the method of Decorative Window.

The engineers created a clickable button on the merchant settlement details page. When users clicked this button, a page containing a text description would pop up (see Figure 2.15), saying that you can leave your mobile phone number if you are interested in this function, then you will receive SMS notification as soon as this function is activated.

The workload for developing this function is listed below:

1. Modify Page 1 by adding an "Instant Withdrawal" button on it.
2. Add Page 2 (a function description page).
3. Save users' mobile phone numbers after their submission.

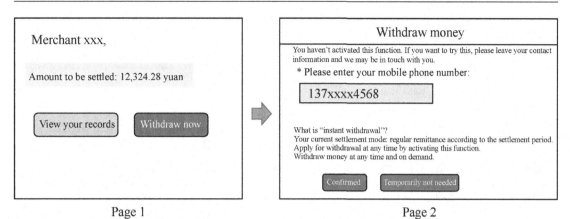

FIGURE 2.15   Page design of Decorative Window.

At this point, the hypothesis that needed to be verified could be described like this: "If we could collect 800 phone numbers in a week without any strong recommend tips, this means that a large number of merchants are interested in this function. Then we can go further".

In fact, this experiment was not advertised after it was released, but only relied on natural traffic. A few days later, more than 1,000 phone numbers were collected, and 120 of them were registered twice or more. It seemed that this function was indeed attractive to merchants, thus making the product owner feel so excited. It was worthwhile to get positive feedback from users with so little resources and time.

2.4.2 Minimum Viable Feature

It is a method that, during the process where the product increases from 1 to N, identifies the requirement hypotheses that are perceivable to users and takes them as the Minimum Viable Feature of a product for prioritized development, and then rapidly increases or modifies a certain product feature at the lowest possible cost, allows users to use it, and collects their feedback. This method highlights improvement of verification function and user experience.

At this point, the hypothesis needed to be verified was like this: "If 50% of the 120 merchants who have repeatedly registered their phone numbers use this function in two weeks, it means that they have strong desire for it. This function is likely to greatly improve merchant satisfaction and further promote the full automation process".

The R&D team didn't implement the intact function in the original solution, but only the part that was directly perceivable to users (see Figure 2.16). So this function could be regarded as completed from users' point of view.

However, it was released with only a rudimentary function. After users had clicked the withdrawal button, the backend service would send an email to the designated engineer, informing him of the necessary information for settlement and withdrawal. This engineer would print the information, and take it to the financial staff to go through the accounting process. The entire transaction process came to an end and all of backend procedure was offline process. It should be noted that when users wanted to turn off this feature, they had to apply through the customer service hotline by phone call, instead of revoking it in the self-service style. Actually, it could be seen as a minimal function subset of this feature, since this subset was easy to implement in a short time and with less workload, and had nothing to do with the financial management system.

By now, the product owner collected data in the shortest time, verified the hypothesis whether users were fond of this feature, and could decide whether to go on developing subsequent functions. For users, the platform has satisfied their demand for Instant Withdrawal and improved their user experience.

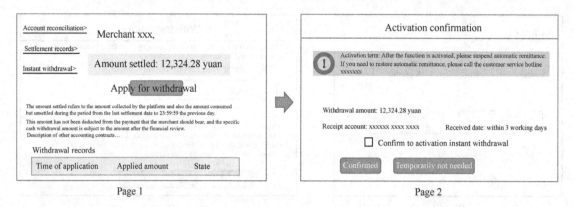

FIGURE 2.16 Minimum Viable Feature perceivable to users.

Consequently, a win-win situation where the supply side and the demand side are free to go forward or back out was thereby formed.

2.4.3 Special Zone

The method of Special Zone is to verify the effectiveness of a new function in a particular segment of users. In this way, even if this new function is invalid or less effective, it will not affect general users. This method is highly recommended for businesses that have limited resources and are cost-sensitive, but still want to provide users with good services. Car-sharing and bicycle-sharing companies have adopted this method. Starting from providing services from a city or an area, this method is able to answer the problems like "Does this demand really exist?" and "Is it an urgent demand?"

After applying the Decorative Window method to Instant Withdrawal, the product owner of the merchant service platform categorized the 120 merchants with repeated entry as Special Zone Users and immediately sent them SMS notification that the function was available. The first Instant Withdrawal occurred that afternoon. However, not many merchants followed his example in the next two days. As a result, the product owner had to notify these 120 merchants once again in SMS messages, together with an on-site notice.

Two weeks later, 45 merchants had clicked the "Apply for Withdrawal" button, but only 33 of them had completed the withdrawal operation; among them, 25 withdrew only once, 7 did twice, and 1 did eight times, failing to satisfy the product owner's expectation: at least 60 merchants would complete the withdrawal operation. The product owner was disappointed, and wanted to know why. So, he used the following method of Directional Explorer to investigate.

2.4.4 Directional Explorer

Directional Explorer is a method that, directing at a specific user group with certain behaviors, explores the motivation behind their behavioral patterns based on a specially designed survey outline. Unlike the common user interview that mainly asks general questions, the method of Directional Explorer is based on facts, and the team is fully aware of the specific behaviors of its interviewees (including behavioral details and time of occurrence).

In view of different user behaviors, the product owner classified users as follows in a directional manner:

1. Users who received the notification but didn't perform any withdrawal operation.
2. Users who visited the page but didn't apply for withdrawal.

3. Users who have applied for withdrawal once.
4. Users who have applied for withdrawal more than once.

To deal with different users, different questionnaires were designed for user interviews so as to learn about user behaviors and provide effective data for subsequent services.

In the end, the product owner came to a conclusion that this function could only satisfy the demands of a few merchants, just like "more flowers on the brocade". But in the process of directional exploration, the team has discovered two new pain points of merchants, thereby pointing out the direction for future improvement.

2.4.5 Corn Dolly

The method of Corn Dolly doesn't implement any function, but pretends that a function is available, and then shows its real effect to users to get their feedback. The difference between this method and the Decorative Window is that it enables users to truly feel the effect of a function, although it is not implemented at all.

This method was already used by IBM in the 1980s. At that time, most people didn't know how to type, only programmers, secretaries, and writers could use typewriters and computers. Being anxious to popularize its PCs, IBM asked its marketing department to conduct a market demand survey. According to the survey result, the marketing department insisted that the company should invent a technology that directly translates speech into text and automatically enters it into computer without manual typing; such kind of computer was sure to be a hot product even with an unbelievable higher price. However, the investment to implement this technology was extremely costly. Then, someone suggested doing a small test to verify the hypothesis that "people are willing to spend the unbelievable higher price on a computer capable of voice input". The test scheme is shown in Figure 2.17.

Potential PC buyers were invited to join in this test to experience the abovementioned technology: in a room where a microphone was directly connected to a display, a potential buyer was asked to speak into the microphone, then what he said would be automatically translated into text and displayed on the screen. In fact, his speech was not translated by a computer, but by a typist sitting in the next room. This typist, with typing speed incomparably fast, was typing out the volunteer's speech simultaneously while he was speaking, and then transmitted the text to the screen in front of him. This typist was asked not to miss

FIGURE 2.17   IBM's experiment of AI translation.

any information, even the pet phrases and pauses of the volunteer. This test had an easy-to-guess result: in those days, no one wanted to shell out a fortune for such a typing machine.

2.4.6 Minimum Viable Product

The method of Minimum Viable Product (MVP) is usually used in the process where the product increases from 0 to 1. It is to quickly develop the core functions of a product at the least possible cost, identify users, collect their feedback, verify real user requirements, and determine the development direction and form of the product. The goal of this method is to find a suitable product form.

Zappos, an American vertical e-commerce platform, didn't have its own logistics management system in its early days. Its co-founders Nick Swinmurn and Tony Hsieh just built a simple photo display website. They took photos of shoes in the shoe store next door and showed them online. If someone placed an order for the shoes in photo, they would first buy the shoes in the store and then ship them by handwriting an express waybill.

This is how to verify the initial business idea with the MVP, instead of forming a software R&D team and building a complete software support system in the first place.

2.5 MATTERS NEEDING ATTENTION

In order to better fulfill the Value Discovery, we need to pay attention to the following six points throughout the whole process.

2.5.1 Multi-Role Participation

The Discovery Loop involves many aspects of the business domain, such as discovery and definition of problems, and establishment and measurement of goals, not as simple as producing a backlog. Therefore, it is advised that all sorts of roles related to business problems and product solutions can participate in this process, and everyone involved should conscientiously play his part.

The above "Instant Withdrawal" case owed to multiple roles in the R&D team, which required the "large and all-inclusive once-for-all" solution to be replaced by the "step-by-step quick testing" solution. After learning about the requirements of the product owner, the engineers decomposed those requirements from a different perspective, and drew on the wisdom of other team members to arrive at the final simplest solution with the highest return on investment (ROI), namely, find the answer to the problem at the fastest speed with less resource (only one person was needed for the implementation, and all the others were still working on originally assigned tasks). From the first step of Decorative Window to the final step of Directional Explorer, it only took about six weeks to get the final conclusion.

According to Mike Cohn, an Agile master and advocate of the Scrum process, it is not necessary for the product backlog to come solely from the product owner; when other people in the team also contribute to the backlog, it is a signal that the team has a greater sense of participation, then it will be more likely for the team to succeed in Agile transformation.

2.5.2 A Cyclic Process

Owing to lots of uncertainties in the process of discovery, the four steps are inevitable to be repeated. This is a normal phenomenon, and more likely to occur when the business domain is complicated and involving multiple aspects and all sorts of roles in the business process. When discussing a viable solution to a problem, we may happen to discover another important but underlying problem.

In addition, "measurement and quantification" are of great significance for the discovery process. During discussions, people's understanding of measurement metrics and quantitative results is often inconsistent, which is likely to cause objections to the previously agreed indicators. But we should be happy with it, because we have discovered understanding deviations that are usually unnoticed in daily communication. When coping with these deviations, explorers may first record them and probe into them later, or record the current result of discussion and start a journey of discovery for a new problem, or even divide themselves into more groups to discuss these deviations separately and then synchronize their conclusions. Whatever the objection is, those joining in the discovery should reach a consensus on their action.

2.5.3 Risk Is Not Equivalent

Through analysis of each business problem, we can discover risks or raise hypotheses. If we develop a variety of verification solutions for each hypothesis and insist on their implementation one by one, it will be too costly and may cause us to miss market opportunities. Given this, we only need to design verification solutions for those hypotheses that contain high risks and try to verify them at a lower cost. In terms of those low-risk hypotheses, the team should determine some measurement metrics when designing solutions and collect relevant data after the verification is done.

2.5.4 Be Aware of God's Perspective

After working for years in a certain field, some people believe that they know users very well, so they are likely to "build air castles" when developing a product and take pride in "caring about user experience". With a work style like this, they might be bound to receive user complaint about product features after the product goes online.

In 2017, the Artificial Intelligence department of an Internet company collected a large number of data in different types that needed to be labeled. Owing to different data types and labeling methods, data annotators were required to have different skills. At the beginning, the recruitment of data annotators was through offline examination, that is, applicants filled in the test paper which were emailed to them and sent it back. It was data operators and consultants that had designed the entire offline process and rules for recruiting annotators.

However, due to the increasing demand for data labeling and the mobility of annotators, a manpower shortage continued to aggravate, and the offline examination was far from able to recruit enough annotators. Through discussion, the company decided to form a product R&D team to develop an online examination system to replace the original offline system and improve the efficiency of recruitment. The product owner of this online examination system, after learning about the business domain knowledge and requirements from the data operators and consultants, wrote a requirements specification. He believed that he had been fully informed of the business requirements by the data consultants, because they were clear about the software requirements of this offline system after it had been running for a period of time, so he directly designed an intact user interface which had the functions of question bank, designing test papers, holding exams, collecting test papers, and scoring. The system had to be served for questions setter, paper form maker, respondent, and administrator.

When the first version of this online system was ready to go, the product owner asked the data operators and consultants to start the acceptance test of this system. After passing the acceptance test, this system was immediately subject to roll-out testing. But on the first day of roll-out, they received lots of feedback from respondents, complaining that several functions of this system didn't work well.

From the idea of an online examination system was born to roll-out, almost five months had passed. After the review and retrospective, the team admitted that they had two major mistakes:

1. The team members thought they had known well all the requirements of the respondents, so they had never verified this system among its real users before all the development work was done.
2. The team members believed that they were fully capable of developing a satisfactory online examination system, so they had never thought of developing an MVP in the first place, but directly designed a "large and all-inclusive" product which required a long period of development.

Later, the team discussed what they would do if the project were to be reworked? After heated discussions, they managed to find several viable solutions to verify the functional requirements in advance. For example:

1. The method of Prototyping on Paper (POP) is to print the system interaction prototype on paper, invite users to experience its functions, observe their behaviors, and communicate with them to get real user feedback. POP is now applicable to lots of electronic tools.
2. The method of MVP is to rapidly introduce a simplified version of test to annotators, that is, the online examination only requires the applicants to label one type of data, and the functions of question bank and questions setter are temporarily performed by internal personnel through manual operation.

2.5.5 All Is Number

After we have established a data indicator system and a testing mechanism, and when we are able to collect a large amount of data, we need to pay special attention to one point: all the collected data can only tell us what the current state looks like, instead of the underlying reasons, and they can't help us fully predict the future, especially when the business market changes and the data cannot be displayed.

The predecessor of the Chinese short video mobile app Kaishou (Fast Fingers) was known as GIF Kuaishou, a mobile GIF generation tool. In its heyday, GIF Kuaishou had tens of millions of users and millions of DAU, but it had a low retention rate which is a common failing of tool-based products. In 2013, GIF Kuaishou transformed into the current short video app Kaishou, with its DAU once dropping to 10,000 level, but by the time of book-written as many as 100 million. Just imagine if the company only cared about the user number and persisted in the GIF business, could it still have such a huge user base?

In short, even if we have obtained the indicator data, we still need to think carefully, analyze the reasons behind these data, think about the future development trend, and even put forward some questions or directions that we can yet make sure, and restart the Discovery Loop.

2.5.6 Snake Crawler Effect

There is another common scenario. The team has figured out the experiment design A in response to the problem and is ready to implement it. But before the implementation is completed or the result yet comes out, the team brings up the new design B; they are so excited about this new idea that they decide to implement it right away. Soon afterward, they come up with the design C, and that cycle repeats, as shown in Figure 2.18.

This scenario often occurs in SMEs when they are rapidly expanding personnel due to availability of funds. Its occurrence may be because the implementation takes too long, or because their CEOs swiftly shift their focus of attention. Although the business problem that we have been trying to solve is likely to become invalid, this scenario still poses a great challenge to lead the team.

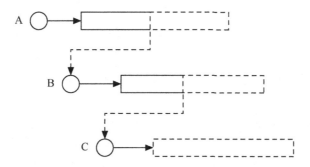

FIGURE 2.18 Snake crawler effect.

2.6 SUMMARY

This chapter discusses the four key steps in the Discovery Loop of the double-flywheels of continuous delivery, that is, questioning, targeting, co-creation, and refining. In order to smoothly implement these four steps, we must follow the principles of "decomposition and quick trial and error", "verify only one point at a time", and "allow failure".

This chapter devotes a large segment of its content on the six methods often used for co-creation and refining, namely, Decorative Window, Minimum Viable Feature, Special Zone, Directional Explorer, Corn Dolly, and MVP. These methods can help the team identify the real user requirements with the least time and cost, avoid the deviation between the final product and the user requirements, and get twofold results with half the effort.

The Minimum Viable Solution in the Discovery Loop has a great impact on the speed of value verification. It is a highly recommended method for achieving more value delivery at the lowest cost.

Fast Verification Loop

3

Peter Drucker (1909–2005), the Mind of a Management Thinker, once taught us that "Neither results nor resources exist inside the business. Both exist outside… Inside an organization there are only cost centers". To put it simply, before the products or services we've created are paid by customers, we can only measure their costs and predict their value. Only when the products or services are genuinely consumed can their value be realized.

After we've agreed on the minimum viable product (MVP) developed in the Discovery Loop, we need to deliver it to users (customers), collect their genuine and reliable feedback, and have it verified by virtue of the fast-running Verification Loop. The speed of the Verification Loop is decided by two parts: one is the size and complexity of the MVP developed in the Discovery Loop (the steps for developing an MVP are introduced in the previous chapter). The other is the speed of the Verification Loop itself, which is the focus of this chapter, as shown in Figure 3.1.

3.1 GOAL OF VERIFICATION LOOP

The basic premise for entering the Verification Loop is that "the team agrees that the selected solution is the best way to verify or solve the business problems in the present situation". The goal of the Verification Loop is, by means of various methods and tools, to deliver reliable solutions to customers as quickly as possible, and then collect and analyze their feedback, and learn from it.

Although quality and velocity are key factors for the Verification Loop, they are often considered mutually exclusive: good quality usually lowers the velocity of delivery, while rapid delivery degrades delivery quality. However, according to *The 2017 State of DevOps Report* presented by Puppet and DevOps Research & Assessment (DORA), in contrast to low-performance information technology (IT) organizations, their high-performance counterparts can achieve both goals (better stability and faster throughput) simultaneously. The principles of Continuous Delivery 1.0, such as built-in quality, small-batch delivery, and automation of all repetitive tasks, have played a crucial role in this regard.

3.2 FOUR KEY STEPS IN VERIFICATION LOOP

The main task of the Verification Loop is to convert the minimum viable solution from a descriptive language into a runnable software package in the most reliable quality and at the fastest speed, deploy it to the production environment for running, and then collect relevant data accurately and show them to the

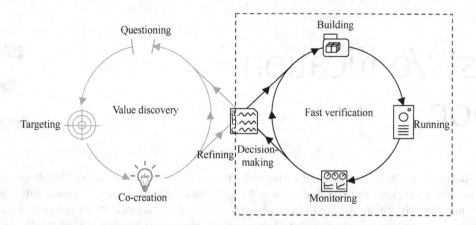

FIGURE 3.1   Verification Loop in the double-flywheels of Continuous Delivery.

team for making judgment and decision. Like the Discovery Loop, the Verification Loop is also made up of four steps, namely, building, running, monitoring, and decision-making.

1. Building: It is to accurately convert a solution into a runnable software package that meets quality requirements based on nondigital descriptions by human beings.
2. Running: It is to deploy the software package that meets the quality requirements to the production environment or deliver it to users and make it at their service.
3. Monitoring: It is to collect data generated in the production environment, monitor the system to ensure its normal operation, and then present business data in time and in an appropriate form.
4. Decision-making: It is to compare the collected data with the corresponding target established in the Discovery Loop, analyze and learn the comparison result, and then decide the direction of the following work.

3.2.1 Building

The step of building is to convert natural language descriptions into computer-executable software, that is, "quality-compliant software packages". This step requires relevant personnel to agree on business problems and pilot scheme, and to be able to accurately convert the team's intention into a software package consisting of "0" and "1"s.

Most personnel are needed to take part in building, including business staff, product owner, development engineer, testing engineer, and operation maintenance engineer, especially when a new product is being developed or an existing product undergoes substantial change. Everyone has different background knowledge and expertise. How to convert their solutions into high-quality and runnable software packages as soon as possible? It has always been a challenge in the field of software engineering. Now that building is the most uncertain step in the Verification Loop, the methods of Timeboxing, Task Decomposition, and Continuous Verification are recommended to deal with these uncertainties.

3.2.1.1 Timeboxing

Timeboxing is a common method for project management. It usually involves deliverables, delivery quality, and deadlines. By establishing a timeboxing management mechanism, the team can learn about the current project status (progress and quality), detect risks immediately, and then work out countermeasures. It also enables the team to keep a watchful eye on the work output, and get timely feedback on progress and quality. The details about Timeboxing are introduced in Chapter 6.

3.2.1.2 Task decomposition

Task Decomposition is one of the core principles of Continuous Delivery 2.0. In the step of building, it is requirements and development tasks that are to be decomposed.

1. Requirements Decomposition. The "requirements" here refer to the minimum viable solutions that are developed at the Discovery Loop, and selected by the team to be implemented, rather than the pristine business-domain requirements. "Requirements Decomposition" is a process for splitting pilot solutions into finer sub-requirements through team discussion, and also a process for team members to further reach consensus; its outputs are sub-requirements, namely, user stories in Extreme Programming or sprint backlog items in Scrum. Through Requirements Decomposition, team members playing different roles can communicate with each other and question each other to make pilot solutions more explicit and less ambiguous. At this point, "whether the team has reached a consensus" can be used as a criterion for specifying requirements. The details about Requirements Decomposition are introduced in Chapter 6.
2. Development Tasks Decomposition is to realize a certain requirement by dividing it into several development tasks; they can either be done by one person or by multiple persons. Upon completion, the development tasks can be hardly checked by other roles rather than developers, which differentiates it from Requirements Decomposition. Development Tasks Decomposition is also a process for further refining requirements and for revealing finer risk items.

3.2.1.3 Continuous Verification

Continuous Verification is to verify the deliverable's quality shortly after a development task or requirement (including sub-requirements) is done, rather than mass quality verification until multiple requirements are completed. This is in essence a fast feedback mechanism: once a requirement is done, there's feedback. The work of quality verification is to verify whether the original functions are destroyed and whether the design requirements are satisfied. The ways of verification include but not limited to code standards check, code security scan, and automation tests. Although the work results at this time are yet delivered to users, such verification can at least confirm if they can meet quality standards that the team has agreed upon.

If the continuous verification has to rely on massive manual operation, then it is sure to incur high costs. "CI" and "automation test" happen to be effective means to reduce the cost of continuous verification.

As a practice in Extreme Programming, Continuous Integration (CI) has been widely accepted by software industry: after a developer finishes a code change, it is to be integrated with the codes developed by his teammates (or other functional modules in the system) immediately, in an aim to verify the quality of the code change. In other words, the current development task shall meet the quality requirements and avoid from damaging the original functions. Only in this way can developers get feedback on code quality as soon as possible without leaving defects to the follow-up work. CI is expounded in Chapter 9.

In the practice of CI, automation test is the most important means for quality verification. It cannot be ignored since its coverage, execution time, and credibility of test results directly affect the reliability and credibility of the quality feedback itself. The details about automation test – a guarantee for quality protection – are covered in Chapter 8.

3.2.2 Running

The step of running in the Verification Loop is to deploy the software package in the production environment and make it at the service of external users. Whenever a new version of software is deployed and released, we don't want to see its normal use be disrupted. In short, our top concern in the Internet era is to upgrade and update software without users being aware of it. Even the most traditional financial industry is constantly looking for better solutions to optimize user experience while ensuring transaction security and data consistency.

This step tends to trigger the most frequent conflicts between Devs and Ops, and create the most repetitive manual operations. Because of this, the team should spare no effort to make improvement and optimization, and free themselves from toil.

3.2.3 Monitoring

The step of monitoring is to collect data, keep statistics, demonstrate the statistical results, and timely detect the problems in production and the abnormal fluctuations in business indicators. It is one of the most important data sources for the team to make decisions. Only based on credible and accurate data, the team can make reasonable analysis and judgment. In case of data loss or error, the team may make wrong decisions or even miss business opportunities. Besides, in order to discover the stability defects and hidden dangers in the production in time, it is imperative to collect the monitoring data as soon as possible, and then locate and analyze the relevant problems.

In order to collect the necessary data in the first time, the team must determine the data requirements for verification at the start of the Verification Loop, define data standards as soon as possible, formulate logging criteria, create data logging and metadata, and satisfy data requirements simultaneously with functional requirements. Otherwise, the unavailable data may delay decision-making after the corresponding functional features are put online.

3.2.4 Decision-Making

The step of decision-making is to compare and analyze the real feedback data in reference to the measurement metrics determined in the Discovery Loop, and then verify whether these data satisfy the initial expectation. On this basis, the team can confirm whether their requirements hypotheses are valid and whether they should follow the original direction or take a pivot. By this time, the next step for the team is either to select next experiment from the minimum viable solutions decided in the refining step or to return to the starting point of the double-flywheels of continuous delivery and discover new problems.

3.3 WORKING PRINCIPLES

The working principles of the Verification Loop mainly include building quality in, eliminating waiting, automating routine work, and monitoring everything. Many software development methods have brought about excellent practices and eliminated wastes. But some practices are beyond the capacity of current development teams, thus requiring their managers to invest more.

3.3.1 Building Quality in

Although the traditional software development method, which is represented by the Waterfall Model, highlights the quality of input and output at each stage, only a large number of detailed documents are produced in the early stage of the project, and no runnable software is developed. It is until the stage of integration test that all code modules are run together. This method has led to late discovery of software defects and higher costs to fix defects. In the book *Code Complete 2*, the cost arising from defects is described as follows:

> *"In general, the principle is to find an error as close as possible to the time at which it was introduced. The longer the defect stays in the software food chain, the more damage it causes further down the chain.*

TABLE 3.1 Average cost of fixing defects based on when they're introduced and detected

TIME INTRODUCED	REQUIREMENTS	DESIGN	BUILD	INTEGRATION TEST	AFTER RELEASE
Requirements	1	3	5~10	10	10~100
Architecture	-	1	10	15	25~100
Construction	-	-	1	10	10~25

Source: Code Complete 2.

Since requirements are done first, requirements defects have the potential to be in the system longer and to be more expensive. Defects inserted into the software upstream also tend to have broader effects than those inserted further downstream. That also makes early defects more expensive".

Table 3.1 shows that the relative expense of fixing defects depends on when they're introduced and when they're found. To be specific, the cost to fix a defect rises dramatically as the time from when it's introduced to when it's detected.

This attempt to satisfy software quality through large-scale inspection at a later stage runs counter to Dr. Deming's viewpoints. The "14 Points for Management" proposed by Dr. Deming, father of Quality Management, have been taken as an important theoretical basis for total quality management. The third point is as follows:

"Cease dependence on inspection to achieve quality. Eliminate the need for inspection on a mass basis by building quality into the product in the first place."

"Building quality in" emphasizes the output quality from the initial stage of the production process, and insists on quality assurance at each stage to eliminate rework and rising defective percentage caused by quality problems, which is able to reduce the quality risks at the final stage and ensure project progress.

3.3.2 Eliminating Waiting

In Chapter 1, we've learned about the definition of "wastes" in *Lean Thinking*. Apparently, "waiting" is an unnecessary waste. In our daily work, waiting is so commonplace that we've been used to it. Nevertheless, we'd better eliminate waiting at each stage, which is the most effective way to improve work efficiency.

3.3.2.1 Make value flow through "pull"

When managers lay emphasis on the efficiency of "people", everyone is likely to get their hands full, yet the output doesn't necessarily increase. By this time, there may be backlog of intermediate products waiting to be further processed (see Figure 3.2). Since the downstream processing capacity is relatively insufficient, it may impede the flow of work items; however, everyone may keep running at full capacity. If developers continue to implement more requirements, it will increase the pressure of testers instead of doing any good to the output of the team. And overpressure may cause more problems. For example, if developers continue to develop more functions on the codebase with uncertain quality, it may give rise to more defects. In order to solve this problem, managers must shift their focus from "people" to "output".

A correct approach is to strengthen the "debottlenecking" capacity and deliver more requirements. We can temporarily add more full-time testers to expand the testing capacity. But it is unlikely for us to keep the input and output of each link in an ideal state by increasing manpower. At this time, an expedient is to transfer some developers or other team members to assist in testing, which helps to expand the testing capacity and maximize the output of the entire system. The real cases described in Chapter 15 will illustrate how to expand the testing capacity expediently and guarantee the output of the team.

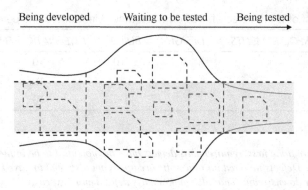

FIGURE 3.2   Backlog of intermediate products caused by insufficient downstream processing capacity.

Of course, it is only an expedient. Looking at the entire system, the upstream production rate should be determined by the downstream production capacity, that is, let the downstream production pull the upstream demand (see Figure 3.3). Once there is a vacancy in the wait queue, it will be immediately filled by an upstream demand, and so on in a similar fashion.

In order to achieve such a smooth effect, the size of requirements needs to be homogenized. To put it simply, in the phase of building, a large requirement is broken down into several small ones with similar workload, which will make the work smooth and efficient. Let's draw an analogy, when there are only small cars travelling on a highway, the traffic capacity is fairly loose, but when there are both trucks and cars, the traffic capacity will become tight.

The bottleneck is usually dynamic. Despite of decomposed requirements, we cannot guarantee that the entire flow system will run smoothly at any time. So we may resort to another solution: invest on tooling to expanding the downstream basic production capacity, which will then permanently ramp up the overall production capacity of the team without adding more testers. Of course, the same goal can be achieved by improving the personnel skill of team members, as shown in Figure 3.4.

3.3.2.2 Self-service tasks

Companies should change their way of thinking in the construction of a tool platform. For example, they are advised to adopt advanced technologies that enable everyone to "help themselves" in toils such as deployment of dev environment and data monitoring and analysis, instead of relying on some dedicated teams. Then everyone can work smoothly, and those "experts" can concentrate on their duties free from being "interrupted" from time to time.

Take microservice architecture as an example, if developers cannot build an environment for microservice development and debugging on their own at any time, but rely on the assistance of testers, it will interrupt the productive work of testers, and developers themselves have to suspend their job at hand and cannot carry it on until testers have finished debugging. Why not developers build a practicable debugging environment all at once and all by themselves? If so, it will neither disturb others nor waste their own time. In addition to this, there are lots of similar scenarios. For example, when a product specialist needs some data statistics, he has to turn to the data analyst or engineer for help, which also needs a period of waiting.

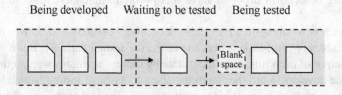

FIGURE 3.3   Flow and pull value.

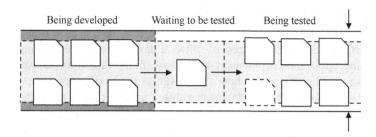

Being developed   Waiting to be tested   Being tested

FIGURE 3.4 Increased output by investment on tools, improved employees' skills, or added manpower for debottlenecking.

Silicon Valley-based Dot-com companies have invested a lot of resources in tooling and infrastructure for these scenarios (Figure 3.5 shows the interface of the real-time data monitoring system used by Facebook in 2012). With this platform, mobile development team can view statistics about users' devices, operating systems and app versions in real time; advertising team can monitor changes in ad exposure, click rates and revenue, quickly locate the country, advertising type or server cluster when any problem occurs, and find out the root cause of this problem; and site reliability engineering (SRE) team can detect server errors, quickly locate the physical problem of the terminal, data center or server cluster, and then report the problem for monitoring.

Based on the query conditions on the left side of Figure 3.5, different business teams can draw a time series chart that contains three measurement dimensions (upper, middle and lower comparison curves) related to the data dissemination scheduling on the page of Facebook. The dotted line represents the data at the same time one week ago, and the solid line represents the data at the current time. This chart clearly shows the daily and weekly changes in user behavior. Thousands of monitoring queries are run every hour, problems are found from massive user feedback and then grouped by different dimensions (such as geographic location, age, and number of friends).

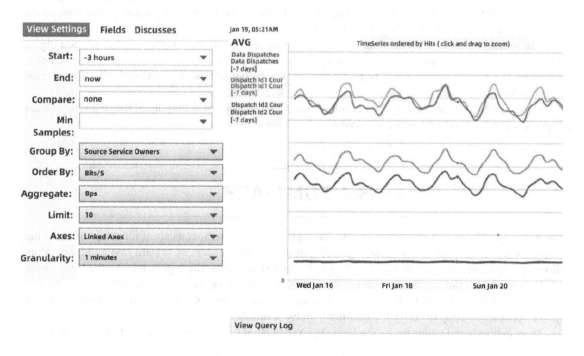

FIGURE 3.5 Real-time monitoring interface of Facebook in 2012.

3.3.3 Automating Routine Work

There are lots of repetitive tasks in the process of software development, like building a testing environment, regression testing, application deployment, and release. In the case of low delivery frequency, these activities will not take up a lot of working hours. However, as the Verification Loop operates faster and faster, software release will become more frequent within a fixed period of time, and the fixed costs of such routine work will account for a larger proportion. For example, if the software was released only once a month in the early stage, but now released eight times each month, then its fixed costs will increase by eight times. It should be pointed out that this kind of routine work is mostly repetitive, it should be done by machines rather than manpower.

Therefore, we must effectively reduce these fixed costs by optimizing processes and automation measures, and avoid unnecessary errors in man-made operation in order to make automation routine work sustainable. In the case introduced in Chapter 16, the team increased software release from "every three months" to "every two weeks", which then resulted in higher costs; such problem was also resolved through automation in the end.

3.3.4 Monitoring Everything

After the software is run in the production environment, we need to collect and analyze its generated data in a timely and accurate manner. The monitoring of the production system is for two purposes: One is to confirm that the software is running smoothly; once an abnormality is found, we can promptly take measures to correct the error so as not to affect the user experience. The other is to obtain valid business data in time to verify the hypotheses that are put forward in the Discovery Loop.

The first purpose of monitoring is known as "application health monitoring". Generally speaking, most system monitoring software in the traditional operation maintenance field is developed for this purpose, such as the most basic hardware and software system (including CPU, memory, storage space, and network connection). Further application health monitoring is for the running status of the application itself, such as service response delay, page fault, and cache size.

The second purpose of monitoring is known as "business health monitoring", since its main object is business indicators. Although some basic log collection platforms are able to display some business indicators, the business indicators to be monitored are usually defined by business team according to their own business context and requirements.

Only through comprehensive system monitoring and discovery of anomalies at the first time can we respond in time to ensure business sustainability.

3.4 SUMMARY

The Verification Loop, which centers on fast and high-quality delivery, consists of four steps as building, running, monitoring, and decision-making. Being guided by the concept of "identifying and eliminating all wastes" in Continuous Delivery 2.0, we should stick to the four working principles of the Verification Loop, namely, building quality in, eliminating waiting, automating toils, and monitoring everything. Besides, we must continuously discover and eliminate wastes in our work, only in this way can we speed up the Verification Loop to verify the minimum viable solution.

More methods and pathways to accelerate the Verification Loop are discussed in following chapters.

A Suitable Organizational Culture for Continuous Delivery 2.0

4

The Continuous Delivery 2.0 Double-loop Model requires the cooperation of multiple disciplines and roles within a company, and its goal is to shorten the end-to-end (from idea to idea) closed-loop cycle, which will inevitably affect the internal cooperation mode and process. The thoughts, ideas, and principles of Continuous Delivery 2.0 may be greatly different from the existing management style and code of conduct that are known to the members of an organization, and there may even be conflicts. Therefore, the top leadership must learn to lead this transformation, establish a corporate culture that is compatible with it, and make Continuous Delivery 2.0 the genes of their business, so that they can continue to reap the benefits it brings.

4.1 SECURITY, MUTUAL TRUST, AND CONTINUOUS IMPROVEMENT

Continuous Delivery 2.0 emphasizes "continuous discovery" and "fast verification", while discovery is bound to be accompanied by failure, which makes people feel frustrated and insecure. But failure also brings learning and growth. Given this, an organization must establish an organizational culture of "security, mutual trust, and continuous improvement".

4.1.1 Don't Be Afraid of Failure

How to deal with "failure", whether it is a failure in experiments or in organizational improvement, is of great significance for an organization. We have identified lots of hypotheses in the Discovery Loop in the double-flywheels of Continuous Delivery, defined metric for these hypotheses, and verified the results of the Verification Loop. The experiment's results should not be used directly for judging individuals, since it may drive members of the organization to develop solutions for "confirmation" rather than for "falsification". And it will be unlikely for us to learn much from such "continuous success".

It's the same when it comes to organizational improvement. An organization is a complex system, no wonder its improvement is more complex. If members of an organization are to be punished for "making a mistake", they will no longer make any risky decisions for fear of being blamed.

In a highly uncertain environment, no one can make sure that their decisions will not go wrong. If members of an organization cannot feel secure when encountering a failure, they are prone to take

DOI: 10.1201/9781003221579-4

care of their own business and reduce cooperation in order to avoid making mistakes and shirk their responsibility.

4.1.2 Mutual Trust

Mutual trust is the basis for efficient cooperation between members of an organization, and also for uniting everyone and boosting their morale. Members need to trust each other's personal quality and professional ability. It is a kind of mutual trust. Lacking trust between each other may cause mutual suspicion or even accusation. And it will not take long for members of an organization to feel insecure and then no longer work as efficiently as before.

Over the past decade or so, many organizations have attempted the Agile Software Development Model, but failed to achieve their goal. In addition to some technical constraints, a nonnegligible reason for their failure is the lack of a "mutual trust" culture. Without this kind of culture, members of an organization tend to blame each other, such as "product specialists are disappointed with developers' performance" and "developers complaining about unreliable product specialists".

4.1.3 Continuous Improvement

In his *Toyota Kata* (2009), Mike Rother made the following remark:

> *"As we conducted benchmarking studies in the 1980's and 90's and tried to explain the reasons for the manufacturing performance gap between Toyota and other automobile companies, we saw at Toyota the now familiar 'lean' techniques such as kanban, cellular manufacturing, short changeovers, andon lights, and so on. Many concluded – and I initially did too – that these new production techniques and the fact that Western industry was still relying on old techniques were the primary reasons for Toyota's superior performance."*

It is the companies that are good at "continuous improvement" and able to make it as their culture will constantly make progress.

The culture of continuous improvement features "full participation" and "constant improvement". "Full participation" requires everyone in an organization to assume the responsibility for "continuous improvement", while "constant improvement" means that it should be routine work, instead of something only taking place at specific times or conditions such as post-event analysis and correction.

4.2 FOUR STEPS IN CULTURE SHAPING

Culture is intangible and hard to change. But when it influences the behaviors of organization members, it is also under an imperceptible impact of their behaviors. How organization members act and react is mainly determined by the actions of their leaders and managers. In *Lean Enterprise: Adopting Continuous Delivery, DevOps, and Lean Startup at Scale*, Jez Humble, Joanne Molesky & Barry O'Reilly. made the following conclusion:

> *"As Mike Rother points out in Toyota Kata, 'what is decisive is not the form of the organization, but how people act and react.' This is determined primarily by the actions of leadership and management".*

For example, do the leadership and management trust people, allow them to act independently, and bear risks and responsibilities together with them? Do the leadership and management punish people for their failure, or do they encourage cross-discipline communication?

So, how do companies establish and maintain an organizational culture that they uphold? Let us look at what Toyota has done in this regard.

4.2.1 Behavior Determines Culture

In the early 1980s, General Motors Corporation (GM) had been bearing a high cost in manufacturing cars, while its Japanese counterpart – Toyota Motor Corporation – spent much less in manufacturing high-quality cars. It was eager to learn about Toyota's management style and manufacturing techniques. Toyota was at that time looking for a United States (US) partner to cofound a local vehicle plant for opening up the US domestic auto market. Both sides hit it off and decided to establish a joint venture known as New United Motor Manufacturing, Inc. (NUMMI). But GM insisted that this joint venture must be built on basis of its old vehicle plant in Fremont, and it must reemploy the workers of the old plant. These two conditions were indeed "harsh", because the Fremont plant was the one notorious for poorest vehicle quality and undisciplined workers among all GM plants. For example, many workers were drinking alcohol, gambling or making trouble at work, going on strike or filing complaints once in a while; the proportion of absent workers often exceeded 20%; and some workers were found deliberately sabotaging production materials and cutting corners during manufacturing.

Just one year later, the level of absenteeism of this new company plummeted to 2%, and its car quality was upgraded from the worst to the best within GM. How did Toyota's leadership make it? Its management method is illustrated in the following example:

> *Toyota firmly believes in "respect for humanity", and requires every employee to find problems and think about ways for improvement, which is similar to Facebook's creed that "nothing is someone else's problem". As a Toyota manager, if he wants employees to discover problems, seek improvement and achieve self-fulfillment, he shall explain to them why it is important to do so. Toyota brought its culture to NUMMI. A typical component of this new culture is the famous "Stop-the-Line System", which is also known as "Andon System".*

The system of "andon", a Japanese word meaning "signal light", is depicted in Figure 4.1. Every worker will receive the following training: once encountering a problem on the production line and unable to solve it when reaching the "Warning Prompt Line", the worker should pull the signal light without

FIGURE 4.1 Diagram of Toyota's andon system.

delay and report to the foreman who must come to his help immediately. If the problem is yet solved when approaching the "Completion Prompt Line", the worker shall pull the signal light again, then the entire production line will cease working right away and do not resume until this problem is solved.

At the beginning of the establishment of NUMMI, some original GM managers questioned the significance of the andon system, arguing that management should not give frontline workers such great power to stop the entire production line by themselves, but report to their superior for instruction and let him make the decision. But the manager from Toyota disagreed with them. "We empower them to stop production as soon as possible once they find a problem, and have it solved immediately, instead of leaving the problem to the next step. In this way, first-line producers can enhance their quality awareness, and the plant can minimize the defective product rate".

In fact, andon is not just an operation manual, principle, or training program but a system teaching everyone to "get their job done with high quality". As an epitome of Toyota's beliefs and commitments, the andon system urges all employees to take production quality as the first standard.

The transformation of the corporate culture of NUMMI has proved that, in addition to "changing people's behaviors by changing their thinking", companies are also able to shape a corporate culture through "changing people's thinking by changing their behaviors". John Shook, the first foreign employee of Toyota, has made great contributions to the company's North American business and is now a master in lean thinking and methodology. Based on his ten years' onsite practice, John Shook has summed up the cultural transformation of NUMMI as a "four-step method".

- Step 1: Define what you want to do.
- Step 2: Define the expectant ways or methods for doing things.
- Step 3: Provide employees with appropriate training.
- Step 4: Design necessary mechanisms or measures to reinforce the behaviors being encouraged.

Through these four steps, employees can master a set of methods for completing their work. And the corporate culture of this company will be shaped in the end. In this way, companies can create a work environment meeting their expectation, and a favorable work environment will have a positive impact on all employees.

Organizational culture, which is the manifestation of a series of behavioral outcomes and reflected in the daily work contact between people, cannot be transformed directly. But we can achieve the purpose of shaping the corporate culture by training employees to master necessary vocational skills and standardize their manners of working. Such approach is quite common in Internet companies too.

4.2.2 Google's Engineer Culture

Google attaches great importance to software quality. Whenever an engineer submits a code change, it must be reviewed by other engineers before being incorporated into the codebase. And these engineers must be qualified to review code readability. Any engineer that intends to take part in a code review shall first file an application and wait for the approval by the review panel.

Google's code quality culture is also reflected in the automation test behavior of its development engineers. These engineers write automation testcases for their own code. Before each code review, they will run the automation testcases and submit the test results to the reviewers for reference. In the Large-Scale Continuous Testing in the Cloud organized in 2013, John Penix mentioned that Google had about 10,000 engineers in 2012, every day they could run 50,000 builds and 50 million testcases.

Google engineers weren't working like that at the beginning; manual testing had been playing an important role before 2005. As result of rapid expansion of project teams and increasingly complicated businesses, test engineers had become terribly busy. At the same time, development engineers had to deal with endless production problems, looking like fire fighters rushing to put out the fire. In this context, Google began to build an engineer culture by taking the following four steps:

Step 1: Define what you want to do.
- Improve code quality, reduce production problems, cut back on manual testing workload, and accelerate software release.

Step 2: Define the expectant ways or methods for doing things.
- Software engineers write automation testcases.
- Proactively run automation testcases.
- Kick off code review.

Step 3: Provide employees with appropriate training.
- Organize trainings for code design and automation test within the company.
- Assign a mentor to each team to help team members improve their automation test skills.

Step 4: Design necessary mechanisms or measures to reinforce the behaviors being encouraged.
- Establish a test-certification mechanism, which splits into three large levels with multiple sub-levels, for evaluating the test maturity of each product team. Based on the quarterly distribution statistics of the number of teams at each level, it is possible for evaluating the progress of automation test culture within the company.
- Build a test group and assign a test mentor to help the team improve its automation test capability.
- Create Readability Certification.
- Code review is mandatory before the code is merged into the version repository.
- Before code review, automation testcases must be passed and a testing report must be submitted to code reviewers.

The above four steps are not easy to be implemented, thus costing Google's four years around to do so. The details in this regard are not discussed here.

4.2.3 Etsy's Continuous Testing Culture

In 2012, the website of Etsy was capable of deploying code for about 25 times and configuration information for about 30 times every day on average (see in Figure 4.2). The total number of employees of this e-commerce company was no more than 200, meaning that each deployment was done by one person in 15 minutes. This must be attributed to Etsy's "continuous testing" culture.

Its concrete measures are introduced as follows:

Step 1: Define what you want to do.
- Don't be afraid of failure, release quickly, and test continuously.

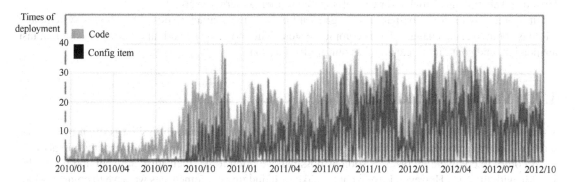

FIGURE 4.2   Etsy's software configuration deployment frequency.

Step 2: Define the expectant ways or methods for doing things.
- Deploy to the production environment multiple times a day.
- Collect data and make statistical analysis immediately after deployment.

Step 3: Provide employees with appropriate training.
- Every new employee is asked to post his photo on the website of Etsy on the first day at work. This is a simple task for newcomers to find where is the template file and how to put their photos on it. In this way, they will learn how to log in to their virtual machine, where to put the code, how to run automation tests, how to push the code to the production, and where to view the matrices to make sure everything is running properly. The purpose is to enable new employees to acquaint with the deployment process from the beginning and do away with fears of deployment.
- Organize trainings for "continuous testing". For example, the search box reconstruction case introduced in Chapter 2 expounds how to decompose a large project into multiple sub-projects, and then collect relevant data about each sub-project, in an aim to verify the initial hypothesis for a sub-project.

Step 4: Design necessary mechanisms or measures to reinforce the behaviors being encouraged.
- Each change requires data measurement.
- Learn from real data regardless of failure or success.
- Develop corresponding tools to improve the capability of deployment and of data collection and analysis with minimal cost.

Facebook has a similar culture. Every engineer has to attend a four-week newcomer training camp in the initial days. In the first week, the code submitted by most engineers will be released to the production environment. By the second week, the code written by almost all new engineers will be released at least once.

4.3 ACTION GUIDE

The above four-step method for shaping corporate culture looks easy, but its implementation will encounter all sorts of challenges, because in the area of organizational management, a company is usually taken as a complex system that has the characters of both a simple system and a random system. A complex system, with a moderate number of intelligent and adaptive components (also known as "subjects"), acts on basis of local information. Existing in every part of the world, a complex system is hard to be defined. It is neither a simple system nor a random system, but a nonlinear complex system, and it contains interdependent subsystems available for coevolving due to their synergistic effect.

It is precisely because companies or organizations have the characteristics of a complex system, any action is about to bring changes to this complex system. Therefore, we should take "value orientation, fast verification, and continuous learning" as our guide of action.

4.3.1 Value Orientation

Although everyone agrees that "we should be value-oriented when doing things", it is often overlooked and hard to be judged while working. It is overlooked because we are dealing with too many things every day. In order to complete all tasks as soon as possible, we often forget their ultimate goal and their relationship with the goal. However, if we want to make right judgments, sometimes we have to come to a halt to think about whether the things we are doing are valuable or most valuable.

It is hard to be judged because everyone in the organization has his/her own backgrounds and experiences, they perceive the external market environment in different ways, and they even have different sense of value from the same workplace. Therefore, when we discuss "value", we should place it in a certain business context and avoid getting too far from the topic. Besides, we should try to provide a full context for discussion, and listen to other people's plans and suggestions.

Despite of sufficient communication and discussion, we may still fail to reach consensus amid multiple solutions to the same problem. At this time, we can apply the second action guide, namely, "fast verification".

4.3.2 Fast Verification

In a highly uncertain environment, it is not easy to judge the value of all solutions in advance, so we need fast verification to get real feedback and make decisions. In a safe working environment, as long as we can actively embrace the guide of "fast verification" and give full play to the subjective initiative of employees, we can find multiple solutions for fast verification.

Fast verification is also available for improving organizational management. For example, when dealing with specific problems, we can assign different pilot teams to perform fast verification, and then make adjustment and optimization according to the actual output of these teams.

4.3.3 Continuous Learning

We cannot guarantee that every decision is right. The team should learn some new knowledge from each feedback, and actively sum up successful experiences and lessons of failure. In addition to in-depth understanding and learning of the business area through the business results generated by experiments, it is also necessary to keep reflecting on the process of doing things, continuously optimize the workflow, and improve the efficiency of each link.

There are two common ways to learn and reflect on the daily workflow of the team: one is regular retrospective, and the other is event-replay mechanism.

4.3.3.1 Regular retrospective

As a meeting initiated by the team periodically, regular retrospective is for team members to analyze the strengths and weaknesses of their collaboration in the past period, and discuss the countermeasures for sustaining progress and making improvement. Regular retrospective is akin to the "retrospective meeting" – an important practice in agile software development.

In his book *Project Retrospectives: A Handbook for Team Reviews*, Norman L. Kerth proposed that the team should repeat the retrospective declaration at the beginning of each retrospective meeting, that is, "Regardless of what we discover, we understand and truly believe that everyone did the best job they could, given what they knew at the time, their skills and abilities, the resources available, and the situation at hand". This is to emphasize a team culture characterized by "safety" and "trust".

In addition, it should be noted that after the retrospective meeting is over, there should be measures and plans for improvement, and the results of their implementation can be tracked. At the same time, do not set too many improvement items for fear of falling into the situation of "repeated proposal and implementation, but no actual progress".

4.3.3.2 Event-replay mechanism

The event-replay mechanism is to analyze the problems that have occurred for the purpose of avoiding the recurrence of the same kind of problems. The team shall first collect and sort out the relevant information before and after the problem occurs, determine its severity, and examine its development process (in case of any difficult problem, an offline simulation test or even online test may be required to reproduce the problem and find out the reasons). Then the team needs to conduct root cause analysis, summarize experiences, work out measures and plans for improvement, and track the results of their implementation.

For root cause analysis, the following points need to be noted:

1. Relax and share.
2. Distinguish "cause" from "effect".
3. Adopt the "Five Whys" approach.
4. Give full play to group wisdom.
5. Look for underlying cause instead of focusing only on superficial effects.
6. Verify the answer.

It is worth mentioning that there should be records and summaries for each replay, and these records and summaries shall be shared among all employees in the company. Only in this way can the company maximize its profits.

The method of "System Thinking" is applicable to both regular retrospective and event-replay mechanism. System Thinking is to think about various forces and interrelationships that affect the system behavior as a whole, so as to cultivate people's understanding and decision-making ability of complexity, interdependence, change, and influence. To put it simply, it is to think about things comprehensively, not just consider something as it stands, but to study a series of issues (such as the desired result, the process of achieving the result, process optimization, and the impact on the future) as an integral system. In terms of the traditional mode of thinking, we usually assume that there is a linear relationship between "cause" and "effect", that is, "cause" produces "effect". But in System Thinking, neither "cause" nor "effect" is absolute, they may have circular interaction between each other, that is, "cause" produces "effect", and this "effect" becomes the "cause" of another "effect" and even the "cause" of another "cause". A specific case is listed below to illustrate the use of System Thinking.

PRACTICAL APPLICATION OF SYSTEM THINKING

It was a case occurred in a foundation product department of a well-known Internet company. This department, which consisted of about 120 engineers, was engaged in collecting public data from internet. They were evenly divided into five teams to deal with different domain areas.

The problem in front of this department was like this: by the end of each quarter, all the five teams always failed to fully complete the key projects that they had committed at the beginning of the quarter. The leader of each team explained that the project progress was hard to control, their plans were often disrupted, and they didn't have enough time. The heads of specific projects also complained that they had so many things to do, but they never got anything done, so they couldn't have a sense of achievement.

Consequently, the department head and the managers of the five teams sat down together to summarize and analyze these issues. Their analysis result is depicted in Figure 4.3.

In Figure 4.3, each node is both the cause and the effect of the other's being and they are mutually reinforcing. For example, once the period of a project was prolonged, another urgent and important requirement would be added into its schedule, thus occupying the resources and extending the current project. Moreover, if the newly added requirement was a new project, there would be multiple projects in parallel. In the case of insufficient resources, in order to meet the deadline as set by multiple project owners, all team members had to work overtime to catch up with the schedule. However, exhausted personnel were prone to make errors or omissions, create more defective products, and lower the quality of deliverables in the end. Then, they would need more time to repair and verify defects, which would further prolong the project period. Moreover, since testers

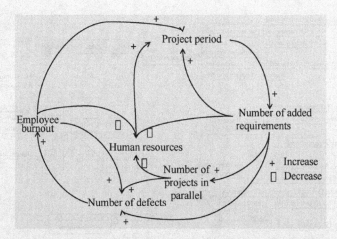

FIGURE 4.3 Schematic diagram of System Thinking in organizational management.

and developers were not in the same team, any delay would lead to changes in project plans and frequent transfers of testers, making it difficult to arrange testing manpower for project acceptance. As a result, upon submissions for test, developers had to wait for testers to be in place, which once again lengthened the project period.

The causes and effects of these problems were interlinked, and it seems that these teams were bound to have such an outcome. But all of them blamed their failure for "shortage of resources". While doing consultation for my customers, most of them would complain for "being short-handed" or "too many requirements".

Like the "lengthened project period", the abovementioned phenomena were merely the operation result of the entire system. Further analysis is needed to find the causes of these phenomena and work out a countermeasure (the reason why it is known as a "countermeasure" is that we are sometimes not sure whether it is indeed the solution to the problem). As a result, the managers of these teams further analyzed each phenomenon and found more information.

By the end of each quarter, this department had to formulate a work plan for the next quarter and each team should establish 3~5 department-level projects for itself during the quarter. This type of projects was classified as P0-level projects. Generally speaking, P0-level projects dealt with important businesses with a large input of resources, and had strict time limits. In addition, this department also had P1, P2, and P3-level projects that accounted for a higher proportion. But they had less resource input and a shorter term. In order to meet the tight deadline, these teams had to save time from business planning period. Because of poor preparation and inadequate consideration, the next-quarter plan was not reasonable enough, meaning that the same problems would repeat themselves in the next quarter.

Figure 4.4 shows that these problems are related to all aspects of organizational management, including organizational planning, personnel capability, software architecture, workflow system, and incentives, as well as many uncontrollable factors from the outside.

The manifestation of these problems in organizational planning:

- Too many goals, lack of details, and insufficient time for preparation, resulting in unclear planning.
- Less attention was paid to goal setting.
- Inadequate time for planning, resulting in nonbinding project commitments.

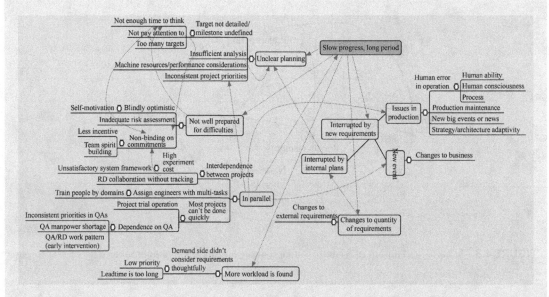

FIGURE 4.4 Schematic diagram of information mining.

The manifestation of these problems in personnel capability:

- Blindly optimistic, and insufficient assessment of difficulties.
- Misoperation due to lack of awareness and ability caused online problems.
- Insufficient analysis ability (thoughtless about machine resources and software performance), resulting in unclear planning.

The manifestation of these problems in software architecture:

- Poor software framework and high cost of testing, resulting in heavy dependence between projects.
- Low adaptability of algorithm strategy and framework, resulting in online problems.

The manifestation of these problems in workflow and incentives:

- Lack of an effective incentive mechanism, resulting in hasty project evaluation and commitment.
- Poor management of external requirements, resulting in inaccurate estimates of workload.
- Incongruous work patterns of developers and testers, poor communication, and collaboration between them, resulting in multiple projects in parallel.
- No tracking of the modules designed by developers through collaboration, resulting in a waste of time in waiting and communication.

The manifestation of these problems in uncontrollable factors from the outside:

- Abnormal fluctuations in traffic caused by new Internet conditions.
- Changes in the market environment, resulting in temporary adjustments in business direction.
- Urgent needs of other business departments.

After discussion, the managers of these teams finally agreed that the core problem of them was "unclear planning". The department was used to developing the quarterly plan with each team as a unit, triggering these teams to only think for itself. All of them wanted to take over more major projects and receive more input of resources, thus depriving the department of key emphasis in work.

Therefore, in the subsequent planning, the five teams were taken as a whole, there were no more than six P0-level projects in a quarter, and all of these projects should be discussed and agreed by the managers of all teams. In each monthly meeting, these managers could adjust the priorities of these projects according to the actual situation, so as to make "breakthroughs" each month and complete the work related to core business.

4.4 IMPORTANCE OF MEASUREMENT

"If you cannot measure it, you cannot improve it", or "you can't manage what you can't measure", said Peter Drucker, the Father of Modern Management. What he wanted to tell us is that success must be defined and tracked, otherwise we cannot know whether we've succeeded or not. This shows the importance of measurement to business management. In the process of organizational improvement, we need to collect data to measure our progress.

However, as managers, we have to admit that there are matters unable to be managed in our daily work, even if we must do so, especially in a highly uncertain environment. This is a premise for discussing the principle of measurement.

4.4.1 Four Attributes of Measurement Indicators

Measurement indicators are divided into leading indicators, lagging indicators, observable indicators, and actionable indicators, which are separately introduced as follows:

4.4.1.1 Leading and lagging indicators

Leading indicators refer to the indicators that play an important role in achieving predetermined goals. Generally, a good leading indicator has two basic characteristics: it is predictable, and it is available to be influenced by team members almost immediately.

Lagging indicators refer to the traceability indicators for achieving the most important goals, such as sales revenue, profit margin, market share, and customer satisfaction. But these indicators are in fact historical data, since the events that have led to them already came to an end when we've obtained these data.

For example, when all other factors are the same, a software product with better quality and performance is more competitive, it is able to draw more customers and have a higher sales volume. In this case, software sales are a lagging indicator, while software quality and performance are a leading indicator. We can influence software sales by improving its quality and performance, but its sales, as a lagging indicator, are not guaranteed.

As the ultimate posterior indicator of a company, customer value is also a lagging indicator. By comparison, all other indicators can be regarded as leading indicators.

4.4.1.2 Observable and actionable indicators

Observable indicators refer to the indicators that can be objectively monitored but cannot be changed through direct actions. Actionable indicators refer to the indicators that are accessible and available to be directly changed through team effort.

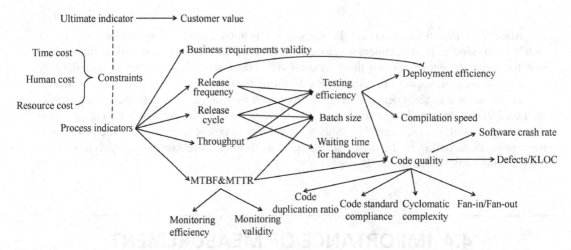

FIGURE 4.5   Correlation between software measurement indicators.

For example, "defects per thousands of lines of code" (Defects/KLOC) is an observable indicator. It cannot be changed directly, but influenced through more extensive quality assurance activities, such as writing high-quality code and doing more comprehensive tests.

Code compliance, cyclomatic complexity, and duplication ratio are at the same time observable and actionable indicators, because the team can directly influence and change these indicators by modifying the code, but they cannot ensure that Defects/KLOC, as a posterior observable indicator, could be reached.

According to the *DevOps Status Report 2017*, IT high-performance organizations have four measurement indicators, namely, release frequency, release cycle, mean time between failure (MTBF)/ mean time to repair (MTTR), and throughput. Among them, release frequency refers to the frequency at which the software is deployed and run in the production environment. For example, the release frequency of the Facebook Mobile App is once a week. In the *DevOps Status Report 2017*, release cycle refers to the time period from code submission to its release. MTBF denotes the mean value of time from the start of work to the first failure of the new product in a given work environment. MTTR denotes the time period from the occurrence of failure to its reparation. Throughput refers to the quantity of deliverables completed by the system in a given time period.

As shown in Figure 4.5, if the above four indicators are taken as lagging indicators, then compilation speed, test duration, and deployment efficiency may become their leading indicators. We can infer that starting from lagging indicators and deriving step-by-step forward, we can find lots of actionable leading indicators. It should be noted that there may be a time delay effect on correlated indicators, that is, the improvement made to an indicator is reflected in its correlated indicator after a period of time. And the longer the indicator chain is, the lower the predictability it will have.

4.4.2 The Goal of Measurement Is to Improve

We can improve our working process by trying to manage process indicators, and compare the final effect with our expected result indicators, so as to confirm whether the improvement is effective, and decide whether we need to change the direction of improvement or keep moving forward. If the process indicator is farther away from the result indicator, its influence on the final result will become less clear and its contribution will be less direct.

Therefore, we shall keep making analysis based on the feedback measurement results before determining the direction of improvement: whether to continue or find another way. Measurement is a double-edged sword. For the actionable process indicators, "you'll get what you've measured", but not necessarily in the way that you want. For example, when measuring unit test coverage, engineers can write useless unit tests (in case of no assertion) to achieve unit test coverage indicators, but this test coverage doesn't make any sense. Therefore, managers shall keep in mind that the goal of measurement is to improve the organization. If the measurement fails to achieve its goal, they have to employ other measurement indicators or do a good job in management.

4.5 THE "IMPROVEMENT KATA" FOR CONTINUOUS IMPROVEMENT

The "Continuous Delivery 2.0 Capability" can be improved in more than one way. For companies, "*N* times of software release per day*" may not be their best choice considering their current situation. Each company shall choose its own path according to the characteristics of its industry, competitive environment, specific forms of products, and competence of personnel.

So, how can we improve our "Continuous Delivery 2.0 Capability"? In his book *Toyota Kata*, Mike Rother introduced a method known as "improvement kata". It consists of four circular stages as shown in Figure 4.6.

- **Stage 1: Understand the direction, vision, target, or need.** Managers need to understand that a company must always take the vision as its target and make continuous improvement. Despite of the difficulties on the way forward, they shall keep experimenting and iterating to achieve our target.
- **Stage 2: Grasp the current condition.** The team needs to know well about the current condition and collect relevant data, so as to have a full knowledge of themselves and make a reasonable description of the next target condition.
- **Stage 3: Establish the next target condition.** The target condition refers to the condition that the team wants to realize. In order to do so, the team should set a desired date to realize that condition and define measurement indicators.
- **Stage 4: The PDCA Cycle.** The plan-do-check-act (PDCA) cycle is a four-step problem-solving iterative technique used to improve business processes. The method was popularized by quality control pioneer Dr. W. Edwards Deming in the 1950s. The PDCA cycle can help a company streamline its processes, reduce costs, increase profits, and improve customer satisfaction.

This "improvement kata" is not for any particular domain, but a universal method. It is a general framework and a set of routine practices for achieving the goal when the path to the goal is uncertain; it is directly applicable to the process of organizational improvement. Since it doesn't tell us exactly what to do, we have to look for some clues to start this process.

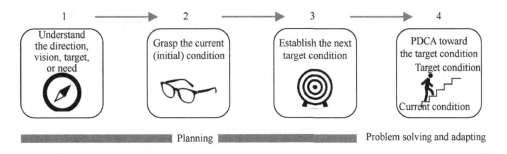

FIGURE 4.6 The improvement kata.

4.6 SUMMARY

In this chapter, we've discussed the cultural atmosphere required for companies to practice continuous delivery, and come up with the following four steps to create a corporate culture based on the case of NUMMI.

- Step 1: Define what you want to do.
- Step 2: Define the expectant ways or methods for doing things.
- Step 3: Provide employees with appropriate training.
- Step 4: Design necessary mechanisms or measures to reinforce the behaviors being encouraged.

In order to improve the "Continuous Delivery 2.0 Capability", a company or organization needs to abide by three principles of action, namely, value orientation, fast verification, and continuous learning. Some specific methods of continuous learning, such as iterative review and replay mechanism, are also analyzed. Moreover, we've discussed the benefits and risks in organizational measurement, and emphasized that the goal of measurement is organizational improvement, rather than performance comparison between individuals.

Companies should follow the "improvement kata": after setting a goal, they should first work on simple tasks and then maintain optimization so as to improve their "Continuous Delivery 2.0 Capability".

Software Architecture for Continuous Delivery

5

Back in 2000, the e-commerce giant Amazon still relied on the Monolithic Application, instead of the Microservice Architecture that prevails nowadays. At that time, each deployment of the Monolithic Application was a matter affecting the entire website, which was bad for the stability of the website during large-scale promotional campaigns. Although the technical team had made capacity expansion in advance, the huge traffic during the campaigns far exceeded its anticipation. Consequently, production incidents occurred from time to time; when one problem was fixed, another one soon propped up.

The management of Amazon reviewed this phenomenon and blamed it for a high degree of coupling and complexity of the Monolithic Architecture. However, amid too many business requirements and a tight schedule, engineers who were busy with the features at hand had no time for communication and learning about the overall architecture. To solve this problem, engineers should have more in-depth discussions before developing requirements. But the company's CEO Jeff Bezos recommended to reduce the communications between teams, and increase those within individual teams. To this end, the Monolithic Architecture of the website should be fully transformed into the Service-oriented Architecture (SOA), and the following requirements should also be satisfied[1]:

1. All teams must provide data and various functions in the form of service interface.
2. The communication between teams must be via interface.
3. No other forms of interoperability are allowed, such as direct reading of data from other teams, shared memory, and any form of backdoor. The only permitted communication is to be via a Web service call.
4. The specific implementation technology is not specified; Hypertext Transfer Protocol (HTTP), CORBA, Pub/Sub, and user-defined protocol are all available.
5. All service interfaces must be designed to be open from the beginning, without exception. That is to say, when an interface is designed, it is assumed to be open to outsiders, and there is no room for bargaining.
6. Anyone who doesn't abide by the above rules will be fired.

As of 2011, the deployment frequency of Amazon's production environment had been greatly improved. On a workday there was deployment every 11.6 seconds on average, and the deployment in an hour even topped 1,079 times[2]. This must give the credit to the transformation of the Monolithic Architecture into the SOA. Clearly, Continuous Delivery is indispensable for better response to business development; and the principle of "big systems to be made small" for software architecture is a necessary condition to achieve this goal.

---

[1] See Steve Yegge's *Programmer's Rantings*.
[2] See the speech "Velocity Culture" delivered by Jon Jenkins at O'Reilly Velocity Conference 2011.

DOI: 10.1201/9781003221579-5

5.1 DIVIDING THE SYSTEM INTO MODULES

5.1.1 Requirements for a Continuous Delivery Architecture

In order to accelerate delivery and obtain Continuous Delivery capability, the following factors need to be taken into account for designing a system architecture:

1. **Design for test.** After we've written out the code, if its testing requires lots of energy and preparations, there will be a long time from writing the code to completing the quality verification, thus making fast release out of the question.
2. **Design for deployment.** After we've developed a new feature, if its deployment is time-consuming and even calling for a downtime, then it cannot be rapidly released.
3. **Design for monitor.** If we cannot monitor the feature after it goes online, and fail to discover its defects until receiving user feedback, then the benefits of Continuous Delivery will be greatly discounted.
4. **Design for scale.** The scalability here involves two aspects: one is to expand the scale of teams; the other is to expand the scale of the system itself.
5. **Design for failure.** An old Chinese goes, "If you always walk around the river, your shoes must be wet". We are bound to come across issues in case of fast deployment. Therefore, before we start developing a software feature, we should think about how to deal with a failed deployment or release in an easy manner.

5.1.2 Principles for System Decomposition

The approach of "dividing the system into modules" is not something new. In 1971, D.L. Parnas published a paper *On the Criteria to be Used in Decomposing Systems into Modules*[3], discussing modularization as a mechanism for improving the flexibility and comprehensibility of a system while allowing the shortening of its development time. As for today's system architecture, are there any the principles for guiding the "system decomposition"?

A large system should consist of many components or services that usually appear in the form of jar/war/dll/gem, and their granularity is larger than a class, but much smaller than the entire system. Components are usually integrated during compilation, construction or deployment, and services may be composed of multiple components that are started and run independently, and able to communicate with the entire system at runtime, thus becoming a component of the entire system. In reference to the paper of D.L. Parnas, and in combination with the development trend of software and requirements for Continuous Delivery, the following principles for system decomposition should be followed:

1. As a part of the system, each component or service has clear business responsibilities and can be modified independently or even replaced by another implementation scheme.
2. "High cohesion, low coupling" makes the entire system easy to maintain. Each component or service relates to as little information as possible and performs a relatively independent single function.
3. The entire system is easy to build and test. After the system is decomposed, these components still need to be combined to provide services for users. Therefore, if there is any difficulty in

---

[3] Reprinted from *Communications of the ACM*, Vol. 15, No. 12, December 1972 pp. 1053–1058.

building and testing the system, it will be unlikely to shorten the development cycle and achieve the goal of Continuous Delivery.

4. Make communication and collaboration between team members smoother.

But this decomposition has brought new problems. For example, for a system composed of multiple services, a request may be completed after many mutual calls between different services, but the call chain is too long. When there are hundreds of services, a request can hardly be completed without a service discovery mechanism. If the service maintained by another team is called in the code, it will be more difficult to find the problem. Unless there is a uniform way to run all services in the sandbox, it will be almost impossible to perform any debugging.

In view of the above problems, we need to establish reasonable building, testing, deployment, and monitoring mechanisms while the system is decomposed. The establishment of these mechanisms is as important as system decomposition. Only in this way can we obtain the benefits of system decomposition, and in the same time manage the complexities caused by the decomposition. For example, Google's C++ code is stored in the same code repository where there are many interdependent components. Google specially developed a powerful compiler platform "Blaze" (now is an open source as "Bazel") to build these components.

5.2 COMMON ARCHITECTURAL PATTERNS

There are already many books on software architecture. This book only discusses three architectural patterns: Microcore Architecture (applicable to client software to be distributed to users); Microservice Architecture (used by companies in their own controllable backend server software); and Monolithic Architecture (preferred by startup companies for software development).

5.2.1 Microcore Architecture

The Microcore Architecture, also known as the Plugin Architecture, denotes the relatively small core framework of software with main business functions and business logic implemented through plug-ins (see Figure 5.1). The core framework usually contains only the basic functions for system startup and operation, such as communication modules, rendering, and overall interface framework. Plug-ins are independent of each other, and their communication is only carried out via the core framework to avoid interdependence.

This architecture boasts the following advantages:

- Good extensibility: Whenever a function is wanted, we only need to develop a plug-in.
- Easy to release: Plug-ins can be loaded and unloaded independently, making them easy to be released.
- Easy to test: Functions are isolated, and plug-ins are fit for isolation test.
- Highly customizable: Satisfy different requirements.
- Iterative development: Functions can be added step by step.

However, this architecture also has some shortcomings:

- Poor scalability: The core is usually an independent unit that is hard to be distributed, but this is not a serious problem for client software.

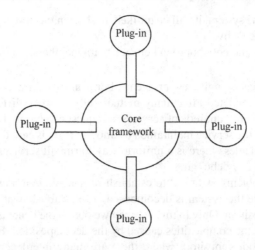

FIGURE 5.1   Sketch diagram of Microcore Architecture.

- Difficult development: The communication between plug-ins and the core, coupled with the internal plug-in registration mechanism, has resulted in sophisticated development.
- Highly dependent on the core framework: Despite of the convenience brought by the core framework, this architecture may interfere with all plug-ins and result in a large amount of transformation work when the framework interface is upgraded.

Considering its characteristics, we've included the Microcore Architecture into the architecture transformation of client software, which has greatly benefited the team's Continuous Delivery. A case in Chapter 14 will illustrate how this transformation makes it easier to increase the release frequency of PC-based client applications while ensuring software quality.

5.2.2 Microservice Architecture

The Microservice Architecture is to divide a single application into a set of small services that coordinate and cooperate with each other to provide users with ultimate value. Each service runs in its own process, and they communicate with each other via a lightweight communication mechanism (usually RESTful API based on HTTP or Remote procedure call, aka RPC). Each service is built around a specific domain and able to be separately deployed to a production or production-like environment. In addition, a unified and centralized service management mechanism should be avoided as far as possible. In order to build a specific service, appropriate languages and tools should be selected according to its business context.

This architecture boasts the following advantages:

- Good scalability: Low coupling between various services. Individual services can be expanded separately, such as the service node *D* shown in Figure 5.2.
- Easy to deploy: Each service is a deployable unit.
- Easy to develop: Each component can be developed and deployed separately, and upgraded continuously.
- Easy to test separately: When a single service is to be modified, we only need to test this service.

However, this architecture also has some shortcomings:

- Services may be finely divided due to the emphasis on mutual independence and low coupling. This causes the system to rely on a large number of microservices and therefore becoming disordered and cumbersome, and the network communication to be energy-intensive.

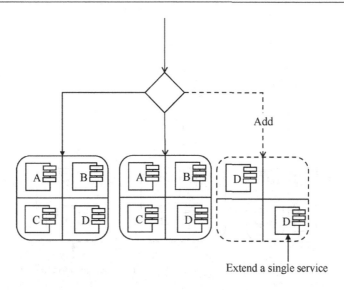

Add

Extend a single service

FIGURE 5.2 Add microservice node *D* separately as required.

- An external request may involve communication between multiple internal services, which makes debugging and diagnosis of problems more difficult and calls for support from more powerful tools.
- It brings difficulties to atomic operations (such as scenarios requiring transactional operations).
- The testing of cross-service composite business scenarios is quite difficult, usually requiring deployment and startup of multiple microservices simultaneously.
- The upgrade of public libraries is rather difficult. Given multiple microservices are using a common library, when the library have to be upgraded, we have to re-build and update each microservice.

Because of these difficulties, when we use the Microservice Architecture, we must ensure that each service can be deployed independently and that its downstream services are not affected during deployment and upgrading (such as to make multiple versions of API compatible), and at the same time establish an all-round monitoring system.

5.2.3 Monolithic Architecture

The Monolithic Application, also known as the Monolithic Architecture, describes a single-tiered software application in which the user interface and data access code are combined into a single program from a single platform. The word "monolith" is often used to describe buildings made from a single huge rock extracted from the earth. The Monolithic Architecture is a self-complete system independent of other applications. Its design philosophy is to go through all the steps for performing a function, not just to implement one of those steps. This architecture usually manifests as a complete package, such as a Java Archive File or a complete directory structure of Node.js or Rails. We can have everything as long as this package is held in our hands.

This architecture boasts the following advantages:

- Convenient for development and debugging: All the current development tools and IDEs support the development of the Monolithic Architecture that is simple and convenient for debugging.

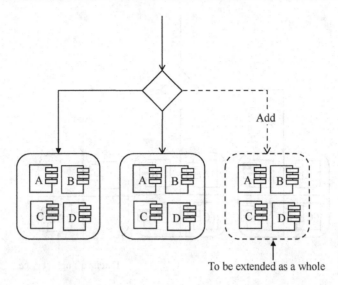

FIGURE 5.3 The Monolithic Architecture can only be extended as a whole.

- Easy to deploy: For example, only a WAR file (or a hierarchical structure of directory) needs to be deployed.
- Good scalability: The application can be extended by running its multiple copies behind the load balancer.

However, this architecture also has some shortcomings:

- For people who are not familiar with the overall program, this architecture is easy to produce messy code, pollute the entire application, and make it difficult to learn and understand.
- Hard to adapt to new technologies.
- The application can only be extended as a whole (see Figure 5.3).
- Continuous deployment is very difficult. In order to update a component, the entire application must be redeployed.

For startup companies or small and medium enterprises (SME) projects, the Monolithic Architecture can be iterated quickly without consuming too many resources. Moreover, it is easy for them to access to human resources, because they usually don't need highly skilled technicians to handle the Monolithic Architecture, a single technology stack may be enough.

The Monolithic Architecture also facilitates Continuous Delivery, but it needs to be properly designed and powerful infrastructure. For example, Facebook had deployment once a day in 2011, and its deployment package was about 1 GB in size. But the time spent on compiling such a large binary package was only about 20 minutes, and its distribution to almost 10,000 machines cost no more than two minutes.

In fact, no matter what kind of architecture, as long as it is not properly designed for the entire life cycle of the code (development, testing, and deployment), there will be difficulties for "fast delivery". For example, a Chinese Internet company once implement a framework, which builds microservice quickly and deploys easily. However, when they made an attempt on the practices of Continuous Delivery, the team found that this framework, when multiple people were developing new versions of multiple services in parallel, would encounter great difficulties in both debugging and testing. It was because this framework only one version for each services, and its registration and discovery must be based on the service's name; the coexistence of multiple versions of the same service was not supported. When two developers

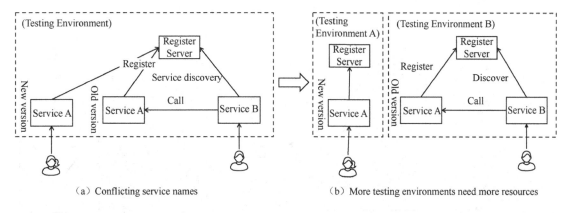

(a) Conflicting service names   (b) More testing environments need more resources

FIGURE 5.4 A microservice framework regardless of debugging environment.

were developing respective service modules A and B at the same time, if the new version of Service A was not yet developed, its joint debugging with Service B had to be based on its old version. In cases the two versions of Service A were concurrently deployed to the debugging environment, they would conflict with each other (see Figure 5.4a). So, it seems feasible to prepare two debugging environments for them (see Figure 5.4b). In other words, it is one exclusive environment for one developer; if more people are involved in parallel development and debugging, more resources must be invested.

There are other ways to solve the above problem. For example, an Internet company had a large number of backend microservices, but it couldn't create a physical isolated testing environment for each developer. Given this, they managed to develop a routing mechanism that operates like this: In a baseline microservice testing environment, developers can separately deploy the microservices that they are modifying, and then through the routing mechanism, form a virtual testing environment with other microservices in the baseline testing environment for self-debugging (see Figure 5.5).

5.3 ARCHITECTURE TRANSFORMATION PATTERNS

For legacy systems with low deployment frequency, we seldom think over the three factors as "easy to test", "easy to deploy", and "easy to extend". In order to enable business agility, software architecture also needs to remain agile (the word "agile" here refers to the ability to make changes quickly and

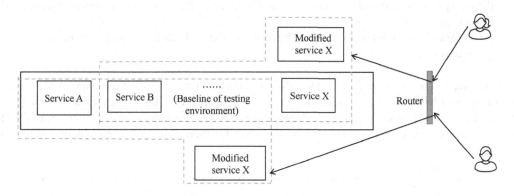

FIGURE 5.5 Create a shared microservice testing environment through the routing mechanism.

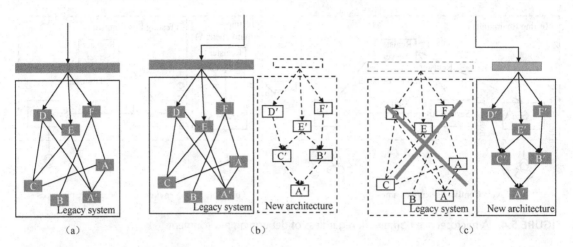

FIGURE 5.6   Demolisher Pattern.

easily). That's why there is demand for architecture transformation from time to time. Generally, there are three patterns for implementing such transformation, namely, Demolisher Pattern, Strangler Pattern, and Decorator Pattern; the latter two patterns are conducive to Continuous Delivery, and able to mitigate the risks of architecture transformation and release.

5.3.1 Demolisher Pattern

The Demolisher Pattern is to redesign the software architecture according to current business requirements, and organize a separate team to redevelop a new system that can completely replace the legacy one at one time (see Figure 5.6).

The advantage of this pattern is that it has nothing to do with the legacy application, so the new one can be designed as expected. But the risks of the Demolisher Pattern cannot be ignored:

1. **Missing business requirements.** In the legacy application, lots of functions are still used but no one knows.
2. **Changes in the market environment.** Since the new system cannot be developed overnight, the changes in demand may have led to lost market opportunities.
3. **Large consumption of human resources.** In addition to the personnel assigned to maintain the old system or deal with urgent requirements, there shall be adequate resources working on the new one.
4. **Development divorced from reality.** The new system fails to meet business requirements after going online.

Of course, this is not to say that the Demolisher Pattern cannot be used. The firmware architecture transformation of HP LaserJet is a successful case in this regard[4]. In 2008, the team was weighed down with developing new features of printers, because only 5% of the team members were available for doing so. Thanks to their constant efforts, the resources for their development had increased by eight

---

[4] Gary Gruver, et. al., *A Practical Approach to Large-Scale Agile Development: How HP Transformed LaserJet FutureSmart Firmware.*

times by 2011, with total development cost dropping by 40%. The software architecture of the LaserJet was transformed into the "Microcore Architecture", that is, each printer is installed with a minimal initial version of firmware. After the printer is connected to the Internet, this firmware can download the necessary functional modules from HP's website according to actual requirements, and then install them automatically.

In the process of rewriting it, the team also replaced the original "hell-like multiple branches" model with the "trunk-based development" model (see Chapter 8), and established its own deployment pipeline for Continuous Delivery.

There are cases of failure in implementing the Demolisher Pattern. For example, Netscape Communications Corporation, an American computer services company, was once famous for its web browser "Netscape Navigator". Since its old version had made user experience worse and worse, and was hard to catch up with the development trend of Internet browsers, the company's leadership decided to transform the browser's software architecture with the Demolisher Pattern. However, before its transformation was completed, Microsoft rose to dominate the browser market with its successful development of Internet Explorer and Windows Operating System, leaving Netscape never recover after this setback.

5.3.2 Strangler Pattern

The Strangler Pattern is a popular design pattern to incrementally transform your monolithic application into microservices by replacing a particular functionality with a new service. Once the new functionality is ready, the old component is strangled, the new service is put into use, and the old component is decommissioned altogether (see shown in Figure 5.7).

The advantages of this pattern are as follows:

- Do not miss the original requirements.
- By providing value stably and delivering versions frequently, this pattern enables the team to better monitor the progress of its transformation.
- Avoid the development divorced from reality.

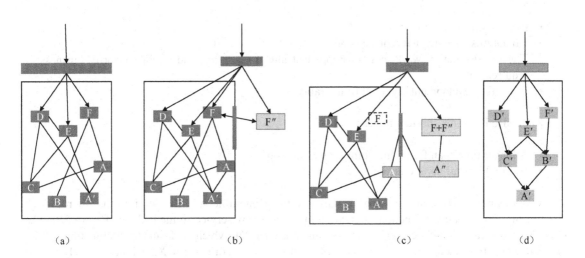

(a)   (b)   (c)   (d)

FIGURE 5.7   Strangler Pattern.

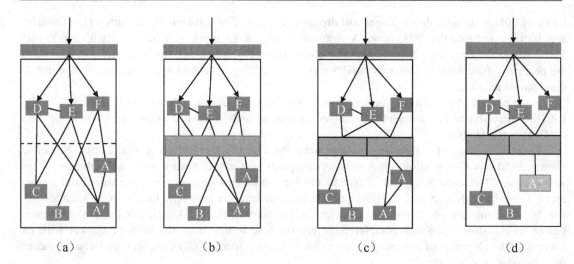

      (a)   (b)   (c)   (d)

FIGURE 5.8   Decorator Pattern.

But it also has some shortcomings:

- A longer time span for architecture transformation.
- Incur additional iteration cost.

5.3.3 Decorator Pattern

The Decorator Pattern is to isolate part of the functions of the legacy system from the rest, and then separately improve them with a new architecture; when improving these functions, the team must ensure that they can still work with other functions, as shown in Figure 5.8 (these steps are the same as the technique of "Branch by Abstraction" to be discussed in Chapter 12). Though it is similar to the Strangler Pattern, this pattern only makes transformation inside the same legacy system.

The advantages of this pattern are as follows:

- Nonperception system.
- Do not miss the original requirements.
- The transformation work can be stopped at any time to respond to high-priority business requirements.
- Avoid the development divorced from reality.

But it also has some shortcomings:

- A longer time span for architecture transformation.
- Incur additional iteration cost.

When using the Decorator Pattern to transform the Monolithic Architecture into the Microservice Architecture, the separated functions should be made as a new service in the end (see Figure 5.9). The Code X at the seam should be divided into X1 and X2; then X1, which performs to the functions of the original application, should be retained in the Monolithic Architecture, while X2, which is closely related to the separated microservices, should be integrated with the Microservice Architecture. Repeat this step until all microservices are separated out.

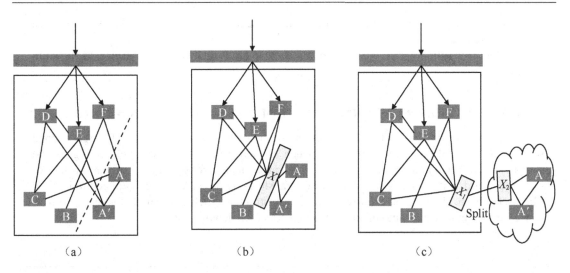

FIGURE 5.9 Transform the Monolithic into the Microservice.

5.3.4 Database Sharding

Generally speaking, relational database is likely to be the biggest coupling point in the Monolithic Architecture. For this reason, when transforming stateful microservices, we need to split the database very carefully by taking the following steps (see Figure 5.10):

1. Learn more about the database structure, including foreign key constraint, shared variable data and transactional boundary, as shown in Figure 5.10a.
2. Split the database and perform data migration as described in Subsection 12.3.2, as shown in Figure 5.10b.

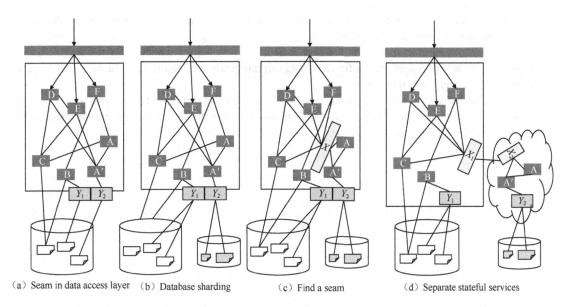

(a) Seam in data access layer　(b) Database sharding　　(c) Find a seam　　(d) Separate stateful services

FIGURE 5.10 Database sharding during the transformation into the Microservice Architecture.

3. If the database is correctly double-written, find the seam in the program architecture, as shown in Figure 5.10c.
4. Combine the split program modules and the database to form a new microservice, as shown in Figure 5.10d.

ARCHITECTURE TRANSFORMATION SHOULD CENTER ON BUSINESS GOALS

When transforming the Monolithic Architecture, we should first split it into relatively large-grained services. If the goal of splitting is reached (such as more frequent release), the splitting can be stopped. Don't seek for architecture or technology transformation for something without substantive meaning. Besides, it should be noted that when transforming the Monolithic Architecture into the Microservice, we shall establish corresponding infrastructure, such as the tools for service governance, service monitoring, automation test, and automation deployment.

5.4 SUMMARY

This chapter discusses the requirements of "Continuous Delivery 2.0 Capability" for designing software architecture, namely, "design for test", "design for deployment", "design for monitor", "design for scale", and "design for failure". The principles for system decomposition are also introduced.

We've also analyzed and compared three common software architectures and their applicable scenarios, namely, Microcore Architecture (applicable to client software to be distributed to users); Microservice Architecture (used by companies in their own controllable backend server software); and Monolithic Architecture (preferred by startup companies for software development).

Finally, we've discussed three patterns to transform the legacy system:

1. The Demolisher Pattern, which is the most common in use, is to rewrite all the code at once.
2. The Strangler Pattern, without changing or free from greatly changing the legacy system, is to keep replacing the original functions by adding new services.
3. The Decorator Pattern is to gradually transform the legacy system through iteration and development of new functions at the same time.

Besides, the ways for database sharding and data migration while implementing the Strangler Pattern or Decorator Pattern are also introduced.

In order to achieve Continuous Delivery and mitigate the risks of architecture transformation, it is recommended that the team should implement the Strangler Pattern or Decorator Pattern to transform the legacy system based on the actual situation.

Collaborative Management around Business Requirements

6

The entire life cycle of a product can be divided into five phases: concept phase, incubation phase, verification phase, operation phase, and withdrawal phase. Each phase has an unfixed time period and a different goal. In concept phase, we need to know well about market opportunities, urgency of customer requirements, competitive edge of our company, product feasibility, and capability of our product team. In incubation phase, we need to examine the completeness of the core functions of the product, satisfaction of typical target users' core demands, and user feedback of small-scale experiments. In verification phase, we need to care about the user experience of the minimum core function set, early user feedback, profit model, technical stability of the product team, and possibility of increasing resource investment. In operation phase, our focus is placed on changes in the market environment, existence of generalized customer requirements, and the input-output ratio. Once any of the four phases fail to meet the company's expectations, we have to think about the product's withdrawal.

Except for concept phase, all the other four phases contain at least one software release life cycle, as shown in Figure 6.1.

Each software release life cycle could be further divided into inception period and delivery period. Both of them are composed of multiple iterations, and each iteration contains at least one double-flywheels of Continuous Delivery for solving one (or a group of) business problem, as shown in Figure 6.2.

Collaborative management around business requirements runs through the entire software release life cycle, involving all roles related to software delivery, like business staff, product personnel, developers, testers, and operations staff. The aim of this collaborative management is to, by improving the interaction and collaboration between different roles at each link of the double-flywheels of Continuous Delivery, effectively and efficiently analyze business problems, implement business solutions, and verify the implementation results, and also ensure that all requirements are taken into account and able to be fully tracked.

6.1 OVERVIEW OF SOFTWARE RELEASE LIFE CYCLE

Each software release life cycle is further divided into inception period and delivery period. The goal of inception period is to enable all roles involved in the release life cycle to agree on the business problems that are expected to be solved and the minimum viable solution. The goal of delivery period is to finally verify or solve these business problems through rapid iteration.

6.1.1 Inception Period

Inception period is a process where team members jointly explore, discover, and make decisions; its primary task is that team members can reach a consensus on business problems and goals. This process

DOI: 10.1201/9781003221579-6

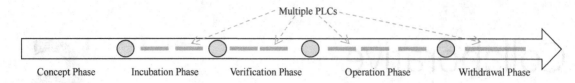

FIGURE 6.1   Five phases of software's full life cycle.

is characterized of first divergence and then focusing: business and product staff, developers, Quality Assurance (QA), and operation personnel first discuss the business problems to be solved, learn about the full picture of these problems, then define business goals and measurement indicators before selecting all possible solutions, and finally determine the minimum viable solution to be verified by the means of refining. Sometimes, inception period is also known as "iteration 0" or "start-up period".

Participants in inception period usually include representatives of the various roles of both the customer side and the implementer side, all of them need to have right to be involved in the process of decision-making, because they have to agree on the minimum viable solution and make relevant decisions ultimately before entering delivery period. In addition, when conditions permit, it should be made to ensure representatives of all parties (at least those playing a major role) involved in inception period to take part in the subsequent delivery period. Only in this way can the business domain knowledge and decision-making context be effectively brought into delivery period, so that the decisions made during delivery will be more accurate.

Generally speaking, in addition to determining the minimum viable solution, the question as "how long would its implementation and verification take?" also needs to be answered in inception period even though it may not be accurate – a key decision point in software release life cycle. In inception period, participants must reach consensus on the minimum viable solution and preliminary delivery plan. And this delivery plan, as long as it can support managers to make decisions, doesn't need to be very precise.

The work in inception period mainly includes:

1. **Describe and understand business goals:** Business representative elaborates on the important business goals that need to be achieved in the current software release life cycle and the related business context. Participants should actively join in the interaction to fully understand the business.
2. **Identify business roles and process, and explore solutions:** All participants need to identify the main process and roles related to the given business problem through discussion, and find as many solutions as possible.
3. **Identify and verify major risks:** Identify business and technical risks in various solutions, and organize people to quickly verify the major risks that can affect decision-making lately.

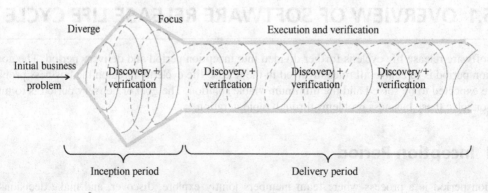

FIGURE 6.2   Composition of a single software release life cycle.

4. **Determine the minimum viable solution through refining:** Select a possible solution and refine it into the minimum viable solution.

5. **Estimate and plan:** Preliminarily estimate the workload and man-hours of the minimum viable solution, and develop a corresponding delivery plan.

With complexities to varying degree, different problems in different business domains have an iterative inception period of different length. For a mature team skilled in collaboration, it may have a short inception period, which takes a week if team members could work closely with each other without any interference.

6.1.2 Delivery Period

Once the team agrees on the preliminary plan conducted in inception period, they can kick off delivery period right away. This period also consists of multiple iterations, and each iteration cycle should be as consistent as possible. In each iteration, there may be several double-flywheels of Continuous Delivery, which largely depends on whether each iteration contains multiple verification points, and on the implementation difficulty and verification cycle of the solution corresponding to each verification point (see Figure 6.2).

Some teams adopt an iterative development approach, that is, to divide a big waterfall process into several small waterfall processes (see Figure 6.3). At the beginning of each iteration, all team members sit together to analyze and discuss the requirements for the current iteration, and then immediately start the development work. In the early stage of the iteration, almost no requirement is fully developed, but by the end of the iteration, a large number of requirements are completed almost concurrently and about to be tested at the same time. The disadvantage of this approach is that team members are not fully aware of the requirements for the current iteration, which is easy to cause rework afterward. Moreover, it may lead to concentrated testing in the later stage of the iteration. This is not the continuous and rapid flow that caters to the goal of Continuous Delivery 2.0.

The team should, right after the current iteration is started, carefully analyze the requirements to be developed in the subsequent iteration, and before entering the next iteration, ensure all participants to have a consistent understanding of the acceptance conditions of the requirements and reach a consensus on them. There are two benefits of making a requirements analysis in advance: one is to identify the risky requirements earlier, and make communications and preparations in advance. The other one is to, if the current iteration is finished ahead of time, select some requirements to be developed in the following iteration and realize continuous development. In this case, some requirements may be developed across iterations, as shown in Figure 6.4.

When employing this operation mode, every team member will take on multiple tasks in the same iteration. For example:

Product manager or business analyst needs to:

1. Answer the questions raised by other team members on the requirements of current iteration without delay.

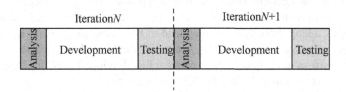

FIGURE 6.3 Wave delivery in iteration.

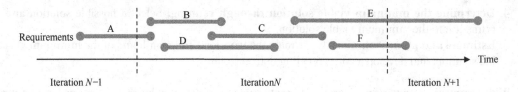

FIGURE 6.4   Continuous development of requirements across iterations.

2. Check and accept the requirements completed in current iteration without delay.
3. Organize other team members to screen and analyze the requirements to be developed in subsequent iteration.

Developers need to:

1. Develop the requirements falls in current iteration;
2. Fix the defects detected by QAs or others in time.
3. Join in requirements analysis and testcase review for subsequent iteration.

QAs need to:

1. Check and accept the requirements just completed without delay;
2. Check and accept the fixed defects;
3. Join in the requirements analysis for subsequent iteration, conduct testcase analysis of these requirements, and organize testcase review.

Besides, developers and QAs also need to analyze the problems that arise in production environment, and address them in a timely manner.

The team should not only deliver qualified and workable software by the end of each iteration but also continue to improve their Continuous Delivery 2.0 capability to ensure they could "deliver the software both workable and up to quality standard even in the iteration process", and realize continuous development of requirements.

6.2 PROS AND CONS OF REQUIREMENTS DECOMPOSITION

When using the traditional waterfall method, the general task is decomposed by stages into requirements analysis, preliminary design, detailed design, coding, and integration testing. Then a specific task at each stage can be further split into requirement analysis, preliminary design, coding, and testing of different modules, as shown in Figure 6.5.

Through this way of task decomposition, the modules cannot be put together for debugging until the integration test stage. As a result, lots of defects would be detected in debugging and testing, which may cause delay. In addition, a long delivery cycle may lead to two consequences: (1) Even if the software is inconsistent with expectations, the business side cannot find it until its delivery at the end. (2) Due to market changes or rapid business development, the software just developed may fall behind actual demand. Therefore, this type of task decomposition should be abandoned.

We should, by starting from the business perspective as possible as we can, split a large business requirement (see Figure 6.6) into several small requirements (a, b_1, b_2... x_n), and describe them from the

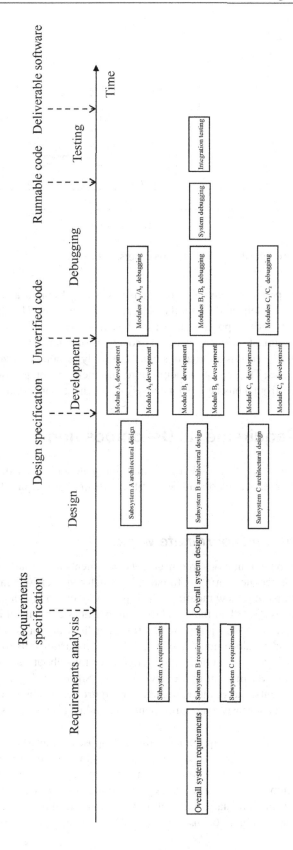

FIGURE 6.5 Task decomposition for traditional waterfall method.

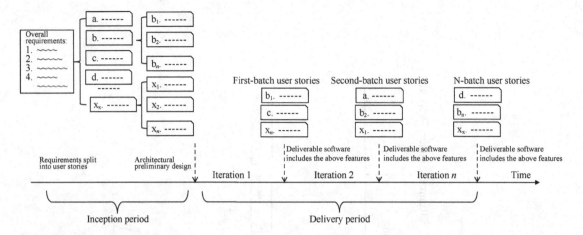

FIGURE 6.6   Requirements decomposition from a business perspective.

user perspective, so as to draw people's attention to their business value. Being evaluated and prioritized, these small requirements are to be delivered in small batches through iteration. This approach enables the team to get runnable software as early as possible, and allows business personnel to track the development progress so that they can communicate with engineers to find any inconsistency with their agreed requirements as early as possible. Moreover, this approach is able to flexibly respond to temporary requirement changes and rapid market changes. The general principle of requirements decomposition, that is, "sticking to requirements decomposition from a business perspective", is to benefit Continuous Delivery.

6.2.1 Benefits of Requirements Decomposition

The small-size requirements after splitting allow the team to integrate and verify them earlier, discover potential problems and defects in time, and obtain deliverable software with required features by the end of each iteration at least.

6.2.1.1 Build consensus and coordinate work

When using traditional development methods, requirements documents are usually written by business analyst or product manager. After the writing is finished, product manager will call together relevant technicians to attend a requirement review meeting which is very likely to take a long time. There are two drawbacks in these methods: (1) When facing a large number of documents, it is hard for the team to thoroughly discuss all requirements in a review meeting that lasts one or two hours. Most of the time, product manager will read the documents one by one for other participants to think about, which is prone to leave out many risk items. (2) Once some tough questions about requirements are raised, product manager can hardly answer them at the review meeting. Since developers and QAs are given less time to pore over requirements, the situation depicted in Figure 6.7a often occurs, that is, all roles believe that they have reached a consensus on requirements, but in fact each one has a different opinion about the same thing.

With the Continuous Delivery mode, requirements are decomposed in advance. During requirements decomposition, all relevant roles should be present, and they need to fully discuss the bounded context of each requirement so as to agree on its goals, quality standards, and acceptance conditions. In fact, the process of requirements decomposition is for all roles to share knowledge and carry out requirements modeling for the concerned business domain. Through this process, the entire team will have the same understanding of requirements (see Figure 6.7b).

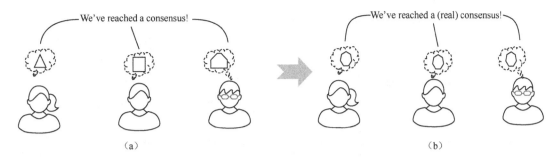

FIGURE 6.7   Reach a real consensus.

Many teams always kick off development in a hurry in order to save time. However, in either development or verification process, they may find different understandings of requirements or incomplete consideration of abnormal scenarios, which then leads to repeated discussions and confirmations. In many cases, they fail to save time, but cause unnecessary wastes instead, such as interrupting other people's work and frequent changes of tasks.

6.2.1.2 Small-batch delivery to speed up the flow of value

After a large requirement is split, the small ones can be developed and tested in batch, which is able to achieve fast delivery and allow users to use the software as early as possible. In order to illustrate the benefits of small-batch delivery, we can first simplify its value model as follows: there is a software project with ten requirements, each requirement takes ten days to develop and two days to verify. After each feature is delivered, it generates a value of US$ 1,000 per day. As shown in Table 6.1, the small-batch delivery has produced a cumulative value of US$ 480,000 by the 120th day, while the bulk delivery has a revenue of zero.

6.2.1.3 Embrace change at a low cost

In case of small-batch delivery, when any unforeseen circumstance occurs during the development process (for example, a high-priority requirement needs to be developed first due to changing market demand), the team can quickly finish or call off the task in hand to work on the inserted high-priority requirement. As shown in Figure 6.8, when a high-priority requirement is inserted on the 72nd day, we can remove the existing requirement without affecting the previous deliverable.

6.2.1.4 Multiple integrations and timely feedback on quality

Even if the small requirements cannot be delivered to users immediately after they are developed, debugging and testing on them can still be executed. If any defect is found, it can be fixed as soon as possible. In case of too many defects, there are three possible reasons: (1) Developers fail to fully understand the

TABLE 6.1   Cumulative value comparison between big-batch delivery and small-batch delivery

CUMULATIVE VALUE (USD)	BIG-BATCH DELIVERY (DELIVER 10 FEATURES AT A TIME)	SMALL-BATCH DELIVERY (DELIVER 2 FEATURES AT A TIME)
24th Day	0	0
48th Day	0	48,000
72nd Day	0	144,000
96th Day	0	288,000
120th Day	0	480,000

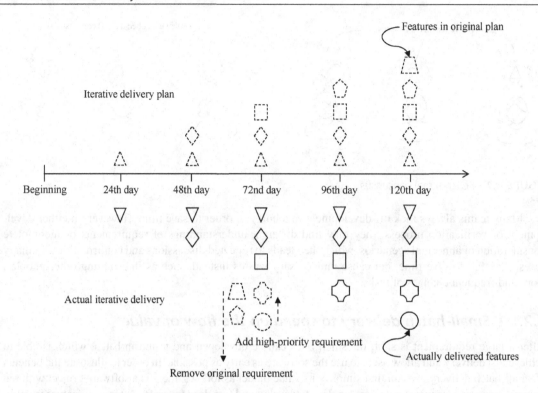

FIGURE 6.8   Replacement with a high-priority requirement.

requirements. (2) Software quality standards are not strictly implemented. (3) Insufficient communication between team members may cause "false alarms" (for example, QAs believe they have detected a defect, but developers don't think so). Regardless of the reason, unlike the big-batch delivery process where we cannot discover software defects until the later stage of development, the small-batch delivery enables us to collect quality feedback in advance and then make adjustments immediately.

6.2.1.5 Boost the morale of team members

If all new features developed in each iteration could be delivered immediately and the real feedback from end users was soon collected, the team was sure to get inspired (whether such feedback is positive or not), because the product is being used and they are about to hear users' suggestions or comments.

6.2.2 Costs of Requirements Decomposition

Of course, requirements decomposition and iterative development not only generate benefits but also incur some additional costs as follows:

6.2.2.1 Explicit cost arising from requirements decomposition

Business requirements are usually collected and complied by someone without a strong technical background, such as product manager or business analyst. However, if a requirement is decomposed only by them, then the effect of decomposition is hardly guaranteed. Therefore, other roles need to take part in requirements decomposition and arrive at a unanimous conclusion in the end. But in doing so, there will be a higher communication cost in the early stage of development in contrast to the waterfall method.

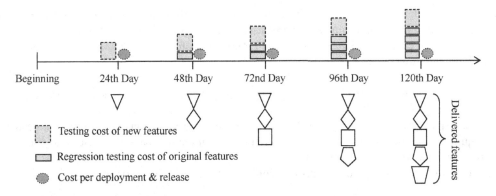

FIGURE 6.9 Fixed cost of iteration.

6.2.2.2 Iterative cost arising from small-batch development, testing, and deployment

An important goal of requirements decomposition is to achieve small-batch delivery through iteration. In order to guarantee the delivery quality, verification must be carried out at least before the end of each iteration to ensure that all delivered software features (including those delivered in previous iterations) could operate correctly. As the frequency of verification increases, the resulting cost will also go up.

If the features developed in each iteration were deployed to production environment, there will be a higher deployment cost (including labor and time costs). Moreover, if downtime is required for deployment, then there will be loss of revenue due to system shutdown, as shown in Figure 6.9.

Although the benefits of iterative development are understandable, they are not easy to measure. But the fixed cost of iteration is clear at a glance. Therefore, when deciding the length of an iteration cycle, its fixed cost should be taken into account. Some methods for reducing iteration costs are to be introduced from Chapter 7.

6.3 WAY OF REQUIREMENTS DECOMPOSITION

Although we have obtained a list of requirements for the minimum viable solution upon the end of inception period, the granularity of these requirements may not be fine enough or definite enough for direct development. Given this, we still need to analyze and refine requirements in each iteration by following the principle of "gradual clarity".

In addition, should the overall requirements list include only the requirements put forward by business personnel? Are there other sources of requirements? After entering delivery period, among the requirements to be delivered in each iteration, how detailed should each requirement be? How to ensure that a requirement is split according to the business orientation and also small enough? These questions are to be discussed in the following subsections.

6.3.1 Sources of Requirements

The initial list of requirements is usually drawn up by the business personnel; however, as other roles join in analysis of requirements, they will find other requirements not noticed by the business personnel. Let's draw an analogy, we usually don't pay attention to air and water, as if they don't exist at all, but we can't live without them, not even for a minute. The nonfunctional requirements, such as for performance, ease of use and response delay in the field of software technology, and those for monitoring and flexible system configuration in production environment, are inconspicuous but as vital as air and water.

In short, before entering delivery period, the requirements for the minimum viable solution come from the following three sources:

1. Business requirements put forward by business personnel. They are basic functional requirements of software.
2. Nonbusiness requirements that must be met to ensure the realization and operation of business requirements, such as performance requirements to guarantee page response time and automatic scaling to guarantee cost control.
3. Security development requirements that comply with security regulations.

After entering delivery period, the requirements to be developed in each iteration come from the following seven sources:

1. The requirements chosen from the initial requirements list to be fulfilled.
2. Newly discovered requirements in the process of refining requirements.
3. Any defect in online production system that is already known and ought to be fixed.
4. Requirements for operating online technologies.
5. Pre-research requirements (the preparations made to achieve a certain business requirement which the team is currently unable to fulfil).
6. Technical debts (the technical improvements to be made to ensure development progress in the early stage).
7. Requirements for assisting tests (the test tools to be developed to facilitate the acceptance of requirements).

6.3.2 Technical Debts Are Another Requirement

"Technical debts" is a concept put forward by Ward Cunningham, the founder of Wiki, in 1992. It means that in the process of architectural design or development, the technical team chooses an easy-to-implement solution based on short-term goals, yet this solution may bring about lasting negative effects in the long run. Technical debts should be properly managed as financial debts, otherwise the accumulated interest may make someone crushed.

Generally speaking, technical debts are deeply hidden and no one will actively alter a seemingly perfect system at present. Therefore, people can't notice technical debts until they have accumulated to a certain level and seriously slow down the speed of software development. By this point, the software is on the verge of collapse; greater costs (both time and resources) must be invested to repay these "debts".

Technical debts occur for the following two reasons:

1. Only care about immediate requirements without further consideration. Even if additional features are developed, the current system is not reconstructed.
2. Low-quality code (the simplest manifestations are hard coding, magic numbers, confusing naming, repetitive code, and high cyclomatic complexity; all of them are technical debts related to code).

In case of Continuous Delivery, there is another type of "technical debts", that is, all the repetitive and time-consuming manual operations that affect the speed of software delivery or business response, such as manual preparation of testing environment, manual regression testing, manual deployment and release. The reason why these operations are defined as "technical debts" is that they can be automated through technical means to a large extent, thus saving lots of man-hours. For example, in many Internet companies, product managers can't obtain user behavioral data right after new features are put online; they have to send a request to technical staff who will write a script for a specific purpose, and then run it to collect the user behavioral statistics two or three days later. In contrast, as early as in 2012, the real-time data analysis system of Facebook only took one minute to have the data displayed on engineers' screen from their landing on the server, and each data query only took one second to get the query results returned[1].

How to deal with the abovementioned "technical debts"? It must be decided in combination of the specific status of the team and product at present. Just like "mortgage loan", although you don't have to pay it off immediately, you still have to make a comprehensive evaluation of your current financial strength and future income expectations. Nevertheless, technical debts must be put on the agenda for company or team managers to make decisions. This is not just a technical issue, but a business issue. Once the decision is made to repay the "debts", they should be included into the requirements list for iteration as a special "user story".

6.3.3 Roles Involved in Requirements Decomposition

When the traditional waterfall model is used, it is product manager (or business analyst) who writes the requirements specification. So, it makes many people believe that user stories should also be split by product manager himself in the scenarios applying the Continuous Delivery model. But this is a serious misunderstanding. Beyond question, product manager is responsible for the list of requirements, but he can't write all user stories on his own, otherwise there may be user stories of "bad smell".

Many product managers don't have a profound knowledge of technical implementation methods. So the user stories directly split by these persons may differ greatly from the actual workload and fail to achieve the goal of continuous and rapid flow of requirements. When splitting user stories, there must be a basic estimation of the workload after splitting. If this is not possible, the split user stories may be not small enough to be finished in an iteration cycle, or there may be too many ultrafine user stories that incur more maintenance and management costs. As a result, multiple roles must be involved in the process of requirements decomposition.

For one thing, the first benefit of involving developers and QAs in requirements decomposition is to make them learn more about the context of product requirements. This may make the development team feel that they are developing their own product, which helps to mitigate the antagonistic emotions between team members and deepens their understanding of business requirements and user stories.

For the other thing, if more roles could join in the writing of user stories, they can learn more about product requirements and the overall intent of these user stories, and then think of more and better ways to achieve these requirements from their own perspective. For example, in the case of "withdraw now" in Chapter 2, developers proposed a cost-optimal quick verification plan; even if only part of its features were implemented, it was still enough to verify the hypotheses of the product manager.

6.3.4 The Unequal "INVEST" Principle

The "INVEST"[2] principle, which consists of the initial letters of six English words, is a combination of six principles for examining whether user stories are split properly.

1. Independent: User stories should be independent of each other with low coupling.
2. Negotiable: Before the start of development, story cards are used to remind the team to discuss with stakeholders, rather than a direct contract between product managers and developers.

---

[1] Lior Abraham, et al., *Scuba: Diving into Data at Facebook*.

[2] The INVEST principle for fast verification of user stories comes from an article *INVEST in Good Stories, and SMART Tasks* written by Bill Wake in 2003. It was recommended by Mike Cohn in his book *User Stories Applied for Agile Software Development* in 2004.

3. Valuable: User stories must be important and valuable to users or customers.
4. Estimable: Development team must be able to estimate the workload for implementing user stories.
5. Small and similar-sized: User stories should be small enough to be completed within one iteration as far as possible (the development of user stories should not be longer than three workdays, at least most of them); and the workload for developing multiple user stories should not differ greatly.
6. Testable: All user stories must be testable.

In practice, there are a small number of very complex user requirements that are hard to meet the six principles at the same time. In this case, some compromises can be made, that is, these requirements shall be at least estimable, small and similar-sized, and testable (EST>INV). Even if these requirements cannot be delivered independently, as long as they can be independently developed and verified in a short time without affecting the completed software features, it is also feasible. In fact, the small requirements after decomposition have become a task that conforms to the "SMART" principle, that is, "specific", "measurable", "achievable", "relevant", and "time-bound".

6.3.5 Five Ways to Split User Stories

Five ways for better splitting user stories are to be introduced as follows. With more practices, everyone can be more skilled in utilizing user stories.

6.3.5.1 Splitting by path

The way to split by path is to split user stories according to different paths in a usage scenario. For example, after a user places an order on an e-commerce website, he or she may pay for it either through PayPal payment or bank card payment. For such a scenario, if the workload for supporting two patterns of payment at the same time is large, then it can be divided into two user stories as shown in Figure 6.10.

1. Users can make payments via PayPal.
2. Users can make payments via bank card.

Assuming that the payment via bank card needs to support different types of bank cards (debit card and credit card), or cards of the same type but from different banks (such as China Merchants Bank and Industrial and Commercial Bank of China), thus resulting in excessive workload, then the user story can be further split according to different cards and banks. For example, you have already finished lots of basic work for enabling the payment via CMB debit card, you can write the payment via debit cards of other banks into another user story (see Figure 6.11). It can be written like this: "to support the debit cards of other two banks except CMB", but it might be indicated that it relies on the user story "to support CMB debit card".

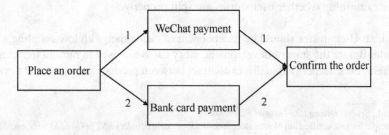

FIGURE 6.10 Schematic diagram 1 for path splitting.

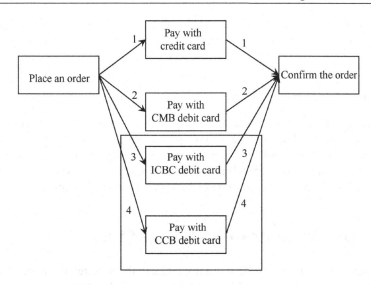

FIGURE 6.11   Schematic diagram 2 for path splitting.

6.3.5.2 Splitting by contact point

The so-called "contact point" refers to the interaction channel between users and the system. For example, mobile applications and PC browsers are two different contact points. User stores split by PC browser is based on different browsers such as Safari, Chrome, Firefox, and IE. Since the adaptation workload is large for the browsers with Internet Explorer (IE) core, but relatively small for other browsers, there can be two user stories:

1. Use browsers with IE core.
2. Use browsers with non-IE core.

6.3.5.3 Splitting by data type or format

For example, a software platform is for data statistics and analysis. One of its requirements is that users can import data to the system in the form of files. And these files shall be in the format of CSV, XML, or Excel. Then, this requirement can be split into three user stories:

1. Upload data in a CSV file.
2. Upload data in an XML file.
3. Upload data in an Excel file.

6.3.5.4 Splitting by rule

There are business rules or technical rules. If a distribution planning system for maritime shipping is to be developed, one of its requirements is to input departure and destination, and then choose the best shipping route according to the type of cargo. This requirement is made up of two parts: type of cargo and route. And it can be split by route into two user stores respectively for basic requirement and optimal requirement.

- Basic requirement: Users input departure and destination, and the system will select a route.
- Optimal requirement: Users input departure and destination, and the system will select the shortest route.

In a relationship of progressive dependency, these two user stories can be realized separately. In addition to the rule of "the shortest route", other rules can be added if users want a new way to choose the "best route".

6.3.5.5 *Splitting by exploration*

During the development process, the team always encounters something that is unfamiliar to them or an uncertain implementation plan. For example, they may be asked to use a new framework or technology, but no external expert could help them. At this time, their experimental exploration of strange things can be gradually split into different user stories. With great uncertainties, these exploratory user stories should be managed as high-risk points and their progress should be watched at all times.

6.3.6 Seven Components of Each User Story

In the current software industry, "user story" usually refers to the requirement in iterative delivery. The concept of "user story" stemmed from the 12 practices of Extreme Programming. We should write a user story in the following form so as to always keep user demand in mind:

> As a user of XXXX…
> In order to fulfill the business of YYYYY…
> I want to use the features of ZZZZZ…

But this is only the initial form of user story when it was created, it needs be continuously improved until it is able to accomplish its mission, that is, serve as a bridge for different roles to collaborate and reach a consensus during iteration, until its functional requirements are achieved and acceptance conditions are met. To this end, each user story usually contains seven components as follows:

1. Serial Number: Convenient for recording and tracking.
2. Title: Summarize the feature and goal of a user story.
3. Description: Briefly introduce the context, business purpose, and requirements of this feature.
4. Technical memo: Simply record some important technical points (there may be some design information) during each discussion.
5. Prerequisites: Some prerequisites should be met when estimating the user story or starting the implementation.
6. Dependency: Both the internal and external requirements on which the user story depends.
7. Acceptance criteria: The user story must meet the definition and description of the delivery standard.

6.4 REQUIREMENTS ANALYSIS AND MANAGEMENT TOOLS

After requirements decomposition, we will have a bunch of story cards, especially when we are working on a large and complex project. We need a better way to have them properly organized and managed. Are there any tools for us to do so?

In addition to Measurable Impact Mapping and User Journey Mapping (see Chapter 2), some other tools for requirements analysis and management are to be introduced in the following subsections.

6.4.1 User Story Mapping

User Story Mapping, a concept comes from Jeff Patton's book of the same name, is a tool for team communication and for requirements analysis and management. It is often used in inception period of software release life cycle. It uses a structured two-dimensional view to unify the thinking of team members, and analyzes requirements from two dimensions of user process and business urgency; the mapping can be regularly taken out for review and revision.

On each user story map, the horizontal axis is the main activity path of a specific business role, and above the horizontal axis is his (her) main activity description which is known as "epic story" (or feature set). These activities are arranged from left to right in the order of their occurrence. Under the horizontal axis and below each epic story are the finer user stories split from this epic story. The vertical axis represents the priority of user stories based on their business goals, that is, critical user stories are placed on the top, followed by less important ones, while lower-priority ones are placed at the bottom. In this way, user stories are about be delivered in batch according to their priority. If this product has different types of users (such as merchants and customers), then each user type may have a corresponding story map.

An example of User Story Mapping for book buyers of a book-selling website is shown in Figure 6.12. All user stories are divided into three batches. The set of requirements corresponding to Goal 1 "Buy Books" can be made as a minimum viable solution for the first-batch delivery. Of course, when dealing with actual business requirements, which user stories are high-priority ones need to be determined according to the business goal and marketing policy of the company.

6.4.2 User Story Tree

In order to view the full picture of product features, user stories can be managed in a tree diagram, that is, user stories are organized according to multiple levels such as "product – feature set – user story" or "product – user – feature set – user story", and the completed user stories are marked so that everyone can

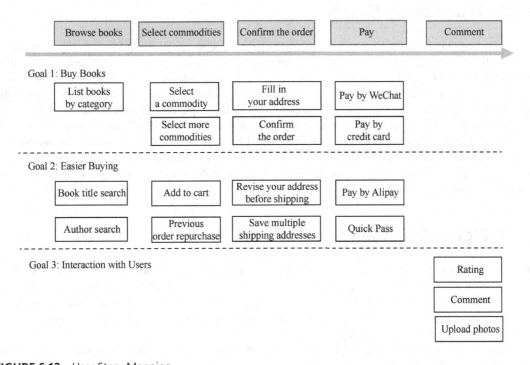

FIGURE 6.12 User Story Mapping.

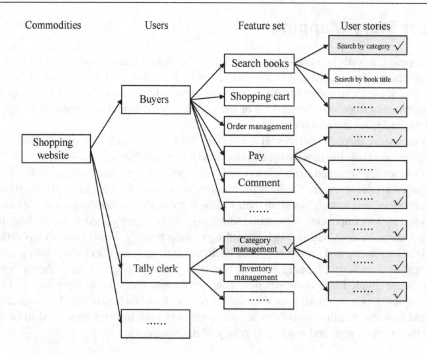

Commodities   Users   Feature set   User stories

FIGURE 6.13   User Story Tree.

track the development progress. As shown in Figure 6.13, the card marked with "√" represents a "completed requirement".

6.4.3 Dependency Graph

User Story Mapping is to define user stories from a business perspective, while Dependency Graph is to establish the relationship between user stories from an implementation dependency perspective. Although we hope all user stories are independent of each other, it is hard to come by in reality. Dependency still exists between some user stories. This dependency may be functional enhancing. For example, in a freight route planning system, "find the cost-optimal route" is usually implemented after "find the basic route" (see Figure 6.14). The context of these dependencies can also affect the workload estimation.

A large and complex project is usually undertaken by several teams. There will be dependencies between user stories developed by different teams, and these dependencies will influence the cycle and plan of software iterative delivery. Dependency Graph can make it easier for teams to manage these requirements and their delivery schedule.

6.4.4 Digital Management Platform

After a requirement is split into several user stories, in order to improve the efficiency of collaboration between team members, better store and organize user stories and contents of requirements, and even achieve automatic association between requirements and source code, we need to use a digital platform to manage these requirements. And this kind of platform should support the above-mentioned tools for requirements analysis and management.

Especially for a project engaged by distributed teams, Digital Management Platform is an essential tool to improve team collaboration efficiency.

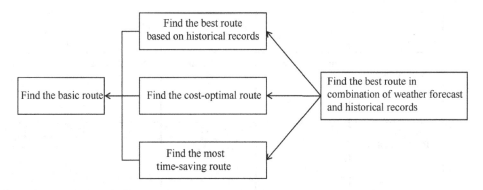

FIGURE 6.14   User Story Dependency Graph for a freight route planning system.

6.5 TOOLS FOR TEAM COLLABORATION

No matter in which period of the software release life cycle, we can use some methods or tools to help team members collaborate more efficiently. In addition to raising the work efficiency of individuals, we care more about that of the entire team. The prominent characteristics of these collaboration management tools is information transparency and visualization. I'd like to introduce some general methods and tools that I have used.

6.5.1 Shared Calendar

When several team members work on the same task, it is a big challenge to efficiently coordinate their working hours. Shared Calendar is an effective tool for team time management. There are two types of Shared Calendar: Team Timetable and Individual Non-work Timetable.

Team Timetable refers to the scheduling of routine activities involving multiple roles in advance; it allows all roles to plan their own working hours and rhythm according to this fixed schedule, thus reducing unnecessary coordination costs. Team Timetable specifies the time and content of various routine collaborations in an iterative cycle. The formulation of such Timetable is up to the negotiation between multiple roles, so as to suit their time arrangement as far as possible and avoid any failed schedule caused by conflicting events.

Figure 6.15 is an example of the Team Timetable for a team's iterative delivery. This team makes every two weeks as an iteration cycle, designates participants, and defines goals and time requirements for every event.

Individual Non-work Timetable is a work calendar for the entire team. Every team member can mark down their predictable non-work hours in advance on this calendar, such as planned annual leave or predictable casual leave (see Figure 6.16). An important prerequisite for this Timetable to work is "timely updating".

6.5.2 Retrospective Meeting

In addition to the management tools for all sorts of event, retrospective meeting is a management tool dealing with people. At a retrospective meeting, all team members can sit together to review the state of their collaboration for some time past, so as to maintain their good work habits and try to make further improvement.

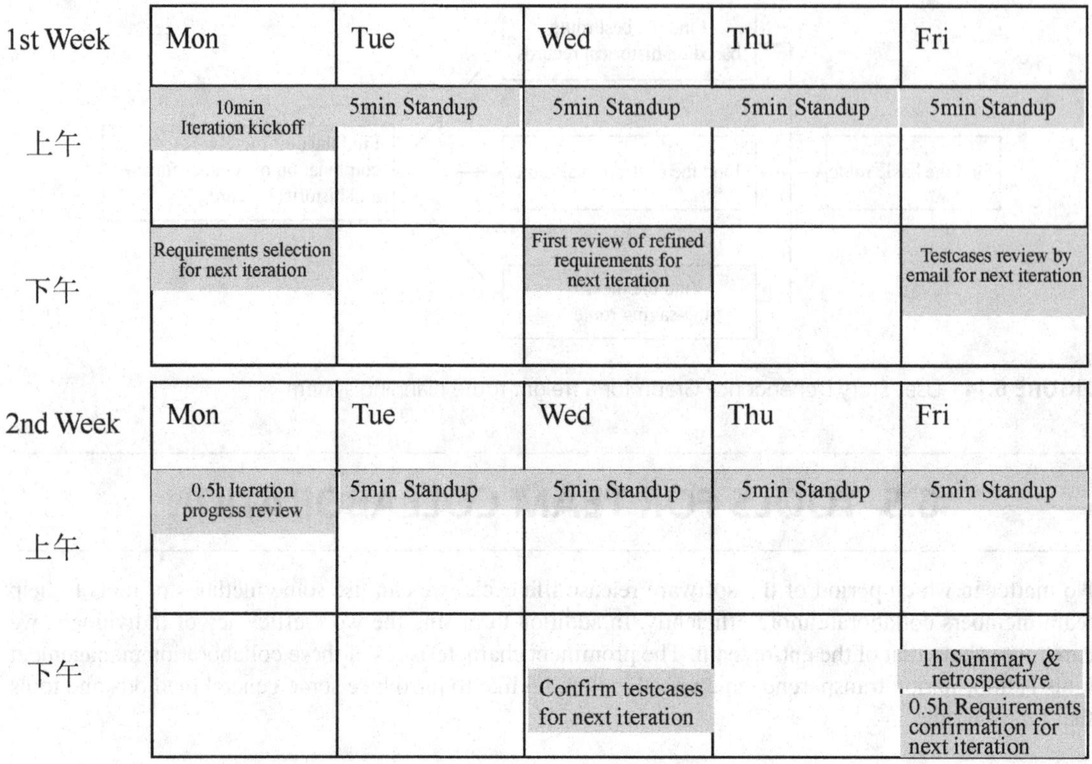

1st Week	Mon	Tue	Wed	Thu	Fri
上午	10min Iteration kickoff	5min Standup	5min Standup	5min Standup	5min Standup
下午	Requirements selection for next iteration		First review of refined requirements for next iteration		Testcases review by email for next iteration

2nd Week	Mon	Tue	Wed	Thu	Fri
上午	0.5h Iteration progress review	5min Standup	5min Standup	5min Standup	5min Standup
下午			Confirm testcases for next iteration		1h Summary & retrospective / 0.5h Requirements confirmation for next iteration

FIGURE 6.15   Team Timetable.

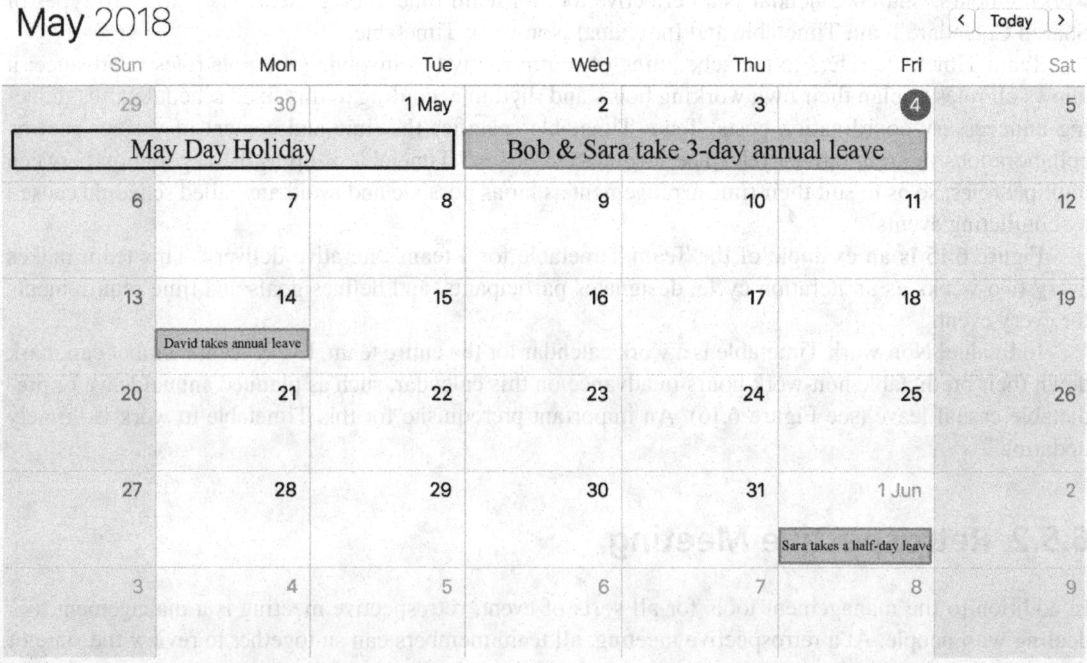

May 2018

‹ | Today | ›

Sun	Mon	Tue	Wed	Thu	Fri	Sat
29	30	1 May	2	3	4	5
	May Day Holiday		Bob & Sara take 3-day annual leave			
6	7	8	9	10	11	12
13	14	15	16	17	18	19
	David takes annual leave					
20	21	22	23	24	25	26
27	28	29	30	31	1 Jun	2
					Sara takes a half-day leave	
3	4	5	6	7	8	9

FIGURE 6.16   Individual Non-work Timetable.

Participants in a retrospective meeting should include all members who have joined in product inception or delivery in the past period of time. This kind of meeting, which does good to team collaboration, should be held regularly without frequent absences. It embodies the principle of "continuous improvement" of Continuous Delivery 2.0. Since every team member is ought to be present, this meeting could be hosted by someone beyond the team. If conditions do not permit, every team member can take turns to preside this meeting.

When team members are still unaware of the essence of retrospective meeting, the host must be skillful enough to take the reins. He shall make all participants feel "safe" before and throughout the meeting. In the course of discussion, team members may talk about some unpleasant matters such as poor collaboration, then the host shall remind the speaker to use proper expressions, such as "I saw...", "I felt...", I thought...would be better", "What do you think?" Once the speaker or listener gets agitated, the host should promptly intervene and help this person to calm down.

The output of retrospective meeting is an actionable list of improvements agreed by team members; moreover, a special person is assigned to take charge of an improvement item, track its implementation and report the result in the next retrospective meeting. It should be noted that the list of improvements should not be too long, with focus only placed on certain foremost items to ensure their implementation; otherwise, a retrospective meeting may become a mere formality without any positive effect on daily work.

As we've discussed in Chapter 4, the atmosphere of retrospective meeting directly reflects the organizational culture. Since it is an important means for constructing organizational culture, every manager should pay attention to the role of this meeting in improving team collaboration. We can even think that the quality of retrospective meeting is an indicator of the quality of team collaboration.

6.5.3 Visualized Story Wall

At present, many teams like to use a "card wall" to manage requirements, that is, write down user requirements on cards and place them in appropriate locations on the wall according to their current status or stage. There are two basic types of card wall:

1. The wall only displaying task status (to do/doing/done), as shown in Figure 6.17a.
2. The wall displaying the iterative development status of requirements (to develop/being developed/to test/being tested/tested/to go online), as shown in Figure 6.17b.

Lean Thinking highlights the flow of value which can eliminate waiting at each link. The two card walls in Figure 6.17 cannot demonstrate the complete value flow: Figure 6.17a reflects the completion of each task with no sign of the value flow. Figure 6.17b reflects the local value flow which may prompt the team to only care about the content of the current iteration, as if they only "see the trees but not the forest".

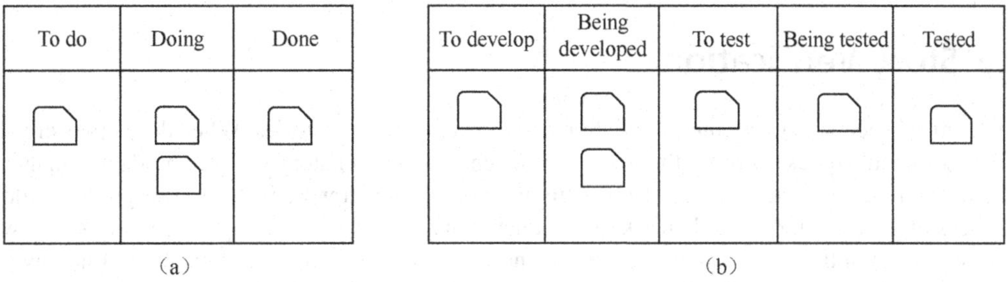

FIGURE 6.17   Two types of card wall.

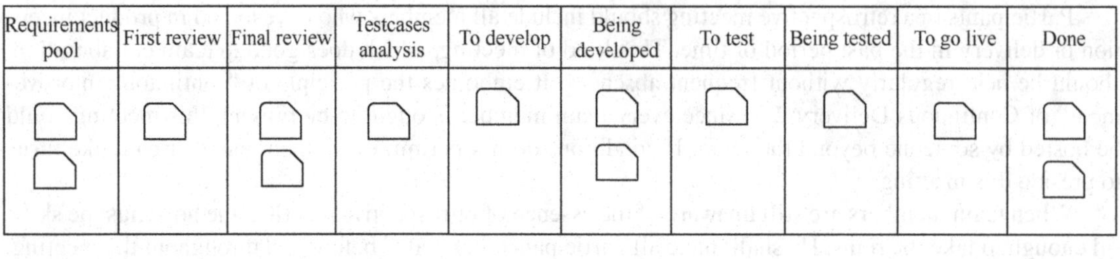

Requirements pool	First review	Final review	Testcases analysis	To develop	Being developed	To test	Being tested	To go live	Done

FIGURE 6.18   Whole-process story wall.

The complete value flow during software development is an entire process from generation of requirements to release of features (see Figure 6.18).

Only by visualizing the work of everyone can it be easier to identify and solve the problems occurring in the process of team collaboration. The visualized story wall can be used not only in the software development process but also in daily operation and maintenance.

6.5.4 Definition of "Done"

The process of team collaboration is most prone to the problem of inconsistent understanding between members. Therefore, the team should to its best to define the "Done" standards for each type of task, which is also a manifestation of the quality built-in principle of Verification Loop. For example, in order to move the cards on the wall from one location to another, what activities the team members need to complete? And what standards the deliverables must satisfy? By defining the "Done" standards, team members will pay more attention to product quality and standardized behaviors, so as to avoid unnecessary rework. These "Done" definitions should be made known to everyone and posted in a prominent location to get everyone noticed while working.

In the actual case analyzed in Chapter 15, the team, by relying on a powerful impetus for improvement (based on the tools of "visualized story wall" and defined "Done" standards, and the guidance of Lean Thinking), succeeded in making multiple changes to the team collaboration process and thereby improving their collaboration efficiency.

6.5.5 Continuous Integration

After decomposing a requirement into smaller ones, multiple team members can work in parallel. Moreover, the work results should be continuously integrated to meet the quality standards. More information about continuous integration is to be discussed in Chapter 9.

6.5.6 Story Verification

In the iterative process, team members collaborate for developing user stories. When developers are about to work, they should quickly review the seven components of the user story with the product manager and QAs, and then reach a consensus with them. After their development work is done, developers should run a self-check of the user story, and then ask the product manager do a quick acceptance test (also known as "mini-showcase") in their development environment. If the product manager is unable to find any obvious or serious problem, they should transfer the user story to QAs for a full acceptance test, as shown in Figure 6.19.

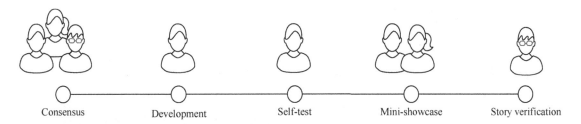

FIGURE 6.19   Verification process of user stories.

6.6 SUMMARY

This chapter elaborates on the inception and delivery periods of software release life cycle, benefits brought by requirements decomposition and the resulting fixed costs. Greater value can hardly be reaped if these fixed costs cannot be reduced. In order to truly obtain the benefits of requirements decomposition, the INVEST principle (INV<EST) must be followed as far as possible when splitting user stories. In order to help readers do better in this regard, this chapter summarizes five ways to split user stories and seven components of each user story.

There are multiple methods and tools for requirements analysis and management. Such common tools as User Story Mapping, User Story Tree, and Dependency Graph are introduced in this chapter.

In addition, this chapter also introduces the tools for improving team collaboration during the iteration process, such as Shared Calendar, Retrospective Meeting, Continuous Integration, and Story Verification.

Principles for Deployment Pipeline and Tool Design

7

As the kernel pattern of Continuous Delivery 1.0, deployment pipeline is a visual presentation of the software delivery process, showing the entire process from code submission, building, testing, deployment, and to release, so as to provide visualized software status and instant feedback to the team. The design of deployment pipeline is affected by software architecture, branch strategy, team structure, and product form. So each software product has its own evolving deployment pipeline.

In order to build and run a deployment pipeline, the product team needs to follow some basic principles, and the company must have tool chain support by powerful build platform with multiple subsystems, such as an automation testing platform, an environment management system. These issues are key contents of this chapter.

Now let's start our discussion from a simple deployment pipeline case.

7.1 SIMPLE DEPLOYMENT PIPELINE

We'll take an on-shelf Software GoCD (original name was Cruise) as example to explain the concept of Deployment Pipeline. GoCD, released ThoughtWorks in 2008, is to extend continuous integration to the testing and deployment phases of a software application at release management platform. Its concept originates from the open-source software (OSS) Cruise Control of enterprise version. Since GoCD first came out in 2008, its commercialized version was released every three months for global corporate users to try and buy. As of 2010, GoCD had accumulated more than 50,000 lines of code (LOC), 2,350 automation unit test and integration testcases, and 140 end-to-end functional testcases. At the time of writing this book, ThoughtWorks put GoCD on the website of GitHub and its community version was open sourced.

7.1.1 Simple Development Process

GoCD is in a typical server/agent architecture, with server and client starting and running independently. The server itself used to be a typical Monolithic Application at the beginning, including relational database and Java Application Server. Users can access its Web services through a browser. There is also a REST-style application programming interface (API) facilitating the application extension of users. The schematic diagram of GoCD is shown in Figure 7.1.

All the code of server and agent (including automation test code) were stored in the same code repository. Mercurial, a distributed version management tool like Git, was adopted for version control. All team members were empowered to modify any code in the code repository, and the number of engineers remained at around 12. During the delivery period, the iteration cycle took one week. The team itself also used GoCD for continuous integration and continuous delivery. Upon the end of each iteration, the team

DOI: 10.1201/9781003221579-7

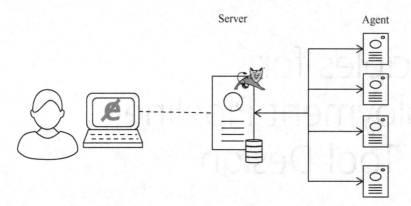

FIGURE 7.1   Architectural diagram of GoCD.

would replace the version they had just used with the latest one. Every two iterations, the trial version would be deployed on the public server inside the company for other teams to try out. If its internal trial running was up to the quality standard, then this trial version would be delivered to external corporate users for early experience (see Figure 7.2).

Since the team employed the test-driven development (TDD) method, developers had to write test-cases for both automation unit test and automation functional test, and then maintain them. The line coverage of unit test fluctuated between 75% and 80%.

7.1.2 Initial Deployment Pipeline

The team that applies GoCD takes the six-step check-in dance for CI (see Chapter 9). After anyone submits the code, an instantiation of the deployment pipeline is automatically triggered. The eight stages of deployment pipeline are shown in Figure 7.3.

1. Stage 1: "Check-in build". Seven tasks are to be completed at this stage: Compilation and packaging, static scanning of coding standards, and parallel running of five sets of different automation unit/integration testcases. An automatic trigger mechanism is put in place. The automation integration test is also implemented by the unit test framework, and some of them run together with the unit test at the stage of check-in build to verify the package to be runnable. Since GoCD supports multiple operating systems, software packages for different operating systems will be generated at this stage, such as .deb files, .exe files, .zip files, and so on. These installation files are applicable for all subsequent stages free from recompilation and repackaging.

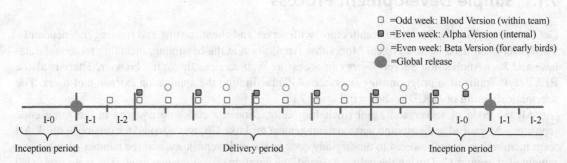

FIGURE 7.2   Continuous delivery process based on GoCD from 2008 to 2010.

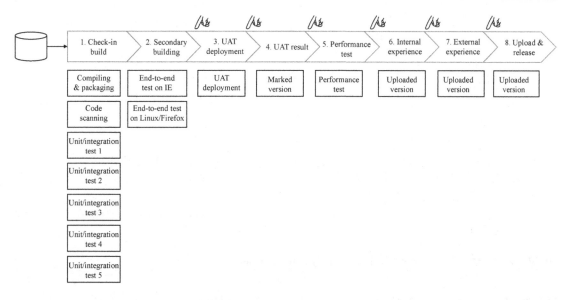

FIGURE 7.3 GoCD deployment pipeline in 2008.

2. Stage 2: "Secondary build". Two tasks are to be completed at this stage: Run the same set of automation functional testcases in two types of environments in parallel, namely, Windows with IE and Linux with Firefox. An automatic trigger mechanism is put in place.
3. Stage 3: "UAT deployment". The software assembly is deployed to the User Acceptance Environment (UAT) for manual verification. Starting from the third stage, each stage will have only one task.
4. Stage 4: "UAT result". After Quality Assurance (QAs) have finished manual verification, the deployment pipeline will be marked as "Acceptance Passed".
5. Stage 5: "Performance test", namely, automation performance test.
6. Stage 6: "Internal experience". The Alpha version is deployed to the internal server of a company for trial use by other teams.
7. Stage 7: "External experience". The Beta version is delivered to external corporate users for trial use.
8. Stage 8: "Uploading and releasing". The determined commercial release version is uploaded to the designated server for users to download by logging into the product website.

After each check-in, the stage of check-in build will be triggered automatically. After passing the first stage, the secondary build will be triggered automatically. Regarding the seven tasks to be completed at the stage of check-in build, there are more than 2,350 unit test and integration testcases that are divided into five test sets; one of them takes the longest time as about 15 minutes to be done. As for the two parallel tasks for secondary build, there are more than 140 end-to-end functional acceptance testcases, and one of them takes a maximum implementation time as about 30 minutes.

The third stage (UAT deployment) is manually triggered by QAs. Based on the completion status of specific requirements, QAs will select a version of software assembly from these builds that have passed the stage of secondary build, and deploy it to the UAT environment for manual acceptance test. If this version was passed, QAs will manually trigger the fourth stage, and the system will automatically mark this version as "Acceptance Passed".

The fifth stage of performance testing is also triggered manually.

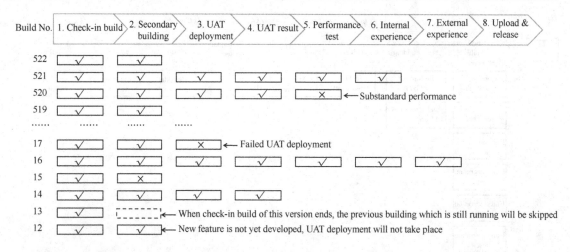

FIGURE 7.4   Example of running a GoCD deployment pipeline.

7.1.3 Execution of the Deployment Pipeline

Each check-in will trigger an instance of the deployment pipeline. Among the versions of software assemblies that have passed the secondary build, QAs only choose a version that contains new features for UAT deployment and manual acceptance test. The end of acceptance test will trigger the UAT result. And the performance test is triggered at regular intervals. An example of running a deployment pipeline is shown in Figure 7.4.

Each developer checks in at least once a day, thus making the deployment pipeline triggered multiple times every day. Of course, not every change can reach the "uploaded and released" stage, and not every check-in runs into the stage of UAT Deployment, because developers submit code whenever they have finished a task, instead of waiting until a feature is fully developed. Each feature requirement may be fulfilled by several development tasks, so developers must ensure that each check-in for the new feature not fully developed will not affect those implemented ones.

7.2 DESIGN AND USE OF DEPLOYMENT PIPELINE

Although the GoCD deployment pipeline as described above is a simple one, its design and operation mode can reflect the design and collaboration principles of the team when using the deployment pipeline.

7.2.1 Principles for Designing a Deployment Pipeline

A deployment pipeline must be designed according to the following five principles:

7.2.1.1 Build once, run anywhere

When a running instance of a deployment pipeline builds an artifact (such as a binary software assembly), it can be used directly in the subsequent stage of this pipeline if required, instead of being rebuilt. If this running instance triggers the downstream pipeline, which uses the same artifact, then it must be guaranteed that this artifact is the one coming from the same upstream deployment pipeline. Only in this way can we build up our confidence in the quality of this artifact as the deployment pipeline progresses. For example, Figure 7.4 depicts a deployment pipeline running instance with Build No. 521, the binary software assembly used for internal release is the same one produced by Build No. 521 in the stage of check-in build.

All the codes, installation scripts and configuration information of the GoCD, released in 2008 as mentioned above, are stored in the same code repository. After the deployment pipeline is triggered each time, if the subsequent stage requires the artifact produced from the previous stage, then it can be taken from the artifact repository instead of being rebuilt.

Even if multiple instances of the same deployment pipeline are running at the same time, the artifact and source code used for each instance in subsequent stage should be consistent with the version and source of the same deployment pipeline running in previous stage.

7.2.1.2 Loosely coupled with business logic

The deployment pipeline platform should be separated from the specific deployment and building task. We should not tightly couple the code building and deployment process with the selected deployment pipeline platform for the purpose of convenient automation, like storing software deployment scripts or required information in the platform. Instead, we should provide a separate script and put it in the code repository of the concerned software application, which will be easier for us to track and review the modification of these scripts.

In other words, the deployment pipeline platform is merely a scheduler, executor, and recorder of a specific deployment and building task. It only needs to trigger and schedule a deployment pipeline, and has nothing to do with the ways for building and deploying a software application.

7.2.1.3 Parallelization

When designing a deployment pipeline, parallelization should be taken into account as far as possible. In the deployment pipeline of GoCD, there are parallel jobs in many stages. For example, there are five automation test jobs in the stage of check-in build; each of them contains different testcases that are running on different computing nodes. Given this, quality feedback should be provided as early as possible to fix all emerging problems without delay.

If any resources are unlimited and free to use, then we hope every change would trigger all types of tests at the same time, and all automation testcases could be implemented in parallel. In this way, the overall feedback time will be greatly shortened.

7.2.1.4 Quick feedback to take precedence

In case of insufficient resources, the deployment pipeline of the tasks that are ought to provide quick feedback should be run as soon as possible. For example, in the deployment pipeline of GoCD, unit test is ahead of end-to-end automation functional test and automation performance test. This is a kind of trade-off between speed and quality of feedback. In order to quicken feedback, we may take some risks in prioritizing the execution of the automation verification sets that run faster, while delaying those that run more slowly and consume more resources.

7.2.1.5 Important feedback to take precedence

But the feedback mechanism cannot be put on the back burner just because of its slow execution speed. It is a necessary means of QA in some cases, although it seems to contradict the previous principle. For example, the installation test of an installer runs slower than the unit test, but the installation feedback is more real and valuable, so this test is still executed at the front stage of the deployment pipeline for fear that the failure in starting software cannot be detected until all unit tests are finished.

7.2.2 Principles for Teamwork

There are two principles for guiding teamwork:

7.2.2.1 Stop the line

The principle of "stopping the line" means that team members should promptly stop what they are doing when the running of deployment pipeline goes wrong due to a problem in a certain stage, and then try to fix it up rather than let it go unchecked. Furthermore, before the problem is fixed, except for the code check-in for fixing the problem, no one is allowed to submit any modified code to the code repository.

As a concrete manifestation of the built-quality-in concept, this principle draws on the rationale of Toyota's "Andon System" (see Subsection 4.2.1 of Chapter 4). On the production line of Toyota, as long as the front-line worker is unable to complete his work with high quality due to any problem, he can pull down the warning light to stop the entire production line; and this production line will not restart until his problem is solved.

The GoCD developers adopted a similar approach to run the deployment pipeline. If the stage of check-in build fails and the submitter cannot fix the problem within ten minutes, the code could be rolled back so as not to hinder other team members from submitting the code.

7.2.2.2 Security audit

When multiple roles are working together, if code or software assembly is to be transmitted between each other, it should come from a controlled environment. In such an environment, all operations are audited and all components (such as source code, binary code package, and installed program) have passed the audit. In each stage of an instance of a deployment pipeline (marked by a unique build number), the artifacts generated from the deployment pipeline should be used, and all of these artifacts are subject to controlled management. For example, QAs should not pull code in private and manually build software assembly for testing, or accept the software assembly sent by developers through various means (such as instant messaging tool) for testing. When each role verifies the deliverable, they should ensure that it comes from a shared and trusted source, that is, a unified version control or artifact repository.

A security audit on all the products of the deployment pipeline should be performed as early as possible. These products include third-party software assemblies used in the building process and class libraries or SaaS provided by other teams in the same company.

7.3 COMPOSITION OF A DEPLOYMENT PIPELINE PLATFORM

No matter it is a company or a team, it needs a flexible and powerful platform to setup its own deployment pipeline quickly. What components and capabilities are needed for a platform to be flexible and powerful? These questions are to be answered in the following subsections.

7.3.1 Overall Architecture of the Platform

The deployment pipeline almost runs through the Verification Loop in the Double-flywheels of continuous delivery, involving the entire process from code submission to deployment in the production environment. The platform that supports the deployment pipeline is composed of a tool chain that contains three

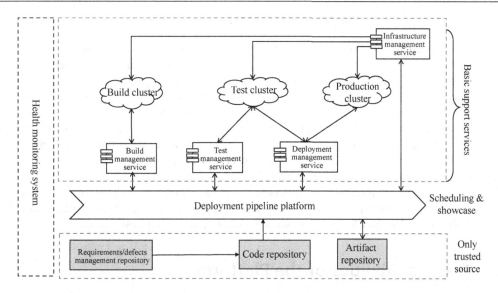

FIGURE 7.5   Architectural diagram of the deployment pipeline platform.

parts: The first part is the "True North Source" as the basis of the deployment pipeline, providing raw materials (code and third-party components) for running the deployment pipeline, and storing the artifacts and products arising from the running of the deployment pipeline. The second part is the core of itself, responsible for scheduling various tasks and unified display of results, and fulfilling the entire delivery process by cooperating with other special tools or subsystems (see Figure 7.5). The third part is the infrastructure subsystem layer, which is made up of diverse special tools, providing basic capabilities such as software building, testing, and deployment.

7.3.1.1 True north source

The True North source is an authoritative arbiter for the information needed in the team's daily work. In Figure 7.5, the three repositories at the bottom (in gray boxes) are the True North source for a company. When different roles question an information item, they can trace back to the True North source and take it as the benchmark. The True North source should persist the relationship between items of information. For example, for any artifact in the artifact repository, its source code can be found in the codebase; for any code in the codebase, its source of requirements is stored in the requirements/defects management platform.

For the software installed and running in any environment (even the operating system itself), its corresponding binary installer should be found in the artifact repository, as well as other binary packages it depends on. Despite of limited storage space, we should be able to find its exact source, such as the downloaded URI.

For any code stored in codebase, its associated information should be traced back to the requirements/defects management platform. In other words, when different roles disagree whether a feature meets the acceptance condition, we can find a correct and unambiguous answer on the requirements/defects management platform.

7.3.1.2 Deployment pipeline platform

According to the product team's definition, the deployment pipeline platform shall be able to connect trusted sources and different basic services in a certain manner, coordinate and schedule different tasks, complete the operation of an entire delivery process, and display both the current progress and historical information of all deployment pipelines.

7.3.1.3 Infrastructure service layer

For a software company with years' operation, it is likely to have formed necessary basic services (building, testing, and deployment). According to the original division of responsibilities, these services are already distributed in different functional departments, and some of them may have been repeatedly built.

For example, the QA department manages multiple testing environments, while the operation team strictly controls the right to access the production environment. Besides, each department defines its own verification system and norms. For example, the development department has created self-testing and code specifications. The QA department has built a set of automation testcases, established an automation test system, and used it to verify the quality of software submitted by the development team. The operation team has built a tool system for themselves to improve operation and maintenance efficiency and reducing work intensity.

When software delivery increasingly relies on the continuous delivery model, the above services must be in line with a continuous deployment pipeline, so as to maximize the benefits of continuous delivery. To this end, the original supporting platform should undergo a series of transformations.

7.3.2 Basic Capabilities of the Platform

The deployment pipeline platform, which is the central system for team collaboration, mainly deals with the value flow efficiency of the software itself, covering information about the entire process from code submission to deployment. It is able to accurately display the status of each stage in the deployment pipeline, automatically collect the data generated in each stage without increasing the burden on the team, and evaluate the efficiency of value flow through data measurement. For example, this platform measures the development cycle time of a feature, that is, the time span from the submission of the first line of code of a feature to its deployment to the production environment or delivery to the customer (see Figure 7.6).

The platform must have traceability of two aspects: (1) It is able to trace all information about an event that occurs in the deployment pipeline, such as "What operation was performed?" "When and why did it happen?" "Who was accountable?" "How about the operation process and the corresponding script?" Only in this way can we support the work of security audit. It is also favorable for rapid location and analysis of defects, and diagnosis of online problems. (2) It is able to trace all the products from the deployment pipeline, including any artifact and its source, the script and environment when it is built, and other components it depends on and their version information.

The platform must be able to reconstruct previous builds. For example, when an old software version goes wrong and its binary installer cannot be found in the artifact repository – although it is an extreme

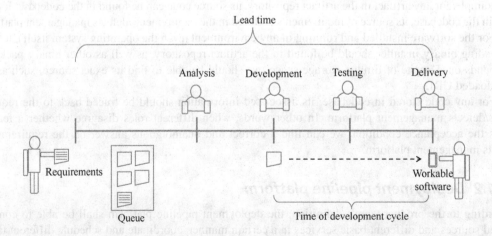

FIGURE 7.6 Development cycle time of a feature.

scenario, as long as the content of the True North source remains intact, the deployment pipeline platform may immediately retrieve the deployment pipeline configuration at that time and enable this old version to be rebuilt the same as before. In addition, we often have to go over certain stages in the deployment pipeline. For example, if we suspect that a failed automation test is caused by some factors related to the operating environment, then we may want to repeat the relevant stage.

7.3.3 Strategy for Tool Chain Construction

Figure 7.5 illustrates the architecture of the deployment pipeline platform for continuous delivery in a highly abstract manner, but it doesn't mean that it is a Monolithic Architecture. In fact, it is integrated by several different tools and subsystems. Since different companies may use different technical architectures, programming languages, operation system, their deployment pipeline platforms are not necessarily identical.

For start-ups or small-sized companies that don't have a large team, multifold business scenario or complex software architecture, they can build a suitable deployment pipeline platform through the assembly of open-source tools in relevant fields.

For medium-sized companies founded years ago, they are likely to have more legacy systems and code to be maintained, as well as few tools, so they only need to develop certain tools to fulfil some customized requirements, in an aim to solve specific problems in certain fields and improve management efficiency. When there is a large number of automation testcases, more systems for managing and distributing these testcases should be put in pace. For example, with too many automation testcases, the GoCD team developed a grouping plug-in which automatically allocates all testcases to different tasks, and then distribute these tasks to multiple test environments for parallel execution.

But for large-sized companies with a complex production environment, a large number of software applications, and intricate relationship between product components, they have to satisfy more customized requirements. And in order to exert the power of continuous delivery, cloud management of various supporting services have become a must choice of these companies. For example, Amazon, Google, Facebook, and Netflix have developed their own tool chain for the continuous deployment pipeline platform, and even contributed some of these tools to the open-source community.

The deployment pipeline platform itself is only used for the definition and task scheduling of the software deployment pipeline, as well as for displaying its current status. The execution of specific tasks is undertaken by the infrastructure services that are associated with each other, that is, the input of one system may be the output of another one. Now, let's talk about the relationship between these systems from the content flowing in the deployment pipeline.

7.4 CLOUDIFICATION OF INFRASTRUCTURE SERVICES

Industry-leading Dot-com companies are known for their highly frequent deployment of server-side programs (see Table 7.1). These companies have created their own cloud-enabled infrastructure services to facilitate their internal large-scale continuous delivery practices; they also encourage the use of unified platforms and tools to improve delivery efficiency, increase resource utilization and reduce management costs. Some companies argue that these internal tools are used by their own employees, they only need to be workable, better use experience or unification doesn't matter at all. However, when applying the continuous delivery model, poorly performed tools will greatly affect work efficiency. Amazon was aware of this as early as 2006, that's why its internal support tools are one of the best in the industry in terms of functionality and usability, thereby allowing Amazon – a super-large and complex e-commerce website – to run smoothly. All of its tools, which are developed and maintained by a dedicated team, are used uniformly throughout the company and updated in a timely and unified manner.

TABLE 7.1   Deployment frequency of top Internet companies

COMPANY	DEPLOYMENT FREQUENCY	DEPLOYMENT LEADTIME
Amazon	23,000/day	Minutes
Google	5,500/day	Minutes
Netflix	500/day	Minutes
Facebook	2/day	Minutes
Twitter	3/week	Hours

Source: Gene Kim, et al., 2015, *The Phoenix Project: A Novel About IT, DevOps, and Helping Your Business Win*, IT Revolution Press.

7.4.1 Interpretation of the Collaboration Process of Infrastructure Services

To better understand the positioning and responsibilities of various infrastructure services, let's first look at a simple deployment pipeline in Figure 7.7. This example illustrates the collaboration process between various infrastructure services for implementing the deployment pipeline for continuous delivery.

This simple deployment pipeline only contains three stages, namely, "check-in build", "secondary build", and "production deployment". Among them, the stage of "check-in build" involves building and packaging, unit testing, and code static check. The stage of "secondary build" involves end-to-end automation test. The stage of "production deployment" directly deploys the code that has passed the first two stages into the production environment. Each subsequent stage is automatically triggered by the previous one, as shown in Figure 7.7.

The collaboration results of all relevant services will be displayed on the deployment pipeline platform. However, in order to make the schematic diagram in Figure 7.8 more concise, the scheduling operations of the deployment pipeline platform are omitted. In this schematic diagram, the direction of the thick arrow points out the advancing direction of the deployment pipeline, the circled serial numbers indicate different stages in the deployment pipeline, and the number "0" denotes the initial preparations of basic environments. As shown in Figure 7.8, all of the configuration information, descriptions and code come from the code repository. The binary packages are put into the binary library after the first build is generated from the check-in stage, and then reused in the next two stages free from being rebuilt.

- Step 0: Prepare environments. After obtaining the base environment configuration information from the code repository, the environment management system provided by the operation team will automatically prepare the base environments for the deployment pipeline, such as the environment for compilation and packaging, the test environment for unit test, the UAT environment for manual acceptance test, and even the production environment.

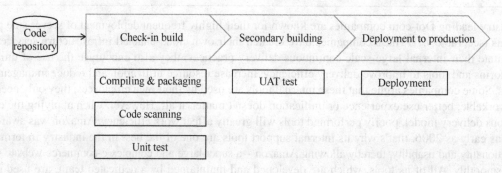

FIGURE 7.7   Example of deployment pipeline.

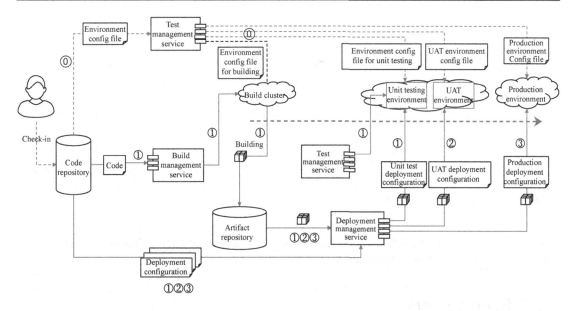

FIGURE 7.8 Schematic diagram of one implementation process of deployment pipeline.

- Step 1: Check-in build. This step is to compile and package software, and execute basic verification of software assembly by unit test, code check, and installer check. To this end, the build system takes out the source code from the code repository, builds and packages it, and puts the artifact into the artifact repository. Afterwards, the deployment system deploys the artifact to the test environment. If a special configuration is needed for this stage, the source config code will be pulled from the code repository for that. After the successful deployment, the tests specified by the pipeline are to be executed, and a signal of whether all tests have passed is returned.
- Step 2: Secondary build. The deployment management system takes out the artifacts generated in Step 1 from the artifact repository, and extracts the deployment config information from the code repository, has them combined and deployed to the UAT environment, and then runs the end-to-end automation testcases. After that, a signal of whether the tests have passed is returned.
- Step 3: Deploy to the production environment. The deployment management system takes out the artifact generated in Step 1 from the artifact repository, and extracts the deployment configuration information from the code repository, has them combined and deployed to the production environment.

THE SIMPLEST DEPLOYMENT PIPELINE – IMVU'S 50 DEPLOYMENTS PER DAY

Founded in 2004, IMVU, Inc. is the creator of IMVU (imm-view), the world's largest avatar-based social network headquartered in Redwood City, California. As of 2009, it had about 50 developers who were busy with 50 times of deployment to the production environment per day. The deployment pipeline only had two stages: "check-in build" and "deployment to production environment"; and both of them were automatically triggered. The automation test suite was run in parallel on 30~40 machines, and it took nine minutes to run in total (including six minutes' deployment to the production environment). The two stages were run continuously, meaning that a change list was pushed to the website every nine minutes in average, so there was six times of deployment within an hour and an average of 50 times of deployment per day.

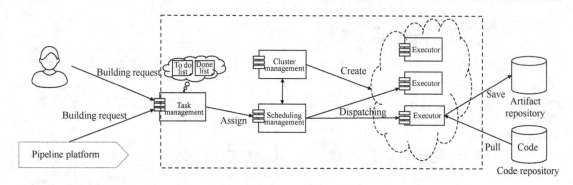

FIGURE 7.9   Architectural diagram of the build management system.

After learning about the collaboration process between the services, the following subsections will interpret the logical structure of these services one by one.

7.4.2 Build System

The build system is responsible for receiving and scheduling builds, managing build clusters, and executing builds (see Figure 7.9).

The task service includes two sub-services: receiving and notification. The receiving sub-service is to receive a building request from the developers or the deployment pipelines (or CI server), record the information about the request (requester, content, and type of request), and add it to the to-do-list. The notification sub-service is to take out relevant information from the done-list, and send build result to the requester.

The scheduling service is to fetch a building task from the to-do-list according to a certain scheduling algorithm, and dispatch to the corresponding build machine. For example, the building of C++ code should be sent to the machine with a C++ compilation environment.

The build cluster service is to manage all sorts of build environments, including the creation and destruction of them, and their status (occupied, idle, or unconnected).

The build executor is an agent that performs building tasks. There are many executors in a cluster; even a computing node may have multiple executors. Based on the received information, each executor checks out the code from the corresponding code repository URI, and then compile and build it. After the build is completed, the build executor will store the artifacts in the location specified in the building description (usually the artifact repository of a company), and report the execution result to the scheduling service system. The executor itself doesn't perform the building task, but calls special build tools to do so. For example, Ant, Maven, and Gradle are the build tools available for the Java project.

At present, many open-source CI servers (such as Jenkins and GoCD) are capable of scheduling management, which are enough to meet the needs of small and medium-sized companies in most cases. A customized build management system is suitable for large-sized companies that have a large number of building tasks. Among the building requests shown in Figure 7.9, some come from the deployment pipeline, and others come from the engineers, which implies that the build service also supports engineers to attempt for personal building before check-in. Therefore, engineers can take advantage of this powerful service while writing code locally. The case introduced in Chapter 16 adopted a similar approach to quicken the feedback on individual building in the six-step check-in dance of CI.

In fact, every infrastructure service should support this work pattern, so as to maximize the usage of resources and fasten high-quality feedback.

7.4.3 Automation Test System

The automation test system is responsible for testing task management, testcase scheduling, and test cluster management. For companies with a large number of automation testcases, they may also need health management of them.

The tasting task service is made up of the sub-services that are to receive task requests and feedback their results.

The testcase scheduling service is to select test tasks from the to-do-list according to a certain scheduling algorithm. This scheduling service has two work patterns: one is to implement testcases in sequence, that is, distribute all testcases to an eligible test device for implementation. The other is to implement testcases in parallel, that is, divide all testcases into several subsets and distribute them to multiple test devices for implementation.

The test cluster service is to manage the testing environment, including its creation and destruction, as well as its state (occupied, idle, or unconnected). This service manages more types of cluster than the build cluster service, such as unit test cluster, functional test cluster, and performance test cluster. Since every product line has different requirement for the testing environment, the test cluster needs to be further divided.

In the case of running a large number of automation testcases, flaky testcases is a serious problem. Some companies will design a testcase health service to automatically identify flaky testcases according to certain rules. Any testcase, if identified as flaky, would be removed from the set of healthy testcases and put into the pool of flaky testcases. Therefore, when the original test set is called later, this flaky test would be automatically ruled out.

Besides, this health service can also detect the flaky tests by different strategies (for example, repeatedly run a test for 100 times based on different network nodes and different node resources). If the times of failure exceed a given number, it is marked as a flaky test, and to be assigned to the team that owns it for fixing (see Figure 7.10).

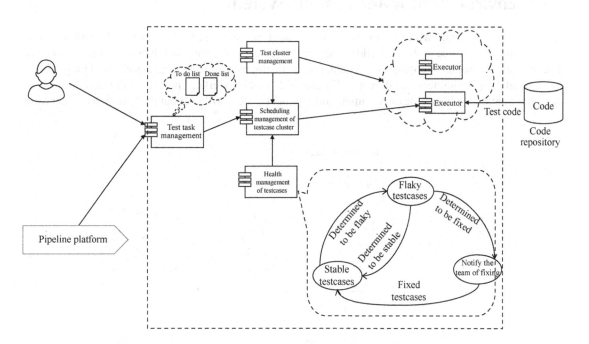

FIGURE 7.10 Architectural diagram of the automation test management system.

7.4.4 Deployment System

It happens all the time that "the package goes well in the test environment and the pre-production environment, but goes wrong in Production". A main reason is the difference between the Production and the test environment. For example, more than a decade ago, lots of companies used the commercialized J2EE application server in production, for example, WebSphere. This kind of server is so RAM consuming that developers and QAs preferred to Tomcat for debugging or testing. Tomcat is not strict with grammar checking. Therefore, even though Web application works with Tomcat, when the Web applications were launched, it could report errors once in a while due to mismatched Html tags in production. This was in fact caused the inconsistency between environments.

In addition, the tension between operators and developers has been a long-standing issue. The former is responsible for the stability of the production, while the latter is responsible for delivering new features as fast as possible. The interface between them is a formal artifact repository. After putting the accepted software assembly into this artifact repository, the development team would mark the work done. Then the operators take the software assembly from the artifact repository, and deploy it to the production according to the online deployment manifest provided by the development team (see Figure 7.11).

After employing the continuous delivery model, everyone should use the same toolkit. Anyone with permission can issue a deployment by one-click button. Upon receiving the instruction, the deployment system will deploy the designated software assembly in the specified environment according to the configuration. These environments could be the environment for developing, testing, staging, and production.

At this time, the deployment system can accept deployment requests from different roles, so it will respectively take out the specified software assembly from the artifact repository, and the deployment script and configuration from the code repository, and then distribute this software assembly to the node on which it runs according to the deployment descriptions, install and start it correctly. Now, there are many deployment tools on the market, such as Puppet, Chaf, Ansible, and SaltStack; all of them are able to work together with the deployment pipeline platform to fulfill the deployment.

7.4.5 Environment Management System

The environment management system provides environment prevision, management and monitoring services for the above three systems (build management, test management, and deployment management). It accepts the environment request from build, test, or deployment management system, and prepares the corresponding environment, as shown in Figure 7.12. To be specific, upon receiving a request from the three front-end systems, the environment management system will take out the specified content from

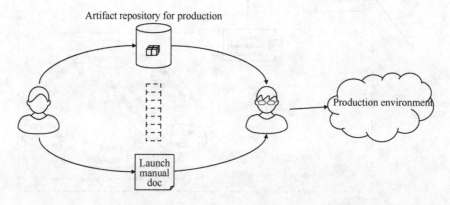

FIGURE 7.11 Wall between development and operation maintenance departments.

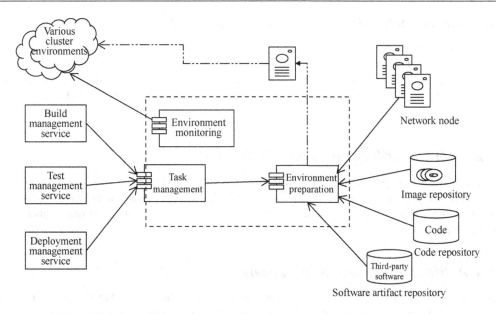

FIGURE 7.12 Architectural diagram of the basic environment management system.

the code repository, artifact repository, prepare the environment after processing this content, and put it in the corresponding cluster and send back a notification.

Usually, the operation team is responsible for production environment, rather than the environment for developing and testing. The development team only deals with the environment for build and test.

As the Docker technology matures, more and more companies begin to use it, which greatly simplifies the environmental preparation. Any software application, configuration and a base environment can be constructed as a Docker image, which can be directly pulled and started during deployment.

7.5 MANAGEMENT OF ARTIFACT REPOSITORY

For a company, the artifact repository is one of the True North of the tool chain for deployment pipeline, and also a very important node in the corporate information security management. Only the binaries that have passed security audit can be stored in the artifact repository. The security audit section should regularly perform security check on the contents stored in the repository, and clean up those with potential safety hazards.

7.5.1 Classification of Artifact Repository

The types of artifact repository are shown in Table 7.2.

TABLE 7.2 Category of artifact repository

ARTIFACT REPOSITORY	INSIDE THE COMPANY		OUTSIDE THE COMPANY
	TEMPORARY	FORMAL	
For packages	A	B	X
For images	C	D	Y

7.5.1.1 Internal artifact repository A (temporary)

The temporary artifact repository stores all packages generated from any stages of the deployment pipeline, which may be not fully checked, such as the binaries generated whenever the check-in build is triggered. So, the software assemblies in this repository cannot be directly deployed to production until finishing the quality check. The historical contents of this repository could be cleaned up to save the space.

7.5.1.2 Internal artifact repository B (formal)

The formal artifact repository stores the software assemblies that have been fully verified and will be deployed to production or delivered to users. Once verified, these software assemblies should be moved from the temporary artifact repository to the formal one. The software assemblies stored in this repository should be kept until they are withdrawn from the market.

7.5.1.3 Artifact repository X (external)

The external artifact repository stores the software assemblies that are acquired by the company from the Internet or third-party organizations; they are necessary for the company to develop its own products, but the source code is not managed and maintained by themselves.

In the external artifact repository, software assemblies are probably stored in three forms: a direct binary form; copy of the source code; or an external link address (for example, the link of GitHub repository for a module of Golang).

A company builds an external artifact repository under its unified management for the following reasons: (1) It is convenient to use. The internal team can acquire these software assemblies on their Intranet without connecting to the Internet. (2) It is subject to unified auditing. The internal team only obtains external software assemblies from this repository, thereby avoiding the same software from different sources, and avoiding the use of unsecure versions in violation of regulations. (3) It is secure. The company can perform security checks on the external software assemblies that are stored in the same repository, so as to keep its own software products from going wrong due to any unsecure software assembly from the outside; even if any security loophole exists in an external software assembly, the internal team can immediately patch it or replace it with a new one.

7.5.1.4 Temporary mirror C, formal mirror D, and external mirror Y

The responsibilities of the three mirrors are similar to those of the software repositories, except that they store the docker images or the virtual machine images. The way for managing software repositories is also applicable to these images.

7.5.2 Principles for Management of Artifact Repository

Each artifact in the artifact repository should have a unique identification; its source, components and usage shall be stored together to constitute the meta-information of this artifact. And all artifacts can be traced back to their sources; those in the temporary artifact repository are no exception. No matter when and where, any artifact obtained from the artifact repository is the same for its unique identification. If an artifact is deleted or lost, the company can regenerate the same one through the original deployment pipeline and based on its meta-information retained in the artifact repository.

7.6 A VARIETY OF DEPLOYMENT PIPELINES

Software has different forms, for example, web applications and distributed assemblies that are built by different teams for users from different industries. Also, different teams may use different branching strategies for the source code. Therefore, the deployment pipelines would be different too. However, they have a few basic patterns.

7.6.1 Multi-Component Deployment Pipeline

If a software application consists of multiple components that have their own code repositories and are maintained by other teams, the deployment pipeline is similar to the one shown in Figure 7.13. A passed deployment pipeline of each component will trigger the integration deployment pipeline of a downstream product. At this time, the recently successful software assembly of each component will be automatically fetched from the artifact repository to go through integration packaging, which will then trigger the subsequent stage of the integration deployment pipeline.

7.6.2 Individual Deployment Pipeline

When GoCD used Mercurial, which is one of the distributed version control systems, every engineer created his own deployment pipeline for quick quality feedback before he pushes the code to the team's repository. This individual deployment pipeline will not be deployed to the integration environment of the team, but only to the environment for the engineer, as shown in Figure 7.14.

Each developer uses a template of the team deployment pipeline, and deletes all other stages except for the first two stages, namely "check-in build" and "secondary build". In this way, the individual deployment pipeline will monitor the developer's own code repository and be automatically triggered by changes. In other words, whenever a developer check in code to his own code repository, his personal deployment pipeline will be automatically triggered.

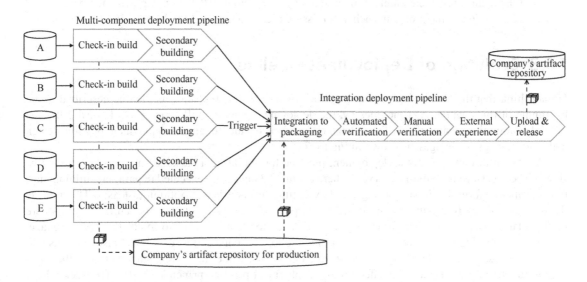

FIGURE 7.13   Multi-component aggregated deployment pipeline.

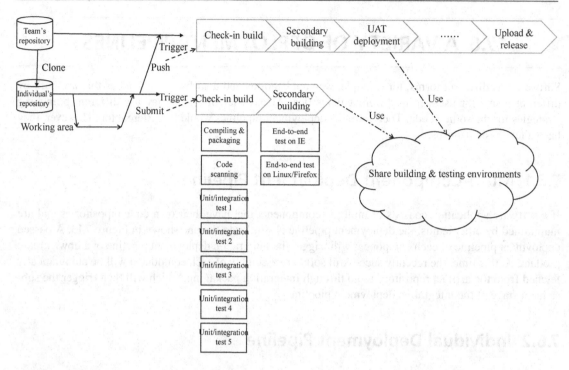

FIGURE 7.14 Improve feedback speed and quality through individual deployment pipeline.

The individual deployment pipeline boasts the following three benefits:

1. It shares the same configuration of building and automation test cluster environments with the team deployment pipeline. This means that these building and automation test environments of individuals are consistent with those of the team at any time.
2. It enables all engineers to speed up personal verification with more powerful testing resources.
3. The testcases in the individual deployment pipeline are identical to those in the first two stages of the team deployment pipeline. In case of any failed build in the team deployment pipeline, it is easy to locate the problem, such as a missing file, which is ought to be submitted.

7.6.3 Evolution of Deployment Pipeline

Do not think that the GoCD deployment pipeline always remains the same as the one described at the beginning of this chapter. As time goes by, the deployment pipeline will evolve. As of April 2018, the official community version of GoCD had been released once a month, and its deployment pipeline design had undergone great changes, as shown in Figure 7.15.

As shown in Figure 7.15, the deployment pipeline for "building a package on Linux" contains two stages. The first stage is "build-no_server" where a total of 39 tasks are executed in parallel: building multiple .jar files to form the Server package, and executing Java and JavaScript unit testcases. This reflects the deployment pipeline principle of "trying to be parallel". The second stage is "build-server" where multiple Jar packages that are preliminarily verified at the first stage are used to conduct a Server package.

As shown in Figure 7.15, the deployment pipeline for "acceptance test on Linux" also contains two stages. The first stage is to run high-priority functional tests, while the second stage is to run the automation functional test of plug-ins, reflecting the deployment pipeline principle of "fast feedback taking precedence".

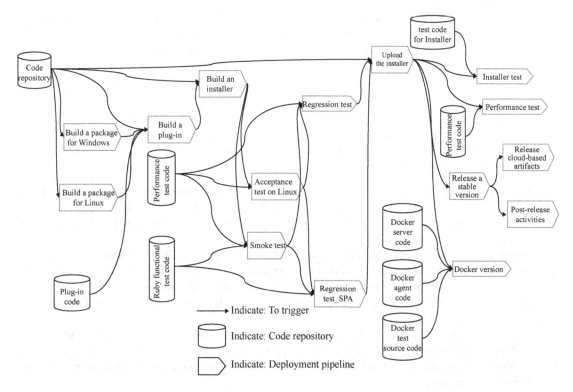

FIGURE 7.15 Complex deployment pipeline design.

In the subsequent tests, including acceptance test, regression test, and functional test, all the binary packages to be tested are the output from the previous stages of the deployment pipeline, and they must be based on the same version of source code.

The deployment pipeline for performance test contains eight stages: generating test scripts, preparing testing environment, starting Server, starting Agent, configuring testcases, getting ready, running, and stopping.

7.7 BUILD SELF-SERVICE TOOLS FOR ENGINEERS

In many companies, the tools built by each role are used by themselves. For example, the automation testcases developed by testers is mainly to reduce their own workload on manual regression test; and part of the core testcases are often used as a gate to shift the responsibility.

There are other scenarios as well. In a large Internet company, the test platform maintained by QAs only allows to write testcases in the browser and to save them by clicking a "Save" button. Sometimes, it may accidentally lose half-written testcases by network issues. Considering its poor performance, how could developers accustomed to the local IDE like to use this test platform and run those testcases? More than that, the operation team has setup a complicated process in order to maintain the stability of production. The production management platform built by them is fairly suitable or even powerful for production. However, according to the environmental consistency principle for continuous delivery, if developers and QAs also use this platform, they may encounter lots of difficulties, because such platform is not suitable for daily debugging and testing.

The world's leading Dot-com companies have embraced another design philosophy for environment tooling, that is, "design tools for developers that they prefer". Just like what Amazon CTO Werner Vogels has said: "you build it, you run it", which has become a working policy of developers. It all started in a 2006 interview with Werner Vogels:

> "Giving developers operational responsibilities has greatly enhanced the quality of the services, both from a customer and a technology point of view. The traditional model is that you take your software to the wall that separates development and operations and throw it over and then forget about it. Not at Amazon. You build it, you run it. This brings developers into contact with the day-to-day operation of their software. It also brings them into day-to-day contact with the customer. This customer feedback loop is essential for improving the quality of the service."

This approach requires a powerful platform that can support developers to deal with operations of product services. Amazon has invested a great deal of resources to build the entire support platform. Besides, the company asks for a shift in the way of thinking about tool construction, that is, all DevOps tools should provide self-service.

In another case, developers of Facebook can see the deployment progress of their changes and how many active users are using new features by the internal platform without turning to others for help (see Figure 7.16).

In e-commerce company Etsy, it is convenient for developers to view the number of changes to their code since its last deployment to the production environment, and find out the differences before and after each change (see Figure 7.17).

To sum up, in order to implement the way of working of "you build it, you run it", companies should, in light of the working scenarios of developers, build powerful DevOps tools for them. They are not only the operation tools but also the infrastructure for business indicators monitoring in the entire workflow. The DevOps tools include:

- Self-service platform for development, like the one for various environments (building, testing, and production).

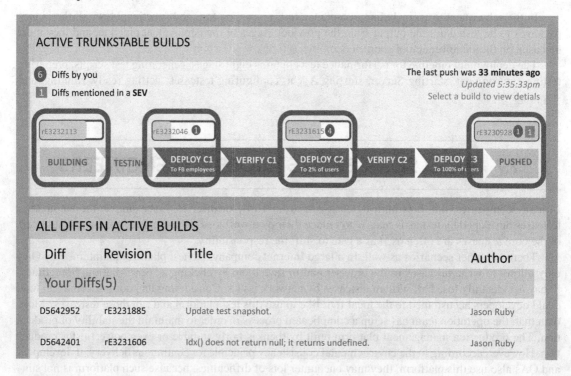

FIGURE 7.16 Visualization tool for Facebook's code deployment progress.

Log

¡¡ Commits since last prod deploy !!

☑ Auto scroll command output?

Add an arbitrary log message:

PROJECT-### to link to jira and add a comment [   ] [log]

- [web] | 2010-06-07 23:20:38 | PRODUCTION | jwong | Production Deploy: old 26721, new: 26722 diff
- [web] | 2010-06-07 23:18:22 | PRINCESS | jwong | Princess Deploy: old: 26721, new: 26722 diff
- [web] | 2010-06-07 23:16:37 | QA | jwong | Adding Jonathan and Any to about.php old: 26721, new: 26722 diff
- [web] | 2010-06-07 23:08:57 | PRODUCTION | ncook | Production Deploy: old 26697, new: 26721 diff
- [web] | 2010-06-07 23:06:57 | PRINCESS | ncook | Princess Deploy: old: 26697, new: 26721 diff
- [web] | 2010-06-07 23:06:30 | QA | ncook | transaction link fix old: 26697, new: 26721 diff
- [web] | 2010-06-07 21:46:25 | PRODUCTION | ncook | Production Deploy: old 26658, new: 26697 diff
- [web] | 2010-06-07 21:42:29 | PRINCESS | ncook | Princess Deploy: old: 26658, new: 26697 diff
- [web] | 2010-06-07 21:38:00 | QA | ncook | transaction should have all images old: 26658, new: 26697 diff

FIGURE 7.17 Etsy's deployment to production.

- Self-service data platform (including three-layer data monitoring).
- Experimental platform for fast trial of business (for example, AB testing).
- User engage platform for mobile devices.

To build a platform in this way of thinking, a company will become a learning organization composed of multiple fully functional teams that are truly self-driven, self-service, and business-oriented.

7.8 SUMMARY

This chapter introduces the principles for the team to design and utilize deployment pipelines, as well as the key points for companies to build customized deployment pipelines, and capability requirements of necessary tools. The four infrastructure services for deployment pipeline (compilation and building, automation test, deployment management, and environment management) are briefly introduced. There is also an analysis of the relationship among the three True North sources (requirements management repository, source code repository, and artifact repository), and the requirements for their management.

This chapter also lists several different product scenarios and corresponding deployment pipeline design schemes for your reference. In order to maximize the effect of deployment pipeline, developers should do their best to abide by the following five principles:

1. Any software package must be fetched from controlled sources, rather than through private channels such as emails and instant messaging tools.
2. Automate processes as many as possible and continue optimizing execution time.
3. Each check-in can automatically trigger the deployment pipeline.
4. Try to avoid manual triggering.
5. The principle of "stopping the line" must be implemented.

Branch Strategy Conducive to Integration

8

Chapter 6 has discussed how to split a requirement into multiple deliverable and acceptable user stories, and how to fit them into the iterative delivery process. This chapter introduces the branching strategy to realize efficient multiperson collaboration with the source code repository. It has a great impact on the cost and effect of Continuous Delivery.

8.1 PURPOSE OF THE VERSION CONTROL SYSTEM

The version control system (VCS) is mainly used to store and track all revisions of directories (folders) and files (the revisions here include "add", "modify", and "delete"), which enables its users to go back to any revision of any code under its control. Its most essential role is to answer the "4Ws", that is, When the revision was made? What was revised? Who did it? Why it was revised? The answer to the last question is included in the comments attached with the submission of code changes.

Now, the VCS has become an important collaboration management mechanism applicable to the software delivery process through teamwork, and it is also the infrastructure of a software development company. It is designed to support software configuration management, track and record the development, and for maintenance activities of multiple versions.

According to their mode of operation, the mainstream VCSs on the market are divided into two types: centralized VCS (CVCS) and distributed VCS (DVCS).

8.1.1 CVCS

The typical representative of the CVCS is subversion, or SVN for short. The emergence of the CVCS solves the problem of how multiple people collaborate with each other in code modification. The CVCS has a single centralized version control server that records and saves the historical revisions of all files. When someone intends to exchange code with his teammate, he has to connect to this server through the client to get the necessary files. For anyone who needs the latest revision submitted by others, he has to access it in the CVCS. At this point, the client doesn't have all the contents stored in the central repository, but acquires a snapshot of the code file in the repository at a time according to user command. The schematic diagram of the CVCS is shown in Figure 8.1.

When a developer has a modified part of the code but has not yet completed his work, if he wants to save this intermediate result as a temporary version for backup, he usually has only two options: one is to copy it to another local directory; the other is to submit it directly to the central repository. However, direct submission of semi-finished products to the central repository without quality inspection may affect the existing features and hinder the work of his teammates.

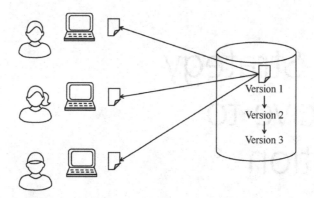

FIGURE 8.1 Schematic diagram of the CVCS.

The CVCS has two disadvantages:

1. In the case of a poor network environment, synchronization of a large number of files often fails. At the end of 2007, the GoCD team was using SVN for version management. The developers of the team were working in Beijing, the sales staff and after-sales personnel were respectively distributed in the US and India, and the SVN server was hosted in Chicago. Once a developer was on a business trip from Beijing to Bangalore. After he arrived at the India office, he borrowed a workstation to modify and submit the code. He was going to get the source code from the SVN to the computer. However, the codebase was a bit large, and the poor network condition of the local office could hardly support file transfer. Despite of hours' trying, this developer was still unable to pull the code from the SVN server.

2. The CVCS server is exposed to the risk of single point of failure (SPOF). If the SVN server is down for an hour, then no one can check-in or get files from the server during that time. In the worst case, if the hard disk goes wrong, and the backup is either delayed or undone, there will be the risk of losing large amounts of data. After the Bangalore incident, the GoCD team migrated the source code repository from SVN to Mercurial (or HG for short) – a kind of DVCS also used by Facebook.

8.1.2 DVCS

Unlike the CVCS, the DVCS has multiple servers in coexistence, each node is a code repository, and all nodes are equal. In the process of team collaboration, a certain node is usually specified as the team's central server, as shown in Figure 8.2.

The characteristic of the DVCS is that any changes can be checked locally without going through the server, so the speed is faster. It is only when files need to be synchronized to other people or remote servers that they will be pushed to or pulled from remote repository via the network. Therefore, even in the absence of network connections, we can still check in frequently. In the network environment, these files can be pushed to the remote code repository. When it comes to currently mainstream DVCS, Git is no doubt the king.

In the case of the GoCD above, when they shift to Mercurial, the engineer in Bangalore could pull the code conveniently despite of an unstable network at first and sync the code later, as shown in Figure 8.3.

1. Bob clones Sara's codebase via the network in the Bangalore office (Bob and Sara are in the same office).

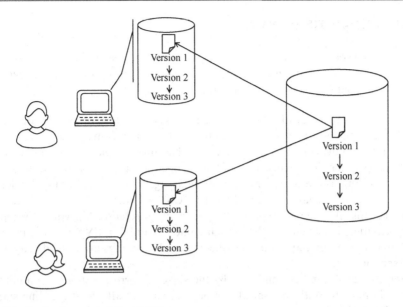

FIGURE 8.2   Schematic diagram of the DVCS.

2. Bob pulls the codes from the Chicago-based central codebase which are different from those in the local codebase.
3. Bob modifies the code file and commits it to the local codebase to generate a new version.
4. Bob pushes this new file version to the central codebase.
5. Sara can pull all the different codes from the central codebase.

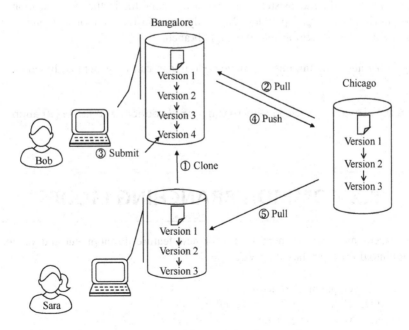

FIGURE 8.3   Acquire code by cloning other's codebase via local network.

8.1.3 Basic Concepts in VCS

The core problem to be solved by the VCS is the file version management in the process of multiperson collaboration. Before discussing the multiperson collaborative pattern in detail, it is necessary to uniformly define some similar concepts in multiple VCSs.

- "Codebase" refers to a logical unit recording the revision history of a set of files; it is usually used to store all file information about a software or a certain component.
- "Branch" refers to the copy of the selected code baseline. People can operate the files in this copy; these operations are independent of the file operations of the original code baseline.
- "Trunk (or Main)" is a branch with special meaning. It is usually created by default automatically when a codebase is created by the VCS, and each codebase has one and only a branch like this. Its special meaning lies in its close relationship with development and release activities. For example, the branch named "trunk" in SVN and the branch named "Main" in Git are both main branches (their special meanings are to be discussed in detail in next section).
- "Revision", a serial number generated by the system, corresponds to a commit operation on a certain branch. With this serial number, we can get all file at the time stamp of the commit. In SVN, revision is a continuously varying positive integer. In Git, it is a 40-bit hash value, similar to a combination of letters and numbers such as "734713bc047d87b... 65ae793478c50d3". For ease of use, Git can use the first few characters of a hash value to identify a commit, as long as the SHA-1 that we provide has no ambiguity and no less than four characters.
- "Tag" is an alias for a specific revision of a branch for easy memory and lookup. We can create an alias with the command provided by the tool.
- "Head" refers to the revision corresponding to the latest revision on the main branch.
- "Merge" is to combine all contents on a branch with those on a target branch, and then create a new revision on the target branch.
- "Conflict" refers to the inconsistent contents of the same file in the same position on the two branches during the merge operation. Normally, manual intervention is required to confirm how to modify before merging with the target branch.

According to the above definitions, a unique code image can be generated based on the following word string:

```
{Codebase name}:{Branch name}:{Revision} or {Codebase name}:{Branch
name}:{Tag}
```

8.2 COMMON BRANCHING MODES

Currently, the branch-based development modes for new feature development and version release are mainly classified into three types based on VCS:

1. Trunk-based Development & Release.
2. Trunk-based Development & Branch-Based Release.
3. Branch-based Development & Trunk-Based Release.

Their respective characteristics are introduced as follows:

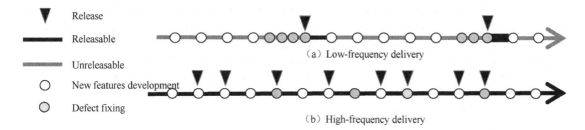

FIGURE 8.4   Trunk-based Development & Release.

8.2.1 Trunk-Based Development and Release

As the name suggests, "Trunk-based Development & Release" means that developers submit code to the trunk (or the life cycle of each branch is as short as several hours or less than one day), and use the trunk code for release (see Figure 8.4). In other words, the code for all new features is submitted to the trunk; when new features need to be released, the code on the trunk is directly deployed to production.

According to different frequency of delivery, there are low-frequency and high-frequency delivery.

The low-frequency delivery is usually seen in large-scale software projects with a long period. It is one of the oldest software development modes born in the era when a delivery cycle had lasted months or even years in the information technology (IT) industry. In the scenario of low-frequency delivery, the trunk code remains unavailable for a long time; the software joint debugging and integration testing cannot start until the code for all required features is developed. In the process of development, the VCS is a pure backup codebase since it is simply used to ensure that no code is lost.

The high-frequency delivery refers to highly frequent release, usually once or even multiple times every day. The high-frequency delivery is preferred by the Internet product teams with relatively comprehensive infrastructure (automation configuration building, automation testing, automation operation and maintenance, automation monitoring, and alarming). This type of delivery is capable of rapid defect fixing, and especially applicable to back-end server-side products, like back-end service for website or SaaS platform.

The Trunk-Based Development & Release boasts the advantage of simple branching and light workload on branch management (such as lower cost of code merging), but it also has some weaknesses. For example, in the case of low-frequency delivery, not every team member is needed in defect fixing in the later stage of the project, which is a waste of resources. In response to this situation, many teams like to adopt the mode of "Trunk-based Development & Branch-based Release" (see Subsection 8.2.2).

In the case of high-frequency delivery, many people frequently submit code to the trunk, thereby causing its code to change very quickly. Suppose a developer pulls out a branch to develop on his own, and then merges his code with the one on the trunk after his work done. At this time, he has only two ways of working: (1) To update the code from the trunk to his own branch every day. The developer may spend one or two hours a day merging the code on the trunk with the one on his branch. (2) Instead of doing daily updates, the developer may merge the code after a period of time (for example, after the features are developed on his branch). However, by this time the code on the trunk may have changed so much that his code can no longer be merged back.

"MERGING TASK" UNACHIEVABLE

In 2011, the R&D team of china.baixing.com (a classified life service website), which only consisted of 12 developers, adopted the high-frequency delivery mode and released to production at 7:00 every workday morning. In order to reconstruct an important module, the chief developer specially created a proprietary branch. However, he announced to abandon all the code on the branch just one week later, because other developers had made too many changes on the trunk, making the code on his branch impossible to be merged back with the trunk.

"Any feature code not fully implemented cannot be added into the version to be released" – once the best practice of quality assurance. However, in the case of high-frequency delivery, this practice is no longer workable; instead, the check-in with uncompleted feature code should be allowed, provided that it does not affect users' normal use and release. Some special technical means (such as feature toggles and branch by abstraction) can be employed to make sure of this, although these means may generate certain managing overhead (see Chapter 12 for details). Besides, the high-frequency delivery also requires quality assurance activities to be fast and comprehensive.

8.2.2 Trunk-Based Development & Branch-Based Release

The mode of Trunk-based Development & Branch-based Release is illustrated in Figure 8.5.
This mode is operated as follows:

- Engineers submit the written code to the trunk directly for daily work.
- Cut out a new branch from the trunk to release when it is implemented or the time to release is approaching.
- Take integration tests and fix defects on the release branch for stabilization. Release it once it meets the quality standard.

This mode is characterized as follows:

- Frequent check-in to the trunk poses a great challenge to guarantee the quality of code on it.
- Branch is only for fixing defects rather than adding new features.
- If any serious defect is found and needs to be fixed immediately, engineers should fix it and release as a patch on the release branch, and then merge it back into the trunk. Another way is to fix the defect on the trunk, and cherry-pick into the corresponding branch. It is adopted by Facebook for developing mobile products.

Generally, the life cycle of the release branch should be short, and any operations on the branch should be terminated after a certain period of time. For example, the V1.0 Branch in Figure 8.5 should end after the V1.01 release point.

In the case of Trunk-based Development & Branch-based Release, the time from cutting out to the point of being deliverable can serve as a quality indicator of the trunk code. This time is known as the "Branch Stabilization Time" (BST), and the shorter the better quality. If the BST is short enough, you can

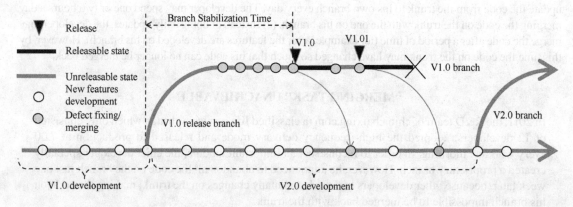

FIGURE 8.5 Trunk-based Development & Branch-Based Release.

switch to the mode of high-frequency Trunk-based Development & Release. Of course, it is not easy, since it requires a combination of the principles, methods, and practices as described in other parts of this book.

The advantages of the mode are as follows:

- The team can keep working on the trunk without being affected by the coming release.
- If any defect is found in the newly release, some developers can fix it on the corresponding branch directly, which is simple and convenient. Even if the code on the trunk has undergone major changes, the branch will not be affected.

The disadvantages of the mode are as follows:

- Generally, the trunk is only for the features of a coming release and no branch is cut until all features are done for it, otherwise it is likely to impede the development plan for the subsequent release. Most open-source projects use this mode.
- It does not restrict the number of release branches; and when keeping more branches alive, it would cause "branch hell", which is commonly seen in products with the strategy of "serialized product family + personalized customization", such as a Branch-based Release for a hardware device as shown in Figure 8.6.

At the beginning, this hardware device (Type A, Model x) only had one software version Ax1.0. After its release, the customer asked for software versions for the same type of hardware device but in different models. In order to satisfy customer requirements, the team cut out a branch from the Ax1.0 branch and named it Ay with an initial version as Ay2.0. Later, an enhanced branch Az was developed on the basis of Ay (its version and release time are shown in Figure 8.6). However, after a serious defect was discovered on Ax1.0, a patch version A1.01 was added. Since this defect also existed on the two branches of Ay and Az, the code for fixing this defect was ought to be ported to both the trunk and these two branches.

With this mode, the team succeeded in supporting hardware devices of more types and models. As shown in Figure 8.6, the team developed hardware device B, and successively released software B1.0 and B1.01 by cutting branches from the trunk. Since the customer demanded some new features on hardware B like Ay2 and Az3, the project team managed to migrate the code of these new features from the Ay2.01 and Az3.0 branches to the B branch.

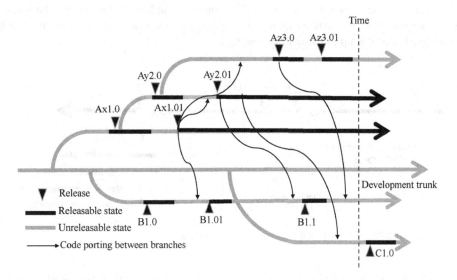

FIGURE 8.6 Branch hell.

HP LaserJet Firmware team (2008)	
Time occupancy ratio	Task
10%	Code integration
20%	Making detailed plans
25%	Code porting between branches
25%	Technical support for released products
15%	Manual testing
About 5%	New features development

FIGURE 8.7   Distribution of R&D resources of HP LaserJet Firmware team in 2008.

Owing to continuous derivation of hardware categories and models, the R&D efficiency of this team has been worsening. And it will eventually be tired of code porting and testing between branches (see the dotted line in Figure 8.6).

This happened on the HP LaserJet Firmware team in 2008 as described in the book *A Practical Approach to Large-Scale Agile Development: How HP Transformed LaserJet FutureSmart Firmware*[1]. Only 5% of the team's resources were consumed for developing new features, and porting code between branches took up 25% of the team's time, as shown in Figure 8.7.

8.2.3 Branch-Based Development & Trunk-Based Release

Branch-based Development & Trunk-based Release is one of the most widely used work patterns, as shown in Figure 8.8.

This mode is operated as follows:

- The team creates branches from the trunk to implement new features or fixes defect.
- The code on branches will not be merged back into the trunk until it is going to be released.
- After merging, defects newly found are usually fixed on the trunk. The code on the trunk will be released once it is up to the quality standard.

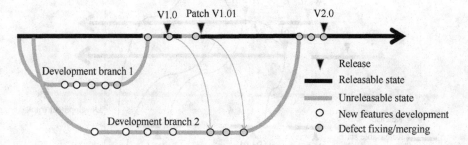

FIGURE 8.8   Branch-based Development & Trunk-Based Release.

---

[1] Gary Gruver, et. al., 2012, *A Practical Approach to Large-Scale Agile Development: How HP Transformed LaserJet FutureSmart Firmware* (1st edition), Addison-Wesley Professional.

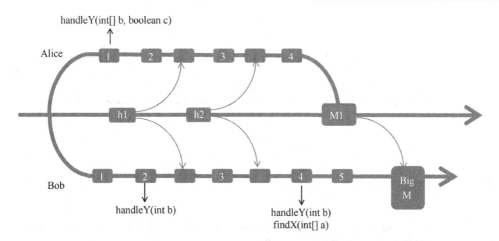

FIGURE 8.9   Huge merging caused by infrequent integration.

The advantages of this mode are as follows:

- Before merging back into the trunk, the changes on each branch are not mutually affecting.
- The team is free to release the features on any branch.
- If any defect is found in the new version, it can be fixed directly on the trunk or on the hotfix branch which is easier and more convenient, since it has nothing to with other feature branch.

However, the advantages of this mode may lead to an undesirable consequence, that is, in order to minimize the mutual impact between branches, developers tend to merge code into the trunk less frequently, thereby failing to discover the conflicts between branches in the first place, which goes against timely refactoring (see Figure 8.9).

The code on the trunk has an original method signature as handleY(int b). Alice and Bob each is assigned to develop a new feature, so they respectively create branch A and branch B. Before fulfilling their task, neither of them merges the code into the trunk. In order to develop her new feature, Alice modifies the handleY method and changes its signature to handleY(int[] b, boolean c). Meanwhile, Bob changes the internal implementation of handleY(int b) on his own branch. Based on the two hotfixes on the trunk, both of them pull trunk into their own branches. After that, Bob extracts a method signature as findX(int[] a) from handleY(int b). By this point, Alice has finished her work and merged the code (from a1 to a4) into the trunk. When Bob intends to submit his code to the trunk, he has to combine Alice's four modifications with his five modifications. Such a combination is probably a huge burden since Alice has made considerable changes. She has not only modified lots of files but also reconstructed the handleY() method. In addition to these textual conflicts which are easy to find and correct, the greater risk comes from the semantic conflict, that is, the logic conflict when the program is running. This kind of situation may discourage team members from refactoring. As time goes on, code changes become more and more difficult to maintain.

Too many branches will lead to the following problem: if the life cycle of a branch (that is, the period from the moment the branch is cut from the trunk to the time it is merged back into the trunk) is too long, the cost of merging and quality assurance will increase rapidly. The cost is directly proportional to the number of branches merged into the trunk within their life cycle.

The key points for successfully using this mode are as follows:

- Keep the trunk in a releasable state as long as possible.
- The life cycle of each branch should be as short as possible.
- Synchronize the trunk with the branch code as early as possible.
- Take the trunk as the norm and try not to merge the branch for different features.

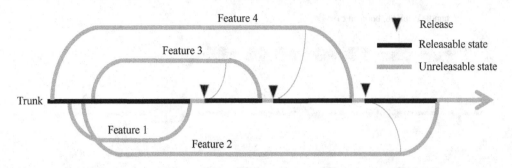

FIGURE 8.10 Feature branch mode.

According to the life cycle and purpose of branches, the mode could be further divided into two sub-modes: feature-based branch and team-based branch.

8.2.3.1 Feature-based branch

During the development, multiple active branches can exist at the same time, and each branch is dedicated to a feature. When a feature is fully implemented, it will be merged into the trunk immediately. As for the feature branch not yet merged into the trunk, it should pull out the trunk and merge with the branch, and then merge back into the trunk as illustrated in Figure 8.10.

The purpose of this mode is to facilitate multiple people to work in parallel at the "feature" level while stabilizing the releasable state of the trunk. Its advantage is easier adjustment of the content of each release. If a new feature is not completed or a defect is not fixed by the release time, it is not necessary to be merged into the trunk, which is of no impact on the scheduled release.

But this mode also has a weakness: too many feature branches will incur more merging costs. For example, whenever a feature branch is going to merge into the trunk, it shall merge with the trunk and undergo quality verification. Once the trunk passes quality verification, other branches should pull out the latest verified code from the trunk. If the feature branches are not merged into the trunk until all work is done, the one-off merge at that time will result in a heavy workload and burdensome quality verification. As shown in Figure 8.10, feature branch 2 needs to merge with feature branches 1, 3, and 4.

What if multiple features are finished at the same time? Two extreme approaches are introduced as follows:

1. Merge all feature branches into the trunk at the same time, and then manage to make the trunk deliverable. This approach is usually rejected by feature teams, because the one-off merger will have the code of multiple features intertwined, making the defects hard to be debugged and rapidly fixed.
2. All feature branches are queued up and merged into the trunk one by one. After one branch is merged into the trunk, the trunk must reach the deliverable state before the next branch can be merged. This is a common approach that manifests the advantage of feature branch. However, when multiple feature branches are lined up for merging, the feature branch at the end of the queue is bound to wait for a long time.

In order to make the feature branch mode perform better, we need pay attention to the following matters:

1. The life cycle of each feature branch should be short; it's better to finish the development and testing on each branch within three days. This requires breaking down "a feature" into smaller batches as far as possible (see the methods for requirements decomposition in Chapter 6).
2. Developers sync the latest deliverable code from the trunk to their own branch every day.
3. Don't pull code from other feature branches.

THE FEATURE BRANCHES LINING UP FOR LAUNCH

In 2011, there was a big web company mainly adopting the code branching strategy of "Branch-based Development & Trunk-based Release" (see Figure 8.11). The release was from trunk, while the features still under development or testing were on their respective branches. Once registered on a version dependency management platform, a project with a few features was allocated with a 3-digit version number like "1.2.1" and its branch was cut from the latest version of the trunk. When the features were done, the stage of debugging and developers' self-testing was kicked off. After that, developers could apply for QAs' testing on the configuration management platform.

Upon receiving the application for testing, the platform automatically generated a 4-digit version number like "1.2.1.1" and notified QAs to verify. QAs started to test manually. If any defect was found, QAs would inform developers to fix it. After fixing the defect, developers would apply for testing again and the platform would generate a next 4-digit version number like "1.2.1.2".

Repeat this process until the quality was up to the release standard and lined up for integration. If there were no other items in the waiting queue, developers could merge the code into the trunk right away and apply for another test round. Once the quality reached the standard, they would prepare deployment documents, write operating steps for release, upload them to the operation platform, and hand them over to the operation team.

According to the regulations of the operation department, there were only two workdays per week for launching, and only one project was allowed to be launched at a time. Therefore, there had been a situation where 14 feature branches were lining up for launch. But it would take as long as seven weeks for these 14 branches, which were already implemented, to be merged and launched. The code of each feature branch must be qualified, and no serious problem was found when each branch was to be launched; otherwise, the code must be rolled back for modification.

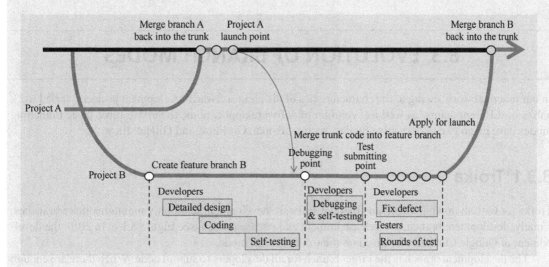

FIGURE 8.11 The Branch-based Release strategy of an Internet company.

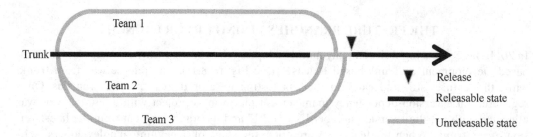

FIGURE 8.12   Team branch mode.

8.2.3.2 Team branch

When employing the team branch mode, a special case of the feature branch mode, a group of people work together on the same branch, and this branch is usually for developing a set of similar or relevant features. Since it is to develop a feature set, the life cycle of the team branch is longer than that of the feature branch.

The team branch is usually employed by a large-sized team (more than 40 people) to work on the same product together. This team is divided into several groups, and each group is in charge of different system components. A new version is not released until the feature set is fully implemented, which is easier to be a typical waterfall process (see Figure 8.12).

The team branch mode is more common in the product development of telecom companies or large-scale client software applications. For example, in the case of Chapter 14, the team had been using the team branch mode before transforming agile mode.

The key to successfully applying this mode is as follows:

1. Each team merges high-quality code into the trunk as early as possible, even if it is not seen by users immediately.
2. Make the code reach the deliverable state as soon as possible after it is merged into the trunk.
3. Other teams merge the deliverable code from the trunk with their own branches as early as possible.

8.3 EVOLUTION OF BRANCH MODES

In our practical work, owing to the characteristics of different software development projects, varied work habits of different teams, as well as evolution of software applications, the above three basic branching modes have given rise to derivative modes, such as Troika, Git Flow, and GitHub Flow.

8.3.1 Troika

Troika (or GitLab flow) mode means that the software development team only maintains three branches, namely, development branch, pre-release branch, and release branch (see Figure 8.13). In 2010, the development of Google Chrome was based on the troika branch mode.

The development branch is the target branch for all developers to submit code. When there are enough new features on the development branch (or approaching the set release date), the features that are ready to be released are cherry picked to the pre-release branch where developers only fix defects, generate documents, and do something related to release, instead of developing new features. When the team believes

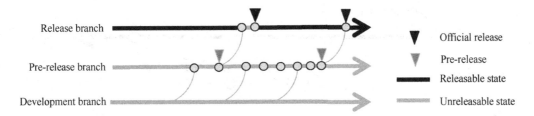

FIGURE 8.13   Troika branch mode.

that the code on the pre-release branch is as qualified as the Alpha version, then an Alpha version will be released to a small number of users for experience. The Beta version will be released next, mainly for early users to feedback the quality problems for timely correction. When the Beta version on the pre-release branch is stable, it will be merged into the release branch, and a Release Candidate (RC) version will be delivered to certain users. As long as its quality becomes stable, the RC version can be marked as an official release version.

8.3.2 Git Flow

Git Flow is now a popular branch mode adopted by many companies, as shown in Figure 8.14.

1. The main branch is the release branch of the official version.
2. The release branch is a pre-release branch for quality polishing. If the quality of the release branch is up to the standard, it can be merged into the main branch and the development branch concurrently.
3. The development branch is for integration of new functions.
4. The feature branch is a branch pulled from the development branch for developing a certain feature. After this feature is fully implemented, its code will be merged into the development branch.

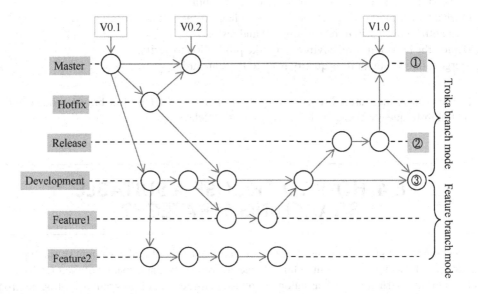

FIGURE 8.14   Git Flow branch mode.

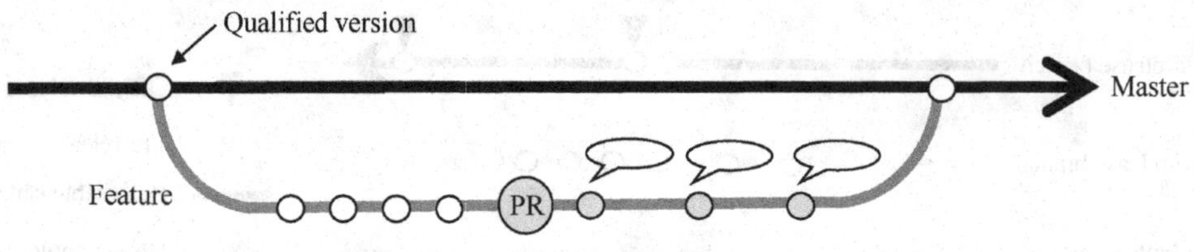

FIGURE 8.15 GitHub flow branch mode.

5. If any serious defect is found in the released version (such as V0.1), developers shall pull a hotfix branch from the V0.1 tag on the main branch, fix the defect on the hotfix, merge the fixed code back into the main branch after quality verification, and then release the patch version V0.2. Since the same defect also exists on the development branch, developers have to port the code of the hotfix branch to the development branch for fixing the defect.

Git Flow, a combination of the feature branch mode and the Troika mode, has clearly defined branches, but more branches are sometimes troublesome like the feature branch mode.

8.3.3 GitHub Flow

The name "GitHub Flow" stems from the work practice of GitHub teams. This branch mode imposes strict disciplines for developers and presents high requirements for quality assurance means (see the GitHub Flow branch mode in Figure 8.15). When developing a new feature or fixing a defect with this mode, developers must implement the following steps:

1. Create a branch from the main branch and name this branch after the number of this feature or defect.
2. Add commit: Check-in code on this newly created branch.
3. Open a pull request (PR) after the developed feature passes the self-test.
4. Invite other developers to review this PR and test it.
5. Deploy the branch into an environment like production to verify.
6. Merge it into the main if its quality is up to the standard.

If the life cycle of the feature branch is very short, then this GitHub Flow branch mode can be taken as a kind of high-frequency Trunk-based Development & Release.

8.4 HOW TO CHOOSE A SUITABLE BRANCHING STRATEGY?

In order to choose an appropriate branching model, companies should take account of the types of software applications to be developed or maintained, release frequency, and capacity of their teams, as well as the level of their infrastructure (such as automation test, management of program operating environment, and team discipline).

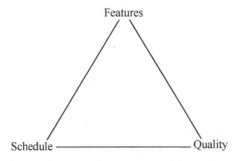

FIGURE 8.16   Three bound variables for release mode.

8.4.1 Release Pattern

There are three basic patterns of release: project release, release train and intercity express. These three patterns have the same constrains, namely, schedule, features, and quality. With relatively fixed resources, the team only needs to pose fixed feature set for two constrains. For example, if schedule and quality are fixed, the features of the version will be fixed accordingly, as shown in Figure 8.16.

8.4.1.1 Project release pattern

The project release pattern predetermines the features to be included in a coming release plan; this version can be released only after all the features are implemented and up to the quality standard. The interval between two releases is not specified, but determined by the time for fulfilling the features and meeting the quality standard.

As the oldest release pattern, the project release is to first determine the features and quality of a specific version, and then estimate its release schedule, which is equivalent to fixing the requirements for the features and quality of this version, then the team will probably have a fixed schedule.

The advantage of this pattern is that we can know exactly which features are included in each version, which is beneficial to the sales mode of commercial software packages (sell copies or authorization of the version, charge software maintenance fees, or charge customers the upgrade fee for the new version containing new features). Moreover, this mode fits with people's safe production practice of forbidding any unfinished feature to be included into the upcoming version.

The disadvantage is a long delivery cycle. In the process of development, in case of changing requirements (to add new requirements, transform the way for realizing original requirements, or replace requirements), the schedule of project needs to be re-estimated, which is sure to affect delay those requirements that can be delivered on time, because this pattern cannot release any deliverable until all of its requirements are fulfilled.

8.4.1.2 Release train pattern

The release train pattern was mainly applicable to the packaged distribution software of traditional large-sized software companies. These companies usually had multiple product lines which were in a complex interdependent relationship. In order to realize the collaborative release of various product lines, these companies tend to determine the release cycle of each version for each product line, making each version look like a train with a pre-set departure timetable. To make sure of punctual release, all teams involved in the same version must be aligned with its process. The reason for such strict time consistency is that any time change of one product line would trigger the change of the others, and these changes were likely to affect the distribution of a shared environment for System Integration Test (SIT). In most cases, due to the

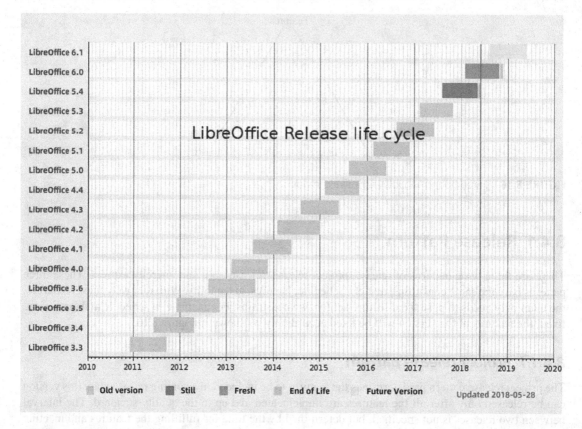

FIGURE 8.17 Timetable of LibreOffice's release train.

dependency between planning and integration, the Release Train Pattern sets a delivery cycle by quarter which is usually no longer than ten months.

Once the train timetable is about to be announced, the release management team will communicate in advance (even months ahead of times occasionally) with the product teams to discuss what to release, and then publish their conclusions in the corporate timetable, which is similar to the timetable of LibreOffice's release train in Figure 8.17. The timetable setting in advance gives business and technical departments enough time for pre-sales and pre-planning and for evaluation of interdependencies and impact.

A release planning is a formal and structured process that requires some formatted data to ensure that the teams involved the release train can determine the feasibility of the official release. These data include release details (relative logo, name, deployment date, risk level, release type-enterprise, plan or portfolio), stages of the entire release cycle, schedule (see Figure 8.18), activities and tasks to be completed at each stage, milestone events, and quality requirements, as well as the key persons responsible for managing the release train.

The advantage of this mode is that companies can, by running multiple trains in parallel, insert an urgent requirement into a release train. Users can experience the new features of the latest product version in advance without affecting the old version currently used on the original production line. After that, users can decide whether to apply this new product version to production. Even if they decide to do so, they can wait for a while until the new version is mature and stable enough. While employing this mode, if more teams get involved, there will be higher costs of communication and coordination.

8.4.1.3 Intercity express pattern

The intercity express pattern is to arrange a release of the features that satisfy the fixed quality standards by the fixed schedule, and the release cycle is as short as one week, one day, or even shorter. It differs from

6.0 release

Basic dates for the initial and bugfix releases

Release	Freeze	Publishing
6.0.0 (freeze: week 2)	Week 42 , Oct 16, 2017 - Oct 22, 2017	Week 5 , Jan 29, 2018 - Feb 4, 2018
6.0.1	Week 6 , Feb 5, 2018 - Feb 11, 2018	Week 6 , Feb 5, 2018 - Feb 11, 2018
6.0.2	Week 8 , Feb 19, 2018 - Feb 25, 2018	Week 9 , Feb 26, 2018 - Mar 4, 2018
6.0.3	Week 11 , Mar 12, 2018 - Mar 18, 2018	Week 14 , Apr 2, 2018 - Apr 8, 2018
6.0.4	Week 16 , Apr 16, 2018 - Apr 22, 2018	Week 19 , May 7, 2018 - May 13, 2018
6.0.5	Week 22 , May 28, 2018 - Jun 3, 2018	Week 25 , Jun 18, 2018 - Jun 24, 2018
6.0.6	Week 28 , Jul 9, 2018 - Jul 15, 2018	Week 31 , Jul 30, 2018 - Aug 5, 2018
6.0.7	Week 40 , Oct 1, 2018 - Oct 7, 2018	Week 43 , Oct 22, 2018 - Oct 28, 2018
End of Life	November 26, 2018	

FIGURE 8.18   Timetable of LibreOffice 6.0's release train.

the release train in two aspects: (1) It has a short interval between two releases, usually within two weeks. (2) The team responsible for features can take time to choose any intercity express, instead of making a decision a long time in advance.

This pattern is mainly applicable to software companies that provide web service or SaaS. The advantage of this is to reduce the cost of coordination between teams and roles. Since everyone is aware of the specific time of each release in advance, they can coordinate their work in advance. Moreover, even if a feature fails to be released in the current schedule, the team knows exactly that it is able to be released on time in the next round. For example, in 2013, Facebook's website was deployed twice a day and a major push was once a week. The release strategy of Facebook is shown in Figure 8.19.

As for Facebook's Branch-based Release, a release branch was cut from the trunk every Sunday, and after passing the automation test, the features in it would be opened to the employees of the company (logging on to the company Intranet and directly redirecting to "latest.facebook.com"). If any defect was found during the operation, it could be fixed on the trunk and then cherry picked to the Release branch.

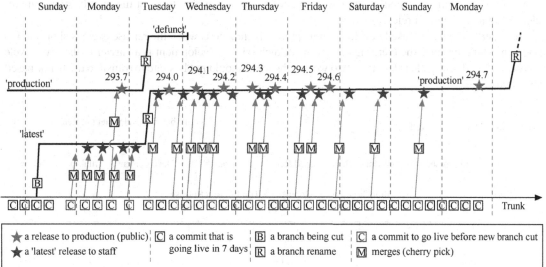

FIGURE 8.19   Facebook's Branch-based Release in 2013.

The code on the release branch was updated twice a day to latest.facebook.com for employees. The version was released to external users twice a day after it became stable. According to reports, since 2017, Facebook has transformed its release strategy from Trunk-based Development & Branch-based Release (releasing twice a day) to Trunk-based Development & Release (releasing 9~10 times a day on average).

This intercity express pattern boasts two advantages: everyone is aware of each release point; quality becomes a focal point.

Of course, it also has some shortcomings. Owing to a high release frequency, the code for unfinished features may be deployed together. There shall be powerful quality assurance means to satisfy higher quality.

If employing this intercity express pattern, how often is it appropriate to release a version? In my opinion, on the premise of not affecting user experience, not increasing costs, and complying with regulations, you can shorten the release cycle to the extent that makes you feel a little nervous. For example, if you released a version once a month, now you can try to do so in two weeks.

8.4.2 Relationship Between Branch Strategy and Release Cycle

There is a certain correlation between the branch strategy and the release cycle, as shown in Figure 8.20. Usually, the teams adopting the project release pattern (longest software development cycle) and the teams adopting the intercity express mode (highest-frequency software release) like to follow the strategy of "Trunk-based Development & Release". The teams, with relatively longer software development cycle and higher-frequency software release, are prone to adopt the strategy of "Trunk-based Development & Branch-based Release". The teams, with a short software development cycle and low-frequency software release, mainly adopt the strategy of "Branch-based Development & Trunk-based Release". Of course, those are not absolute. There are situations of overlapping strategies, which are determined by the size of team, product architecture, and quality assurance infrastructure, and so on.

The project release pattern will not disappear. Each new product needs such an initial start-up process before its first version 1.0 is completed and promoted. Currently, many traditional IT companies still use it.

Being favored by Continuous Delivery 2.0, the intercity express has been adopted by more and more companies. Even in the companies that currently have a long release cycle, the intercity express is sometimes used alternatively with the project release pattern, that is, add iterations of fixed duration into the project lifecycle and obtain a deliverable at the end of each iteration. The deliverable state here means that the software is running normally, and the completed features are able to meet the quality standards for release (not a commercial release).

In general, the trunk-based development is more advantageous when the release cycle is shortened to a certain extent, because the merging cost of the branch-based development is a barrier to the short-cycle release. If the release cycle is less than two weeks, the team should not hesitate to transit to the trunk-based development.

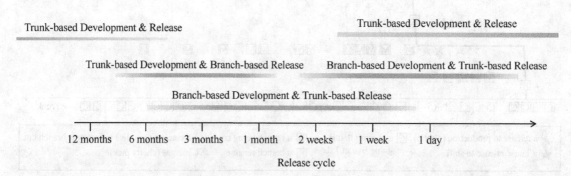

FIGURE 8.20   Relationship between branch strategy and release cycle.

8.5 SUMMARY

With both strengths and weaknesses, each branch strategy has a significant impact on release frequency and efficiency. The current trend is that software is released more and more frequently, and the release cycle has become increasingly shorter. Top dot-com companies in Silicon Valley like to use the Trunk-based Development or high-frequency GitHub Flow branch. When choosing a suitable branch strategy, companies should refer to the specific conditions of their teams. If the relevant supporting conditions (such as software architecture, personnel capability, and maturity of tool platform) are insufficient, then blindly increasing release frequency and shortening release cycle will cause unnecessary losses.

Continuous Delivery 2.0 is in favor of a branch mode for Continuous Integration (CI). An appropriate branch mode can be chosen by observing the principles as follows:

1. The fewer branches, the better; it's better to have only one trunk.
2. The shorter the branch life cycle, the better, preferably less than three days.
3. The shorter the release cycle, the better, as long as the business allows.

The leadership should, under the guidance of the ideas, philosophies, and principles of Continuous Delivery 2.0, establish reasonable goals for making improvements and continuously enhance their software delivery capability, so as to keep up with the development of the times.

Continuous Integration

9

Since 1999, "Continuous Integration", a kind of software development practice and known simply as CI, has drawn attention of the practitioners in software industry along with the rise of the agile movement. Among the numerous principles, methods, and practices advocated by the agile movement, "Continuous Integration" is the first engineering practice that is widely accepted and recognized; some people even mistakenly equate "Continuous Integration" with "Agile Software Development".

This chapter mainly discusses the origin and definition of CI, the CI workflow of team and individuals, the connection between CI, and deployment pipeline guided by different branch strategies, the common problems in the daily work of CI and the corresponding solutions.

9.1 ORIGIN AND DEFINITION

Speaking of the origin of CI, we must talk about the Chrysler Comprehensive Compensation System ("C3" Project for short), which was a well-known software project in the late 1990s. Although this project was not quite successful due to its low return on investment (ROI), it is still well-known since many of the present software development practices, including "CI", are attributed to this project.

Initiated in 1993, the C3 Project was developed with Smalltalk in 1994 with an ultimate goal of supporting a comprehensive personnel and salary system covering 87,000 employees in 1999. However, this system remained unworkable by 1996. In order to bring this project back to life, Kent Beck was invited to preside over the big picture, and he subsequently asked Ron Jeffries to lend him a hand. In March 1996, this new development team estimated that they would take another year to put this system into operation. In 1997, this project was finally delivered after Kent Beck had his team fully adopt a new software development method, namely, Extreme Programming (XP), although it was delayed for a while due to some ambiguous business requirements. Nevertheless, the released software was only available for 10,000 users. Despite of subsequent optimizations, an upgraded version seemed unattainable until this project was called off in 2000.

Interestingly, the C3 Project gave birth to many software development practices, and one of them is CI. When just taking over this project, Kent Beck was forced to address a vexing problem: "integrate all project codes and have them started and run". This process of integration and debugging was so painful that it usually took one or two weeks. So, they decided to increase the frequency of system integration. Although team members felt annoyed at the beginning of frequent integration, they gradually found that they could spend less time on each integration, and it was easier to locate and fix the problems in the process of integration.

As a result, team members came up with an even more crazy idea: "now that increasing the integration frequency can make problems exposed earlier and fixed more easily, why not do it more frequently and integrate code shortly after each code commit?" So, the developers wrote a series of shell scripts for the purpose like this: access the codebase regularly, as long as any change is found, the script

DOI: 10.1201/9781003221579-9

automatically pulls the code to a clean machine with a build environment (the tools or repositories needed for code compilation are installed on this machine in advance) to be built. Once the build is finished, the result will be displayed on the screen.

Although the software tools for CI had not appeared in those years, this did not impede CI practices. The C3 Project also implemented other XP practices; among them, test-driven development (TDD) is closely related to CI. The reason why they are "closely related" is that in the process of CI, software quality must be verified, and the running of automation unit tests is an important feedback of quality.

9.1.1 Original Definition

As early as the 1980s, the Microsoft Office product research and development (R&D) team began to employ a development practice known as "daily build" or "nightly build", which is a kind of automatic execution of software building every day. To be specific, it checks out the source code into a build environment (a clean machine without an integrated development environment) to be compiled, linked, and packaged.

Performing daily build helps teams confirm whether they have introduced any new problem during the code compilation the day before. Daily build usually involves a small number of automation smoke tests to help the team determine whether new changes have destroyed the original features. The key part is that each build must include modifications and tests of new code. The term "smoke test" comes from electronic hardware testing: as long as there is no smoke after the hardware samples are powered on, it means that the basic quality requirements of this hardware are satisfied.

The "CI" practice stems from the XP method proposed by Kent Beck in 1996, and briefly explained in Chapter 10 of his book *Extreme Programming Explained: Embrace Change* as "Continuous Integration – Integrate and build the system multiple times a day, every time a task is completed".

CI got its formal definition from Martin Fowler in 2000, and was further expounded in 2006 as follows:

Continuous Integration is a software development practice where members of a team integrate their work frequently, usually each person integrates at least daily - leading to multiple integrations per day. Each integration is verified by a build (including test) to detect integration errors as quickly as possible. Many teams find that this approach leads to significantly reduced integration problems and allows a team to develop cohesive software more rapidly.

It can be seen that CI is a quality feedback mechanism whose purpose is to "detect integration errors as quickly as possible".

9.1.2 Integration Process

To date, there have been no less than 35 platforms or tools that provide CI functions, including priced software such as TeamCity, open-source software such as Jenkins, GoCD and Buildbot, and SaaS tool platforms such as Travis CI. And all of them have the same CI process, as shown in Figure 9.1.

1. Engineers commit code to the codebase.
2. The CI server polls the codebase at a regular interval (such as every minute) and detect if there is any change.
3. The CI server automatically checks out the latest code to the prepared dedicated server that can be CI server if the application scale is not large.
4. Run the build script or command specified by the CI server on the dedicated server to check the latest code by means of dynamic and static code scanning, code compilation and packaging, unit test, deployment, or functional test.
5. After finishing the operation, the verification result (success or failure) is fed back to the team.

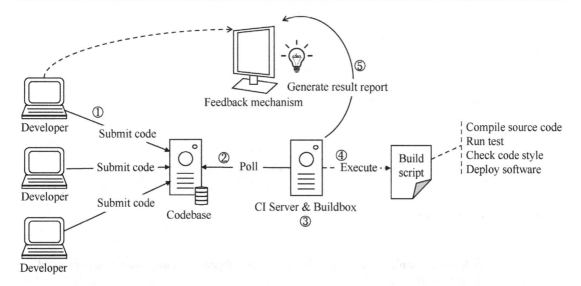

FIGURE 9.1 CI process.

In order to "save both time and labor", a large number of quality verification items (including automation test, code check, and security scan) can be run automatically. The "Continuous Integration" practice directly embodies the basic working principle of the fast Verification Loop, that is, "quality built-in, rapid feedback". Whenever developers complete a development task, they must run a series of automation quality tests to verify whether his code is qualified enough to be accepted by the team.

9.2 SIX-STEP CHECK-IN DANCE

Like other XP methods, the CI practice also stresses discipline. Especially when there are more developers and they work in parallel, discipline is to guarantee efficient team collaboration. In the process of CI, what work steps should everyone follow? If someone in the team (developer, tester, or operation maintenance personnel) intends to make a change, he must adopt the "six-step check-in dance" (see Figure 9.2) as follows:

1. **Check out the latest green build:** When a developer starts to work (for example, he takes on a new user story in the morning of a work day), he shall check out the code of the latest green build from the trunk to his own workspace.
2. **Modify the code:** The developer modifies the code in his own workspace for new features including automation tests.
3. **First personal build:** When his task is done and about to be committed, the developer shall run automation tests for verification in his own workspace to verify the change's quality. This is the first build (or known as "local build") for his own.
4. **Second personal build:** During the period from "checking out code" to "completion of first personal build", other members may have committed to the trunk and passed the quality verification for CI. At this moment, the developer needs to merge his code with that of others, and perform another quality verification to make sure that no code is problematic. This is the second build for his own code with others.

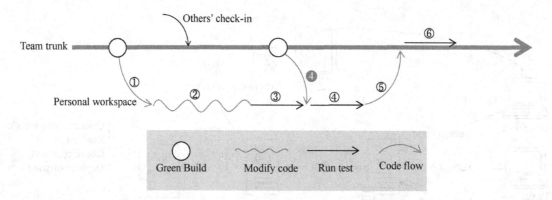

FIGURE 9.2   Six-step check-in dance for CI.

5. **Submit code to the trunk:** Once succeeding in his second personal build, the developer should commit his code to the trunk.
6. **Trigger the build:** When the CI server discovers this change, it will immediately trigger the build and run automation tests for quality verification. If this build fails, the developer should fix it immediately and notify others right away to stop committing code to the trunk and checking out the failed build.

The team's trunk means that there is a branch jointly owned by team members, that is, after each developer completes his own task, he shall submit the code to this branch and merge with others' code. Personal workspace refers to the local working directory used by each engineer. Personal build refers to the activity of an engineer to run automation task on his branch before submitting it to the team trunk, in an aim to ensure that his code could meet functional requirements without disrupting other functions. It is also known as "local build" or "local verification" – a kind of legacy of history, because this verification activity used to be performed in one's own local development machine. Presently, as software applications have a larger scale, more complex architecture, and higher input of resources, many companies have started creating cloud infrastructure, thus making the unsubmitted code built and tested on it. Therefore, "personal build" is a more accurate term in this day and age.

9.2.1 Four Key Points of Check-In Dance

9.2.1.1 Effect of the three times of verification

Among the six steps of check-in for CI, Step 3, 4, and 6 is to conduct a quality verification. Make sure that the same commands and scripts are executed for the three verifications. For example, for a Java project built with Gradle, such command could be "Gradle test", because it is easy to debug by comparing the output of the three steps when any of them goes wrong.

Now that identical commands and scripts are used, why the verification should be implemented for three times? The verification in Step 3 (first personal build) is to confirm whether the code modified by the engineer is correct. The verification in Step 4 (second personal build) is to ensure that all of the code is up to the quality standard after merging with others' code from Team Trunk. The verification in Step 6 (submit the build), which is in a clean and controlled environment, is the same with the one in Step 4, namely to make sure that the code submitted is complete, qualified, and without omission.

The verification in Step 3 and Step 4 has different content: The verification object in Step 3 is the code checked out and modified by an individual engineer. In addition to this engineer's own code, the verification object in Step 4 also includes the code from Team Trunk just submitted by his team members.

Theoretically, the verification in Step 4 and Step 6 has the same codebase but running on separate environment. The verification in Step 4, which is performed on the engineer's own machine, is to verify the code that he has modified but not yet submitted. The verification in Step 6, which is performed in the team's standardized environment, is to verify the version of code he has just submitted. If the verification in Step 4 succeeds, but the one in Step 6 fails, it is probably attributed to three reasons: (1) The code submitted by the engineer is incomplete and some of the modified code is missing. (2) The engineer's own verification environment differs from the standardized environment of the team. (3) Other team members have submitted new code again before his own submission, yet the engineer pays no attention to it.

9.2.1.2 Twice personal verifications are a necessity

The first personal verification is to verify whether the code modified by an engineer meets the quality expectations, while the second one is to verify whether the code, merged with the code submitted by his teammates, is still up to the quality standards. If the code passed the first verification but failed in the second one, it means that the code on the Team Trunk has distorted his own code. It can be seen that it is easier to locate the problem through twice verifications.

As a confident engineer, you may conduct personal verification only once, but it is advised that you should do a second personal verification. Once the second verification succeeds, you'll be most likely to pass Step 6, which is the verification at the stage of check-in build. It is conducive to efficient integration as well.

9.2.1.3 Ensure the performance of a personal build before code submission

The people in charge of CI workflow often ask a question: How can we ensure that each engineer has performed personal verifications before submission? One way is that when the code is about to be submitted, the CI platform captures the submission event through a hook and enforces the second personal verification before the code is merged into the trunk, which is also called "pre-submit". Of course, the team may ask everyone to comply with this requirement through a verbal agreement. Based on the statistics of the number and distribution of failed verifications and cause of failure in build submission, we can easily learn about the behavioral patterns of each member.

9.2.1.4 The contents of quality verification to be included in each build

Automation unit tests cannot cover all operating scenarios of the software. Therefore, in addition to unit tests, we would run a richer test set for quality verification in the processes of personal verification and check-in build, such as code dynamic and static scanning, code check, and build verification test. If conditions permit, it would be even better if more large functional tests could be run. Build verification test is to check the following contents:

1. Whether the binary package generated after the end of building contains the correct content, such as the integrity of some specific configuration file.
2. Whether this building result can be correctly installed and normally started and run.
3. Whether the most basic functions (such as user login) are workable after starting.

The tools for code check are not only ample and mature, but also the easiest to implement. Compared with automation tests, code check has a lower execution cost. The team has no need to write any code as automation tests, but formulate their coding style and specifications, and configure the corresponding scanning rules with check tools. However, for the large legacy codebase, code check is likely to bring a problem like this: A huge number of existing problems may expose through code check. How to deal with such problem? Clear them all at once? The following two measures can be adopted at this time:

1. Reduce rules and focus on the key points. Most check tools classify problems into multiple types such as serious, important, and warning. The team should identify the most important code rules through discussion, focus on serious problems in the early stage, and then gradually increase more rules.
2. Implement the Boy Scout Rule. If a large amount of legacy code has been running for a long time in production, and there is no need to have it modified in the short run, then it can remain unchanged for the time being. Even if all the problems cannot be eliminated immediately, it is necessary to ensure that the number of problems will not increase each time the code is submitted. It would be better if they could decrease every time.

THE BOY SCOUT RULE

The Boy Scouts is an educational practice for minors in American society. Children who join the Boy Scouts must learn and abide by certain rules, and then try to win various medals.

There is a rule as concise as "Always leave the campground cleaner than you found it". If applying to a software development project, this rule can be rewritten like this, "Always leave the code cleaner than you found it". In other words, every team member is obliged to improve the code.

9.2.2 Synchronous and Asynchronous Modes

The six-step check-in dance can be implemented in two modes: "synchronous mode" and "asynchronous mode". The difference between them lies in the behavior of engineers after the Step 5 (submit code to the trunk).

In the synchronous mode, the engineer has to wait for the completion of Step 6 (submit the build) and return of the building result before deciding the next action, that is, "each engineer performs an integration immediately after programming for a while, and the time for integration should not exceed 10 minutes. Confirm whether the code quality is up to standard upon completion of this build and end of the entire automation tests, move on to the next task if no code will be rolled back".

In the asynchronous mode, after completing Step 5, the engineer can move on to the next task without waiting till the end of the stage of check-in build. It is possible that the CI server does not execute the build including his submission immediately; instead, it is likely to trigger the build later. It could be every 30 minutes or other rules that the team has agreed.

According to Kent Beck, although CI in asynchronous mode is a big improvement compared to daily build, it is not recommended because of possible "wastes". For example, while working on his next task, the engineer is notified that the code submitted half an hour ago has failed build. At this point, he has to spend some time recalling what he has done, and then debug and fix the problem, and finally submit the modified code again. After that, he has to make some effort to concentrate on the new task that is interrupted just now. Such switching between tasks is regarded as an unnecessary "waste" in lean management theory.

9.2.3 Self-Check Sheet

If readers want to know whether their team has reached the best state of CI, they can run a self-check in the following six aspects:

9.2.3.1 Trunk-based Development and frequent submission

The Trunk-based development means that all team members involved in the same software development project or service submit code to the trunk of the project's codebase, at least the life cycle of most of branches does not exceed three days. Frequent submission means that everyone submits code at least once a day, preferably every few hours while working.

9.2.3.2 Content of each submission is a complete task

The content of each submission should be meaningful, not just to submit code randomly to satisfy the required submission frequency. We hope that the code submitted every time will revolve around the same task, and the automation tests corresponding to this task will be submitted together.

9.2.3.3 Finish check-in build within 10 minutes

Developers usually have no patience to wait, so it is better for them to spend less time in each build verification. When the team uses the "synchronous mode", the run time of build verification is particularly crucial. If the execution time is too long, it will undoubtedly slow down the quality feedback. If the check-in build fails, the engineer has to put more energy into recalling the work context of that code so as to locate the possible problems.

9.2.3.4 After a failed check-in build, do not submit new code or check out the problematic code

When an engineer checks in code and fails the build, it indicates that there may be a problem or risk in the overall quality of the software. At this point, the entire team should no longer submit new code changes, which accords with the "Stop the Line" principle (see Chapter 7) in Toyota Production System (TPS). The guiding ideology of TPS is: when any problem is detected on the production line, it must be stopped immediately for the problem to be solved. If the production line keeps running before the problem is solved, it will only increase the rate of defective products.

Similarly, for a software, after the code has failed to pass the quality verification test, if someone else keeps submitting new code before the problem is fixed, the check-in build is sure to come to nothing. Is this failure caused by the last failure or is the new code itself is problematic? Such situation will make the resolution of the problem more complicated.

9.2.3.5 Fix the check-in build or roll back within ten minutes

According to the previous discussion, after the check-in build fails, team members cannot submit new code until the problem is fixed. This will break the development rhythm of others and even hinder the progress of the entire project, so the problem should be solved immediately. A common phenomenon in reality is that engineers who are fixing problems often claim that they can make it in a few minutes, but in fact it could take much longer than it. Therefore, the team needs to setup a principle like this: If the problem cannot be fixed within x minutes, the code will be rolled back. This not only allows the engineers to have enough time to think about and solve the problem so as not to make mistakes in the rush, but also allows others to proceed with their own work. If it takes a long time to fix the problem, the entire team will accumulate too much unsubmitted code, and there may be more potential integration problems. After the problem is fixed, the submission of a large amount of accumulated code will make the build more likely to fail and require more time to be spent on fixing (see Figure 9.3).

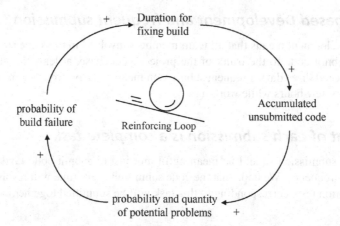

FIGURE 9.3   Systematic thinking diagram of bugfix time.

9.2.3.6 Passing the automation build will boost up the confidence in software quality

The real purpose of CI is to get fast and effective quality feedback, that is, as long as the automation building is successful, the team will gain confidence in their software quality in a high degree. I once met a team that practices CI, it is able to fully satisfy the previous five requirements. While talking about with the team leader, I thought they had been doing well. However, team members didn't think their CI was useful. Through communications with them, I learned that although they had many automation testcases, they didn't have enough newly-added testcases. As such, after the original automation testcases failed, they would delete them if it was difficult to have them fixed.

9.3 TRADE-OFF BETWEEN SPEED AND QUALITY

In order to obtain a more comprehensive feedback on software quality, we can add more automation functional testcases. However, with the continuous increase of automation tests, we are bound to encounter the problem of time-consuming tests and failed feedback on test results within ten minutes. How can we solve this problem?

9.3.1 Staging Build

With the development of software, the number of automation testcases will inevitably increase, and the run time will sooner or later exceed our endurable limit. Well then, how can we get quality feedback while giving consideration to engineers' work efficiency? One way is to employ secondary build, which is explained by Martin Fowler in his article *Continuous Integration*, as shown in Figure 9.4.

In Figure 9.4, the team divides all automation testcases into two parts: one part is the testcases that run fast and have high feedback quality and would run at check-in build, the other is the testcases that run slowly or do not fail frequently and would run the secondary build to verify the quality. After the check-in build, the execution of the secondary build is triggered immediately. Careful readers are sure to notice that this is the prototype of the "deployment pipeline".

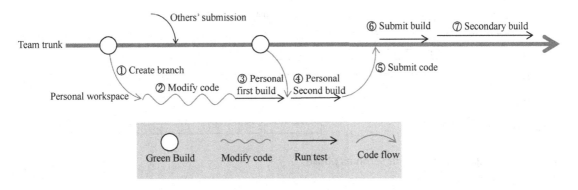

FIGURE 9.4 Hierarchical construction of CI.

When a secondary build is employed, developers can move on to other tasks as long as the check-in build passes, and don't have to wait for the result of the secondary build. However, once the secondary build fails, relevant engineers should be notified immediately, and start fixing the problem without delay. Moreover, everyone on the team should be notified that no more code is allowed to be submitted until the problem is solved.

How does the team decide the content of the secondary build? Generally, the testcases that are run a long time or less likely to fail should be included in the secondary build, while those that are run quickly or prone to fail should be put into the commit build. Of course, the testcases in those builds are not invariable. Team should regularly evaluate the testcases in each stage of building to ensure of high-quality feedback in case of short-time check-in build, which will build up their confidence in the check-in build feedback.

9.3.2 Builds Submitted by Multiple People at the Same Time

If the secondary build runs for a long time (such as more than 30 minutes), it is likely to run into the case that a few newly commit build is completed, but the prior secondary build is still running. What should be done at this time?

In the case of unlimited computing resources, we can immediately trigger the corresponding secondary build after each successful commit build. But this approach would waste resources. For example, as shown in Figure 9.5, when the secondary build triggered by the Rev121 submitted by Sara fails at 10:40, the secondary build triggered by the submission of Bob and Martin is already running. Since Sara has no time to do fixing, the secondary build of Bob, Martin, and David will definitely fail.

In order to utilize resources more efficiently, secondary build can include the content submitted by multiple people. For example, a team has their check-in build run for ten minutes and a secondary build

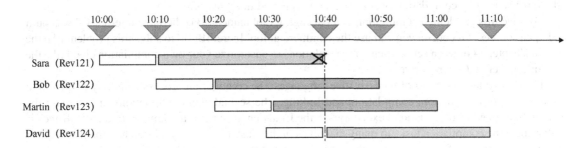

FIGURE 9.5 Trigger secondary build immediately after each submission.

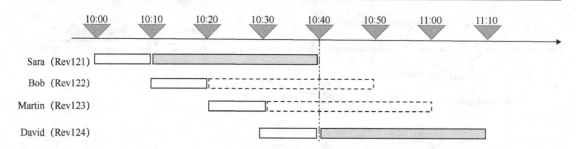

FIGURE 9.6 Delayed triggering of secondary build.

run for 30 minutes. After Sara submits the code (Rev121) at 10:00, the commit build starts to execute. When Bob submits the code (Rev122) at 10:10, the check-in build for Rve121 has just completed and triggers the secondary build of Rev121. Then the check-in build of Rev122 also gets started. By parity of reasoning, Martin submits the code (Rev123) at 10:20 and David submits the code (Rev124) at 10:30. When the check-in build of Rev124 is completed, the secondary build of Rev121 also comes to an end. At this time, the secondary build containing Rev122, 123 and 124 will be triggered, as shown in Figure 9.6.

Because of limited computing resources and unknown result of Rev121, the secondary build of Rev122 and Rev123 in Figure 9.6 is not triggered automatically. After the secondary build of Rev121 has succeeded, in order to save time and resources, the secondary build of the latest version of Rev124 can be directly triggered. If this secondary build fails, in order to find out the cause of failure, the secondary build of Rev122 or Rev123 can be triggered to locate the version the problem was introduced in.

9.3.3 The Power of Cloud Platform

Nowadays, the cloud computing infrastructure provides more resources and convenience to support CI practice. We can execute those time-consuming and resource-consuming steps on the cloud and notify the owner after the execution. This approach is applicable to many cases, such as compilation, code style-checking, automation unit tests, and functional tests. Here, we only discuss the issues related to compilation optimization.

Not all projects will encounter compilation optimization, but this problem does exist, especially in large C/C++ projects. Although there are methods such as dynamic and static libraries, considering the characteristics of C language itself, the full compilation of source code in C/C++ projects is fairly common so as to achieve a high degree of control.

The so-called full compilation of source code means that the source code available for the current project is put together with the source code in a third-party library, and then subject to compilation and packaging, which would cost more than ten minutes to do so. This problem has not only happened to the two cases to be discussed later but also occurred to Google's C/C++ project, which also uses source compilation. The lengthy compilation of source code is depicted in Figure 9.7.

To solve this problem, a compilation and packaging tool named "Bazel (Blaze internally)" was built and open sourced. Of course, you can use the commercial tool IncrediBuild to solve this problem like the case in Chapter 14 or use a set of open-source solutions to customize your own compilation cloud like the case in Chapter 16 (see in Figure 9.8).

For C language and most of its derivative languages, the compilation process is mainly divided into three steps: pre-compilation, compilation, and linking. The second step (compilation) can increase the compilation speed through parallel execution. In the Linux environment, the famous free tool "distcc" is to distribute the compilation tasks to many machines in the cluster in the second step (compilation). After each machine completes it compilation task, it will return the result for implementing the third step (linking). However, the threshold limit value for speed increase is three times. After Distcc of version 3.0 came

FIGURE 9.7   Consequence of time-consuming compilation in synchronous mode.

out, a new Python-based tool "pump" was introduced. It can perform distributed processing of part of the pre-compilation tasks in the first step, thereby improving compilation efficiency. The official website makes it clear that pump can improve the efficiency of file transfer and compilation by up to ten times.

Distcc only distributes compilation tasks according to the order specified by the server but cannot dynamically distribute these tasks based on the load of the boxes in the compilation pool. The free tool "dmucs" is capable of simple load balancing.

Now that the compilation speed cannot be increased indefinitely, how can we further solve the problem? In the C/C++ field, the free tool ccache, which is used together with distcc, is to cache the intermediate files generated from compilation through the hash table according to the pre-compilation results for the next use. Of course, only by hitting the cache can the compilation speed be improved. For C/C++ projects, this incremental compilation has a certain risk of error, so a source full compilation is usually done before the final official delivery.

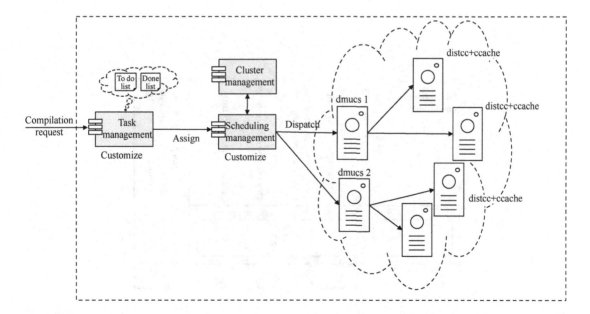

FIGURE 9.8   Build C/C++ compilation cloud platform in Linux with open-source tools.

There are also Java-based tools that can accelerate compilation. For example, Facebook's open-source project Buck, which is in reference to Google's C/C++ distributed compilation system, complies source with a customized Java tool. And the open-source tool "Gradle" is also capable of incremental compilation.

If the duration of compilation remains unable to meet the requirement after trying all of the above methods, the build script and product code need to be optimized. For example, for C++ projects, try not to write the function implementation of the code in the header file, because each .cpp file containing this header file will compile the function implementation in this header file into the corresponding .obj file during compilation. In the processing of "linking", these duplicate compilation results will be filtered out, and only one is retained.

For the application on the Windows platform, you can optimize part of the compilation time by reorganizing the Solution file. When dealing with Java projects, you can decompose a large project into multiple sub-projects. Just like the GoCD team described in Chapter 7, you can split a large Java project into multiple components, compile and pack them separately, and then assemble them together. If you do so, please beware of package dependency management (see Chapter 11).

9.4 IMPLEMENT CI PRACTICES IN THE TEAM

With the development of IT infrastructure and technology and the continuous improvement of tool chains, the threshold for CI practice has become lower and lower. So, how to quickly start CI practice in your team?

9.4.1 Quickly Establish a CI Practice for the Team

There are six steps for the team, which has to maintain the legacy codebase, to establish CI practice, as shown in Figure 9.9.

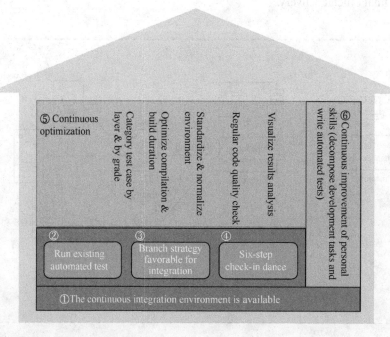

FIGURE 9.9 Six steps for implementing CI.

9.4.1.1 Scripted build and setup CI tool

1. Choose a CI tool and complete its installation and deployment. Most CI tools have nothing to do with software development language, so they can be chosen to rest assured. Currently, Jenkins is the most popular tool in China. If your project is to develop a cloud-native application, you can also use cloud CI services.
2. Create a building task on this CI tool, and pull the code from your codebase.
3. Write a script file to automatically complete the compilation, building and packaging of the software project.
4. Modify the building task just created on the CI tool so that it can call the written script file.
5. Submit the code to the codebase, verify the CI tool to find newly submitted code, pull the correct version of code, and run the specified build script.

9.4.1.2 Add an existing automation verification script to the build

1. Add automation testcases to the build. Generally speaking, many large teams with legacy code usually have some kind of automation testcases. If this is the case, find a way to put at least one automation testcase into the build as soon as possible so that it can be automatically executed after being triggered.
2. Add code scanning to the build. There are many tools for automatically scanning code specifications and health in the market, such as SonarQube, Android Lite, CCCC, cppcheck, Clang, and Pc-lint, as well as Coverity as one of the commercial tools. If the team already has a coding specification for the programming language, you can add one of these tools into the previously created build to perform automatic code scanning.

9.4.1.3 Choose a branch strategy that is conducive to CI

After implementing the first two steps, the team will have the foundation for CI. Now, it needs to choose a branch strategy that benefits CI. Each branch should have a corresponding environment for CI. But too many branches will do no good to the team's CI effect. Therefore, the team should choose a branch strategy favorable for CI based on the actual situation and build an automation deployment pipeline.

9.4.1.4 Adopt the six-step check-in dance

So far, the team has gone through the entire process of CI. Although only a small number of quality verification activities are included in the build, it is already a good starting point. If the compilation of the project takes an excessively long period, you can refer to the above discussions about "compilation optimization" to solve it. If the code scanning takes a long time due to an over-large codebase, you can take a step back and use incremental scanning to shorten the time.

After the time requirements of the six-step check-in dance are basically satisfied, team members can attend trainings to learn to do daily work by employing the six-step check-in dance for CI.

9.4.1.5 Continuous optimization

The next job is to continue optimization. Generally, for the companies with massive legacy code and a large number of automation testcases, it is difficult for them to meet the time requirements set by the check-in dance, and many new problems will come out. For example, QA team developed dozens of automation testcases; however, owing to poor-quality code, the results of batch execution of these testcases without manual intervention were very unstable, and random failures occurred from time to time. Random failure refers to inconsistent testing results from repeated execution of automation testcases for two times when all conditions remain unchanged. For example, some testcases are "successful" in their first running, but "failed" in their second running, with overall operational stability of only 80%. In this case, the team is unable to practice CI. Since this build result is untrusted, the utilization of check-in dance will waste time.

If the project lasts a long time, more automation tests may be added. If so, the team must maintain conscious optimization in a bid to continuously reap the benefits of CI. The optimized content includes but not limited to the following items:

1. Time spent on compilation and packaging. Introduce various tools or reorganize and optimize the compilation and building scripts, as well as split or combine system modules.
2. Branch strategy. With the deepening of CI, the team will choose a branch strategy that is conducive to CI.
3. Layered and staged management of automation testcases. As the types and numbers of automation testcases increase, different types of automation testcases need to be managed by layers and by stages. Layered management is to manage different layers of objects under testing, such as unit test, integration test and end-to-end test (see more in Chapter 10). Staged management is to manage testcases according to speed and quality of feedback; in the case of limited resources, various testcases are placed in different stages (such as check-in and secondary build), and they are executed in a linear manner.
4. Prepare the testing environment. Sometimes the preparation of the testing environment costs a long time, which delays the time of CI. Therefore, we need to sort out the preparations of the testing environment and reduce manual participation, so as to raise the efficiency of previsioning. If there are many testcases, we may need to prepare multiple testing environments concurrently. At this time, the automation preparation of the testing environment becomes even more important.
5. Optimize code scanning. Previously we've used the least amount of compilation specifications. With the deepening of practice, the team can gradually increase, modify, and adjust the coding specifications to make them meet the code quality requirements.
6. Generate data reports. Let everyone easily keep aware of the code quality status at any time.

9.4.1.6 Engineers change habits and improve skills

CI is an active teamwork practice that requires engineers to proactively integrate in advance instead of delaying integration. This runs counter to people's mentality of "delaying risks", thus requiring engineers to change their work habits and split large tasks into small ones as far as possible. Meanwhile, frequent running of automation test suite depends on the stability and reliability of automation testcases. Therefore, engineers need to invest some time to learn related methods and techniques. Refer to Chapter 10 for how to implement and write automation testcases.

9.4.2　Branch Strategy and Deployment Pipeline

Careful readers may have noticed that the check-in build and secondary build in the CI practice have formed a simple deployment pipeline. As mentioned in Chapter 1, the concept of deployment pipeline was initiated on basis of the CI practice. But when multiple teams have to work together to develop large-scale and complex software (such as a mobile phone operating system), they need to carefully design a CI approach.

Generally speaking, the CI approach between teams is closely related to their branch strategy. What is certain is that every time a branch is created, a corresponding deployment pipeline should be created immediately until the life cycle of the branch is over (abandoned or merged back).

9.4.2.1 Trunk-based Development & Release

If the software product only has one repository, and the team adopts the strategy of "Trunk-based Development & Release", then they only need to do CI of the code trunk. In other words, this team only

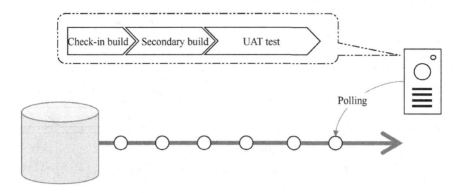

FIGURE 9.10   CI strategy of "Trunk-based Development & Trunk-based Release".

needs to set up one deployment pipeline and focus on the code changes on the trunk. The GoCD team used this approach for CI before their product was officially released (see Figure 9.10).

9.4.2.2 Trunk-based Development & Branch-based Release

If the software product only has one repository, and the team adopts the strategy of "Trunk-based development & Branch-based release", then they need to create a new release branch by the time of each release, and create a corresponding deployment pipeline for this branch, because team members will fix defects and submit code on this branch (see Figure 9.11).

9.4.2.3 Branch-based Development & Trunk-based Release

If the software product only has one repository, and the team adopts the strategy of "Branch-based Development & Trunk-based Release", then the team needs to set up a corresponding deployment pipeline for each development branch, and immediately triggers this pipeline whenever the branch code is merged into it. When the submission of branch code is no longer active or the branch is directly deleted, its corresponding deployment pipeline may also be deleted (see Figure 9.12). This CI approach is more common for the development of large and complex software products undertaken by multiple teams.

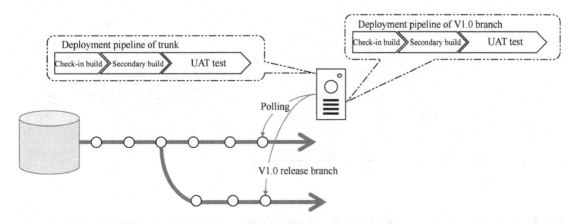

FIGURE 9.11   CI strategy of "Trunk-based Development & Branch-based Release".

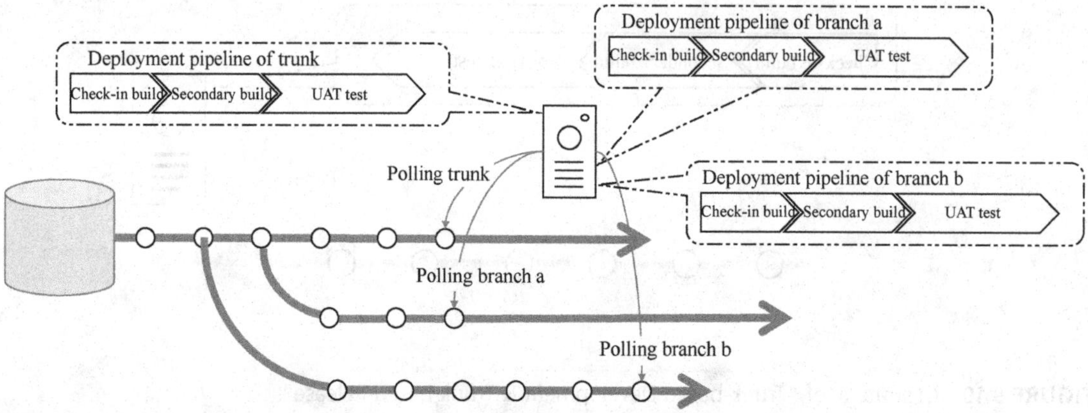

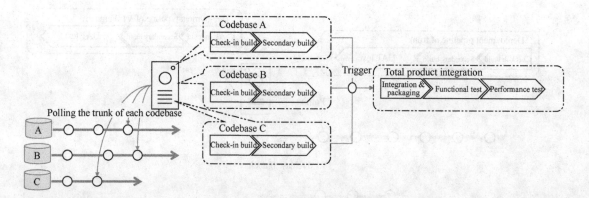

FIGURE 9.12 CI strategy of "Branch-based Development & Trunk-based Release".

9.4.2.4 Multi-component integration

This strategy means that a software product is composed of multiple services (or components), and each service (or component) has an independent repository, while the code of each codebase is contributed by multiple people. Each independent repository may have its own unique branch strategy. According to the three strategies described in Chapter 8, a separate deployment pipeline is created for each independent repository. Afterward, another deployment pipeline is created for integration; this pipeline does not poll any repository but is triggered by upstream deployment pipelines. Once the upstream deployment pipelines are completed, this integration pipeline will verify the integration build of the software assemblies produced by the upstream pipelines.

For example, if each component of a product uses the strategy of "Trunk-based Development & Release", then its multicomponent integration strategy is like this: each trunk corresponds to a deployment pipeline, and all deployment pipelines of trunk correspond to the same integration deployment pipeline (see Figure 9.13).

The four CI modes described above are the most basic ones. In the life cycle of software products, an actual deployment pipeline is usually a combination of these four modes depending on the team size, product form, componentization level, and release strategy.

FIGURE 9.13 Deployment pipeline for multicomponent integration based on "Trunk-based Development & Release".

9.5 COMMON PROBLEMS IN IMPLEMENTATION

During employing CI practice, we usually encounter many difficulties, some of these come from the original work habits of team members (for example, engineers don't want to integrate their code with that of others until finishing their work; QAs prefer centralized testing after a batch of features are fully developed), and others are caused by poor management of technology R&D. For example, the environment of development, test, and production are not separated or incompletely separated, the same testing environment shared by multiple engineers, and preparations of various testing environments greatly complicated. In this chapter, we only discuss three problems associated with people's work habits, and other issues are to be discussed in subsequent chapters.

9.5.1 Work Habits of Engineers

Before the popularization of the CI practice, many companies did not have many requirements for the granularity and frequency of the code submission, especially the companies relying on the traditional waterfall development model. In 2009, when I was offering consultation services a communications company, I found its team only took the SVN codebase as something that protects code from loss during the two-month development period, and no one cared about whether the code could be complied at all. Even someone didn't submit code for two months, but kept their code on their own development workstation. Until it is time to centralize integration for testing, developers set about submitting code to the SVN codebase.

If a developer has been accustomed to non-integration with others' code in a long time, it will be hard for him to reach the "best state of CI" shortly after he has just attempted the CI practices, such as small-step submission, complete coding, and zero impact on existing features. However, if he is capable of requirements decomposition (refer to Chapter 6), he will obtain faster quality feedback and receive a good result of CI. Highlighting development quality and continuous shortening of build stabilization time (BST) is the starting point to improve the work habits of developers.

9.5.2 Code Scanning is Often Ignored

An important task of CI is to "quickly verify the quality of the current artifacts". We usually have a series of means to complete this quality verification. Among them, the means of "build verification test" and "dynamic/static code scanning" have a relatively low input cost and a low execution cost, and they are easy to implement; so, they are available for all teams to have a try.

However, it is worth noting that the results of scanning are often ignored by developers. The reasons may be in two aspects: (1) Team members haven't reached an agreement on the scanning rules, and some developers have doubt about them, but team leader ignores these dissonant voices. (2) Too many problems have been scanned out, making team members at their wits end.

The first problem is attributed to poor technical management of the team, and no uniform standard for code. The technical leader should learn the code specifications together with other team members, formulate the team's code standards through discussions, record the agreed items to be scanned, and then perform automation scanning.

The second problem usually occurs in case of a tight schedule for product development before. At this time, the Boy Scout Rule should be implemented, that is, to keep quality indicators from deteriorating. For example, "Try to reduce the number of problems whenever the code is submitted, at least prevent them from increasing"; or make rectification within a time limit such as "eliminate serious problems within three months". Meanwhile, the development of convenient and easy-to-use tools is encouraged, so as to facilitate engineers to detect nonstandard code more easily and fix it in a timely manner.

9.5.3 Lack of Automation Testcases

Testing activity is currently one of the most important quality assurance activities of the team, and centralized manual testing by Quality Assurance (QAs) is a kind of "slow feedback", that is, testcases can only be executed when the code features are developed and the software is workable, and the work schedule of developers and QAs shall be well coordinated.

If there are automation testcases, we can find a way to have them automatically executed at the time of any integration points. It would be even better if each developer could execute these automation testcases at any time without the help of others.

Currently, most automation testcases are still written by hands, so developers with good coding skills are in great demand. In CI practices, these automation testcases play an important role and need to be executed stably and correctly. Otherwise, the feedback results (such as random failure) can easily be misleading and waste working time of developers.

How to work out a test strategy? How to do a good job in test management? And how to write appropriate automation testcases? These questions are to be answered in Chapter 10.

9.6 SUMMARY

This chapter mainly talks about the origin of CI, the principles for CI, the check-in dance, and the six steps to quickly establish a CI practice in team. It is not the case that as long as a CI server is installed and deployed and used for automation compilation and packaging every day, then the team has been done with CI practices. To truly achieve CI while obtaining the largest benefit therefrom, attention must be paid to the following six points:

1. Trunk-based Development, and frequent code submission.
2. The content of each submission must be complete and meaningful code.
3. The check-in stage is completed within ten minutes.
4. Upon failed commit build, fix the problem immediately; no more code is allowed to be submitted before the fixing.
5. The defect should be fixed within ten minutes, otherwise the code that causes the failure will be rolled back.
6. After fulfilling the automation build is fulfilled, the team becomes more confident in the software quality.

Automation Test Strategies and Methods

10

The previous chapter introduces the definition of Continuous Integration, the six-step check-in dance for CI, and the CI model available for a team. To truly play the role of CI, an important part is the automation test strategies.

This chapter mainly discusses the automation test management before the software is deployed to the production environment, including the positioning of automation tests, the dilemma of traditional automation tests, the automation test strategies that facilitate feedback, and how to write easy-to-maintain code for automation tests.

10.1 SELF-POSITIONING OF AUTOMATION TEST

Generally speaking, there are four basic testing activities: problem recognition, analysis, execution, and decision-making. Among them, "problem recognition" refers to the understanding and knowledge of the business problem itself. Its main information comes from the Discovery Loop in the double-flywheels of Continuous Delivery. "Analysis" denotes "test analysis and design". Based on recognition of business problems, we will analyze and design ways and methods that verify various solutions, minimize testing cost through continuous optimization under the premise of ensuring the quality of verification. "Execution" is to execute the testcases generated from the stage of test analysis to obtain test results or data. The "decision-making" is to decide the next action according to the test results.

Among these four activities, only "execution" has a lot of repetitive labor, many of which can be undertaken by machine, and automation testing is to take advantage of machine and free people from repetitive manual labor (one type of toils). Well then, which tests can be automated? In reference to Brian Marick's agile testing quadrants (see Figure 10.1), we can put different types of tests into the matrix. "Business Facing" is to realize barrier-free communication with business experts by business examples. "Technology Facing" means that it is easy to reach consensus with technicians. "Supporting the Team" means that the goal is to help the whole production team to build the features that meet the requirement. "Critique Product" is to judge the output of the product.

The test types in the second and third quadrants can be automated, including functional acceptance testing, unit testing, component testing, and system integration testing. Among them, the functional acceptance test is to accept the software function from the user's point of view, while the unit tests, component tests and system integration tests (SITs) are all verifications for the realization of the software technology. Some of the nonfunctional acceptance tests (including safety tests, performance tests, etc.) in the fourth quadrant could be fully automated, but most can be at least semi-automated. The test types in the first quadrant are usually only run manually, such as software demonstration, user experience testing, and exploratory testing. This chapter mainly discusses the types of tests in the second and third quadrants.

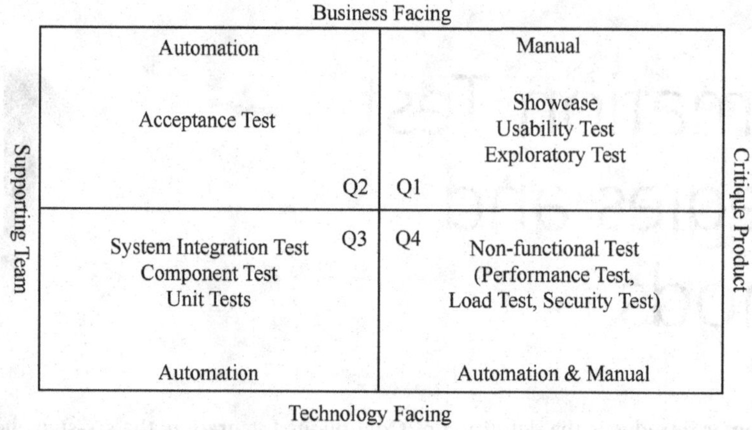

Business Facing

Automation Acceptance Test Q2	Manual Showcase Usability Test Exploratory Test Q1
System Integration Test Q3 Component Test Unit Tests Automation	Q4 Non-functional Test (Performance Test, Load Test, Security Test) Automation & Manual

Supporting Team ← (left vertical label)   Critique Product → (right vertical label)

Technology Facing

FIGURE 10.1 Brian Marick's agile testing quadrants.

10.1.1 Advantages of Automation Test

Compared with manual testing, automation test has greater advantages in the following aspects:

- **Reduce errors and improve accuracy.** Automation test performs the same steps whenever it is executed, records detailed execution results each time, and is not affected by "human" factor. When people perform repetitive tasks, they are likely to have different effects on the execution results due to their personal experiences and emotions at that time.
- **Save time and execution costs.** In the entire life cycle of software, testing activities need to be repeated frequently to ensure its quality. Software testing should be repeated every time the source code is modified. Before any version is released, it must be tested on all supported operating systems and hardware configurations. Once automation testcases are created, they can be run unattended, and even run in parallel on multiple computers with different configurations, and their run time may be faster than that of manual testing. Automation test can reduce the time of repeated manual testing from days to hours. Especially when the software life cycle is long and the release frequency is high, the time cost can be saved to a great extent.
- **Widen test coverage.** Automation test can increase the depth and scope of tests, which is able to improve software quality. For example, automation test can view the internal operating conditions of applications, such as memory usage and content, data sheet, file content, and internal program status, so as to determine whether the product is operating as expected. Automation test can execute thousands of different and complex testcases in each run, thereby providing coverage that cannot be achieved by manual testing.
- **Do tests that cannot be done manually.** Even the largest software quality assurance department cannot manually simulate network application tests controlled by thousands of users concurrently. In contrast, automation test can simulate thousands of virtual users and interact with networks, software, and Web applications.
- **Speed up quality feedback.** Before submitting the software package to Quality Assurance (QA) team for verification, developers can run these shared automation tests to quickly find out whether or not they have bugs. Whenever a change is checked in, the test can be run automatically, and the team will be notified if it fails. This will save developers' time and increase their confidence of code quality written by them.
- **Shore up team morale.** Morale is something difficult to measure, but perceptible. Using automation test to perform repetitive tasks allows the team to spend time on more challenging and valuable

activities, such as exploratory testing. Team members can improve their skills and confidence, and at the same time, the improvement of skills and confidence will be given back to their team.

10.1.2 Investment Required for Automation Test

Everything has two sides. While automation test brings benefits, it also incurs costs and cannot be covered. Its costs are made up of the following items:

- **Investment for tools.** Since automation test requires tool support, investment must be poured into research and development (R&D) of testing tools. Moreover, team members need to be trained to use proprietary testing framework and tools.
- **Maintenance of testcases.** Throughout the software's entire life cycle, features are added, deleted, or modified continuously. As a result, the original code for automation testcases also needs to be changed accordingly, which brings a certain cost of modification.
- **Skilled personnel.** Code must be written for automation testcases. The creators of automation testcases must be capable of software design and code writing.
- **Equipment resources.** Since automation test cannot completely replace manual testing, we not only need to retain the testing environment required for manual testing, but also prepare the corresponding testing environment for executing automation testcases.

Compared with manual testing, the shortcoming of automation test lies in its "unobservable execution process". When an automation testcase is executed, it only does what the execution script specifies, and does not have the capabilities of active observation, cognition, and analysis.

Automation testcases are best at answering the question "Does the software system run correctly in our pre-defined way?"; and the "pre-defined way" is set by developers who write code.

In short, automation test is mainly used for batch regression verification of software features. Such mechanical and repetitive verification is exactly what machines are good at. On the contrary, the core value of manual testing is to answer the question "Are we developing a correct software system that meets user expectations?", because in the manual testing process, we can actively observe, learn and analyze, and perform more creative work, such as exploratory testing, user-friendliness verification, or user experience improvement. This type of work is not the field of expertise of machines, and beyond their capability at present.

Suppose a piece of software needs to perform quality verification only once, then it is certain that manual testing is the most beneficial at this time, because it can't give full play to the advantages of automation test. However, this assumption is basically untenable in reality. We always need to do regression testing, and as the delivery cycle shortens, the frequency of regression testing has been increasing. If we rely on automation test, more automation tests will be executed, which will increase its input-output ratio, as shown in Figure 10.2. At which point the two curves will intersect? It depends on many factors, such as average labor cost, time cost, equipment cost, frequency of test execution, and product life cycle.

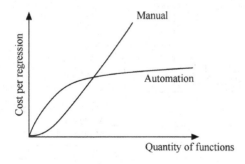 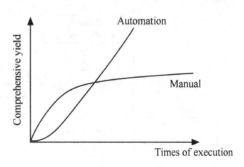

FIGURE 10.2   Cost-benefit comparison between automation test and manual test.

10.2 BREAK THROUGH THE DILEMMA OF TRADITIONAL AUTOMATION TEST

Automation test itself is not new. Since the birth of software, many product teams have devoted themselves into automation of testcases to eliminate repetitive manual labor. These testcases, which mainly cover the most basic functions of software, are written, maintained, and utilized by QAs in most companies. A common usage of them is to serve as an automation verification standard before QAs accept to test it manually. The typical creation process of these automation testcases is shown in Figure 10.3.

- Step 1: Test analysts design testcases and have them documented.
- Step 2: Test executors execute testcases and report bugs.
- Step 3: Developers fix bugs.
- Step 4: Test executors execute testcases again until they pass the verification.
- Step 5: Test automation experts select some important testcases, which are important and less likely to change, from the testcase documents.
- Step 6: Write automation scripts for selected testcases and put them into the automation regression testcase system.

10.2.1 Characteristics of Traditional Automation Test

The automation regression testcases created in the above process usually have six characteristics:

1. Costly execution. Blackbox automation testcases are the most common, and they usually go through SIT driven by simulated user interface (UI) operation. This kind of tests need to simulate the operation of real users, and at the same time capture the results returned by the system in the interface. In addition to the initial data required to start the system under test (SUT), data must be prepared for each testcase before their running, and dirty data must be cleaned up after that. Due to a long processing flow, more data need to be prepared for each testcase, thereby consuming more time and energy.

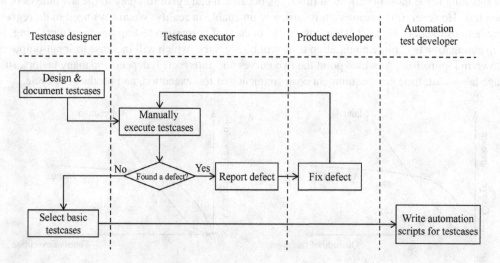

FIGURE 10.3   Creation process of traditional automation testcases.

2. Low-frequency execution. In many companies, automation testcases are only used as a gate keeper for QAs to verify the packages at the end of development stage, and also used for system regression test.

3. Lagging quality feedback. Most testcases, which are used for regression test of the main operating procedures of software applications, cannot cover the new features being developed for the current release. In addition, in order to guarantee the security of running the testcases, commands like Sleep are sometimes given to suspend the process to wait for the end of system processing, and then continue the following operation procedure. The entire process is really time consuming.

4. Costly prevision. The automation testcases wrote by QAs are usually end-to-end, it is necessary to prepare a full data set and a complete operating environment. There could be lots of manual operations in the process of setting up the testing environment, and even more people are involved, thus incurring a high cost.

5. Low reliability of test results. Affected by multiple factors such as machine hardware configuration, network condition, and length of process flow of testcases, end-to-end automation testcases may fail randomly; that is to say, when all conditions remain unchanged, running the same automation testcase multiple times, there will be different results, sometimes successful, sometimes not. The instability of the automation testcases themselves greatly reduces the credibility of the test results. In addition, collaboration between large-sized teams also brings difficulties to end-to-end testing. For example, testers are not informed of the changes in interface requirements in time, resulting in delayed updating of the original automation testcases, and ultimately leading to failed running of the testcases that are affected by those changes. These factors will make software development teams more inclined to ignore the existence of automation testcases.

6. Strong dependence on personnel. The writing of automation testcases relies heavily on a small number of dedicated QAs.

The mode of writing and executing automation testcases came from teams developing software a long delivery cycle and employing traditional waterfall development model. As result of increasingly variable software requirements, more complicated software features, and close human-computer interaction, the iteration of software is getting faster, but the return on investment (ROI) of such automation testcases is getting lower and lower.

10.2.2 Layering of Automation Test

As shown in Figure 10.1, the automation tests of the second and third quadrants are layered from big to small according to the scope of the objects under testing (se Figure 10.4a), we can find that the traditional automation testcases are mostly used for user acceptance tests (UAT) and SIT; these testcases have a large scope of tested objects, and the execution time of a single testcase is quite long. Moreover, the testcases are in a large number. Since developers usually do not participate in the creation of automation tests, there are fewer automation tests in the two layers below, forming in a "top-heavy" situation, which is described as "a cone ice cream easy to melt" (see Figure 10.4b).

This "cone ice cream" model is not conducive to CI. Chapter 9 makes it clear that automation testcases need to be executed before and after code submission, and automation test should provide fast and high-quality verification feedback to the tested software. Therefore, "fast, convenient, timely, and credible" are four basic measurement dimensions of automation tests in CI area.

1. "Fast": Automation testcases are executed at a fast pace. If a set of automation testcases takes 30 minutes to complete, then the cycle of its quality feedback is sure to exceed 30 minutes considering the operations of compilation, packaging, and deployment. And 30 minutes is far from enough for the teams that write a large number of end-to-end automation testcases. However, the requirement of CI is "better within 10 minutes, not more than 15 minutes".

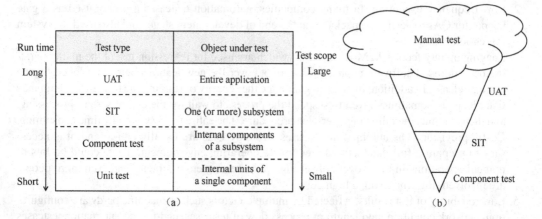

FIGURE 10.4　Correspondence between test categories and scope of tested objects.

2. "Convenient": Every engineer in the team can execute automation testcases anytime and anywhere, without asking others to lend a hand or disrupting others. If convenience cannot be guaranteed, people will tend to "delay feedback" until they believe it is cost-effective to execute them.
3. "Timely": Once a feature is changed, team members can immediately learn about its impact on original functions and the quality of newly added functions by running automation testcases. If developers have finished a new feature, but there is no automation testcase to verify it and its impact on other features in time, the feedback speed may be slowed down.
4. "Credible": The results of running automation testcases are trustworthy, and there is no random failure (or success). Random failure arises from instable running of testcases. As required by CI practices, once automation testcases fail, they must be fixed immediately. Random failure will greatly increase the "ineffective input" of engineers, deprive them of confidence in the results of CI, and finally drive them to turn a blind eye to the testcases that really fail, which will make CI meaningless.

The automation testcases created in the tradition model are hard to meet the above four basic requirements. In order to be "fast" and "credible", the number of automation testcases at different layers must be adjusted. As Mike Cohn has pointed out in his book *Succeeding with Agile: Software Development Using Scrum*, the number of upper-layer testcases with a large scope of tested objects should be reduced, while the number of lower-layer testcases with fine-grained tested objects should increase, so as to form a stable regular triangle, known as "golden test pyramid" as shown in Figure 10.5.

The costs of lower-layer testcases (including code maintenance cost, test preparation cost, and run time cost) are lower than those of upper-layer testcases. For example, in a J2EE Web Application development

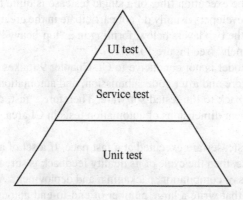

FIGURE 10.5　The Test Pyramid proposed by Mike Cohn.

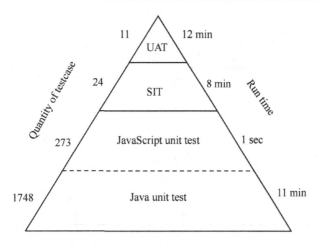

FIGURE 10.6 Number and run time of automation tests of a J2EE application.

project (the number of automation testcases at each layer is shown in Figure 10.6), the number of lower-layer unit tests is far more than that of SITs and UATs in the upper layer, but the run time of the former is very short. Therefore, we should encourage the use of lower-layer testcases to verify functional logic, which will be easier to meet the four basic requirements of automation test for continuous integration, thus forming a virtuous work cycle.

For a certain software application or service, not all layers of tests are necessary, the selection of tests should be based on the characteristics of the software application itself, the delivery requirements, and the ability of the team. And the lower-layer testcases cannot fully replace the upper-layer ones. However, if we have a choice (for example, choose the logic and scenarios that are associated with the lower-layer testcases), in order to speed up test running and reduce costs, we should use the lower-layer testcases as much as possible.

AUTOMATION TEST PYRAMID OF GOOGLE

Google's software development relies heavily on automation testcases. Before merging into the trunk, extensive automation testcases are automatically run. If any automation testcase fails, the team cannot move on to the next step of the workflow, that is, "code review". Moreover, Google has its own "pyramid structure" of automation testcases. In other words, its automation testcases are divided into three types: large, medium, and small (see Figure 10.7).

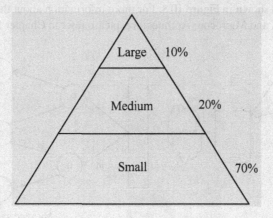

FIGURE 10.7 Google's Test Pyramid.

TABLE 10.1   Category and definition of Google's automation testcases.

WILL IT BE USED IN TESTCASES	SMALL TEST	MEDIUM TEST	LARGE TEST
Network access	N	Access only localhost	Y
Database access	N	Y	Y
File access	N	Y	Y
Use external services	N	Not encouraged	Y
Multithreading	N	Y	Y
Sleep statement	N	Y	Y
Use system property settings	N	Y	Y
Time to execution (ms)	60	300	900+

The differences among the three automation tests are listed in Table 10.1.

Of course, this is not a mandatory standard for distributing testcases within Google, but a guiding recommendation. The company has lots of product lines; different products have varying number of tests. It is still changing now, but there is not much change in the relative quantity proportion among them.

10.2.3 Different Types of Test Pyramid

Thanks to the robust development of technologies, the number of Internet users have risen sharply. In order to cope with the exponential increase in the number of Internet users and network requests, dot-com companies have begun to transit their software architecture to servitization and microservices, setting off a wave of large-scale distributed application services. Many back-end services have been splitting from the Monolithic Architecture into the Service-Oriented Architecture (SOA). Multiple services have been interacting with each other via Remote Procedure Call (RPC) and other means.

Since 2011, various mobile devices have sprung up like mushrooms, mobile Internet users have been increasing rapidly, and the number of mobile dot-com companies has even shown explosive growth. There is also a great demand for information exchange between companies via service interface. The Microservice Architecture came out as an achievement of continuously developing SOA. The back-end service module is split into microservices. Furthermore, the client software has been developing toward componentization or micro-core architecture, as shown in Figure 10.8. For more information about the Monolithic Architecture, Microservice Architecture, and Microcore Architecture, please refer to Chapter 5.

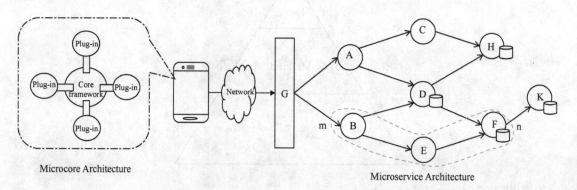

FIGURE 10.8   Schematic diagram of Microcore Architecture and Microservice Architecture.

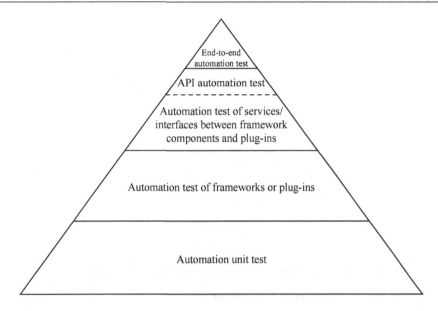

FIGURE 10.9   Test Pyramid of Microcore Architecture.

10.2.3.1 Test Pyramid of Microcore Architecture

The Test Pyramid of Microcore Architecture is shown in Figure 10.9. The top-level end-to-end automation test is driven by simulated UI calls from perspective of end users. The Application Programming Interface (API) automation test refers to the automation test that drives the underlying business logic through the API interface below the UI layer. The interface automation test of the service between components or plug-ins is mainly to verify the functional correctness of two or more components (plug-ins). The component test is to verify the quality of a single component or the framework itself. The automation unit test is the most fine-grained automation test.

10.2.3.2 Test Pyramid of Microservice Architecture

The Test Pyramid of Microservice Architecture is shown in Figure 10.10. The unit test is to check and verify the minimum testable business logic unit in the software, which is specified by human; the specific meaning of "a business logic unit" is generally specified according to the actual situation. For example, in the C language, a unit may refer to a function (such as an encryption algorithm). In object-oriented languages like Java, a unit may be a Class (such as Request Dispatcher). The unit test is characterized by less external dependency (such as file system and network). Since the SUT does not need to be running during the execution of the test, the test runs fast. Business unit test emphasizes business logic unit rather than the specific code implementation.

1. Business component or service test is to test a single component or service to verify whether the behavior of this component meets the design expectations. A component is a code block composed of multiple minimum business logic units, which provides a set of related business functions externally. It interacts with other components in the system and external integration points. External integration points can be interfaces that interact with external systems, or they can refer to components being developed by other teams. For example, the class MaterialService in the CI tool GoCD is an integration point that deals with Git, Subversion, or other CVS tools. Same as unit test, the component test usually does not require SUT to be running, but it may

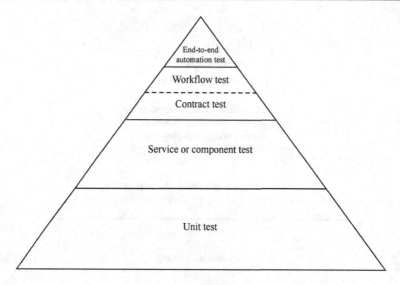

FIGURE 10.10   Test Pyramid of Microservice Architecture.

involve external dependency (such as file system, network and database, and so on), so the execution of testcases may be slightly slower than unit test.

2. Contract Tests are also known as consumer-driven contracts test (CDC tests). Contracts refer to protocols between consumers and providers, as shown in Figure 10.11. Its goal is to test the correctness between the consumer and the provider, verify whether the data offered by the provider is what the consumer needs. Using CDC, consumers of an interface write tests that check the interface for all data they need from that interface and publishes them so that the provider can fetch and execute these tests easily.

3. Business workflow test is executed on two or more running microservices, in an aim to verify whether multiple tested services can work together and support a certain business request. It focuses on multi-services interaction, testing interface connectivity, and process availability. For example, as shown in Figure 10.8, the test of services B, C, and F is a kind of business workflow tests between services. The input to B is m, then after the processing by B, C, and F, the output becomes n.

4. End-to-end test is to test the entire process of software service to verify whether the execution of the workflow from beginning to end meets the design expectations. The purpose of running an end-to-end test is to identify system dependencies and ensure that the correct information is passed between various systems (including external and internal systems). A common end-to-end test is to simulate users to perform various operations on the visual UI. If the SaaS also

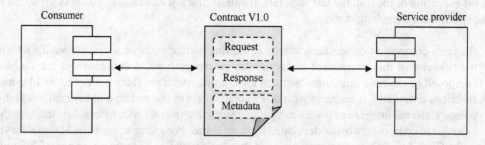

FIGURE 10.11   Contract between consumer and service provider.

provides nonvisual interface services (such as API calls, or even information exchange through files or databases), then this type of test is also classified as end-to-end test. It verifies a few key processes for end-to-end business from the user perspective and does not pay attention to the realization of a small function point.

10.3 IMPLEMENTATION STRATEGY OF AUTOMATION TESTING

Automation testing is a traditional software development practice, instead of something new. At the time when there was no sophisticated test framework, many excellent developers would still write automation tests for their own code. For example, in C/C++ projects, there is a very old practice, that is, add a function called Main to every C/C++ file to verify the implementation of some functions in this file. Nowadays, every programming language has a corresponding automation testing framework, often more than one.

As mentioned earlier, automating testcases are not free, there is certain cost involved, and every company will consider their ROI. Therefore, we need to start automation testing practices smarter, especially when dealing with legacy systems.

10.3.1 Add Starting Points for Automation Testcases

In order to run automation tests of a legacy system, where shall we start? While trying to avoid the testcases distribution like an "ice-cream cone", we can start from the following four aspects:

10.3.1.1 Write tests for code hotspots

Code hotspots refer to the files or functions that have relatively high frequency of code changes, as well as functional components that often have defects. For the code that does not change frequently and runs for a long time, its stability has been proven, so there is no need to write tests for them immediately. Writing tests for code hotspots has the most cost-effective input-output ratio at the beginning.

10.3.1.2 Write tests side by side with new features

It is best to follow the development progress and write corresponding tests that can be directly applied to provide timely quality feedback on new features. If we only supplement the tests for old features, the test coverage for features is likely to lag far away the feature development and fail to act as a safety net in time. This will greatly reduce value to developers.

Since this "parallel" strategy poses high requirements, the team must make sure of timely and smooth communication. In the software companies doing better at engineering management, automation tests are mostly written by developers on their own, because for the same feature, if its production code and test code are written by different persons, they need to communicate with each other, which is to incur communication costs.

10.3.1.3 Expand up and down from the middle layer of the test pyramid

If you just plan to write tests, you'd better start from the middle layer of the Test Pyramid, which can ensure the maximum ROI. For example, in the case of an online video website as mentioned earlier, the installation of a server-side software in the Microservice Architecture should start with the contracts test. But for mobile applications, it is best to start with the component or API test.

10.3.1.4 Quality of automation tests is more important than quantity

Automation tests are also the code in need of maintenance, which is sure to incur costs. Therefore, under the premise of satisfying the quality standard, the fewer automation testcases, the better.

1. It's better to have just enough automation tests. Do not write unnecessary test code, since no customer will not pay for your test code. The quality of automation tests is always more important that their quantity.
2. Do not write testcases for the same logic in different layers of test, such as unit test and component test.
3. Test the corresponding business logic at the layer with the minimum implementation cost. For example, the business logic that can be covered at the component and service levels should not be covered by end-to-end tests. Some tests that are not easy to execute at the unit test level can be verified by the upper-layer tests.

10.3.2 Increase the Execution Frequency of Automation Testing

Once the team decides to invest in automation testing, in order to raise its benefits, it is a good way to increase the execution frequency. Of course, we do not encourage repeated execution of multiple testcases in the same scenario, what we support is to reuse these available automation testcases in different scenarios. For example, in the process of code modification, developers shall run testcases before and after submitting the change, and at the time of integration after multiple people have submitted their code, instead of doing so only at the time of submission for testing. How can we effectively increase the execution frequency?

10.3.2.1 Share automation testcases

All automation testcases, no matter who has written them, are an asset of a company. Therefore, sharing these automation tests within the team to benefit everyone is one of the best ways to maximize their value.

In 2017, I was invited by a web startup to offer consultations. At that time, this company had more than 50 developers and 8 QAs. And all of the QAs were doing test manually. One hardworking QA learned Python and Postman (a testing tool) all by himself. So, he wrote lots of interface tests and ran several tests every day to verify if all interfaces in the production were working properly. However, these automation tests were stored and run only on his own computer, no one could execute them except for him.

If he could refactor these automation tests to a certain extent so that they would be adapted to different environments (such as testing environment and pre-production environment), then these automation testcases could be shared in multiple environments.

If he committed these automation tests into the team's repository, they would be shared with his teammates and used by more people, thus saved more human resources.

If he integrated these automation tests into their continuous deployment pipeline, then they could be executed automatically and unattended.

10.3.2.2 Developers are the first users of automation tests

If every developer could easily run automation tests at any time when writing code, use these tests as a safety net in the development process, and quickly get quality feedback after modifying the code, these automation tests would be run multiple times a day. Therefore, in order to truly exert the power of automation testing, it should be used as a quality protection network for developers in their daily development, rather than a tool used by testers to check and accept the work results of developers.

10.3.3 Characteristics of Good Automation Testing

In order to make it easier for everyone to perform automation tests and meet the basic requirements of "fast, convenient, credible, and timely", we need to write good automation tests. Generally speaking, a good automation testcase should have the following characteristics:

10.3.3.1 Testcases must be independent of each other

Testcases should be independent of each other, that is, the running result of the previous testcase has no effect on the running of the latter one. In automation testcases relying on traditional way of working, it is often seen that the running result of the previous testcase is used as the input of the latter one. This creates a sequential between testcases, resulting in their linear running. Once there are too many testcases, their running will last a long time and greatly reduce the feedback. And once a test fails, it is hard to find the root cause due to the interdependency.

10.3.3.2 The testcases must be stable

"Stable" means that when nothing is changed for a test, the multiple times of running results should be invariable. Flaky testcases will only give false quality signals or cause the team to waste too much time. For CI, flaky tests are worse than no tests.

10.3.3.3 The testcases must run fast

When a testcase is run in multiple steps, each step costs a certain period of time. In order to make the test more stable, each step is usually given sufficient execution time. Therefore, statements like sleep are often used to make the application wait long enough. But this approach will extend the run time of a testcase.

We usually have two ways to deal with this problem: (1) Decompose a testcase into multiple independent smaller testcases, with each smaller testcase only testing a part of the original testcase, so that they can be run in parallel. (2) Transform "waiting" to "polling", that is, to check ceaselessly whether it is available for the next step within smaller time intervals. This could reduce the waiting time, thereby shortening the time of the entire testcase.

10.3.3.4 The testing environments should be unified

In the teams with little experience in writing large scale automation tests, the following situation is often encountered: the automation tests can only be run in a certain testing environment, or even on the machine of a particular engineer. When others want to run these existed automation tests, they have to seek help to get a right testing environment. In this case, these existing automation tests cannot be reused by others, making it difficult to maximize the benefits of automation testing.

10.3.4 Share Responsibilities for Maintenance

In order to maintain a good state of automation testing and protect our investment in this regard, team should share the maintenance responsibilities for automation testcases.

Since automation tests are also a kind of software code, they should be written by people with good design and programming capabilities. Whenever and wherever, the test code should not be treated as a "second-class citizen". It is necessary to spend time on the design and writing of test code in order to make it easy to maintain and avoid from decaying.

When the requirement changes, but the corresponding tests are not updated in time, the testcase will definitely fail. When this happens from time to time, it is easy for developers to turn a blind eye to the running results of automation tests, then the testcases can no longer play a greater role, and it will cause more and more automation testcases to fail without any attention, thereby resulting in a "broken window effect". Given this, it is necessary to make automation tests change with the production code synchronously as far as possible. And the best way to do so is that when a developer fails to run the automation tests, he can modify the corresponding code by himself (maybe a feature goes wrong, or an automation testcase needs to be updated). This is also an indicator to judge whether the awareness of automation testing is deeply rooted in people's mind.

BROKEN WINDOWS THEORY

The "Broken Windows Theory" is a theory of criminology, believing that if undesirable phenomena in the environment are allowed to exist, they will induce people to imitate or even intensify them. For example, there is a vacant building with a few broken windows, if they are not repaired as soon as possible, more windows will be destroyed. Vandals will eventually break into this building. Noticing that no one is inhabited, they may settle there or even set fire. Similar phenomena happen all over the place: If the graffiti on a wall is not cleaned off immediately, a mess of unsightly things will appear it in no time. A sidewalk with a few scraps of paper soon leads to more trash, and eventually people dump it on the ground as a matter of course.

10.3.5 Test Coverage

Test coverage is an interesting indicator. Many people have done research on it and have got some conflicting results. Some people argue it is a useful indicator and a certain percentage of test coverage is a necessity. Some people, although they agree it is useful, believe that it can only tell you "which code are not covered by test", instead of showing you "the code covered by testcases must be the verified one". There are also people saying that test coverage is harmful because it provides a false sense of security.

At its Google Test Automation Conference (GTAC) held in 2014, a speaker made public its statement coverage of automation tests, which only included the coverage achieved by using the unit test framework. The data came from Google's more than 100,000 times of code submissions in 650 projects, and the data collection took one month, as shown in Figure 10.12.

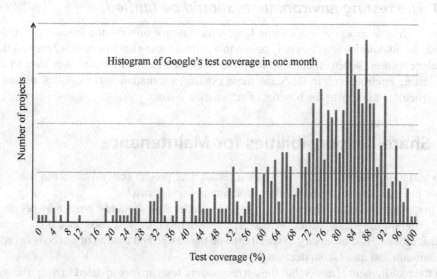

FIGURE 10.12 Google's automation test coverage in 2014.

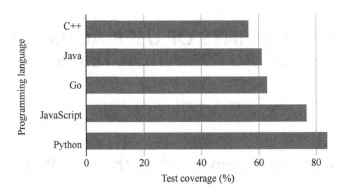

FIGURE 10.13   Google's test coverage for different programming languages.

The median coverage in Figure 10.12 is 78%, the 75th quantile is 85%, and the 90th quantile is 90%. The test coverage of each project is different, and different programming languages have different test coverage. The average test coverage of each programming language is shown in Figure 10.13. Google does not stipulate a unified standard for test coverage, it only has one recommended standard, that is, unit test coverage to reach 85%.

The reality is that many startups do not write automation testcases in its early stages. When Facebook was first online in 2004, it did not write automation tests as well. However, along with rapid development of business, the number of engineers has increased significantly, and the systems have become more complicated. As a result, the quality of software delivery had deteriorated, more defects were found from time to time, and developers had been rushing to make fixes. Therefore, Facebook introduced automation testing practices in 2008, since then the automation tests run before each release of its website code, and the size of tests has gradually increased (see Figure 10.14), but the company has not unified how many tests need to be written, which continues to this day. It is worth noting that most automation testcases in Facebook are within the job responsibilities of developers themselves.

Although people often ask something like "What is an appropriate test coverage?" This kind of problem is either "important" or not by taking account of the above various data. Writing and running automation testcases is not to examine the coverage value, but to confirm one's confidence in the quality of software he is developing.

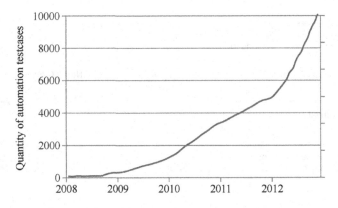

FIGURE 10.14   Growth trend of Facebook's automation testcases over 2008–2012.

10.4 KEY POINTS OF USER ACCEPTANCE OF AUTOMATION TESTS

UAT is at the top level of the Test Pyramid. Before writing more user acceptance automation testcases, careful preparation must be made to maintain healthy testcases at the lowest possible cost.

10.4.1 Build a Layered Framework in the First Place

When multiple people write UAT in large numbers at the same time, a test fixture should be built first. There are many general testing tools and frameworks, but they are not exclusive test fixtures for a particular business area, just like all programming languages. In order to make test scripts easier to maintain, we should first use these general test tools to establish an automation test mechanism with proprietary domain-specific language (DSL) for our own business domain. In this way, automation testcases can be easily maintained and modified, thereby reducing maintenance costs.

Here we take Selenium, an automation tool for web pages, as an example to illustrate the process of forming an exclusive test fixture for a specific domain. Figure 10.15 shows a form for searching domestic air tickets. We can write some testcases for ticket search to verify the correctness of this feature.

If we use the native API provided by Selenium to write automation testcases right away, the test scripts will look like the one as shown in Figure 10.16.

The first line of code means to open the homepage; the code in lines 2 through 5 is to find every input box in the page form and assign a value to it; Line 6 is to find the submit button and click; Line 7 is to pause the program for one second and wait for the response of the search; Line 8 is to find the total number of search results; and Line 9 is to confirm that the total number is not empty.

There are two hidden dangers in this test script: (1) Poor readability. For someone who has just got this test script, if he fails to carefully read the code line by line, he will probably have no idea what each line of this test script is doing. (2) Poor maintainability. Suppose a variety of test data are needed to test this scenario, a lot of similar or duplicate code will be generated.

Are there other ways of writing tests that better express the test intent and easily communicate with others? Let's take the same test script as an example and have it redesigned. Generally speaking, the code framework structure of automation testing can be divided into three different layers:

1. Description layer. It is used for communication between people. The above testcase can be written in text (see Figure 10.17), everyone can easily know the purpose and content of this test.

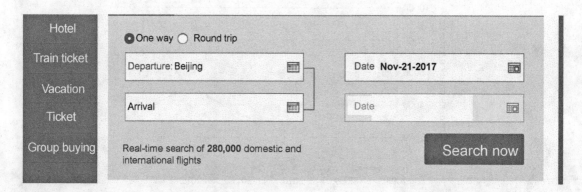

FIGURE 10.15 A web form for searching China's domestic air tickets.

```
0 ... ...
1 WebDriver.open("http://www.mytrip.com");
2 webDriver.findElement(By.xpath("//div[contains(@id,'single_trip')]//input")).click();
3 webDriver.findElement(By.xpath("//div[contains(@id,'from')]//input")).sendKeys("北京");
4 webDriver.findElement(By.xpath("//div[contains(@id,'to')]//input")).sendKeys("深圳");
5 webDriver.findElement(By.xpath("//div[contains(@id,'date')]//input")).sendKeys("2020-09-01");
6 webDriver.findElement(By.xpath("//a[contains(@id,'searchBtn')]//button")).click();
7 sleep(1000);
8 WebElement counterElement= webDriver.findElement(By.xpath("//div[text()='"+counter+"']"""));
9 Assert.assertNotNull(counterElement);
...
```

FIGURE 10.16   Write automation testcases with selenium API.

2. Implementation layer. It associates the upper description layer with the program script and realize the test intent. The sample code is shown in Figure 10.18, in which the function method *flight_search (String date, String from, String to)* is encapsulation of the test API for the air ticket booking domain. Therefore, as long as there are similar operations, this API can be reused. In this piece of code, there are two encapsulated domain objects, namely, *FlightHomePage* and *SearchResultPage*, which are both subclasses of Page and also part of the air ticket booking domain. When we write more tests, we just need to use these encapsulated business-related domain objects instead of the native WebDriver API similar to Figure 10.16. Through the abstraction, code with different test purposes can be concentrated in several files or methods. This makes the writing of large-scale testcases simple and easy to use. Since they are highly readable, they can also improve the efficiency of communication between team members.

3. Interface layer. It encapsulates the API provided by general test tool, isolates the implementation details of the code that is irrelevant to the test field, and provides some reusable basic interface sets for the upper implementation layer (see the sample code in Figure 10.19). This piece of code is encapsulated in the *FlightHomePage* object. Encapsulation of detailed technical implementations into a few class objects is conducive to subsequent modifications.

Which type of features should we choose for automation testing to refine the test fixture of a software application? Generally, we can choose basic or commonly used features in the software and write automation testcases for them based on user process. These features are usually relatively stable and free from drastic change. They are also core features in the business, and easier to abstract commonly used test fixture. Once the test fixture is setup, the tests can be written on a relatively large scale.

```
Search from <from> to <to> flights on <date>
shall include <flight>

Example:
|data      |from      |to        |flight  |
|20190101  |Beijing   |Shenzhen  |CA1305  |
|20190101  |Shenzhen  | Beijing  |CA1306  |
```

FIGURE 10.17   Example of description layer of automation testcases.

```
public void flight_search(String date, String from, String to) {

    FlightHomePage page = applicationFactory.get(FlightHomePage.class);
    this.homePage = page;
    homePage.search(data, from, to);
    ...
}

public should_contains(String flightNumber) {
    ...
    Page searchResultPage = homePage.getResult();
    ...
    assertTrue(searchResultPage.contains(flightNumber));
}
```

FIGURE 10.18   Example of implementation layer of automation testcases.

10.4.2 The Total Number of UAT should be as Small as Possible

As I've pointed out when talking about the Test Pyramid, there should not be a large number of UAT at the top layer. As it is, for a small number of tests, which scenarios should be covered? What is the key point of verification?

1. UAT should verify the core workflow of a software application or service in the form of a User Journey Map – a series of main interactive processes. User Journey Map, by starting from the user perspective, describes the interaction between users and software applications in a story-telling manner.
2. UAT should verify the end-to-end behavior of a software application or service, rather than specific implementation details. For example, when verifying the system login behavior, the main target of verification is to verify whether the entire login process is executed correctly, rather than verifying whether the input information is illegal, because the latter can be covered by lower layer tests and at a lower cost.

10.4.3 Reserve API for Automation Testcases

When writing this kind of testcases, we should try to call the API at just below the Graphical User Interface (GUI) to drive the execution and use less code that simulates the operation of the GUI. The GUI is for human interaction, not for machines. GUI operations are usually slow to respond, it is difficult to locate GUI elements in many cases, and the running of code is prone to be flaky.

This requires that the convenience of writing UAT should be taken into account when designing, and corresponding API-driven methods should be supported. For example, you can use the GUI to create a login account on the system, and at the same time you are able to create an account through RESTful API. Sometimes even for the convenience of testing, you should add necessary APIs but not open them to the outside. When released in a production environment, these APIs can be hidden or removed through technical means.

```
public void search(String date, String from, String to) {
    WebElement dateInput = webDriver.findElement(By.id(date));
    dateInput.sendKeys(date);
    ...
}
```

FIGURE 10.19   Example of interface layer of automation testcases.

10.4.4 Prepare for Debugging

Make the debugging of UAT easier through various means, such as providing complete log files; recording common test failure modes; retaining all relevant system status information like automatic screenshots, on-site image storage in case of errors.

10.4.5 Prepare Test Data

In addition to writing test code, there is another important task for automation testing, which is preparation of test data. The data required for testing can be divided into three categories: the first category is the most basic data required for application startup, such as metadata and dictionary tables for initialization. The second category is the data needed to make a set of tests reach the desired state. The third category is the data needed for executing a particular testcase on the basis of the first two types of data. Of course, every time the test is run, some data may be modified. In order to maintain the independence between testcases, after a test is finished, its impact on the data should be eliminated to make sure that the original state of data should be restored.

For running tests at different layers of the Test Pyramid, the data are prepared in different ways with different costs. For UAT, the corresponding preparations may be slightly more complicated. Generally speaking, there are four common ways to do that:

1. Write programs to automatically generate data based on some domain rules. Its shortcoming is that the data generation program is difficult to write and maintain in case of complex rules.
2. Record the data generated from manual testing.
3. Clone a copy of non-sensitive data from production, or intercept data fragments.
4. Record and playback. Save and backup the production environment data automatically. For example, for search algorithm optimization projects, all query records can be recorded as input data for tests.

The data traffic cloning of the real-time production environment is shown in Figure 10.20. Its principle is to add a request cloner at the entrance of the traffic request. When the request from the production

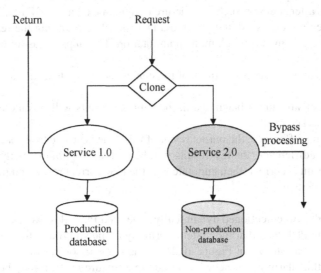

FIGURE 10.20   Traffic cloning in production environment.

enters the cloner, it will be cloned, the original request is still processed normally through the original service (Service 1.0 in Figure 10.20), and the cloned copy is diverted to the new version of the service (Service 2.0 in Figure 10.20), so as to perform the test of the new version. This method is usually used in the testing of Internet products and is an implementation method of dark deployment (see its explanation in Chapter 12).

"VIRTUAL CITY" IN THE PACIFIC OCEAN

A similar approach is adopted for online stress testing of an online car-hailing platform. There is a prominent tidal phenomenon in taxi travel (multiple peaks and troughs per day), which inspired engineers to think of the method of real-time traffic cloning. Of course, it is not only traffic that is cloned, but also cities. For example, the data of Beijing is cloned, and its latitude and longitude are drifted, so as to make this cloned city float on the Pacific Ocean. At the same time, clone the real-time coordinates of the driver and passenger and drift their longitude and latitude. In this way, the code of new version can undergo stress test in this cloned Beijing – a virtual city floating in the Pacific Ocean.

10.5 OTHER QUALITY INSPECTION METHODS

In addition to the methods mentioned above, there are other quality inspection methods that can be used. They are briefly introduced as follows:

10.5.1 Diff-Approval Testing

Diff-approval testing is a kind of semi-automation testing. In some cases, we may not be able to do fully automation UAT. For example, the software system needs to generate a lot of pictures of dynamic data or PDF files (such as electronic invoice). How to run an automate test of products in this binary format? At this time, we can employ Diff-approval testing.

The principle of Diff-approval testing is as follows: when a predefined data set is input into the system, the output results after running (such as a picture of dynamic data or PDF file) are collected, the data that need to be verified are extracted and put into a text file. By comparing the results of two tests, the semi-automatic test is performed through manual annotation. The steps are as follows:

1. After the first running, the correctness of the contents of these text files are marked manually and saved.
2. When these tests are run in batch again, the running results will be automatically compared with the last marked results.
   i. If there is no difference, the output result of this time is considered correct.
   ii. If there is a difference, the test results will be reviewed again manually. If the subsequent running result is correct, then annotate it as the new correct result and make it the basis for the later judgment.

For example, for the aforementioned dynamically generated PDF files, we need an additional conversion tool to convert the PDF files that the system normally outputs into text files that contain important verification information, as shown in Figure 10.21. If the comparison results are inconsistent, then an alarm is needed, but this alarm is not necessarily due to a feature error, it may because a newly added feature logic causes the output PDF file format to change.

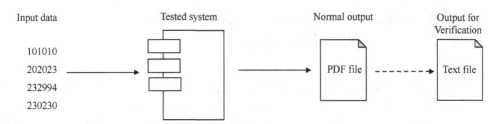

FIGURE 10.21   Process of Diff-approval testing.

In addition, when running a Diff-approval test, we need to pay attention to the processing of dynamic data (such as date, timestamp, and auto-generated random number). This type of data related to real-time timestamp may be automatically generated by the system. When doing this type of test, we need to filter the noise in some way.

Although the effort to creation of Diff-approval tests may not be much, it could require lots of effort to maintain, which is decided by whether there is strong tool support. Moreover, since it is usually really hard to achieve independence of testcases, there will be many assertions. Some of comparison tools are available, such as TextTest or ApprovalTests.

10.5.2 Code Style Check and Code Dynamic/Static Analysis

Code style check is to check the source code through some tools and by complying with the code writing norms defined by the team, and engineers correct the code that violates the norms. These common tools include Checkstyle, PMD, SonarQube, and so on. Regarding code style check, its purpose is to enhance the readability and maintainability of the code. When Google engineers do code reviews, they have very strict requirements for code readability.

Code dynamic/static analysis is to automatically scan the source code with some tools to find problems or potential risks in the code. It is a quality inspection means with a relatively high ROI. It can be divided into static scanning and dynamic analysis.

As for static scanning, it means that after the source code is written, it does not need to be compiled by a compiler but is directly scanned to detect semantic defects and security loopholes in the code. There are two ways to implement static scanning: one is to perform static analysis through pattern matching based on syntax analysis, and the other is to simulate program's full path execution. This way of simulation covers more paths than dynamic testing of program and reveals defects that are difficult to find by testcases. In addition to the lint tools corresponding to various programming languages, there are also commercial tools such as Coverity and Klocwork.

Dynamic analysis is performed by executing the target program on a real or virtual processor. For example, insert specially programmed failure occurrence functions at possible loopholes, the purpose of these functions is to force the execution of the target software to produce exceptions, and then the monitor is used to check for boundary overflows or other anomalies. Commonly used tools include Valgrind and Purify.

The analysis and scanning of the source code with these dynamic and static tools can reveal some issues or defects in time, as well as potential risks. Therefore, same as automation testing, we can integrate checks into the deployment pipeline, and even let the engineers who write the code execute them themselves.

It is worth noting that this scanning work may take a long time when the codebase is large. At this point, we should provide incremental scanning before submitting the build, and scan the entire codebase afterwards or separately. This is to strike a balance between speed and quality of feedback, just as we may separate check-in build from secondary build.

10.5.3 Application of Artificial Intelligence (AI) in the Field of Testing

There are many AI tools for code analysis and defect location, and there are also tools for UI and security tests, including Appdiff, DiffBlue, BugDojo, Microsoft Security Risk Detection, and Facebook Sapienz. Although these smart test tools are still being explored, some gratifying results have already come out.

For example, in May 2018, on the website code.facebook.com, Ke Mao and Mark Harman published an article titled *Sapienz: Intelligent Automated Software Testing at Scale*, which talks about the result of intelligent automation testing of Facebook's own Android apps with Sapienz, and states that "In addition to speeding up the testing process, Sapienz has delivered an extremely low false-positive rate. Our engineers find that 75 percent of Sapienz reports are actionable, resulting in fixes".

10.6 SUMMARY

"Lead time" is a concept in lean production management. It refers to the time period from the date when a user places an order to the date when the user receives his product. A shorter time period is a sign of higher delivery efficiency and better customer satisfaction.

With higher requirements for delivery frequency, the lead time is expected to be shorter, thus making automation testing more important. For the purpose of achieving rapid software delivery, there are four basic requirements for automation testing, namely "fast, convenient, credible, and timely". In order to achieve these four points, we shall use the layered Test Pyramid as a guide to rationally design automation testing implementation strategies, which can increase the benefits of automation testing. For the practical management of automation testing, I hope everyone could remember five important principles:

1. The more frequent automation testcases are run, the lower the average cost and the greater the benefit.
2. Automation testcases should be as independent as possible without affecting each other.
3. On the premise of guaranteed quality, the number of automation testcases should be as small as possible.
4. The writing of automation testcases for legacy code should start from the code hotspots.
5. Automation testcases are supplemented from the middle layer of the Test Pyramid, which boasts the maximum input-output ratio.

Software Configuration Management

11

"Automate everything" is an important principle of the Deployment Pipeline and a key factor in speeding up the Continuous Delivery verification loop. With higher frequency releases, software configuration management (SCM) has become the cornerstone of "automating everything".

For Internet products, in order to grasp the real needs of massive users, multiple versions of the services have to be run concurrently on different servers in production, and the diversity of mobile terminals has also presented the requirements for version management of multi-channel packages. Teams are responsible for rapid iteration of requirements, and maintenance and updating of multiple historical versions.

All these have brought great challenges for managing software development, testing, and operation. To be able to cope with these challenges, SCM is particularly important. This chapter mainly discusses the goals, scope, and principles of SCM, and introduces in detail the content of SCM, as well as the problems that may be encountered and their corresponding solutions.

11.1 PUT EVERYTHING UNDER SCM

In information technology (IT) industry, the term "configuration management" is widely used, but it means different things in different contexts. Regarding software life cycle management, it is similar to version control and baseline management; and when we talk about environmental preparation and application deployment, configuration management is closely related to something like Configuration Management Database (CMDB) in the domain of operation.

In this chapter, SCM refers to the management of related products in the process of production and operation during the entire software life cycle, including the products themselves and their unique identification and revision history, as well as the relationship between different products. Its goal is to record and manage the evolution of software products, so as to ensure that the organization can get accurate product configuration at all stages of the software life cycle, and to improve the efficiency of collaboration between different roles.

11.1.1 Goals of SCM

We need to obtain two basic capabilities through SCM, namely, traceability and reproducibility, so as to improve the security of the entire software life cycle and raise team collaboration efficiency.

Traceability means that anyone can find out all previous changes of the software as long as he is authorized, that is, for any change, he can answer the questions starting with the "4Ws1H" (Who, When, What, Why, and How). This is an important means of information security management in software

DOI: 10.1201/9781003221579-11

companies. For example, the source code version control systems such as Git and Subversion are SCM tools that contain revision information for all the code.

Reproducibility means that anyone can reproduce the software state at any point in time from the past to the present as long as he is authorized. In addition to its effect in information security management, it is also one of the most important means for each role to improve the efficiency of collaboration.

Good SCM not only requires traceability and reproducibility but also requires easy operation and high efficiency, that is, people can easily trace and reproduce the specified state of the software at a certain point in time. In addition, the information needed for configuration management should be obtained automatically free from interrupting the normal activities of team members as far as possible.

11.1.2 Scope of SCM

The life cycle of a piece of software begins when the software requirements are put forward and put into the requirements repository. In order to realize certain business functions, developers take out the requirement from the requirements repository, write code in the development environment, and submit it to the codebase. A software artifact is generated through building and stored in the temporary Artifactory. Then this artifact will be deployed to different environments. After passing the quality verification, it will be stored in the official Artifactory, verified in the pre-production environment, and finally run in the production until it is replaced by another artifact. In this process, there are four types of artifacts: requirements, source code, software artifact (deployment), and environment, which the scope of SCM, as shown in Figure 11.1. If the software you built is to be used externally, you also need to prepare software instructions.

11.1.3 Principles of SCM

The following questions can serve as a benchmark to examine a company's SCM capability.

1. How long does it take to create a new or recover operating environment (such as a testing environment, a pre-production environment, or even a production environment)? How many people are needed to provide support in creating this environment? How much manual intervention is

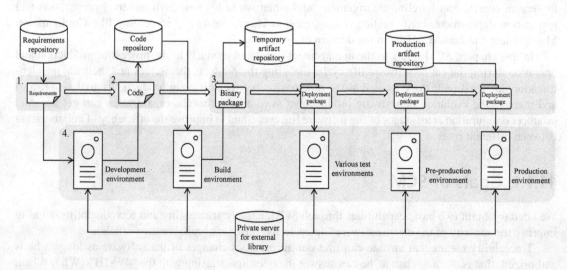

FIGURE 11.1 Scope of SCM.

required? Can anyone use the software operating environment as long as others upon obtaining authorization?

2. How long can you restart and configure a new Continuous Integration (CI) server and restore its normal use if the box that your deployment pipeline is running on is damaged and cannot be repaired?

In order to get satisfactory answers to these two questions, we must understand the three basic principles of SCM: (1) everything has a unique identifier; (2) sharing the True North source; (3) and standardization and automation.

11.1.3.1 Everything has a unique identifier

Version management of the source code of application and the software artifact released online has been the consensus of software industry. However, when software needs to be released faster, this level of version management is neither sufficient nor comprehensive.

In 2017, I had a talk with a developer from an Internet company in China (with less than 200 developers and Quality Assurance [QAs]) about provisioning. I asked him a question: "How long does it take to create a new testing environment for a business software service?" "Two hours by developers, but QAs have not done something like this", replied him. In order to figure out the time for QAs, developers specially wrote a Testing Deployment Instruction to QAs. A QA followed it (see Table 11.1) to perform manual operations, and developers guided him by his side. When the QA was preparing the environment, a developer kept revising this document based on the feedback from the QA. The final result showed that it took one day for QAs to accomplish this task from scratch.

Table 11.1 shows a simplified version of this instructions, but it unfolds all relevant contents that need to be done to make a certain service run. These contents can basically be divided into three levels (see Figure 11.2): operating system level, standard software (or middleware) level, and customed application level. The frequency of changes gradually increases from bottom to top.

1. Operating system level. As the name suggests, this level refers to the operating system, network configuration, as well as general network and system management services just on the top of the hardware (Step 1 in Table 11.1).
2. Standard software level. This level usually includes standardized software assembly on which customed application depends. The "standardized software assembly" means that it exists as an independent process and provides services for upper-level applications, such as data storage, message queues and caching services, and so on. Database software, message middleware or Application server usually exist in the form of software installation packages and seldom change. They are usually provided by external products, such as MySQL database, Redis server, ActiveMQ, Apache2 server, or ZooKeeper (Steps 2~5 in Table 11.1).
3. Customed application level. This level usually includes the applications developed by the team, and the third-party component library and relevant data for running these applications (Steps 6~8 in Table 11.1). Among them, the third-party software service for operation interaction refers to the software runtime service that is developed and maintained by other teams, and unable to be changed or modified by our own team.

In order to run the entire software stacks, in addition to the software itself in the above three levels, we also need the software configuration information and relevant data to initiate and run the services correctly. For example, in Table 11.1, the revised IP address in such configuration files app.conf, advert.conf, db.conf, and redis.conf in Step 6; the modified permission of the upload file directory in Step 7; and the data for database initialization in Step 8.

Is it enough for SCM to cover only the software source code, and the three levels of software, configuration files and data? In addition to managing the contents required for the normal operation of software in

TABLE 11.1   Deployment document of an Internet company's business system

STEP	CONTENT
1	Install the operating system (find a copy of CentOS 6 or above and install it)
2	Download, unzip, compile, install Nginx, and modify the configuration
3	Install MySQL and modify the configuration
4	Install ffmpeg and create a soft link
5	Install PHP 7.1 (start pdo_mysql, curl, mb_string modules): 1. Install dependent software such as gcc and curl-devel. 2. Download, unzip, compile and install php. 3. Install yaf extension. 4. Install redis extension. 5. Start php-fpm.
6	Install and configure the application: 1. Pull the code on the master branch from the project repository. 2. Update the configuration files (app.conf, advert.conf, db.conf, redis.conf), and change the Internet Protocol (IP) and port in the configuration to those used in the project.
7	Create the storage directory for uploading files: 1. Create directories named "uploads", "downloads", and "device" under the directory "www", and enable PHP to have read and write permissions. 2. Create a directory named "var/logs" under the root directory and enable PHP to have read and write permissions.
8	Data initialization: import the table structure and initial data of the ad_zzz from mysql whose IP is xxx.xxx.xxx.xxx
9	Test: visit the login page http://$IP

production, SCM should also manage the contents in the process of software production. These contents include the software testing toolkit or test class library, test-related code, and data for test running, as well as some scripts associated with the test.

In summary, in addition to the source code, we also need to manage all the contents in Figure 11.3. Any change to one piece of these contents will generate a new snapshot (that is, a new version correspondence).

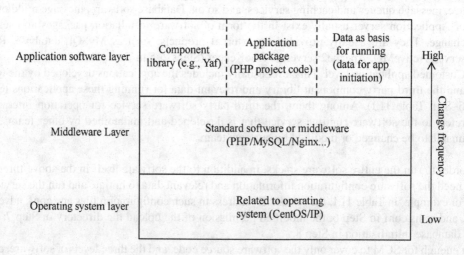

FIGURE 11.2   Three levels of software stack.

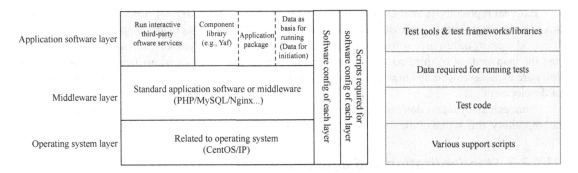

FIGURE 11.3 Version management content in Continuous Delivery.

And each change should come from a business request (either requirement change, defect fixing or technical transformation). Therefore, the first principle of SCM is to carry out version change management for all contents, that is, everything requires version management.

11.1.3.2 Sharing the True North source

In order to grasp the software status at any time and ensure that everyone obtains consistent information, the company shall manage the True North source, that is, the repositories (see Figure 11.1) for storing three types of data: business requirements/defects, source code, and software artifact. All team members should use the contents in these repositories as a benchmark to communicate and collaborate with each other. As are one of the company's assets, these repositories need to be properly kept. Their functions are listed as follows:

- Requirements repository: To save all version requirements descriptions and acceptance conditions of related products, and record each version change when the team reaches a consensus on the requirements.
- Code repository: To save all changes of the source code. In addition to source code, it also covers all contents in the form of code throughout the life cycle of the software artifact, such as test code, automation scripts of deployment pipeline, environment configuration information, and artifact build dependency.
- Artifacts repository: To automatically save the software artifact produced and processed by the deployment pipeline to facilitate the quick access in subsequent stages. According to the usage of different contents, it can be divided into three sub-types: temporary repository, release repository, and external repository.

Artifacts repository should serve as the only software trusted source for different roles in the development team to collaborate and communicate while developing a release, so as to avoid unnecessary risks and waste caused by inconsistent environments or repeated packaging. For example, developers may hand over the software artifacts built in their personal development environment to testers, but the development environment would be uncontrolled, which could lead to security risks or file loss (such as a file modification failed to be submitted to the repository). The correct approach is to transmit software artifacts through the artifacts repository. For example, developers inform QAs of the download location of the artifact to be tested in the temporary artifacts repository, and QAs take out this artifact and perform corresponding testing.

Release repository is used to store all software artifacts that have passed the quality verification and are about to go online or already online. Similar to the management of a temporary repository, the contents stored in a release repository should not come from someone's own build, but verified software artifacts transferred from the temporary repository manually or automatically through the controlled management system.

External repository is also known as private server of the third-party software library. It is used to store the external third-party trusted software artifacts for all internal software to quote, include, or use. It should support third-party software management for the entire life cycle of a software application, not just the management of third-party software artifacts in production, that is, artifacts, class libraries or software tools developed and maintained by external teams but required by our own team in the process of development.

Although many teams don't pay great attention to the management of temporary repository and external repository, this is one of the focuses of Continuous Delivery.

11.1.3.3 Standardization and automation

An important task in SCM is baseline management. The so-called "baseline" is a "snapshot" of all repositories at a certain moment, that is, when the baseline is created, an overall mark or copy of the current version in the repository. For example, when a project reaches a milestone moment, it is necessary to create a baseline for all the documents in the document library to record the results of as of this point.

In order to facilitate team collaboration and version traceability, SCM should have appropriate standards and norms (such as branch strategy, branch naming, branch tag naming, feature naming, storage location, and source code directory structure). In this way, when everyone understands and abides by the management norms, a lot of unnecessary communication costs can be reduced.

With available standards and norms, many daily transactional operations can be automated (such as baseline), thereby freeing up more human resources. For example, in Chapter 14, after redefining the branch strategy, the team standardized the usage of different branches and the naming conventions of software artifacts (such as the meaning of each flag bit, and the automatic generation mechanism of flag bits). Lots of error-prone manual operations, such as pulling branches and tagging, entering version numbers, and uploading them, are replaced by automated mechanisms.

It should be noted that standardization and normalization do not mean rigidity. All standardized management should have corresponding improvement mechanisms to continuously discover and optimize points in standardized management, which is especially important for large-scale teams.

11.2 VERSIONING OF SOFTWARE ARTIFACTS

The release cycle of software services is continuously shortening. At the same time, back-end services are evolving to the Microservice Architecture, mobile applications are evolving to the Microcore Architecture, and various public components are reused. All this makes us bound to face the problem of "package explosion". In other words, the number of managed software packages has grown rapidly over time. How can we carry out effective versioning for these packages?

11.2.1 Anti-Pattern of Package Management

For the packages on which an application depends, a common practice in the past was to put them together with the source code and submit them to the code repository. This approach is as simple as "out of the box" for engineers that develop this application, that is, check out the source code from the code repository, and start working right away. But this approach is not good at identifying the package version. Therefore, when submitting the package to the code repository, it is best to add the version ID to the file name. For example, for the "Java log package slf4j", it is "slf4j -1.7.21.jar" that is to be submitted to the codebase instead of "slf4j.jar". In this way, the version of this software package can be easily identified. Even so, I do not recommend to do that.

This approach is enough for a small project undertaken by a small team. But for a company with a large number of employees and projects, this approach will bring the following problems:

1. A large number of packages exist in the repository in a binary form, but most version control systems (VCSs) are inefficient in the management of binary files, and they also have I/O bottlenecks, making them unable to optimize transmission in a targeted manner.
2. A large number of duplicate packages are stored in the code repository. If a company has lots of projects (including the projects either being maintained or vigorously developed), there will be a large number of duplicate packages in the VCS.
3. The coordination for public packages has increased. When multiple teams work together on developing a complex system, some small teams will use the packages produced by other teams in the organization. These packages change more frequently than those developed externally. Once a package is updated, all items that depend on it have to be replaced manually.

Therefore, although this is a convenient way of package versioning, companies are not advised to save any type of package in code repository once their scale becomes larger, but immediately establish a "centralized package management service".

11.2.2 Centralized Package Management Service

We should establish an enterprise-level unified service for managing packages, put all packages into it, and provide stable inquiry, acquisition, and application services to all internal teams.

Query service means that internal personnel can conveniently find the package they need. Acquisition service means that one can download the required package through the package management service and be ensured with correct version and high-speed download. Application service means that when the required package (usually a third-party software outside the company) is not found in the private server, an employee can apply for the use of this package and get a quick response.

Companies can either develop such library management systems themselves, or use open-source or commercial package management software such as the commonly used Nexus and Artifactory. Both of them have community version and commercial version. By the time this book was written, Nexus Repository Manager OSS 3.x was able to manage multiple forms of repositories, which was used together with Bower, Docker, Git LFS, Maven, npm, NuGet, PyPI, Ruby Gems, or Yum Proxy. For Java projects, the free version of Artifactory is more thoughtful in details and easy to use.

Unified package management has the following advantages:

- Unified storage, and less space occupation.
- Consistency. Uniform copies are used throughout the company and are the only source of all packages.
- Safe and worry-free. It can perform unified security scanning and legal auditing on packages. When a package has any security loophole or risk, we can identify the usage scope in time, locate the risk points, and formulate a unified risk response strategy.
- Fast download. On the company's Intranet, packages are rapidly downloaded.

Of course, this type of management incurs more costs: (1) Someone is needed to manage and maintain this enterprise-level system service. (2) Storing third-party software packages on the company's internal server will take up some storage space. (3) It is prone to cause a single point of failure, so a corresponding solution needs to be formulated.

11.2.3 Meta Information of Packages

We need some information to describe and define each package in the artifacts repository so as to facilitate mutual reference, traceability, and retrieval. This information, which is known as the meta information of package, can be made up of the following contents:

- Unique ID information of the software package itself.
- Source. For example, the person that provides the software package, location of the source code, and current status (available, unavailable, and quality).
- Dependency. Does it refer to other software packages?

11.2.3.1 Unique ID

Each package should have a unique ID. Generally, there are two basic requirements for the ID: easy to understand and remember; and easy to query the index. Although each software development team defines the unique ID format of the package and related semantic descriptions according to its own situation, the ID format of most packages usually consists of two parts: software name and version number. The version number of most software can be divided into four segments, like A.B.C.D, each segment is represented by an integer, and the four segments are separated by a decimal point, such as 1.0.12.1223, and their meaning is as follows:

- Segment A is the main version number: When any important feature is to be added or any feature is to be revised, or when there is backward incompatible change, the Segment A number usually increases by 1. When this number is "0", it means that the software is not yet fully functional and has not been officially released.
- Segment B is the minor version number: It represents the enhancement of some existing features, and the features must be downward compatible.
- Segment C is a revised version: It means that there are only minor changes, for example, some defects are corrected.
- Segment D is usually a custom section, which can be agreed by team members.

In order to facilitate communication with users, the ID of certain software may contain more information. For example, when you visit the packaging page of GoCD, you will see the information as shown in Figure 11.4 in the tab Artifacts.

Figure 11.4 shows that GoCD uses its own software package ID as its file name. Moreover, a lot of useful information can be obtained from the file name. For example, the name of the software, release year and month, minor revision number, as well as build number and corresponding operating system.

Not every software must abide by such rules, but every software should have similar rules as clearly as possible in order to achieve version self-identification and self-interpretation, thereby reducing communication costs and improving communication efficiency.

11.2.3.2 Source

The source information of software package mainly indicates where it comes from, that is, the location of the corresponding program code that corresponds to the Universal Resource Identifier (URI) address, branch name, and RevisionID of the source codebase. Many pieces of software directly include their RevisionID in the codebase into its package name or version number.

As an example, when you visit GoCD website https://build.gocd.org, at the bottom of the page, you can see information similar to Figure 11.5. The string of numbers "18.4.0 (6600-f3e5401fb... c3cdc62a28)" behind "Go Version" is the full version number of the software package, and its format is

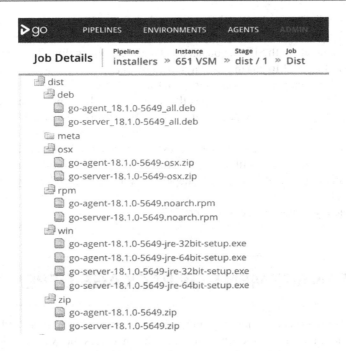

FIGURE 11.4 Example of package naming.

YY.MM.N (buildID-RevisionID). "YY" indicates the year, "MM" indicates the month, and "N" indicates the *n*-th revision in the month. "buildID" is the build number generated by its deployment pipeline, and "RevisionID" is that of the corresponding program code in the codebase.

11.2.3.3 Dependency

Most software products are not built from scratch, but increasingly relying on third-party packages to increase the speed of development. This has directly increased the complex dependencies between packages. Generally speaking, packages have three types of dependencies: build-time dependency, test-time dependency, and run-time dependency.

Build-time dependency refers to the third-party packages used in the process of building a software package with source code. For example, when developing a Java application, you need dependency in Classpath to compile your code. This kind of dependency is caused by referencing a certain "external class or method" in the program source code, for example, directly calling a method provided in an external package, similar to the way of reference.call().

In the world of Java, there are various log libraries, such as Apache log4j, logback, and SLF4j. Among them, SLF4j provides an abstraction layer, and the library that really provides log implementation is other log libraries. For example, when an application uses SLF4j, the usage mode in the program file is as follows:

```
logger.debug("Processing trade with id: {} and symbol : {} ", id, symbol);
```

Copyright © 2018ThoughtWorks, Inc. Licensed underApache License, Version 2.0.
Go includesthird-party_software. Go Version: 18.4.0 (6600-f3e5401fb04e2e732835628b134bb6c3cdc62a28).

FIGURE 11.5 Source information of the software package run by GoCD.

In order to use SLF4j, Classpath not only needs to point to the API jar package of SLF4j (such as slf4j-api-1.6.1.jar) but also needs to have the log implementation class library that you are using. For example, if you use Log4J to cooperate with SLF4j, you need to put the following three Jar files (slf4j-api-1.7.21.jar, slf4j-log4j12-1.7.21.jar, log4j-1.2.16.jar) in the search path of Classpath. At this point, the package you are building has build-time dependency on these three packages.

Test-time dependency refers to the packages that need to be relied upon when automation tests are compiling or running. For example, we need to use testing frameworks such as JUnit, and other test supporting tools.

Run-time dependency refers to the packages necessary for running in production. These dependency packages must be put into in the class library search directory (Classpath) that your program can locate. The .so file in C++ language is a typical run-time dependency. It is not included in your package, but must exist and can be found at runtime.

So, how to efficiently manage these dependencies?

11.3 MANAGEMENT OF PACKAGE DEPENDENCY

The dependencies between packages are their innate characteristic. "Reusability" and "convenience" are the source of these dependencies. We cannot eliminate dependencies, but we can adopt some means to minimize the negative impact of dependence as much as possible. What is proper management of package dependencies? A simple measuring standard is like this: is it possible to generate a finished software package with one click just by checking out the files (or script files) from code repository?

In order to manage package dependencies properly, we should keep eyes on three aspects: explicit declaration of dependencies, automatic management of dependencies, and reduction of complex dependencies.

11.3.1 Explicit Declaration of Dependencies

Explicit declaration of dependencies means that the packages and corresponding version information required by an application in environments for different purposes (such as building, testing, pre-production, or production) are explicitly recorded in files through a pre-agreed descriptive approach (such as build script).

Most programming languages have their corresponding build and packaging tools, and they usually rely on a build file. The package dependencies required by a piece of software are described in the specified format of the corresponding tool and saved in the build files of the project. For example, in a Java project, the default build file is pom.xml for Maven, and build.gradle for Gradle. The following code is a fragment of dependency declaration for a Java project using Maven to manage two log packages:

```
<dependency>
  <groupId>org.slf4j</groupId>
  <artifactId>slf4j-api</artifactId>
  <version>1.7.21</version>
</dependency>
<dependency>
  <groupId>org.slf4j</groupId>
  <artifactId>slf4j-log4j12</artifactId>
  <version>1.7.21</version>
</dependency>
```

The unique ID (groupId-artifactId-version) of each log package in Maven repository is explicitly declared.

Test-time dependency could also be described in text format. For example, for the application Ruby on Rails (referred to as "RoR application" for short), we can use Capstrano, a deployment management tool, to manage test-time dependency. The following is a fragment of a deployment file for a RoR application, declaring the software packages with test-time dependency:

```
...
group :test do
  gem "rspec ", "~> 2.7.0"
  gem "rspec-rails", "~> 2.7.0"
  gem 'factory_girl', '4.2.0'
  gem 'factory_girl_rails', '4.2.0'
  gem 'minitest', '5.10.0'
  gem 'mocha', '1.3.0'
  gem 'spork', '0.9.1'
  gem 'database_cleaner', '~> 1.6.0'
end
...
```

Among them, group: test contains a set of package dependency declarations, indicating that the automation tests of the application in the testing environment and needs to rely on these packages, and each package has the required version number explicitly specified. For example, the package Rspec required should use a version above 2.7.0.

When we put all the files that declare package dependencies into the software's own codebase, and manage them as source code, the versioning of package dependencies is realized.

So far, we have established the correspondence between the application and the packages it depends on, as shown in Figure 11.6. So, in actual work, how to connect them easily and apply them efficiently?

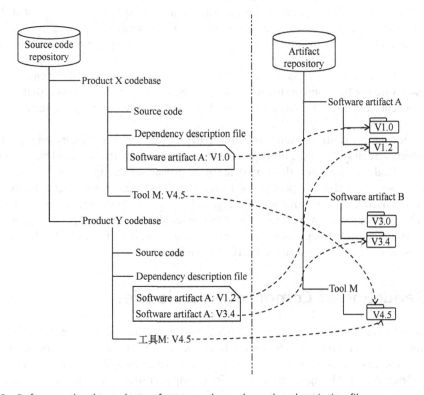

FIGURE 11.6   Reference the dependent software package through a description file.

11.3.2 Automatic Management of Dependencies

With the explicit declaration of dependencies, when we build, test, or deploy the applications that we've developed, as long as there are tools that identify the information in the package dependency description file, we can automatically download and update these packages from repositories. For example, regarding the Gradle used in a Java project, the build.gradle file contains not only the description of package dependency but also the URI of the repository. The fragment of the build.gradle file using Gradle is as follows:

```
01.   apply plugin: 'java'
02.
03.   repositories {
04.   maven {
05.       url "http://repo.mycompany.com/maven2"
06.   }
07.   }
08.   dependencies {
09.      compile group: 'org.hibernate', name: 'hibernate-core', version:
10.   '3.6.7.Final' testCompile group: 'junit', name: 'junit', version: '4.+'
11.      runtime "org.groovy:groovy:2.2.0@jar"
12.   }
```

From this build file, we can learn that there is a public repository whose access address is http://repo.mycompany.com/maven2, and Grade will look for the dependency package required by the application. At the same time, the file also clearly shows the source compilation, test compilation, runtime dependency packages, and their IDs required by the software.

The tool, which identifies the build file and automatically downloads and updates a package, is also a software, so we should also perform version management and explicit declaration of it. Just like the tool M in Figure 11.6, we put the description information of the dependency management tool required by the software application in the code repository, and put the corresponding package in the artifacts repository.

By parity of reasoning, we can manage the tools and packages used for compiling, building, and testing software applications in this way. Now, we basically achieve the goal that "as long as the product code is checked out from the source codebase, a complete software application can be built with one click".

After employing this strategy, even if the third-party private server is lost, as long as we've had the source repository, we can still find the third-party software information that we need based on the description information, and recreate a new third-party software private server repository.

Slightly different from the Java project, the package used in the C/C++ project consists of two parts. The header file is used for compilation and linking, and the .so dynamic library file is used for runtime calls. Google's open-source software Bazel also uses explicit declaration of dependency. For example, in the process of compilation, the dependency calculation needs to be done first, which relies on the declaration of the hdrs, srcs, and deps fields in the BUILD file defined by it.

11.3.3 Reduction of Complex Dependencies

When developing an application, the readymade framework and components can reduce the workload and shorten the time to market. This is like building a house, we will buy readymade doors and windows from suppliers instead of making them ourselves. However, this is where the risk of package dependency arises. Simple dependency does not bring too much risk. For example, software A depends on software packages B and C, while B and C have no dependencies at all. However, when there are too many dependencies and multi-level chain dependencies, thus forming an intricate network structure, the resolution of dependencies will become extremely difficult, there are even fatal errors that can't be resolved.

In addition to storing and retrieving packages, the package repository should provide a capability that can check the dependencies of each software package and identify the dependency problems, risks, and hidden dangers, such as too many dependencies, over-long chains, dependency conflict, or circular dependency. A healthy dependency graph should be a directed acyclic graph, and each node should be a combination of package name and specific version number.

DEPENDENCY MANAGEMENT PLATFORM

There was a large-scale Internet system in C/C++ language jointly developed, built, and maintained by thousands of people. This system was split into many small service units (or known as "microservices"), and the 1,000-person team was divided into multiple sub-teams, each responsible for several service modules. Different service modules had different development and maintenance cycles, but the operation of the entire system and different sub-teams needed to be coordinated. To this end, the company built a software package dependency management platform. Before each service module was released, developers had to login this platform to enter the module information, including its module name and 3-digit version number (such as "A_1.1.1"), the changed feature set, and the upstream module name and 3-digit version number on which it depends. In this way, through this platform, developers were able to query the dependencies of each package.

As shown in Figure 11.7, Engine depends on two Util packages (Histogram_Util and Pie_Util), while the software packages Printer and Reporter depend on Engine. This constitutes a directed acyclic graph. Also in this figure, Engine 7.2.1 depends on Histogram_Util 2.1.1 and Pie_Util 4.2.1, and the three versions of Reporter (1.7.1, 1.7.2, and 2.0.1) all use Engine 7.2.1.

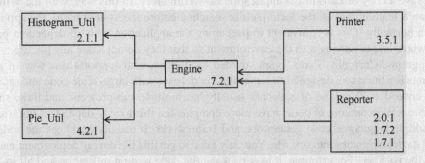

FIGURE 11.7 Directed acyclic dependency graph.

There are three main categories of common package dependency problems that need to be resolved, and the goal is to simplify dependencies as much as possible.

11.3.3.1 Too many dependencies or over-long chains

When a software package depends on too many software packages (see Figure 11.8), it is neither convenient for installation and deployment nor conducive to platform migration. When you install an application, the system prompts you to install package A first, but when you try to do so, the system prompts you to install package B. This a long chain of dependencies can be resolved by a package manager that automatically resolves all dependencies. For example, the default installation package managers of many operating systems are capable of doing so.

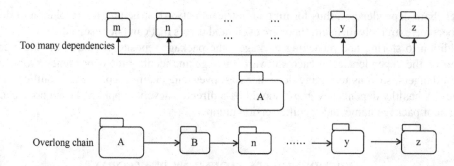

FIGURE 11.8   Too many dependencies or over-long chains.

11.3.3.2 Dependency conflict

When packages A and B are to be run on the same machine, A depends on the version V1.1 of *m*, while B depends on the version V1.2 of *m*; however, the two different versions of *m* cannot be installed on the same machine, which causes a dependency conflict, as shown in Figure 11.9.

There are two ways to resolve such dependency conflict:

1. Try to make two different versions of dependent packages to run in the same box. This kind of dependency conflict is often seen in DLL file dependencies of older versions of Windows. However, since Windows 2000 came out, the concept of Windows file protection was introduced. In addition to preventing applications from overwriting the system's own dynamic link library .dll files, developers are also encouraged to use their own "dedicated DLLs", that is, to save a copy of DLL in the application's own directory. In this way, with the Windows path search feature (that is, the local path is searched before the system path), the application can run normally. This is equivalent to packaging the application with all dependent packages as a whole and deploying it to the environment so that they do not share any packages with other programs. Currently, Pants, open sourced by Twitter, also supports this way of packaging. Pants is a build tool designed to serve those codebases with large-scale code and rapid increase in code size. This kind of codebase usually has multiple sub-projects, and these sub-projects share a large amount of code, have more complicated third-party dependent libraries, and use multiple languages, code generators, and frameworks. It usually packages the codebase with all its dependencies into one file. You only need to get this file during deployment and use it out of the package. For example, it may package the code written in Python and all its dependent packages into a PEX file. Pants currently supports Java, Scala, Python, C/C++, Go, JavaScript/ Node, Thrift, Protobuf, and Android code.

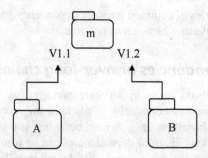

FIGURE 11.9   Dependency conflict.

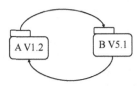

FIGURE 11.10 Circular dependency.

2. Split the dependencies. By changing the code, packages A and B will depend on the same version of package *m*. For example, upgrade the dependency of package A on mV1.1 to depend on mV1.2, as shown in Figure 11.9.

11.3.3.3 Circular dependency

If A depends on B and must be run under a specific version of the latter, and B in turn depends on A and must also run under a specific version of A, then any upgrade to one of these packages will break the other, as shown in Figure 11.10.

There are two ways to resolve circular dependency:

1. Split dependency. Analyze and transform software packages A and B, and split them into one or more dependent sub-packages, so that the original software packages will depend on the separated sub-packages, thereby breaking the cycle and forming a chain, as shown in Figure 11.11. Although the figure shows that the sub-package A.c is separated from package A, in actual work, another sub-package may be separated from package B, or there may be re-conduct A and B, or a combination them together. Which way should be used depends on the actual context and code logic.
2. Use step-wise upgrading method every time you upgrade software packages. In other words, first use the version V5.1 of B to build the new version V1.3 of A, and then use the latter to build the new version of B, thus upgrading them alternately in a stepwise manner, as shown in Figure 11.12.

In Subsection 11.1.3, the software stack is divided into three layers, they are from top to bottom "application software layer", "standard software layer", and "basic operating system layer". So far, the first half of this chapter discusses the package management of the application layer, the following sections go on to discussing the package management of the other two layers, that is, standard software layer and basic operating system layer.

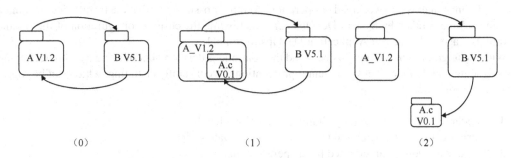

FIGURE 11.11 Resolve circular dependency by splitting.

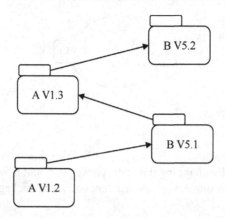

FIGURE 11.12 Step-wise upgrading.

11.4 MANAGEMENT OF ENVIRONMENTAL INFRASTRUCTURE MANAGEMENT

Basic operating system layer and standard software layer, which are the basic context for the operation of application software, are also known as "environmental infrastructure" which is characterized by low change frequency. According to the first principle of configuration management "everything has a version", we also need to perform version management of these two layers. The demand for this part of management gradually becomes stronger with the development of Continuous Delivery and DevOps. In recent years, the development of related support tools has also made it more recognized and valued.

11.4.1 Four States of Environment Previsioning

When employing the traditional mode, most production environments are handled by dedicated operation teams. For companies with a large number of servers in production, these operation personnel belong to the same department, such as the technical operation department (referred to as the DevOps department for short). Due to a large number of servers and business complexities, the management of production is respectively undertaken the personnel engaged in System DevOps and Application DevOps. Among them, the former is responsible for the basic operating system layer, while the latter is responsible for the application software layer. As for the standard software layer, it may be taken over by either one depending on different contexts and workload of operation. Another possibility is that the installation of standard software package is taken by System DevOps personnel, while the custom configuration of the standard software package is the duty of Application DevOps personnel.

With the upgrading of product business and the continuous development of infrastructure technology, the work content and mode of environmental preparation are constantly changing, which can be roughly divided into four states:

1. "Wilderness" characterized by "human brain + handwork".
2. "Normalization" characterized by "document + private script".
3. "Standardization" characterized by "paperless officing".
4. "Automation" characterized by "controlled automated code".

11.4.1.1 *"Wilderness" featured by "human brain + handwork"*

When a software company is just founded, its deployment is usually at the level of handwork: there are neither complicated requirements for software nor a great number of users and customers, and the operation work is not yet a focus of the company. The characteristics of this stage are as follows:

1. Developers themselves can solve all the problems related to software deployment.
2. All the knowledge related to environmental preparation exists in the minds of individual key developers. They are backbone of their team and "heroes" of deployment.

11.4.1.2 *"Normalization" characterized by "document + private script"*

With the success of software, and increasing number of users and customers, and more software requirements will fly over like snowflakes. Since the number of services has also increased due to mounting requests, more work needs to be done for maintenance.

By this time, the backbone team members may run round in circles, so this repetitive work must be transferred to others. As a result, certain team members, are assigned to take care of this job, namely, DevOps personnel. This stage has the following manifestations:

1. A formal deployment document is required. An environmental preparation guide is usually summarized. Every time the software is deployed, developers will also submit an online operation instruction, detailing the online steps of the software, which will be executed by the DevOps personnel. In a startup, the back-end service preparation document (see Table 11.1) has 11 major steps, and each step contains many sub-steps, and a full version of this document has more than a dozen pages. Compared with other startups, this team probably has done a good job in software engineering management. However, the reality is that in many teams, you can't find such a document. Even if it is found, it is probably too outdated to be used.

   Whenever a release of the software is coming, the DevOps personnel always ask the developers for an updating instruction, and it must be clear and precise without missing a word. The common practice of developers at this time is to revise the document written last time and hand it over to the DevOps personnel.
2. There is a standardized deployment process. At this stage, the characteristic of operation work is to establish a collaborative order manually and record each operation in detail, as shown in Figure 11.13.
3. Use private scripts to improve individual work efficiency. In this process, with the development of companies and enrichment of features, we also need to continuously upgrade the software. During each upgrade, some operations will be repeated again and again. The DevOps personnel capable of scripting will spontaneously use shell or other scripting languages to make automated execution.

   Each time of software update, operators may pick up a few of those automation scripts and modify a few lines of code for some config items (because the purpose of each update is different), and then execute them. During the execution of these scripts, the operators might occasionally stop to manually check whether the execution results of these scripts are correct, and then go on to the subsequent steps. These scripts have greatly reduced the labor intensity of operation and maintenance. However, the scripts are usually kept by the DevOps personnel personally, since they facilitate individuals and are not fully incorporated into the corporate assets and put into the code repository for versioning. After any personnel leave the team, some information and tools may be lost.

   This is usually applicable in scenarios with few running machines, uncomplicated environment, and low-release frequency. It is also an important work mode of early DevOps personnel.

Single operation record			
Date	Operator	Operated module	Operation record (difference from the benchmark module)

Summarized inconsistencies in a week		
Module	Benchmark module	Difference from the benchmark module

FIGURE 11.13　Record form of operation and maintenance.

Many companies are still in this state, as shown in Figure 11.14. The industry attaches great importance to the procedural and operational compliance of the production release process, but without technical support, the release process is mostly subject to manual operations, which are painful for both developers and DevOps personnel. And a long release process is prone to cause problems.

After a new version is finished, developers must first prepare a bunch of documents to deploy it into production (the operation steps must be completely mechanized and copied and pasted step by step to complete the deployment). It could take half a month to write documents, then everyone will attend a review meeting and organize drills over and over again before this new version goes live:

The challenges to be encountered at this stage are as follows:

1. The process is maintained by "human", and there are often omissions.
2. Documents are tracked through "email", which is inconvenient to look up.
3. The audit workload is heavy. Due to a large amount of manual work, people often bypass this process.
4. The automated scripts are not standardized and unified, and scattered with mistakes, which may interrupt the deployment process.

11.4.1.3 "Standardization" characterized by "paperless officing"

As result of increasingly mature software development and expansion of companies, the size of operation team has been on the rise, and the deployment incidents in production are mounting. That's why the call for strengthening management and control of operation is growing stronger. With more and more DevOps engineers coming to the fore, an automation operation platform has emerged.

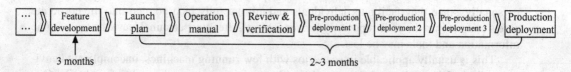

FIGURE 11.14　Schematic diagram of the online process of a financial company.

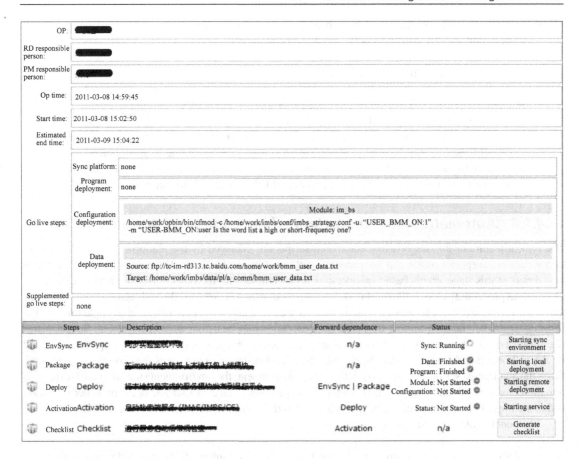

FIGURE 11.15   UI of an operation platform for office automation.

The "automation platform" at this time usually appears in the form of "paperless officing", that is, the online deployment document that was originally filled out offline has become a form that is filled out and saved on a Web page, known as "fill an issue automatically". In fact, it is just an electronic form to write deployment document and operation record.

Certain operation platforms, which are doing better in this regard, are able to automate some simple steps by scripting them in a custom language and run them automatically. However, for those complicated operations, developers are still needed to describe them in the Web form textually, and DevOps personnel will execute them manually.

Another manifestation of standardization is that all the original norms are fully consolidated to the platform to become specific implementation standards. DevOps personnel do not need to ask developers to confirm, but check by themselves on the platform, click "Confirmed" if they are qualified or click "Refuse" if they not, and leave a message. Then developers would receive a notification from the platform, revise the forms, and check "send" again on the platform. Figure 11.15 is a UI screenshot of an operation platform as paperless officing automation.

The benefits of this platform are as follows:

- Fixed workflow on the platform. The interaction and collaboration between developers and DevOps personnel are unified on the same platform, and their collaboration process is under control.
- Unified standards for some contents. For example, simple deployment operations can be automatically executed by the platform through template configuration.

- Partially reusable. Reduce workload through various config items.
- Easier auditing. All information is stored on the platform.

There are also some challenges at this stage:

- Manual participation is still required because of many complicated operations.
- It is still difficult to compare the differences between the two deployments. Although developers can copy a previously used deployment step lists each time when they ask for a new deployment, all lists are stored in the platform's own storage, and each one is an independent copy, thereby saving lots of repetitive data. If you want to compare the differences between the two deployments, you must log in to the platform and look for them with the naked eye.

11.4.1.4 *"Automatic state" characterized by "controlled automation script"*

The typical feature of this stage is that automated scripts are managed by the platform, that is, all automation scripts are corporate assets and are recorded and saved by the platform. There are two forms of operation scripts at this stage: one is based on operational procedures, and the other is based on state declaration. Operational procedural script is the most traditional method, which is executed through automation commands that simulate manual steps. Its main feature is that when automation scripts are executed multiple times in the same environment, the environment state after each execution may be inconsistent or erroneous. State declarative scripts refer to the target state of the environment specified in the scripts, and these scripts are executed by the platform that defines the state declaration specification. Its main feature is that no matter how many times the automation scripts are executed in the same environment, the environment state after each execution remains consistent, which is the so-called "idempotent operation". The characteristic of idempotence operation is that the impact of a program executed multiple times is the same as the impact of one execution.

The benefits of procedural scripts are as follows:

- In line with the original thinking habits. It is enough to implement the original manual operation steps in a scripting language.
- Flexible. No matter what kind of operation you want to do, almost all manual operations can be performed by the procedural scripts without any constraints.

But they also have a shortcoming: calling for lots of energy in management. Two things must be known before execution: one is the original state of the system before these scripts are executed, and the other is what specific operations are done to execute these scripts. Moreover, multiple executions of the same automation scripts in the same environment may eventually leave the environment in an "unknown" state.

The benefits of state declarative scripts are as follows:

- It can be clearly known that no matter who executes these scripts under any circumstances, the system will eventually reach the same state.
- By putting these scripts into the codebase, you can directly compare the differences between the two deployments.

But they also have shortcomings in two aspects:

- A high learning cost. In fact, these state declarative scripts are in a domain-specific language (DSL), which is used to describe the exclusive operation and state in the operation domain of provisioning.
- Hard to manage files in case of a large number of declarative texts. For example, as a code file, such declaration does not have an integrated development environment similar to a high-level programming language, and it is relatively difficult to refactor and debug.

TABLE 11.2 Ratings of various tools on GitHub

REPOSITORY	WATCHES	STARS	FORKS
puppetlabs/puppet	501	4,778	1,958
chef/chef	432	5,137	2,132
saltstack/salt	582	8,374	3,908
Ansible/ansible	1,788	27,218	9,776

At the time of writing the book, the mainstream state declarative tools include Puppet, Chef, Ansible, and SaltStack. All of them are open-source tools on GitHub, and they also have commercial versions. Their ratings as of December 2017 are shown in Table 11.2.

The operating modes of these four tools are slightly different, which can be divided into "pull mode" and "push mode".

- The characteristic of "pull mode" is that an agent must be installed on the target machine in advance, and a "heartbeat" connection with the server must be maintained. The agent on the target machine sends a request command to the control server, and the server packages the relevant deployment information and sends it to the target machine for execution. Puppet and Chef belong to this operating mode.
- The "Push mode" means that the target machine doesn't need to install with an agent in advance. As long as the target machine list is set on the control end and the permission of the machine is given, the control end can send the environment deployment request to the target machine and complete the deployment. Ansible and SaltStack belong to this operating mode.

In addition, there is a type of application deployment tools (such as Capstrano and Fabric) that are usually used for the deployment at the application software layer (the third layer). Such tools can provide convenience for the deployment of applications written in a specific programming language. For example, Capistrano adopts the design philosophy of "customary convention is better than configuration", which is more friendly to Web applications developed with the Ruby On Rails.

11.4.2 DSL Application

All the above tools have their own defined DSL. Using DSL, you can write a text file describing the required environment deployment state. This file can be interpreted and executed automatically by the tools themselves, and it is also highly readable. Let's take Puppet and Ansible as examples for explanation:

First of all, let's briefly describe how Puppet manages the apache2 service, and take it as an example. The following code fragment is part of the content of the environment configuration file:

```
01.  ...
02.  class apache2 {
03.      exec { 'apt-update':
04.          command => '/usr/bin/apt-get update'  # command this resource
     will run
05.      }
06.
07.      package { 'apache2':
08.          require => Exec['apt-update'],          # require 'apt-update'
     before installing
```

```
09.            ensure => installed,
10.        }
11.
12.      service { 'apache2':
13.            ensure => running,
14.        }
15.  }
16.  ...
17.  node ' host1 . example . com ' {
18.            include apache2
19.  }
20.  ...
```

In this fragment of code, the lines 2~15 declare an apache2 service class and define the service to first execute the command "apt-get update", then install apache2, and ensure it could be started and run. Lines 17~19 indicate that the defined apache2 is installed on host1.exmaple.com.

The syntax of Ansible is as follows:

```
01.  ---
02.  - hosts: webservers
03.    vars:
04.      http_port: 80
05.      max_clients: 200
06.      remote_user: root
07.    tasks:
08.    - name: ensure apache is at the latest version
09.      yum: pkg=httpd state=latest
10.    - name: write the apache config file
11.      template: src=/srv/httpd.j2 dest=/etc/httpd.conf
12.      notify:
13.      - restart apache
14.    - name: ensure apache is running
15.      service: name=httpd state=started
16.    handlers:
17.    - name: restart apache
18.      service: name=httpd state=restarted
```

The above information means that the latest version of httpd (service name of apache) is installed on the machine named "webservers", and the file/srv/httpd.j2 is used as the config file of this service and copied to/etc/httpd.conf, and this file is to serve as a new config to restart the apache Web service.

I'm not going to explain the specific usage of each tool, but the above two examples show that each tool defines its own DSL and is very powerful and easy to use. What is the difference between this DSL-based automation specification and a shell script written by an individual?

This type of tools has defined a DSL for environment provision. Programming grammar usually aims to describe the intent (that is, what state the system should have after the environment is prepared), so that all scripts must follow the same DSL, thus reducing the difficulty in understanding scripts and the complexity of maintenance, and making it easier for knowledge sharing.

11.4.3 Infrastructure as Code

Now, we can describe a series of preparations for the environmental infrastructure in scripts and execute them automatically. For engineers, environmental infrastructure is no longer a bunch of machines with network cables, but a "programmable environment". This is commonly referred to as "infrastructure as code". The advantages of doing so are as follows:

- No matter what kind of environment (build, test, production) goes wrong, we can quickly and automatically build a brand-new environment.
- As long as authorized, anyone can complete this task without the needs of others.
- Any changes on an environment can be recorded and audited.
- For different environments, as long as the code is compared, we can understand their differences without having to log in to the actual host to check.

In order to obtain the above benefits, the version management of environmental infrastructure should include:

- Operating system name, version number, patch version number, and system-level configuration.
- The third-party software of all middleware layers that the software package depends on, their corresponding version number, and configuration.
- The external services and their version numbers that need to interact with the application, and the configuration they need.

All the above three points involve the configuration of the application itself. In the subsequent section, we will focus on the management of application config.

11.5 MANAGEMENT OF SOFTWARE CONFIGURATION ITEMS

In this section, the "software configuration items" mean that when the software is built or running in different environments, by setting different specific values corresponding to these configuration items, the software can produce different behaviors.

11.5.1 Separation of Binary and Configuration

A software package usually consists of binaries and config items. A binary is usually compiled and packaged from source code. As a whole, once generated, it remains immutable. During the build process, other packages that it depends on (some people often call it "libraries" or "components") may be integrated into the final binary in some way. Although the program formed by some scripting languages does not require the step of "compiling", as long as it is the final product and provides a set of related functions, it can be regarded as an indivisible whole.

Configuration items are a set of configurable variables independent of the binary. According to the different values of each configuration item, the binary can run in different operating environments and may produce different behaviors. Configuration items usually exist in different forms. A binary obtains specific information about the configuration from files, databases, system environment variables, or process startup parameters.

Modifications to any of the configuration items will form a new two-tuple composed of a binary and a new set of configuration items, and can be regard as a new deployment package. Therefore, whether it is a code change or a config change, we can regard it as one deployment, as shown in Figure 11.16.

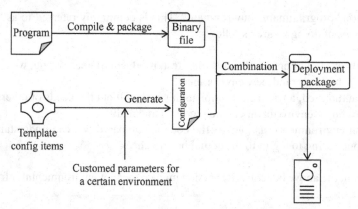

FIGURE 11.16   Separation of binary and configuration.

When we separate the binary from the configuration, we can build the binary once and reuse it at different stages of the deployment pipeline. This can ensure that the binaries that we verify at different stages of the deployment pipeline are exactly the same, but configs with different values are used for different environments.

11.5.2 Version Management of Configuration

Different config is needed when the package is built and run. According to the content of the config, it can be divided into the following three categories:

- Environment config: The corresponding value of this configuration item is related to the environment in which it runs and is often bound to the definition of the environment itself, such as the domain name (or IP address), the service address, and the port for communicating with other systems or services.
- Application config: This type of config is related to health of the application, such as account password, initial allocated memory size, database connection pool size, and log level. It also includes the config of the program itself. For example, in a Java project using the Spring framework, different ApplicationContext.xml is loaded according to different purposes, so that different Beans are used.
- Business config: This type of config is related to the business behavior, and each config is set with a default value, such as feature toggles, or the commodity pricing strategy in the e-commerce system.

According to the time of use, these config can be divided into build-time, deployment-time, and run-time. Configs at build time and deployment time are equivalent to static variables, usually some configs related to the environment. Run-time configuration items are parameters that can be dynamically adjusted. The program will produce different behaviors based on different parameter values, usually the parameters related to technical performance (such as cache size), or the parameters related to business strategies such as discount ratio (see Figure 11.17).

It is generally not recommended to inject environment config at build time. If config is injected into the binary at build time, the binary and the environment config will be bound together. If different environments need different configs, we have to repackage, which can neither meet the requirements of "a set of programs, multi-environment deployment" nor ensure "consistent binaries to be tested in all environments", the quality risk will increase and flexibility will be compromised.

	Build-time (static configuration)	Deployment-time (static configuration)	Run-time (dynamic configuration)
Environment		Data source address Registry address Configuration center address	
Application	application.xml of Spring	Account password & Token license	Cache size
Business			Discount strategy Red pack helper

FIGURE 11.17   Classification of config items.

We can customize version management strategies for different types of config. Static config could be in VCS. For example, in a back-end service of an Internet company, in order to efficiently manage all configs and prevent the omission of configs between different environments in the entire research and development (R&D) process, the related static config and the source code will be in the same repository with different directories for different environment configs, as shown in Figure 11.18.

However, this way cannot be fully applied to dynamic runtime config. Usually, the dynamic config is modified frequently at runtime. When a config is adjusted, the software behavior will also change accordingly. For example, some systems are capable of scaling up or down, which are essentially a config change. According to SCM, we need to perform versioning on runtime config to facilitate auditing and debugging. Also, the config changes could usually be recorded in a log or CMDB for subsequent problem diagnosis and operation audit.

11.5.3 Storage of Configuration Items

Currently, there are many ways to store configs, the easiest way is to use text files. We can write a text file for each type of operating environment, as shown in Table 11.3. It is easier to do versioning and auditing by committing into code repository. It should be noted that some sensitive information (such as passwords) cannot be placed in code repository without encryption. If the host system is a distributed service, the config needs to be synchronized on different nodes. How to keep consistency of config and validify synchronized update is a challenge. Usually, another service will help distribute it.

We can also store the config into database or registry, all of which can be accessed remotely. The security permissions are relatively easy to manage with them. However, with those tools, the team has to deal with change histories by themselves.

At present, there are many open-sourced applications that can provide configuration management, such as ZooKeeper and etcd. To be noted that, you should pay attention to versioning and auditing. Sometimes you have to do it by yourself.

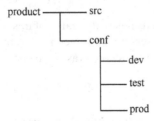

FIGURE 11.18   Static config items are of the same source as the product source code.

TABLE 11.3　Plaintext file of configuration

OPERATING ENVIRONMENT	FILE
Shared configuration	global.cong.php
Development environment	dev.cong.php
foo idc	foo.cong.php
bar idc	bar.cong.php
Environment mapping file (soft link)	env.cong.php

11.5.4 Configuration Drift and Governance

"Configuration drift" means that refers as the time goes by, the config changes made for various unexpected reasons have caused computer or software service to deviate from the desired configuration state. It is a common phenomenon in production. This is usually caused by people's temporary modification. Someone logs in to a machine to modify the service log level in order to debug, and forgets to restore it afterward; or someone temporarily changes the network config of a machine in order to alleviate an emergency event in production. When the configuration drift occurs, the production environment is often in an uncertainty state and may even cause major accidents.

Due to the large number of online and offline hardware and software, configuration drift takes place in many data centers. In disaster recovery and high-availability system failures, configuration drift accounts for the majority of failures. The phenomenon of unknown configuration drift puts organizations at high risk of data loss and extended outages.

> **TYPICAL SCENARIO OF CONFIGURATION DRIFT:**
> **CONFIGURATION MODIFICATION WITHOUT A RECORD**
>
> Bob has been doing an internship in a company for more than six months. He is often praised by company leaders for his good performance. Two months ago, Martin, one of his colleagues, resigned and needed to hand over his work. One of the tasks was to maintain a Web service without huge traffic. Bob was designated as the one to take over the maintenance task.
>
> With a lot of work in hands, Bob didn't spend much time on the maintenance. He just took a quick look at the system that was built with a certain J2EE framework and it has been running relatively stable. Recently, daily active users (DAU) had been increasing slowly. In order to cope with the increase in traffic, the leader had asked to allocate a more powerful computer to deal with it.
>
> However, since the website was migrated to the new host, it restarted every two days due to performance issues. It was very strange that the system was running stably on the original server; how could it go wrong so frequently on this powerful one? He checked DAU trend, and found no significant increase. Bob was sure that he strictly followed the migration instruction. Since he was not experienced enough, Bob sent a WeChat message to Martin who left the company, asking if he could figure out the reason. Martin sent him a brief reply saying that "Allocate more memory for JVM at startup".
>
> It turned out that before Martin resigned, the traffic of this website had been mounting continuously. They had modified the Web service startup command on the original server and increased the JVM memory, but the modification record was not recorded and the original instruction was not revised.

Good SCM can solve the issue of configuration drift. For example, you put static configuration into VCS, and prohibit directly logging in to the host environment to modify configuration. So you have to submit change to the codebase, it would be picked up to the production environment automatically. So you can avoid configuration drift due to human omissions. There is a more rigorous way, namely, "immutable infrastructure".

11.6 IMMUTABLE INFRASTRUCTURE AND CLOUD APPLICATIONS

Imagine if you are building blocks with your kid and you want to change to a different colored brick, would you recolor it? Of course not, you just need to get a block you want and replace it. Immutable Infrastructure is like a building block, which treats the three levels of the software runtime stack as a whole. When any one of the levels needs to be changed, it can only be done by replacing it as a whole (that is, removing before adding), not by updating or modifying the content directly. As an immutable infrastructure, it must meet the following three requirements:

1. Provision (including all levels) is done automatically.
2. Once provision is completed, nothing can be changed in it.
3. If it needs to be changed for some reason, it must be replaced by another one instead of changing the original one.

11.6.1 Implement Immutable Infrastructure

11.6.1.1 Physical machine mirroring technology and virtual machine mirroring technology

Both of these technologies can be used to improve the efficiency of environmental preparation. We can use mirroring tools (such as Full Automatic Installer, SystemImager, and ISO mirroring tool) to perform mirror backups of the installed application running environment, and save the mirrored files in a unified mirror repository. When you need to prepare an environment same as the original system, you can directly take out the corresponding image from the mirror repository, put it into a host, and run.

The physical machine mirroring technology is to make the content of the entire physical machine into a mirrored file, while the virtualization technology allocates the resources of the physical machine to multiple virtual machines running on it, although it may bring some performance losses, but its resource utilization rate has been greatly improved, and the convenience of provision has also been improved. Figure 11.19 shows the use process of physical image and virtual image.

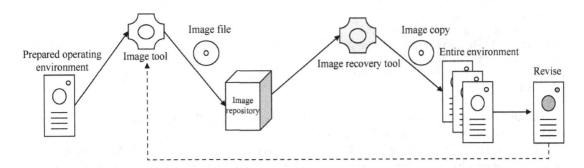

FIGURE 11.19   The process of using physical machine image and virtual machine image.

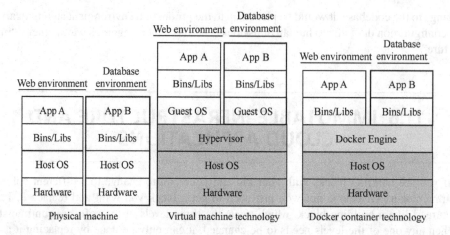

FIGURE 11.20 Differences between different mirroring technologies.

For example, the running environment of a simple Web application originally requires two physical machines, namely a Web application server and a database server. But when we use virtual machine technology, we can start two virtual machines on a physical machine to run the Web application server and database server respectively, as shown in Figure 11.20.

Make each virtual machine into a corresponding image file and save it in the image repository. When others need the same, they can run the compiled environment orchestration file to quickly prepare it in an automatic way with tools such as Vagrant. You can even find and download the basic image file you want in the public repository which Vagrant up provides, instead of making it from scratch.

Vagrant also uses text files as description files for virtual machine orchestration. The following is an example of Vagrantfile:

```
01.  Vagrant.configure("2") do |config|
02.    config.vm.box = "hashicorp/precise64"
03.    config.vm.provision :shell, path: "bootstrap.sh"
04.  end
```

Line 2 declares to use the image file named "hashicorp/precise64" in the public mirror repository; Line 3 declares to run a shell script file after the virtual machine is started, the file name is "bootstrap.sh". And bootstrap.sh file is stored in the same directory with Vagrantfile. Its content is to install the Apache server and link the/vagrant directory to the apache Web directory. The code is as follows:

```
01.  #!/usr/bin/env bash
02.
03.  apt-get update
04.  apt-get install -y apache2
05.  if ! [ -L /var/www ]; then
06.    rm -rf /var/www
07.    ln -fs /vagrant /var/www
08.  fi
```

At this point, as long as you execute the command "vagrant up", the virtual machine you need will be created and the Apache server will be ready.

However, these two mirroring technologies are not easy for code management. Before making a mirror image, you may have to install or update the fundamental system manually. If you need to modify the existing image, the cost of the change is relatively high.

11.6.1.2 Docker container technology

Virtual machine technology runs a complete set of "guest OS" on the host operating system ("host OS"), while Docker is a lighter-weight container technology that uses a part of the host operating system instead of reinstalling a set of guest operating systems, as shown in Figure 11.20.

Docker has developed rapidly since it was open sourced in 2012. It can generate an image through an orchestration file named dockerfile. More importantly, Docker images have a hierarchical design, that is, new images can be built on the basis of other images. The following piece of code shows that you can generate an environment with the Nginx server installed on basis of the basic and latest version of image Ubuntu.

```
01.  FROM Ubuntu:latest
02.  MAINTAINER Derek
03.
04.  RUN echo "deb http://archive.ubuntu.com/ubuntu/ raring main universe" >>
     /etc/apt/sources.list
05.  RUN apt-get update
06.  RUN apt-get install -y nano wget dialog net-tools
07.  RUN apt-get install -y nginx
08.  RUN rm -v /etc/nginx/nginx.conf
09.  ADD nginx.conf /etc/nginx/
10.  RUN echo "daemon off;" >> /etc/nginx/nginx.conf
11.  EXPOSE 80
12.  CMD service nginx start
```

Line 1 indicates that this new Docker image is based on the latest version (latest) of Ubuntu in the mirror repository. The maintainer of Docker file is Derek. Lines 3~7 add the package source to the sources.list in the new system and install Nginx. Lines 8~10 specify the Nginx config. Line 12 is to start the Nginx service.

Usually, the benefit that mirroring brings us is its immutability. That is, once the image is generated, it will not change. Moreover, as long as the layout file (such as the code above) used to generate the image remains unchanged, even if the image generation operation is performed multiple times using the file, the result should be unchanged.

However, in the above dockerfile, there is still a potential risk that the image may change, which stems from the first line of the layout file (base image version). In Line 1, we specify that the base image is the latest version of the Ubuntu image. At the beginning, a Nginx image was generated by the latest version that points to the Ubuntu 17.04 version in the image repository. However, the new version 17.10 of image Ubuntu was just published as the latest. Now you use the same code as above to recreate the Nginx service, it would use Ubuntu 17.10, which is different with original Nginx.

How to fix it? Can we change the first line of code to From Ubuntu:17.04 to ensure that the Nginx images built twice are exactly the same? Actually not. Because "17.04" and "17.10" are just tags for the base image, and Docker's tag can be reused or redefined. Therefore, if we want to ensure the immutability of the base image, it is best to use the unique identifier of the image, that is, a hash string generated when the image is generated, which is similar to the hash code generated when we submit the code to the Git repository, it is globally unique.

The costs of implementing Immutable Infrastructure by the upper three mirroring technologies are obviously different. The highest cost arises from the physical mirroring, followed by virtual technology, and the cost of Docker containerization technology is relatively low.

11.6.2 Cloud Native Application

With the rapid development and popularization of cloud technology, more and more companies put their services on the cloud. This greatly simplifies the time-consuming and energy-consuming preparation of infrastructure, and at the same time facilitates effective use of resources. In the development process, it is also easier to build a test environment similar to the production environment. For example, if you want to deploy a program to Heroku – one of the earliest PaaS (Platform As A Service) providers, you only need to use the "git push" command to push the program to Heroku's Git server, and it will automatically trigger installation, configuration, and deployment procedures. Heroku is an Application Hosted Service. Whenever a new version is deployed, Heroku will build a new instance and replace the old one. Such applications can be seen as a "cloud native applications".

As a pioneer of public cloud PaaS, Heroku proposed the 12 elements of "cloud native applications" in 2012, also known as the 12 principles, to tell engineers how to use the convenience provided by the cloud to develop cloud native applications that are more reliable, scalable, flexible, and easier to maintain. The 12 principles are:

1. Codebase: One codebase tracked in revision control, many deploys.
2. Dependencies: Explicitly declare and isolate dependencies.
3. Config: Store config in the environment.
4. Backing services: Treat backing services as attached resources.
5. Build, release, run: Strictly separate build and run stages.
6. Processes: Execute the app as one or more stateless processes.
7. Port binding: Export services via port binding.
8. Concurrency: Scale out via the process model.
9. Disposability: Maximize robustness with fast startup and graceful shutdown.
10. Dev/prod parity: Keep development, staging, and production as similar as possible.
11. XI. Logs: Treat logs as event streams.
12. Admin processes: Run admin/management tasks as one-off processes.

Although these principles bear traces of Heroku's product promotion, their core still indicates a software architecture conducive to Continuous Delivery, that is, the software service itself is strictly separated from the data processed by the service, making it easier to make software deployment and release based on Immutable Infrastructure. For cloud native applications, Immutable Infrastructure is a piece of cake.

11.6.3 Advantages and Challenges

This Immutable Infrastructure has seven advantages compared with provision by traditional ways:

1. Simplify operation and maintenance. A way of fully automation can be used to replace old components with newer versions to ensure that the system remains in a "known and good" state from the beginning to the end. There is no need to track component changes manually, so that it is easier to maintain a batch of running instances for us. Rollback is also easier. Technically speaking, you just take back the image of the old version automatically.
2. The deployment process is self-documenting. When the deployment is fully automated, you only need to create a declarative plaintext file that explains how to correctly generate an image of the application instead of writing a Word document, but the automation steps in the plaintext file are accurate and in detail. Moreover, as time goes by, this declarative file will not become obsolete due to negligence in synchronization, because it is always updating to date for any deployments.
3. Continuous deployment without downtime and fewer failures. All changes can be managed by code and tracked through the deployment pipeline. Every change to the infrastructure can be made in the form of code. When the new Immutable Infrastructure is ready, the original instance can be replaced directly.
4. Reduce errors and threats. Services are built on complex software stacks, and errors will always occur over time. Through automated replacement instead of reparation, we can recreate

instances more frequently and regularly. This can reduce configuration drift while maintaining or improving Service Level Agreements (SLAs).

5. Consistency of multiple types of environmental infrastructure. Virtualization and containerization technologies enable us to obtain and verify the infrastructure similar to the production in a cheaper way during development and testing, thereby reducing production issues caused by the gap between test environment and production environment.

6. Eliminate "configuration drift". After using Immutable Infrastructure, the three-tier software stack is used as a whole. If you need to modify any of the information, you must regenerate the mirror.

7. What is tested is what is used. Once the code changes are completed, an immutable base image will be generated immediately. And this image will be verified by the entire deployment pipeline, and eventually it will be either discarded due to a quality issue by verification or used in production. It is certain that the images used in production must have been verified.

Although Immutable Infrastructure has many benefits, it is not a free lunch, and it may be a huge challenge for your organization. For example:

1. Establishing a complete automation management system for Immutable Infrastructure requires high costs in the early stage.

2. The repair time for unexpected issues in the production may be slightly longer. Because in this mode, you are forbidden to directly connect to the current problematic server via SSH, and modify it. You can only change the source (may be the source code or config), submit the codebase, regenerate the image again through the deployment pipeline, and finally deploy it online. Of course, you could fix it quickly by rolling back instead.

3. For large-scale services, distributing large-size images to multiple hosts requires a lot of network resources and time, so there must be support by corresponding tools. For example, Facebook uses the BitTorrent protocol to transfer large files.

4. Stateful storage services are not easy to replace directly. We may have huge data stored in the database. It is hard to use this method for quick replacement with data.

11.7 DATA VERSION MANAGEMENT

Every software has to process data, and it is hard to conduct versioning about data. However, we can still improve the efficiency of collaboration among members in development process through versioning data, such as speeding up a test environment provision and improving the execution reliability of automation testcases.

11.7.1 Changes of Database Structure

If you use a relational database system, when the frequency of deployment becomes higher and more people involved in development process, the database schema should be versioned. In addition to auditing and debugging, it is also helpful to integration and automation testing.

From the day when a service with DB was born, whenever the schema changes, an incremental SQL script must be written and checked into the source codebase. In this way, the database can be upgraded or downgraded through tools such as Flyway or Liquibase. GoCD manages the database schema in this way since the project was started in 2007, as shown in Figure 11.21.

After we check in every change of schema, we can easily get a clean initial database when performing automation tests. If there is a defect in a historical version released to a customer, and a clean database is

1_create_initial_tables.sql	2_create_indexes.sql	3_add_build_ignored_column.sql
4_add_check_externals_column.sql	5_add_from_external_column.sql	6_add_pipeline_label.sql
7_add_pipeline_label_counters.sql	8_add_build_cause_buffer.sql	9_add_material_properties_table.sql
10_add_stage_timestamp.sql	11_add_stage_order.sql	12_add_stage_result.sql
13_add_stage_approvalType.sql	14_add_name_pipelineId_index_for_s...	15_add_name_agentId_buildid_index...
16_add_folder_to_materials.sql	17_correct_integrity_issues_in_stages...	18_change_material_properties_valu...
19_change_material_url_to_nvarchar....	20_add_artifact_properties_generator...	21_add_materialId_to_modifications....
22_remove_pipelineId_from_modific...	23_add_index_for_stages.sql	24_add_columns_for_dependency_...
25_change_length_of_revision_to_10...	26_add_table_fetch_artifact_plans.sql	27_set_not_null_on_fetch_artifact_pl...
28_drop_table_fetch_artifacts.sql	29_fix_hsqldb_migration.sql	30_add_buildcause_message_to_pip...
31_add_user_setting.sql	32_add_email_me_column.sql	33_add_unique_constraint_to_name_...
34_add_changed_column_to_modifi...	35_rename_usersettings_table.sql	36_add_notificationfilters_table.sql
37_make_the_pipeline_name_case_in...	38_make_the_stage_name_case_inse...	39_make_the_job_name_case_insens...
40_undo_pipelines_case_insensitive_...	41_add_builds_index_on_name_state...	42_add_counter_to_pipelines.sql
43_alter_modifiedFiles_fileName.sql	44_added_name_column_into_mater...	

FIGURE 11.21 Save schema changes of relational database in text script.

needed to locate the problem, you can check out the corresponding version from the repository and use these scripts to rebuild the database. If you want to upgrade a historical version to the latest version, then the tools of Flyway or Liquibase will use these scripts to help you complete this work.

11.7.2 Data File

VCS for plant text is not good at versioning binary data files. It can be managed in a way similar to File Transfer Protocol (FTP) and remote file system. For example, a company has a large file storage system. You can upload a large file to the system, and it will return a unified URI. So, engineers submit text file with the URI into the code repository. In this way, the data and source code will have the same VCS. The URI is a reference, and this large file storage system is equivalent to a shared repository that stores versioned data. This method is extremely important for the management of test data.

There is another situation: when the application starts or runs with initial data that are dynamically generated by applying some algorithms to a static data set. At this point, as long as we treat the static data set as a binary file and save the algorithms in the codebase, we can also achieve the purpose of version management.

11.8 ASSOCIATION BETWEEN REQUIREMENTS AND SOURCE CODE

So far, we have discussed version control about code, package, and environment in Figure 11.1. So, if you want to associate the code with the requirement item, how should you deal with it? Although in many cases this is not a strong requirement by now, it can be achieved if you want to do so.

We can archive the requirements and associate it with the corresponding software package version. If you need more fine-grained management, you can also associate each requirement item ID (or defect ID) in the requirements platform with the code. For example, each time the code is submitted to the codebase, the ID of the requirement item is used as a part of the code submission comment, and this related

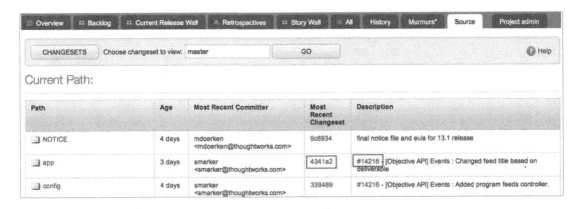

FIGURE 11.22   Association between Mingle and codebase.

information is displayed. Figure 11.22 is the display after Mingle (the agile project management tool) is associated with the codebase, where "4341a2" is the revision number in the codebase, and "#14216" is the requirement identifier corresponding to the requirement on the requirement platform.

11.9 SUMMARY

Good SCM is the cornerstone of building Continuous Delivery deployment pipelines and accelerating continuous verification loop.

This chapter discusses three core principles for SCM:

1. Versioning everything.
2. Share the True North source.
3. Standardization and automation.

The following five questions can be used to verify whether you have done version management of everything:

1. Whether source code and test code are in VCS?
2. Whether the configuration of the software application is in VCS?
3. Whether the system configuration of various environments is in VCS?
4. Whether the automation build and deployment scripts are in the VCS?
5. Whether the package is under version management?

In addition, you can also use the following two questions to check whether the SCM is done well:

1. As long as the source code is checked out from codebase, can a complete package be built automatically with one click?
2. Without the help of others, can any team member automatically setup the blooding version of application with one click to experience new features?

Low-Risk Release 12

The previous chapters mainly discuss the work in the building stage of the Fast Verification Loop. Through improvement in various aspects such as collaboration in business requirements, software configuration management (SCM), Continuous Integration (CI), and automation test, the time for feedback on development quality is shortened, and the speed of software application research and development (R&D) is increased. In this chapter, we will discuss how to deploy and release the software with high frequency and low risk, and let the software run in production as soon as possible, as shown in Figure 12.1.

The main content in deploying and running the Fast Verification Loop includes the motivation and benefits behind high-frequency release; the corresponding methods for mitigating release risks include blue-green deployment, canary release (gray release), and dark launch. The technical means supporting high-frequency release are represented by switching technique, data migration, and Branch by Abstraction.

12.1 HIGH-FREQUENCY RELEASE IS A TREND

Since the birth of the Agile Manifesto in 2001, the Agile model for software delivery has been questioned. Very few software companies in China had taken interest in it before 2007. Some information technology (IT) companies even said, "We don't need to deliver software so quickly, 'Agile' is not fit for us". Dot-com companies also rejected the Agile model, because they thought a release every two weeks in Agile model was too slow. However, the presentation of John Allspaw and Paul Hammond at 2009 Velocity about "10+ Deploys Per Day: Dev and Ops Cooperation" helped start the DevOps movement, and shed a new light on the entire software industry. It turned out that software can be released so quickly!

12.1.1 High-Frequency Release by Dot-Com Companies

Now the world's leading dot-com companies are updating their products through "frequent release". For example, as early as May 2011, Amazon's monthly statistics showed that a deployment was triggered every 11.6 seconds on average, with the highest deployment frequency reaching 1,079 times per hour that month. On average, 10,000 servers would receive deployment requests at the same time, and the highest record was that 30,000 servers were performing a deployment operation concurrently.

In 2017, Facebook pushed front-end code multiple times every day, as shown in Figures 12.2a and 12.2b. And its mobile application was pushed to the App market once a week. Its R&D process is shown in Figure 12.2c. Every day a green version was released to internal employees, while Alpha and Beta versions were respectively pushed to 100,000 and millions of users.

Of course, not all of these pushes were feature releases in Facebook, some contained bugfix. For example, according to the article *Development and Deployment at Facebook* published by Kent Beck and others in 2013 (see the contents of Facebook's daily release in Figure 12.3), we can see that 50% of its releases were related to bugfix for front-end.

DOI: 10.1201/9781003221579-12

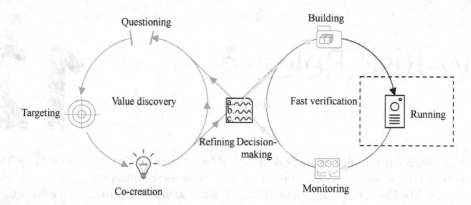

FIGURE 12.1   Deployment and running of the Fast Verification Loop.

Does that indicate that the application quality is worrying? In reference to the article *Continuous Deployment of Mobile Software at Facebook*, co-authored by Chuck Rossi and Kent Beck, as result of more frequent deployment, increasing total amount of code and times of submissions, the number of serious defects has not increased, as shown in Figure 12.4 (the horizontal axis is the times of code submissions per month, and the vertical axis is the number of defects found in production). Despite an increase in the number of defects with medium and low severity, considering more and more engineers, and more complicated systems, and company's attitude toward software quality, it is a level that Facebook was comfortable with.

Etsy is a P2P e-commerce company engaged in trading handmade products. In 2014, it had about 600,000 monthly active users and 1.5 billion page views per month, with sales of US$1.9 billion. In 2017, its product sales reached US$3.2 billion. Chapter 2 introduces its working philosophy as "continuous experimentation". The company has switched to Continuous Delivery since the end of 2009. Before that, they used the waterfall model with slow, complex, and highly customed release process. After 2010, its deployments were characterized by "fast, simple, and consistent", as listed in Table 12.1.

Etsy's each deployment contains the following contents:

1. New classes or functions added to the application software.
2. Images, style sheets, or template files on the page.
3. Content changes, etc.
4. Modified toggle or rolling out. Each deployment may be a quick response to online issues (such as security risks, defects, requests for users, or scaling up/down), or it may be patches for a config.

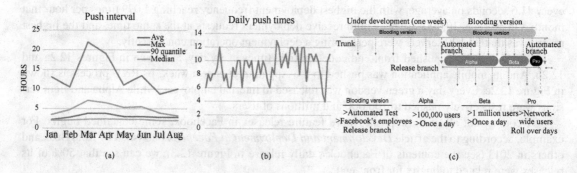

FIGURE 12.2   Facebook's deployment and release.

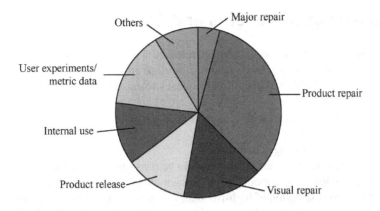

FIGURE 12.3 Content of Facebook's daily release.

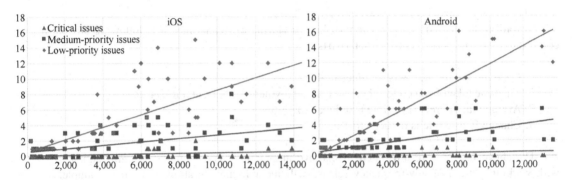

FIGURE 12.4 The function relationship between the number of defects of varied severity and monthly submission times on Android and iOS in Facebook.

TABLE 12.1 Comparison before and after Etsy implemented continuous deployment in 2010

COMPARISON ITEM	BEFORE	AFTER
Leadtime per deployment	Requires 6~14 hours of downtime for deployment	15 mins (configuration change less than 5 mins)
Staff for each deployment	A team dedicated to deployment	1 person
Deployment frequency	Deployment is the company's top priority task, highly planned, and low-frequency	30 times/day (2012), 50 times/day (2014)
Number of code contributors	N/A	170+ persons (2012)
Deployment steps	1. Create a release branch 2. Prepare for database structure changes 3. Prepare for data conversion 4. Package 5. Distribute, deploy, restart 6. Cache cleaning 7. Result	1. Use trunk code 2. Very few links and builds 3. Distribution via rsync 4. End

Source: Mike Brittain, *Continuous Delivery: The Dirty Details*, GOTO 2012 Conference.

12.1.2 Coexistence of Benefits and Costs

In high-frequency release, the amount of content released each time is usually less than that in low-frequency release (it is apparent that fewer features are done in one day than in ten days). Why are so many companies moving in the direction of high-frequency release? Because it has the following benefits:

1. More opportunities to interact with real users so as to quickly decide or adjust the direction of their products.
2. Low risks due to small changes in a shot.
3. The cost of a deployment is reduced and tends to be constant. As listed in Table 12.1, when Etsy used the large-version release model, each deployment called for a great amount of energy and time; after the implementation of high-frequency release in 2010, the energy and time required for each deployment has reduced and remains basically constant. Painful frequent deployment drives people to build a lot of automation facilities, thereby reducing costs and energy.
4. Issues are easy to debug and fix quickly.

The specific comparison is shown in Figure 12.5.

According to the 2017 DevOps report, high-performance teams have the following advantages in contrast to their low-performance counterparts:

1. Code release frequency is 46 times higher.
2. The time taken from code submission to deployment is shortened to 1/440.
3. Average failure recovery time is reduced to 1/96.
4. Change failure rate is reduced to 1/5.

The above benefits are attributed to massive automation. The mandatory high-frequency release with working pattern of low-frequency release will incur higher iteration costs. For example, a team had manual release once a month, but it decides to do it once a week immediately. Not to mention the

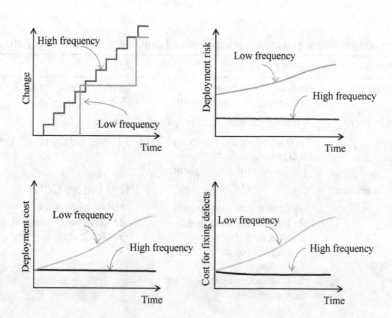

FIGURE 12.5   Comparison between high-frequency release and low-frequency release.

possible change to the quality of each release, assuming that the original manual mode is still applied, the monthly verification workload will increase by four times. Moreover, after the release cycle is shortened, the original relatively low-cost operations (such as compilation time and test work intensity) will become prominent contradictions.

No matter what, we cannot eliminate the release risk once and for all. What we have to do is continuous improvement for risk mitigation.

12.2 WAYS TO MITIGATE RELEASE RISK

Now, let's discuss some mechanism to reduce release risks, such as blue-green deployment, rolling deployment, canary release, and dark launch.

12.2.1 Blue-Green Deployment

Blue-green deployment is to prepare two identical environments, one of which is used as a formal production environment to provide external services. The other environment serves as the pre-production environment for deploying a new version of software and running acceptance tests on them. After confirming the quality of the new version, the access traffic is directed to the environment where the new version is located to make it as a formal production environment, while preserving the environment where the old version is located. Until it is certain that the new version is good, the environment for running the old version is to serve as the pre-production environment for deploying next version. As shown in Figure 12.6, "blue environment" and "green environment" are independent of each other.

Of course, this is an ideal situation. In reality, the time cost of database replication is very high, coupled with a high cost. So, usually blue-green deployment solutions use the same database, but different environments for other applications, as shown in Figure 12.7. In this case, the storage format of the same data must be compatible with the old and new versions, and the same data can be used for the operations of two versions simultaneously.

In addition, there is another issue that needs to be addressed in blue-green deployment. That is how to ensure data consistency for a user request, which is across the transaction processing. Generally speaking, switching is not done in an instant. During the process, new requests are directed to the environment for the new version, and access to the environment for the old version is no longer allowed. For those old requests with no response yet during the switch, they can keep accessing the old environment, but new requests are not allowed to do so.

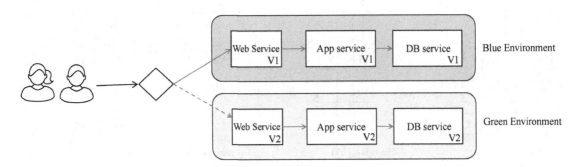

FIGURE 12.6 Blue-green deployment.

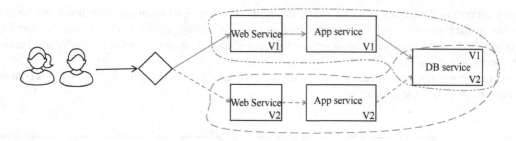

FIGURE 12.7 Blue-green deployment using the same data storage node.

12.2.2 Rolling Deployment

Rolling deployment is to select one or more instances from a cluster, stop the service and perform an update, and then put it back into use. Repeat these steps until all instances in the cluster are updated, as shown in Figure 12.8. Compared with blue-green deployment, rolling deployment saves more resources, the instances can be cut down by half.

When issues are raised with the new version, rolling deployment method cannot simply switch back as blue-green deployment; instead, the instances with the new version have to be rolled back. Another way to fix it quickly is to fix forward, which is to create a bug-patch version V3, and initiate a rolling deployment of V3 immediately. At the same time, there may be three versions as V1, V2, and V3 in production and it is common for rolling deployment.

12.2.3 Canary Release

In a general sense, canary release allows a small number of users to use the fresh version first in order to get quick feedback from real users in advance, thereby avoiding more users from being harmed.

The name "canary release" comes from an ancient practice of miners. In the 17th century, British miners happened to find that canaries are very sensitive to gas. In order to protect themselves, miners would bring a canary with them every time they went down the mine. If there is any harmful gas, the canary will die immediately before humans have any perception of it. Then miners would know there was poisonous gas in the mine, thus stop to ascend to the ground.

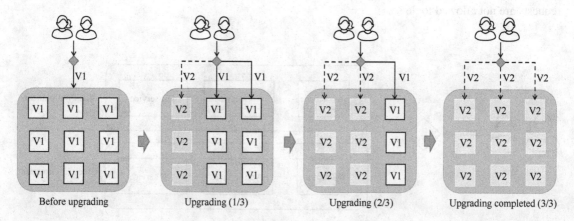

FIGURE 12.8 Rolling deployment.

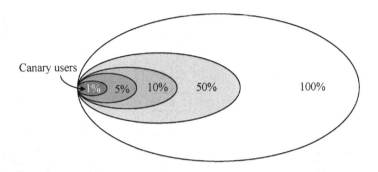

FIGURE 12.9 Canary release and gradient release.

Gradient release is the extension of canary release. It is to divide a release into different stages, and users in each stage increases gradually. If the new version is good enough, it will enter the next stage until it extends to all users, as shown in Figure 12.9. "How many stages are divided and how many users are in each stage?" It depends on the context of the product.

In 2012, Facebook made a major revision of its website homepage, introducing a big change with gradient release. When the number of users was around 1%, indicators of website health (such as page views and clicking rate) declined. After discussion, the team believed that these users were temporarily unsuited to the new user interface (UI) and agreed on further gradient release. However, after this percentage exceeded 10%, various key business indicators were still performing poorly, so Facebook finally abandoned the UI change and restored the original one.

There are two ways for canary and gradient release:

One is achieved through isolation by toggle (see Section 12.3.1 for details of switch technology), which is to deploy a new version to all nodes in production and open the new features to different user segmentation by toggle. For example, the network access layer, Web layer, and business logic layer can all be used for toggles, but an appropriate solution is determined on basis of specific scenarios, such as divert traffic by Internet Protocol (IP), cookie, request parameter, region, traffic percentage, and so on.

The other is achieved by the rolling deployment as mentioned earlier. It is decided by the node on which the version is installed. The two methods are shown in Figure 12.10.

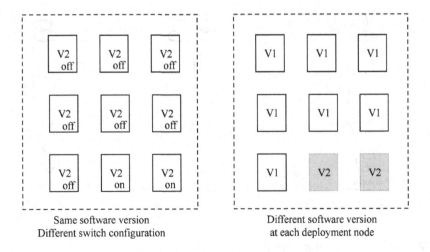

FIGURE 12.10 Traffic diversion by switch and by physical version deployment.

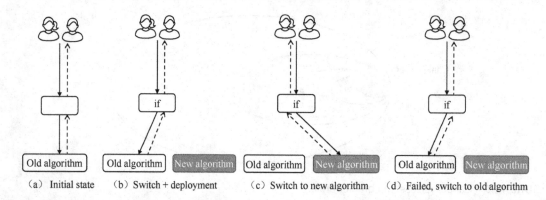

FIGURE 12.11 Dark launch in switch mode.

12.2.4 Dark Launch

Dark launch is to deploy features into production without seen by users, so that the team can test it and find potential issues without affecting end users. The word "dark" here is to describe that "users have no perception", which can be achieved through toggle technology. For example, a team just developed an online recommendation algorithm to recommend more excellent contents to users. However, due to the complexity of this algorithm, they want to know how the performances of the algorithm when there is a large number of real users. What can they do?

We can have a toggle for this algorithm. When this toggle is on, there will be partial traffic entering the algorithm. However, users do not know which algorithm they are using, old or new one. No matter the result is good or bad, we can take an action correspondingly by changing toggle. The steps are shown in Figure 12.11.

We can also use the traffic cloning method introduced in Chapter 10. That is, a copy of each request is cloned and sent to this new algorithm. The responses of this new algorithm will be collected by engineers rather than end users. The workflow is shown in Figure 12.12.

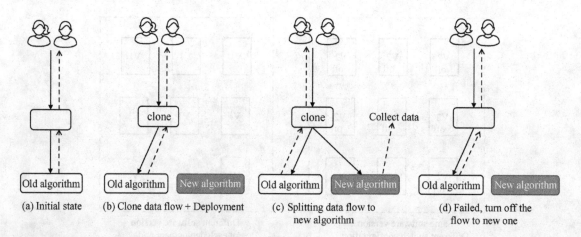

FIGURE 12.12 Dark launch in traffic cloning mode.

12.3 HIGH-FREQUENCY RELEASE SUPPORT TECHNOLOGY

Chapter 8 has mentioned that there is a certain correspondence between release frequency and branch strategy. When the release frequency is higher than once a week, it is more economical to adopt "Trunk-based Development & Release". However, they may encounter a practical difficulty: if a feature is very complex and cannot be done in a release cycle, what should they do to? There are three ways to solve it:

1. Decompose a feature. Split a feature into a set of smaller features that can be completed in a development cycle. Chapter 6 has mentioned that a feature can divided into sub-features (or technical tasks) to deliver directly (see Figure 12.13). Of course, some technicism has to be employed, such as Branch by Abstraction will be introduced soon.
2. Back-end service priors to front-end service. Implement the back-end function before implementing UI. That is, first implement the function that is not visible to users, while ensuring that the other functions are not affected. In this way, even if this code is brought into production, since there is no entry for external users, the release will not be affected. At the same time, dark launch and traffic cloning can be performed to verify the quality of the new function in the back-end server (see Figure 12.14).
3. Feature Toggle technology. Undeveloped features can be hidden with a toggle.

12.3.1 Feature Toggle

What is "Feature Toggle" (same as "Feature Flag")? Speaking of code, the essence of each toggle is an "if......else......" statement block. Let's take an e-commerce website as an example to illustrate. This website uses the PHP programming language to implement. The file fragment of "switch.config" is as follows:

```
01.  $cfg['new_search'] = array('enabled' => 'off');
02.  $cfg['sign_in'] = array('enabled' => 'on');
03.  $cfg['checkout'] = array('enabled' => 'on');
04.  $cfg['homepage'] = array('enabled' => 'on');
```

When designing a new commodity search algorithm, add the above first line of code into the configuration file "switch.config".

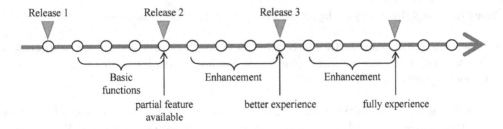

FIGURE 12.13 Decomposition of a big feature.

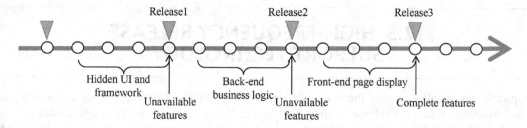

FIGURE 12.14 Back-end service priors to front-end service.

At the same time, add a conditional statement to the relevant code positions of the search algorithm. When the toggle "new_search" is on, "do_solr()" is executed, otherwise "do_grep()" is executed, as shown below:

```
01.  if($cfg['new_search'] == 'on') {
02.          $results = do_solr();      // call a new product search
algorithm
03.  } else {
04.          $results = do_grep();      // call an old product search
algorithm
05.  }
```

When the code is executed here, it will read "new_search" from the config file "switch.config", and select a different path to execute according to the logic we've designed. When we want to invite different user groups to use the new search, we can modify "new_search" to achieve the goal, as shown below:

```
01.  $cfg['new_search'] = array('enabled' => 'on');       // available to all
users
02.  $cfg['new_search'] = array('enabled' => 'staff');    // available to
internal employees
03.  $cfg['new_search'] = array('enabled' => '1%');       // available to 1%
of users
04.  $cfg['new_search'] = array('enabled' => 'users', 'user_list' =>
     'qiao_liang');
05.                                      // available to particular users
in whitelist
```

Feature Toggle itself is not a new technology. Usually, license keys in many commercial software are toggles to activate them. And different keys could activate different features.

For this kind of commercial software, we once tended to include the code for full features only in the official releases, and the unimplemented feature code is prohibited from being brought into such packages. This kind of software licensing is usually used in functional visibility strategy of different charging models. This model is still in use.

Presently, for high-frequency deployment, Feature Toggle has two new uses:

1. Isolation: Isolate the unfinished feature code outside the execution path, so that it cannot affect users.
2. Quick hemostasis: Once a critical issue is raised in production, just set the toggle of the corresponding feature to "Off".

Feature Toggle is a reasonable technical means to achieve high-frequency deployment. It is especially necessary for companies that implement the strategy of "Trunk-based Development & Release" such as Etsy, since all developers submit code directly to the trunk. Of course, Feature Toggle also incurs certain costs: first of all, each toggle has at least two states as "On" and "Off". When they verify features before release, engineers need to consider each state of a toggle in the system, and sometimes even perform combined toggles testing. Larger number of toggles may increase the test costs for combination of toggles. Second, not all toggles can be implemented in an elegant manner, which brings some complexity to design and maintenance. Finally, the longer the toggles exist in code, the higher the cost of maintaining it.

In order to maximize the benefits of Feature Flag and minimize its costs, we need to setup rules to manage toggles, and the following principles should be followed as far as possible:

1. On the premise of meeting business requirements, use Feature Toggle as little as possible. Since the toggle is essentially an "if...else..." statement, it will bring complexity to the program, especially when the code design is confusing and the responsibilities of the code module are not designed, it is more likely to make mistakes.
2. If we have to make a choice between "branching" and "Toggle", it's better to choose Toggle if possible. First of all, Feature Toggle enables iteration development in small steps. Second, it facilitates frequent integration on the trunk, which helps to detect conflicts as early as possible. Finally, branching will bring in subsequent integration of branches and costs for multiple tests.
3. The team shall manage the toggles in a unified manner to facilitate query and status-checking.
4. Use a unified framework and strategy for toggles as much as possible. The strategy here refers to the definition, naming, and config of toggles.
5. Regularly clean up unnecessary toggles.

Here are a few common tools: gflag is a C/C++ open-source tool contributed by Google, the Java community can use Togglz or Flip; Grails can use grails-feature-toggle, while .Net community can refer to FeatureToggle.

12.3.2 Data Migration

Any software will process data, and many of the data will be persisted. As the services last, there will be more and more data. Therefore, the modification of the database schema is relatively complicated, and the update takes more time.

For those enterprise-level applications with a low release frequency, when a new version is released, there would be a shut down in advance, and the schema is modified based on SQLs to reorganize the data. After it is completed, a corresponding version of the software will start to restore the service.

12.3.2.1 Fields only to be added instead of being deleted

For Internet applications that process massive amounts of data every day, in the high-frequency release mode, it is normal for the DB change once a week or two, although it is not a patch on an application that changes several times a day. If DB updating takes longer, shutting down for update is not appropriate. At this point, the easiest way to update DB is to "add fields as much as possible instead of deletion", that is, do not modify or delete the original fields in the DB table.

As shown in Figure 12.15, in the original DB, the delivery address is divided into three fields, and historical data have been stored (the personal information in the figure is not real, but a fictitious example). Since the three fields are always used together, they are ought to be merged into one field. Then we can add a new field as "delivery address" and modify this application in two ways as follows:

1. Since it is impossible to identify whether other applications still use the original three fields, when any information is written into the database, the existing information should be retained.
2. When reading the data, the program can check the field "delivery address" first. If it is empty, it means that this is an old record. Then, it should read the data from the original three fields separately and splice them together.

ID	User name	City delivery	District/county delivery	Detailed delivery address
001	Zhang Xinyue	Beijing	Chaoyang	Bldg 29, Liufang Nanli
002	Li Jianguo	Shanghai	Zhangjiang High-tech Park	Bldg 99, Haike Rd
003	Wang Yongming	Beijing	Haidian	ldg 3, Shangdi St 10

ID	User name	City delivery	District/county delivery	Detailed delivery address	Delivery address
001	Zhang Xinyue	Beijing	Chaoyang	Bldg 29, Liufang Nanli	
002	Li Jianguo	Shanghai	Zhangjiang High-tech Park	ldg 99, Haike Rd	
003	Wang Yongming	Beijing	Haidian	Bldg 3, Shangdi St 10	
004	Sun Xiaodan	Beijing	Dongcheng	Bldg 5, Block 13, Hepingli	Bldg 5, Block 13, Hepingli, Dongcheng, Beijing
005	Qin Jianfei	Beijing	Dongcheng	Bldg 12, Block 8, Hepingli	Bldg 12, Block 8, Hepingli, Dongcheng, Beijing

FIGURE 12.15   Fields only to be added instead of being deleted.

This kind of modification makes minor changes to the application and does not require processing the original data in the database.

12.3.2.2 Data migration

The above process is enough in most cases, but it may be inapplicable sometimes, such as converting the storage from H2DB to MySQL, or splitting the original DB into multiple DBs, or the amount of data in a single table is too large. At this time, a large amount of data needs to be migrated.

There are five steps to do data migration:

1. Add a new change on database schema, for example, a new column in a DB table.
2. Modify the application to write data into two places: old column and new one.
3. Write a script to backfill the original historical data into the new one by way of back-end service.
4. Let the application read data from the old and new versions and compare them to ensure consistency.
5. After confirmation, modify the application to write data to the new one. The original data can be kept for a while for fear of any unexpected problems

THE PROCESS OF MERGING TWO TABLES IN THE DATABASE

A similar situation was seen in a company. Its team was inexperienced at the beginning, so they designed two tables for storing the information of registered users. The tables were respectively named Users (for saving users' basic information) and User_profiles (for saving users' extended information). The purpose was for subsequent business expansion without modifying the Users table, they would simply add information in User_profiles based on different business logic.

However, after a period of time, the team found that User_profiles was not used much, and every time the UserService read information, it had to obtain data from two tables, which was time-consuming. Therefore, the team intended to merge the data in User_profiles into Users and delete User_profiles. So how to do it?

STEP 1: MODIFY THE DATABASE SCHEMA

1. Write a SQL script, and add the same columns in the table "User_profiles" to the table "Users".
2. Modify the application to add three toggles and ship as shown below:

```
01.   'write_profile_to_user_profiles_table'=>'on'
02.   'write_profile_to_user_ table'=>'off'
03.   'read_profile_from_users_table'=>'off'
```

STEP 2: MODIFY THE APPLICATION TO WRITE DATA
INTO BOTH "USER_PROFILES" AND "USERS"

1. Modify the code to write the profile into the original User_profiles table and also into the Users table at the same time.
2. Modify the toggle in line 2 to "On", as shown below and ship it:

```
01.   'write_profile_to_user_profiles_table'=>'on'
02.   'write_profile_to_user_ table'=>'on'
```

STEP 3: WRITE A BACK-END SCRIPT THAT CAN BE EXECUTED
OFFLINE, AND BATCH BACKFILL THE ORIGINAL HISTORICAL
DATA OF "USER_PROFILES" INTO "USERS"

This step does not need to modify the code in production, but write an offline program to write the data originally stored in User_profiles into the corresponding column in Users. Run the offline program until all data synchronization is completed.

STEP 4: READ DATA FROM BOTH THE OLD AND NEW VERSION
TO COMPARE THEM TO ENSURE CONSISTENCY

1. Modify the source code. When there is need to read data, read the corresponding data from the two tables and compare them in the memory to verify whether the data are consistent. In case of any inconsistency, it can be written to the log and then processed offline. The data can also be repaired according to a pre-defined revision strategy.
2. Modify the toggle in line 3 so that internal employees can use the data in Users, and modify the toggle "read_profile_from_users_table" to "staff", as shown below:

```
01.   'write_profile_to_user_profiles_table'=>'on'
02.   'write_profile_to_user_ table'=>'on'
03.   'read_profile_from_users_table'=>'staff'
```

Release this version of modification after it is done. At this time, it is equivalent to the release of an internal experience version. Employees will verify the consistency of data until they are confirmed to be correct.

STEP 5: AFTER CONFIRMATION, MODIFY THE CODE TO
WRITE DATA TO THE NEW VERSION STRUCTURE

Modify the configuration switch in line 3 so that 5% of users can use the information in the Users table, and modify the switch "read_profile_from_users_table" to "5%", as shown below:

```
01.   'write_profile_to_user_profiles_table'=>'on'
02.   'write_profile_to_user_ table'=>'on'
03.   'read_profile_from_users_table'=>'5%'
```

Release this version and confirm that the operation is correct. After that, repeat this step to allow more users by toggle "read_profile_from_users_table" from "5%" to "On", until 100% of them use the data.

STEP 6: ABANDON THE OLD VERSION (THIS IS AN OPTIONAL STEP)

When running for an enough time and no issue is raised, change the toggle "write_profile_to_user_profiles_table" to "Off" and no longer write data to User_profiles, as shown below, and ship it:

```
01.    'write_profile_to_user_profiles_table'=>'off'
02.    'write_profile_to_user_ table'=>'on'
03.    'read_profile_from_users_table'=>'on'
```

12.3.3 Branch by Abstraction

When making big architectural changes, it usually takes a long time. The traditional approach is shown in Figure 12.16: create a new branch from current branch for large-scale rewriting, and then port new features to the new branch continuously if needed. The new branch, which has been extensively rewritten, cannot be released for a long time until the big architectural change is completed. Continuous Delivery cannot be achieved in this way, and the realization of requirements will fall into periodic stagnation. There will be greater probability to discover problems at the end of this change, so a long stabilization time for the new branch is required.

The "Branch by Abstraction", which is from Jez Humber, is to decompose a big refactoring change into multiple small steps without creating a physical branch, so as to gradually complete big refactoring. The process of Branch by Abstraction is shown in Figure 12.17.

To deal with Spaghetti code shown in Figure 12.17a, you would define the scope of modularization with a seam. As for the situation shown in Figure 12.17b, a piece of code should be inserted in the seam to isolate the new module with other part of the system. So, both parts can interact through the seam code. In terms of the situation shown in Figure 12.17c, the new implementation replaces the old one gradually. Regarding the situation shown in Figure 12.17d, the work cannot cease until all original code is replaced.

In this way, we can still achieve the result of "refactoring" without branching. The benefits are as follows:

- Deliver business requirements while refactoring.
- Gradually verify the direction and correctness of the architectural adjustment
- It is easy to suspend if there is any emergency, and the previous workload is not wasted.
- Strengthen the team's cooperation.
- Make the software architecture more modular and easier to maintain.

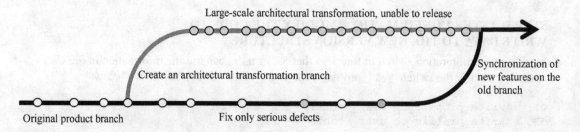

FIGURE 12.16 Refactor and release through real branches.

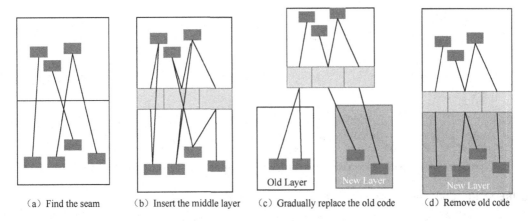

(a) Find the seam   (b) Insert the middle layer   (c) Gradually replace the old code   (d) Remove old code

FIGURE 12.17   Technical transformation based on Branch by Abstraction.

Using the Branch by Abstraction also has costs. For example, the entire modification period may be extended; because it is iteratively completed, the overall workload is larger than that of one-shoot completion.

The GoCD team once used Branch by Abstraction to successfully replace iBATIS with Hibernate. There were two formal releases containing those two Object Relational Mapping (ORM) frameworks. Before using Branch by Abstraction, the tech lead planned to replace the framework on a dedicated branch and merge it back after the change completed, but failed. Because most engineers merge their code into the trunk every day, there are too many diffs between the trunk and the branch. This shows that if big changes will be done by branching, we usually have to stop most work for new features, otherwise it will be difficult to succeed.

12.3.4 Fix-Forward Instead of Rollback

As the saying goes, "If you often walk by the river, how can you not wet your shoes?" We will definitely encounter some issues to be fixed immediately after deployment. It could be an easy task when you are employing the Feature Toggle. The only need is to find the toggle about the issue and turn it off to hide the feature. But what if the Feature Toggle is not practiced?

In their co-authored article *Development and Deployment at Facebook*, Dror Feitelson, Kent Beck, and others recommended to replace rollback with fix-forward as much as possible. A typical fix-forward is to backout the commits related to the issue and wait for the next push, so that engineers do not have to fix the issue with a rush. All of this is due to the principles that engineers follow, such as small steps, atomic tasks, frequent check-in, and high-frequency releases. Facebook engineers submit code 0.75 times a day on average, and each person submits about 100 lines of code change per day, as shown in Figure 12.18.

12.4 FACTORS AFFECTING RELEASE FREQUENCY

Although this chapter talks much about the benefits of high-frequency release, it does not mean that daily release is suitable for all types of software. For example, for any embedded software that needs to follow the hardware release, the cost of public release is still high. Once the recall rate rises due to software defects, the loss may be quite high.

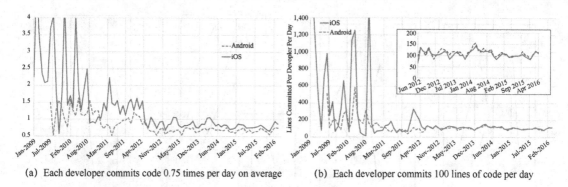

(a) Each developer commits code 0.75 times per day on average   (b) Each developer commits 100 lines of code per day

FIGURE 12.18   Code submission habits of Facebook engineers.

When we determine the frequency of software release, we need to consider the following factors:

1. The benefits and possibilities of incremental release.
2. The execution cost of each release or deployment operation.
3. The probability of problems and their costs.
4. The costs of maintaining multiple versions.
5. The skillset of engineers to accomplish high-frequency release.
6. The completeness of infrastructure required to support high-frequency release.
7. Team's attitude and cultural orientation toward high-frequency release.

Among these influencing factors, 5, 6, and 7 will also have a direct impact on the results of the previous four factors. It is possible that due to these three factors, the cost of high-frequency release will remain high, thus making the benefits relatively small. In this case, the leadership team should make more efforts and invest more energy in the latter three factors.

Everyone is prone to postpone risks, but any deployment and release do have risks. In case of a longer interval between two releases, more code changes will be cumulated, which means more risks, thus requiring more time in quality verification. This forms a progressive enhancement loop, as shown in Figure 12.19. After we adopt the methods introduced in this chapter, we could reduce the risk of deployment and release, and increase the frequency of release while boosting team morale. After all, everyone wants to see the fruits of their labor used by real users as soon as possible.

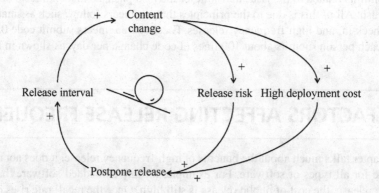

FIGURE 12.19   Progressive enhancement loop for motive of delayed release.

12.5 SUMMARY

In this chapter, we've discussed how to reduce risks through a variety of technical means in the case of frequent deployment and release, such as Feature Toggle, database migration, blue-green deployment, canary and gradient release, Branch by Abstraction, and dark launch. It should be noted that even if Feature Toggle is not used, if the team can keep following the strategy of "small-step, atomic tasks and frequent check-in", they are still capable to roll back the defect quickly.

In some scenarios, we cannot realize formal release frequently for outside. However, if we can use the methods described in this chapter to continuously release and deploy software internally, we still obtain quality feedback of the software as soon as possible, thereby reducing the risk in the official release afterward. When we reduce the release cost to low enough, it will directly change the team's development process.

Monitoring and Decision-Making

13

The previous chapters mainly discuss how to build high-quality software and how to release frequently with low risk. These are the first two steps of Continuous Delivery Verification Loop. The first step is to transform the minimum viable solution (MVS) wrote in a human language into deliverables. The second step is to run the deliverables in production (or deliver it to users). An effective business closed loop is not yet formed. Only when the deliverables provide customers (users) with continual service and collect effective feedback data, can we see the real verification closed loop (see Figure 13.1) to verify whether it meets the business goals and expectations decided in the Discovery Loop.

Not every change can achieve the desired effect. After some changes are deployed, the performance might be declined, which will affect user experience and even lead to a decline in revenue. Large international dot-com companies have experienced instances of damage or even interruption of services due to software changes.

- Case 1: In October 2012, a load balancing software upgrade at Google failed, causing damage to the global Gmail business, which lasted for 18 minutes.
- Case 2: In December 2014, there was a bug in Dropbox's routine upgrade of the operating system, which caused the Dropbox to be interrupted for 3 hours.
- Case 3: In June 2014, a configuration change of Facebook's system caused a 31-minute interruption of services.
- Case 4: In November 2014, an upgrade of Microsoft Azure caused damage to Azure Storage services.

Once software changes occur, quickly and accurately assessing the impact of changes, discovering production problems in time, and quickly debugging and fixing them have always been important tasks in Software Life Cycle Management (SLCM). In this chapter, we will discuss the last two steps in Verification Loop, namely "monitoring" and "decision-making".

13.1 SCOPE OF PRODUCTION MONITORING

According to the different monitoring content, it can be divided into three layers, namely, resource (or system) monitoring, application monitoring, and business monitoring. Resource monitoring has always been the top priority in the field of system operation and maintenance, and its basic operation and maintenance system construction and tool support are relatively mature and complete. Now, the application monitoring has also got attention of development department. Many tools support the collection of relevant data on the market. Especially in the era of the mobile Internet, the diversity of devices and the focus on user experience have made the operation quality monitoring of application software an important data support for measuring the quality indicators of mobile Internet products. For mass-oriented Internet services or products, the unpredictability between providers' expectations and real user feedback makes more and more companies pay attention to the monitoring of business data trend.

DOI: 10.1201/9781003221579-13

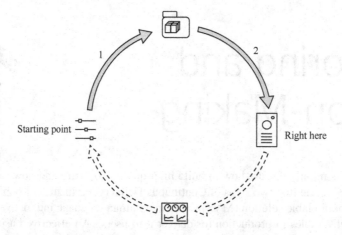

FIGURE 13.1 Closed fast Verification Loop.

At present, software ship is in two main forms, one is back-end service, which is maintained easily; the other is a software package distributed to users themselves, such as mobile App, PC-side software, and embedded software in hardware devices. We should try to monitor both of them comprehensively.

13.1.1 Monitoring of Backend Services

For the back-end service monitoring:

1. System monitoring is to monitor the health of the system infrastructure, including network connection and traffic congestion status, CPU load, and usage of memory and external storage space, and so on.
2. Application monitoring is to monitor the running health of the application, for example, whether the process is still alive, whether it provides service normally, whether it connects the database normally, whether there are timeouts, thrown exceptions, and alarms, whether scaling up/down properly deals with emergency such as a large number of requests increase suddenly.
3. Business monitoring is to monitor the health of business indicators. For example, for an e-commerce website, it should include, but is not limited to, real-time user visits, specific page views, conversion rates, order, transaction volume, and so on.

13.1.2 Monitoring of Consumer-Host Software

Since the environments in which consumer-host software runs are not controlled environments, the monitoring is restricted by objective conditions. Generally speaking, we need to collect the running status of our own software and of the host devices on user equipment upon obtaining user authorization and send the collected data to the back-end regularly. The back-end server will analyze and show the collected data. If the consumer-host device is running in a non-networked state, the software needs to cache the monitor data locally, and upload the data once it is connected to the Internet.

Like the monitoring of back-end services, the monitoring also includes three layers. System monitoring is to monitor the operation of the basic environment (such as mobile device model, operating system, and memory) in which the software runs, and the connection to the server. Application monitoring is to monitor the health status of the application itself (such as memory usage, program crashes, unresponsiveness, and communication with back-end). Business monitoring is to monitor users' operation data, such as which page is opened, stay time, and so on.

Of course, the monitoring is not only from the report of the software itself but also the information on the Internet, such as the scoring of mobile software applications, and user comments of the software itself published in various new media. More extensive channels are used to collect information in a comprehensive way, and to fix bugs and loopholes in the software in time to provide users with the best experience.

13.2 DATA MONITORING SYSTEM

In order to obtain effective data, the acquisition process and processing flow of data must be comprehensively managed, including data sources, data formats and collection cycles, and data processing algorithms.

13.2.1 Collection and Processing

The processing of data is shown in Figure 13.2.

Each step in Figure 13.2 involves a large amount of platform processing and calculation, and their responsibilities are as follows:

1. Collection and reporting: Collect and report the predefined event data locally.
2. Data sorting: Collect, clean, and sort the data reported from each data source.
3. Real-time analysis: Analyze and process real-time data.
4. Offline analysis: Extract model or rule through large amounts of data.
5. Result output: Display the results of real-time and offline analyses for decision-making reference.
6. Decision-making: Based on the result output, the decision of next action is made artificially or automatically; at the same time, the decision-making record is saved to provide a basis for subsequent decision-making.
7. Data storage: Save offline raw data, analysis data, and processing records.
8. Interface with Ops managing systems: It could send instructions to ask the Ops managing system for fixing issues.

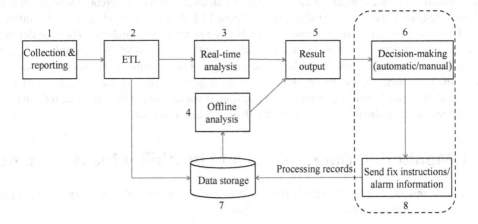

FIGURE 13.2   Collection, processing, and application processes of monitoring data.

13.2.2 Standardization

To obtain data, we have to plan and track the events generated by the software in advance. Especially for business data, planning ahead is a necessity. In the Discovery Loop of Continuous Delivery, one of its most important inputs is real user feedback. In order to improve the timeliness of "verification", we need to do two other things in addition to discussing the implementation before coding: The first is to define business indicators, that is, what are the business indicators related to the success of a feature? What are the correlations with other business indicators? And how to calculate this business indicator? The second is to define the events. In order to get the data of this business indicator, where should the event be coded in the program? What is the input and output format? What is the relationship with other events? These two things are the prerequisite to ensure data accuracy.

Startups often encounter data collection problems at the beginning. The root cause of these problems lies in the neglect of data indicator system construction in the development process, or even no consideration at all. Once entering into the bottleneck period of product development, since there is no corresponding data system, it is impossible for these companies to observe user behavior, but guessing.

Usually, the research and development (R&D) team and the operation team pay more attention to system layer events (such as CPU, memory, hard disk, and network) and application events (such as service response time, page loading speed, and App startup speed), but not take too much interest in business events. Inexperienced product owners pay much more attention to feature implementation than data collection.

Do you often encounter the following scenarios in daily work? When the product owner intends to collect data for some back-end support for improving the existing features or reporting to his superior, he will hurriedly push data requirements to the data team. Each data request may have to wait two or three days to get, or even longer. Unfortunately, the data obtained are often inaccurate, and data inconsistencies often occur caused by no attention to data daily.

For a highly uncertain environment, we are sure that business data collection is more important than feature implementation. Product owners who are not data-conscious can only make decisions based on gut feeling. This would cause a great waste, especially in the highly competitive market.

In order to facilitate statistical analysis, the team must define the data log format and collection standards and rules from the beginning, and make regular presentations. Standard definitions can make data collection and processing more convenient, reduce unnecessary dirty data or data classification errors, and improve the timeliness and accuracy of data processing.

The format of the data log itself is not complicated, and is usually divided into basic information and extended information. Basic information needs to describe the most basic background information of the application, including 4Ws, namely who, when where, and what, such as basic application information, event time, level, environmental information, event code, and indication position. Extended information is for better scalability of data to meet the monitoring and statistical needs of different businesses. It is usually defined, analyzed, and used by each business team. Figure 13.3 shows an example of extended information.

The definition of events and log standards needs to be continuously updated. With the development of businesses and continuously changing features, the specific event collection standards and log format as well as their contained content will change accordingly. For example, if some features are merged or deleted, the corresponding events and logs also need to be updated, and these updates will affect the original statistical formula or analysis report. In addition, if some fields in the extended information exist for a long time, the team should consider defining them as basic information.

13.2.3 Monitoring Data System and Its Ability Measurement

Many decisions rely on a large amount of data analysis, so the quality of these data is very important. Monitoring data can be measured from three dimensions:

1. "Correctness" indicates the consistency between collected data and facts.

Uniform format

The fields should be in order of serial number: between first-level fields, use the first-level separator '\001'

Serial number	Format name	Description
1	Event name	Such as, 1.1 concept description, uploaded by the client
2	Event details	Record the specific tracking point, check each log description specifically, and upload it by the client
3	Event expansion	Check the description in the event expansion table below, uploaded by the client
4	Atomic package	Added by the point service, assembled and added in order at the server-side
5	record_time	Added by the tracking service, with unix timestamp recorded at the server-side, without involving the client

Description

- The format of the tracking log file should be assembled from small to large according to the serial number, and unified according to the format convention in the above table
- The unified request for the tracking client is POST request:
    - Serial number 1~3: uploaded by the client, assembled in POST and uploaded.
    - Serial number 4~5: added by tracking service, and the atomic package will be uploaded uniformly after adding the parameters at the end of the request URL
- Separator:
    - Level 1 separator: '\001', event name, atomic packaging, event details, etc. (serial number1~5), using level 1 separator

FIGURE 13.3 Example of extended log information.

2. "Comprehensiveness" means that the collected data should be sufficient to support the team's decision-making.
3. "Timeliness" is that the processing time from data occurrence to decision-making is short enough.

At the beginning, we may encounter situations where collected data are inconsistent with actual business performance. If so, we can verify data quality in the following two ways:

1. Rely on the judgments by business experts. We can invite business experts to join in the construction of a data system at the early stage.
2. Comparison and verification by multi-party data. Multi-party data indicate that the data may come from the sources outside the company (such as general data in the industry, and data performance of similar companies), or from different dimensions in the system (such as browsing data, order data, and financial data). Through mutual verification between different dimensions of data, quality problems are found and gradually improved.

Timeliness is important for business agility. It includes the timeliness of data reporting and processing. Whenever system behaviors change, we'd like to know the impact on business indicators as soon as possible, such as registration rate, detail page open rate, order rate, and so on in e-comm website.

FACEBOOK'S REAL-TIME DATA ANALYSIS AND STORAGE SYSTEM

According to an article entitled *Scuba: Diving into Data at Facebook* published by Lior Abraham et., al. in 2012, Facebook's real-time data analysis and storage system "Scuba" handled one million rows per second and processed one million queries per day in 2012. The processing delay of each event was less than one second. It only took one second from the data landing on the log server to its display on the dashboard or seen by the monitoring personnel, as shown in Figure 13.4.

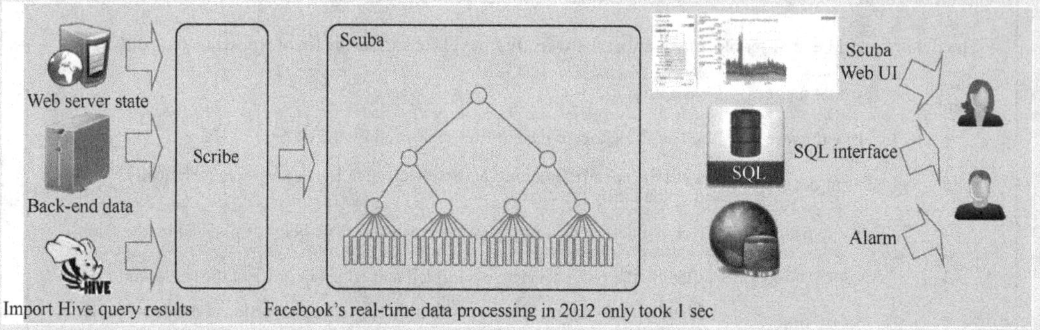

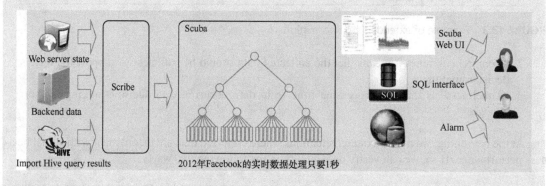

FIGURE 13.4   Facebook's real-time data monitoring system in 2012.

Scribe is a log collection service, and Scuba is a data processing service cluster. The system provides three data usage methods. One is through the dashboard, which may directly display a weekly data comparison chart. Second, you can customize the query conditions visually, or write your own script to query, and each query takes less than one second. The third is automatic alarm processing. Figure 13.5 shows Facebook's data trend after the code changes.

FIGURE 13.5   Facebook's real-time monitoring dashboard in 2012.

In addition to the above three measurement dimensions, the monitoring system should also have sampling capabilities, that is, according to the actual data volume needs, engineers can configure the sampling density of each data sampling point and put it into effect quickly. This is conducive to reducing the total data size when production is running normally, and the most detailed log information can be quickly obtained when production is abnormal.

13.3 ISSUE HANDLING SYSTEM

After a data monitoring system is established, the next step is to identify and fix issues by the data with two ways. One is manual discrimination. The other is automatically identified by AI. Faced with a large amount of monitoring data, it is unrealistic to rely entirely on manual processing. Usually, suspected issues would be identified by machines according to rules as many as possible. When it cannot be handled automatically, it would be used as an "alarm" to generate a ticket for the designated recipient.

13.3.1 Alarm Storm and Intelligent Management

In a Chinese domestic Internet company, an operation engineer received more than 6,000 alarms every day. If each alarm had to be checked, he would check four alarms per minute on average, and would be on standby 24 hours a day. However, although the alarms had been storming, whenever a production accident occurs, two action items in the accident reanalysis would come again and again: one is to sort out the current log monitoring and alarm points, and reconfigure all relevant personnel to avoid missing anyone; the other is to add more monitoring points and alarms.

The alarm storm has been formed, and you are trying your best to reduce alarms but also adding more to avoid missing something. The final winner is usually the latter. In fact, the receiver would ignore most of them without reading. There are two main reasons:

1. The receiver is not the first person to be responsible for it in the process. For example, after a postmortem, it is believed that this type of alarm should not only be sent to colleagues but also to his leader so that the leader could be a backup just in case. In this way, an alarm point has at least three recipients.
2. The alarm is a preliminary warning and doesn't need to be processed immediately. For example, an alarm about disk space shortage occurred in production. After checking, it was found that the threshold was 50 GB, but the data increment on this server is 40 GB/day normally. So, there was enough time (about 24 hours) to deal with it. However, current case caused by an incident that consumed 50 GB in a short period of time, resulting in an accident of insufficient disk space. So, in order to avoid a similar situation happening again, the operation engineer added one more alarm with a lower limit of the threshold, say 200 GB/day. If you are the man receiving an alert like this, you might ignore it too.

Of course, we don't rule out the correctness and authenticity of many alarms but we also need to improve the quality of the alarm in the other two dimensions: One is timeliness. The other is actionable for alarms. Actionable means that the alarm receiver should take an action when getting the alarm. Otherwise, the alarm should be blocked for him like a spam. If a real alarm is submerged in a large number of "false" alarms that do not need to be processed, it is easy to cause a production accident. How can we alleviate or resolve "alarm storm"? We can start from four aspects:

1. **Bring the monitoring point closer to the problem by correlation analysis.** Currently, back-end services have begun to move toward microservices, and the call chain is relatively longer. Sometimes the problem of a certain terminal service is caused by the front-end service, and the front-end service can also detect this anomaly, so you should setup a monitoring point in the front-end service instead of adding a monitoring point to the back-end service.
2. **Set reasonable alarms through dynamic thresholds.** Initially, we may write a fixed value when setting the threshold. If this value is set too high, then the problem has already occurred, and the alarm may not have been triggered. If it is set too low, it may cause invalid alarms and waste employees' time and energy. Therefore, we can dynamically adjust the threshold through some algorithms automatically. Taking the case of insufficient disk space as an example, we can dynamically adjust the threshold according to the growth ratio of the disk space occupancy curve. The growth ratio is slow, the algorithms can set it to 40 GB, or 200 Gb if it is fast. In this way, we don't need to set two alarm points like the example above. Of course, to ensure the accuracy of the algorithm requires a certain period of observation and accumulation, as well as big data analysis.
3. **Regularly sort out the alarm settings and clean up unnecessary alarms.** Unnecessary alarms fall into two categories: one is that the alarm event itself is unnecessary. This situation

mostly occurs when the software feature changes, and the original meaningful alarms become no longer meaningful. The second is that the recipient doesn't need to receive this alarm at all.

4. **Dynamically clear the alarm through artificial intelligence (AI).** This is a new hot spot in the current operation field. Some regular relationships between different events in the production can be found through artificial intelligence (AI) algorithms. In this way, problems can be identified earlier, alarms can be sent early, and even problems can be handled automatically without warning. The field of AIOps is still in the exploratory stage and has not yet been able to achieve large-scale applications in the industry.

Through continuous efforts, we can control the number of alarms at a certain level, but it is difficult to eliminate them. For those common alarms, we may already have a way to deal with them. What really needs time to deal with is those abnormal alarms that have not occurred before, because they are likely to be "production issues".

13.3.2 Problem Solving Is a Learning Process

The handling of "production issue" is also an important part of the development management process. If there is no good process, more management problems are likely to arise. The general process is shown in Figure 13.6.

When the team size is small, this process is performed manually, mainly through email, IM tools, or "calling out". Once the staff size becomes larger and the system becomes complicated, this process becomes very time-consuming. For example, due to the inaccurate judgment of problem location, it is often necessary to transfer the processing between several teams or divisions, and the context is often lost during the transfer. In order to improve efficiency, it is usually necessary to solve the manual part of the process through automation as much as possible, including automatic tracking of tickets, additional records of related information, timeliness measurement of the entire handling process, timely notification mechanisms with multiple channels, and issue escalation mechanism. This requires a ticket system to support. Moreover, when we review the issue, such a ticket system can provide us with a lot of information in a timely and correct manner.

In many teams, postmortem events are often regarded as a "accountability meeting", and the meeting atmosphere is quite tense. In a learning organization, postmortem is a good learning opportunity. At the time of replaying, all relevant people will compare the results, review the process, analyze gains and losses, and summarize the rules. This is the best process of mutual learning, and it is an opportunity for everyone to improve. The law summarized through replaying is an action guide for latecomers to deal with similar things, and it is also the best knowledge inheritance of an organization, which can help latecomers to progress to the greatest extent.

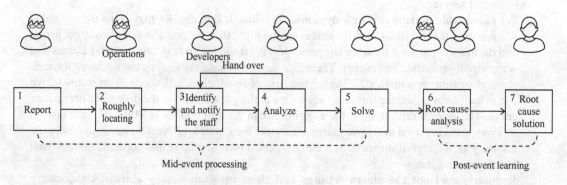

FIGURE 13.6 Process of handling production problems.

One of the most important prerequisites for replaying is that there must be a detailed record of the ticket handling process, and the full participation of all participants in the whole process (including the party that just transfers issue without handling). As for the questionable points in the replaying process, a second scene reappearance should be performed in order to get a better prevention program and a fundamental solution.

13.4 TEST IN PRODUCTION

The production environment is unique. The non-production environment created for the purpose of "pre-quality verification" can never guarantee to discover all the problems that may occur in production. With the increase in requirements for rapid software release and the increase in the probability of non-enumerability of test scenarios, test scenarios in non-production environments have become increasingly inadequate. Therefore, people have begun to consider how to test in production without affecting production.

13.4.1 Flattening Trend of Testing Activities

In the traditional waterfall model, test execution and decision-making are usually concentrated in the middle of a software project life cycle. However, with the increasing frequency of modern software delivery, things have changed. The testing activities of many teams began to shift to the left and right, as shown in Figure 13.7.

"Shift-left testing" refers to the earlier and more active participation of testers in the early stage of project, such as early participation in the Discovery Loop activities, and definition of relevant testcases before development. Test execution is also shifting to the left, which is expressed like this: in more and more software teams, testers begin to embrace "incremental testing", that is, before the software integration test, perform quality verification of a few developed small features to detect risks in advance. Although this "incremental test" cannot find all issues, it can reduce the pressure in integration phase, as shown in Figure 13.8. At the same time, it will also ensure the quality of software delivery by frequently running automated tests at all levels, and ultimately shorten the time to market and increase the release frequency.

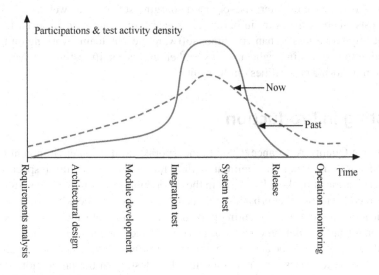

FIGURE 13.7 Shift-left and shift-right tests.

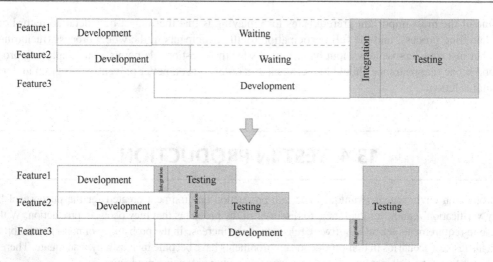

FIGURE 13.8   Shift-left test.

"Shift-right testing" refers to the use of various technical means to place part of the quality verification work in production. This is a kind of "helpless act", because the testing of Internet services is significantly different from the testing of enterprise applications, that is, it has too many scenarios you cannot image. The users of enterprise applications are limited, the environment is relatively controllable, and administrative means can be used to intervene at the worst. Consumer software is installed by individuals on their computers or mobile phones, and there is broad landscape of the devices and operating systems, which makes it an impossible task to test all scenarios in an exhaustive manner by relying on the provider's own resources. More and more providers are increasingly dependent on quality verification in production. To some extent, A/B test is also a form of test in production. Its main goal is to verify the validity of the business design plan, not the correct execution of a certain software feature.

At present, shift-right test is mostly performed on the consumer software, which is not executed crucial tasks, such as searching, gaming, information showing, and recommending. Even if an issue raises, it will have a certain impact on the software brand, but as long as it is discovered and repaired in time, it will not cause essential loss or serious impact on users.

For transactional software or enterprise-oriented charging software, as well as software with higher problem repair costs (such as firmware in hardware devices), once an issue is raised in the production, it will bring relatively larger losses than consumer software. So, the teams working on this kind of software are not willing to shift testing right currently, rather embrace shift testing left. Meanwhile, they are strengthening the monitoring capabilities on the right.

13.4.2 Testing in Production

We should encourage Quality Assurance (QAs) to incorporate production environment testing into their daily work. "Production inspection", a common method for production quality inspection, is to perform regular feature verification of back-end services in the production to ensure that the system offers services normally and correctly. The usual approach is to create a daily health checklist covering the main functions of the application and routinely executing it to check the quality of functions. This kind of testing is different from monitoring. The delivery team does it actively and regularly rather than the operation staff. As a routine verification, it should be automated. Interface testing is a typical representative. Many teams have started to put some testcases for automation interface testing in the production to replace manual inspection.

Test in production should follow the following principles:

1. Create QA's own test data to ensure that they do not pollute the data of real users.
2. The more real the test data, the better.
3. Do not modify the data of real users.
4. Create user access credentials for QA to run tests in production.

13.4.3 Chaos Engineering

Chaos engineering is a discipline of experimenting on a software system in production in order to build confidence in the system's capability to withstand turbulent and unexpected conditions by injecting "problems" actively. The goal is to continuously improve the reliability of the production. This is similar to vaccine injection, namely injecting some small doses of "virus" into the body to help it build up resistance and gain immunity.

Chaos engineering does not mean that everything should be done randomly, especially when the stability of the production is not very high. At the initial stage of chaos engineering, it may just inject known problems (and known solutions) within a limited range and time to verify whether the known solutions can work normally.

In 2013, I used it to find loopholes in the emergency handling process in production. At that time, it was to verify whether or not the emergency handling process is reliable for network products installed on PC. We selected a batch of machines within a certain range and distributed a module with a known issue to these machines randomly. When designing the exercise, we added two more random factors: One is to pick up machines to inject randomly within a specified range rather than all of them, and the other is to select a time within a specified range rather than assigned by us. We discovered two time-consuming operations in the emergency process. The characteristics of this method are "notice in advance and plan ahead".

Once the team has a sense of "design for failure", it can take a more radical approach like Netflix. Netflix has developed a series of chaos engineering called "Simian Army". These tools run on Amazon Web Services (AWS) infrastructure and are specifically designed to handle various cloud computing problems and challenges to help ensure network health, promote efficient traffic management, and find out security issues in the system. For example, Chaos Gorilla simulates the failure of an entire AWS availability zone; Chaos Kong is used to kill an entire AWS Region (such as North America or Europe); Latency Monkey is artificially creating call delays. It is used to simulate service degradation to see if the modules that depend on these services can respond correctly. There are other types of tools, such as finding a malfunctioning AWS instance, and if the person responsible for maintaining the AWS instance does not repair it in time, it will be automatically closed.

This "Failing Injection" type of active detection makes software engineers need to consider some common failures when designing the architecture. In the era of cloud infrastructure, this is an extremely important way to actively discover unknown problems. Of course, this approach will also increase the investment cost of cloud infrastructure.

13.5 EASTWARD OR WESTWARD

As shown in Figure 13.9, in the Verification Loop, we transformed requirements in human language into runnable software, deployed it into production, and collected the feedback. Now is the time to decide the next step "eastward or westward". We will complete the first business closed loop entirely.

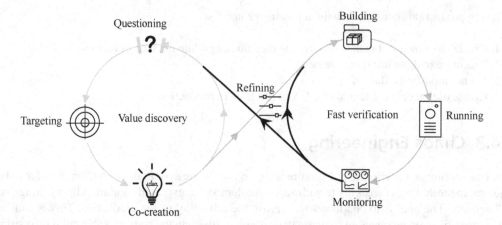

FIGURE 13.9 Eastward or westward.

Through analysis and summary, if the business metrics meets the target expectations as we defined in Value Discovery Loop, we may confirm that the hypotheses in the Value Discovery Loop are true. At this point, we can return to the starting point of the Discovery Loop to pick up next question or hypothesis.

If the results do not meet expectations, there is nothing to be discouraged. At least we have obtained the answer as quickly as possible. Now, just analyze with the team why the results are inconsistent with our expectations, whether we need to fine-tune this experiment again, or choose another experiment from the set of alternatives to continue to run Fast Verification Loop.

Of course, there is another possibility that we've learned new knowledge about the business during the Verification Loop. And this new knowledge shows us that all the alternatives produced in the refining link of the Value Discovery Loop are wrong, and we have to start the journey again, armed with the knowledge we've just learned.

13.6 SUMMARY

The monitoring scope of the production has three layers, which are system layer, application layer, and business layer. Although the means are different according to the characteristics of each layer, the processing flow is basically the same. The monitoring system has the links of collecting, reporting, sorting, analysis, presentation, and decision-making. The measurement of the monitoring system's capabilities has three dimensions, namely the accuracy, comprehensiveness, and timeliness. The sampling capability is an effective method to improve monitoring flexibility, save resources, and enhance user experience.

Alarm handling is a routine work of Dev and Ops. However, if alarm storm is formed, it will reduce work output. We should continue to optimize the alarm points and the thresholds to increase the effective alarm rate as much as possible. Once an alarm is sent out, the ticket handling process needs to be started. The last two links of this process, "root cause analysis" and "root cause resolution", are important characteristics of learning organizations.

With the increase in release frequency and the complexity of test scenarios, more and more teams started to find ways to do testing in production. This is known as the shift-right testing. It occurs mostly in customer software, and the cost and impact are relatively small if a mistake appears. For the software with high recovery costs, the shift-left testing is more applicable by now.

There are two types of shift-right tests. One is to automatically run the testcases in production. The second is chaos engineering by injecting "problems" in production to discover potential stability issues. Netflix has developed a series of destructive testing tools (Simian Army) that can prompt engineers to consider the possibility of various failures in advance when designing and developing software. This is called "design for failure", thereby improving the stability in production and providing users with a better experience.

After collecting real feedback, we can verify the hypothesis or goal we put forward in the Value Discovery Loop, and through active correlation analysis, we can finally determine whether to continue more experiments or take a pivot.

Large Internet Teams to Become Feature Teams

14

This chapter focuses on a real case of a large Internet desktop product team. It was a project for Continuous Delivery improvement that lasted a year or so. I cannot record every improvement decision that the team had made in the entire journey, but I hope readers could understand the main context and ideas for solving problems, so that they can be applied to daily improvement work.

14.1 CASE PROFILE

This case occurred in a large Internet company with multiple product lines. It took place on one of the company's product lines developing Windows desktop products for mass consumers. The entire product line is staffed with more than 300 people who are respectively responsible for product roadmap and planning, development, quality assurance; a small number of them are dedicated to operation and maintenance. It is a full-featured team responsible for the performance of their products in market and is solely responsible for business indicators. After a year of improvement in research and development (R&D) management, successful outcome has been achieved. The comparison before and after the improvement is shown in Table 14.1.

The entire improvement process can be divided into four stages:

1. **Architecture decoupling:** Transform the system architecture of the entire Windows application from "Monolithic Architecture" to "Microcore Architecture" (see Chapter 5 for details), so as to solve the problem of low efficiency and poor quality of multi-person parallel development arising from severe code coupling.
2. **Organization decoupling:** Break the "silos" between functional divisions, reorganize the original organization divided by discipline, establish a business-oriented, multi-role, and full-featured team, and promote small closed loops of business within each team to improve the overall efficiency.
3. **R&D process reengineering:** Formulate new product development and release workflow by improving the management of multi-team code branches.
4. **Automation efficiency improvement:** Through the construction of automation tools, the efficiency of each link can be improved.

In a word, these four stages involve software architecture, organizational mechanism, and infrastructure transformation for Continuous Delivery.

DOI: 10.1201/9781003221579-14

TABLE 14.1   Comparison before and after improvement

	BEFORE	AFTER
System structure	Mudball	Microcore architecture
Organizational structure	Functional organization	Business organization
Release interval	Big Release: 6 weeks (sometimes delayed)	Big Release: 4 weeks (no delay) Beta version: 0.5 days
Product quality	N/A	90% drop in crash rate

14.1.1 State before Improvement

Before the improvement, the product had a history of four years with hundreds of millions of users and had undergone a rapid and wild process. With the rapid growth of the team size, under the pressure of time schedule, the product codebase owes a lot of technical debt. After growth of the product entered a period of flattening, the morale of the team was somewhat low.

14.1.1.1 Team organization structure

- The product team was in a typical functional organization structure, and each discipline had its own responsibilities.
- Product center: Grouped by product managers who come up with more and more effective ideas and creativity to provide users with value and gain more user recognition.
- Development center: Grouped by developers who ensure that the requirements put forward by the product center are realized with high quality as soon as possible.
- Test center: Grouped by Quality Assurance (QAs) who verify the application from developer as soon as possible to ensure that the quality of each release delivered to users is high.
- Operation center: Grouped by operation engineers to ensure that products that have passed the test are launched in time, maintain production, and sustain contact with users to improve their satisfaction.
- Design Center: Grouped by UX staff to ensure excellent user experience.
- Project management center: Grouped by project managers to ensure that all disciplines can collaborate efficiently.

14.1.1.2 Development process and rhythm

The releases have "large version" and "hotfix version". The large version contains many new features, and each large version has a long development cycle. It uses a typical waterfall process (see its different stages in Figure 14.1). After all the requirements are reviewed, the developers will start to work on it. The entire delivery cycle of each release is approximately 29 workdays. The hotfix version is a revision that is urgently released to fix serious online issues.

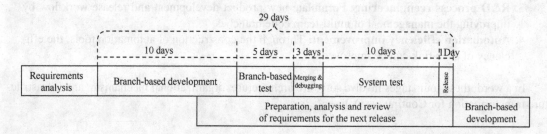

FIGURE 14.1   The product development rhythm in this case.

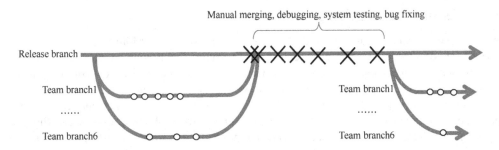

FIGURE 14.2   Branch-based release strategy in early stage.

This product has six major domains. More than 80 developers were assigned to take charge of this Windows desktop application, and they were divided into six groups, and each of them was responsible for one domain.

The branch strategy adopted by the entire team was "Branch-based Development & Trunk-based Release", as shown in Figure 14.2. The "branch" in this chapter refers to the "team branch".

The specific workflow is introduced as follows:

- Development on Team Branch: When the requirements for a certain version are reviewed, each development team cuts a branch from the trunk of the repository for its own feature modules. The development takes about ten workdays.
- Testing on Team Branch: After the features of the current release are developed, the team will test and fix defects on its own branch. It takes about five workdays.
- Merging and debugging: According to the predefined merging sequence, the six development groups merge their code into the trunk in turn, and conduct debugging until the quality is basically up to standard (that is, ensure that there are no defects that seriously hinder the tests, including failed program startup, unworkable main features, and unfinished main features of this release). This stage takes 2~3 workdays.
- System testing: Perform three rounds of testing after merging and debugging. The first round is a comprehensive test, in an aim to find as many problems as possible and notify developers to modify. The second round is a verification test, which keeps verifying the defects that developers fixed. The third round is a regression test, selecting important scenario use cases and defects above the important level as final verification. During this period, developers continue to fix the defects found by QAs until all parties evaluate that the code is qualified for public release before it can go online. System test takes about ten workdays.
- Releasing: This release workflow includes approval, uploading, configuration, and verification until the first user receives the new version. This stage takes one workday without gradient release.

Not all large releases were completed on time with good quality by following this process. Although everyone was working hard and even often worked late into the night, sometimes a large release would take two or three months to be done, and it is so exhausted.

14.1.2 State after Improvement

Almost a year later, the entire product line had made notable adjustments in team organization, software architecture, and R&D workflow.

14.1.2.1 Team organization structure

The product team became a business-oriented organizational structure. More than 400 people (scaling up overtime) are divided into six business centers and five functional groups. Each business center, composed of product managers and developers, is responsible for its domain features with its own business goals. The five functional groups include test center, back-end development center, product design center, operation center, and project management center. The original project management center is split into two parts: some are assigned to six business centers and reporting to the business leader; while the rest, a few people take charge of the coordination related to product R&D workflow. Also, the members of the other four functional centers are grouped according to business domain and work with the corresponding business centers closely.

In the end, the size of each business unit is different, ranging from a dozen to fifty, based on the needs of the business domain.

14.1.2.2 Workflow and rhythm

A high-quality large version is released on time every month now. The product quality has been greatly improved. For example, the crash rate has dropped by 90%. Two Beta versions, which are in product line-level, are released every day, and each business center releases its own Alpha version at any time according to its own needs, and there will be no interference with the Beta version.

14.2 IMPROVEMENT METHODOLOGY

For the overall improvement of a product team, a large number of people and roles are involved. If there is no definite goal, it is difficult for everyone to form a synergy. Therefore, the goal of the team is the same, and "making everyone understand this goal" is the key to success.

14.2.1 Guiding Ideology

"Goal-driven, starting from simple problems, and continuous improvement" is the guiding ideology of the entire improvement.

As an Internet product team, real feedback from users is the most important. However, it usually takes two to three months from "coding" to "getting real feedback" for this team. Therefore, they expected to reach the status of releasing a high-quality network-wide version every month as quickly as possible.

14.2.2 Improvement Steps

Since this was an improvement activity for the entire product team, many people and roles were involved. A senior external advisor was invited to provide guidance, and the improvement work lasted for nearly a year. The improvement steps are as follows:

1. An internal change team was established.
2. A Change Committee was composed of core management and external advisor. The person in charge of the product line was the lead of the committee.
3. Evaluate the current situation and define goals.

4. The Change Committee evaluated the problems in front of them and defined the goal to "inspire individual vitality and improve the efficiency of product development". The indicator for reaching the goal was to "release a high-quality network-wide version every month without delay".
5. Identify specific issues and set short-term goals.
6. Figure out the countermeasure and implement them.
7. Continue to optimize until the short-term goals were achieved according to real feedback.
8. Go back to Step 4 and continue until fulfilling the goal set initially.

14.3 THE JOURNEY

The time span for this improvement was about one year, and the improvement had gone through four stages, namely architecture decoupling, organization decoupling, R&D process reengineering, and automation efficiency improvement.

14.3.1 Architecture Decoupling

Although they had defined the goal to "release a high-quality network-wide version every month without delay", the team was still a bit at loss when they embarked on the improvement work. Where should they start? They'd better define a short-term goal at first. And this goal should solve the biggest pain point they were facing and bring them confidence.

The person in charge of the technical R&D department described the situation at the time like this: "The team had been in a state of rapid response. In order to achieve fast delivery and speed up feature development, the size of the entire team had rapidly expanded, and the communication between sub-teams had decreased, and it was impossible to let all members know about the cause and effect of certain architecture designs. The rapid expansion of the team deprived new recruits of enough training. New members had less time to understand the entire architecture and its evolutionary history, but started writing code right away. Senior developers who were familiar with the product architecture had to fix the defects introduced by newcomers one after another".

After discussion, senior developers agreed that the most painful stages were code merging and joint debugging and later system testing. The duration of these two stages was simply uncontrollable with so many uncertainties. No one could predict the size of defects in each large release and how long would it take to resolve these defects. Sometimes, other modules were broken after fixing the bugs in one module. So, the team decided to solve this pain point first.

This Windows application was a typical three-layer system architecture (UI/Logic/Storage). After years of rapid development, its structure had been messy, and cross-layer calls and cross-calls of multi-service function modules often occurred, as shown in Figure 14.3. The product had six business modules in total, and this kind of cross-calls was seen everywhere. It is common that one module was modified while defects were found in others. So, the team's top priority was to optimize the system architecture by decoupling, and take the lead in solving the accumulated drawbacks in software architecture.

The team had already discussed the architecture optimization plan, but not yet implemented it. After the discussion in the Change Committee, a final decision was made: more than 50% of the R&D force would handle architecture optimization, and the others would maintain the public version, fix serious online defects, and develop urgent mini requirement that might affect user experience. This was a tough decision, because the team had to endure an output without major features for at least three months. This decision also showed that the software architecture problem was really serious.

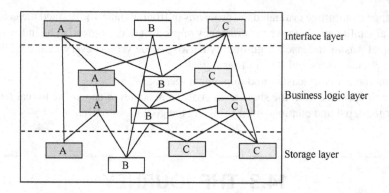

FIGURE 14.3 Pasta-style code.

What were the design principles of this software architecture adjustment? In addition to following the basic principles of software architecture, such as layering (UI layer, business logic layer, and storage service layer), and high-cohesion and low-coupling componentization, there is the "business-oriented plug-in principle", that is, there should be a clear call boundary between multiple modules, and the code providing business capabilities externally should be placed in the module of the concerned business, rather than implemented by the caller, thereby forming the Microcore Architecture in the end (see details about Microcore Architecture in Chapter 5), as shown in Figure 14.4.

After nearly three months of hard work, this new version was finally released. The development of subsequent versions showed that the work efficiency of the team had been improved. Without additional resources and adjustment of the workflow, the merging time was shortened from three days to one day, and the system testing time was shortened from ten days to five days. In this way, the period of large release was shortened from 29 days to 22 days, as shown in Figure 14.5. Due to time constraints, this architecture decoupling was not complete, and some features were still coupled.

More importantly, this improvement of software architecture has brought a greater benefit, that is, the entire team was capable of dual-version alternate parallel development, that is, the features by every three groups were released as one version, and two large versions could be run alternatively, as shown in Figure 14.6.

From the user perspective, the release time between two releases has been shortened, and each version contained certain new features, which has improved users' product perception.

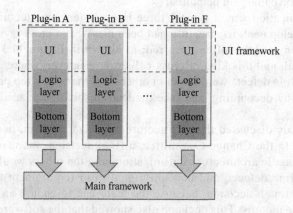

FIGURE 14.4 Service-oriented Microcore Architecture.

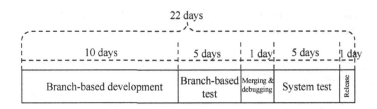

FIGURE 14.5   Release cycle after architecture decoupling.

14.3.2 Organization Decoupling

The product line manager believed that although efficiency was improved, the results were not satisfactory enough. Data exchange between functional departments remained poor, especially when there was problem in the production environment, there would be many complaints after the fixing was made and reviewed. However, it seemed that each role had very good reasons, for example:

- Ops staff: "There is no advance notice for the launch, the time is very tight, and there is no online documentation…"
- Project manager: "This problem was caused by a missed test…"
- QAs: "It was too late to get the candidate package, and the time for testing was compressed too much… Besides, the development quality was too poor and there were too many bugs."
- Developers: "We're at our wits' end. The product requirements have changed too much, and there is too many rework…"
- Product staff: "The requirements were presented long ago, the designers are insufficient, and the design draft comes out too late…"
- Designers: "The product requirements have not been sorted out clearly, there is a conflict with the previous design, and the developed program is different from the design draft…"

And every time, the improvement measures were a "twice-told story" and characterized by "defensive collaboration". For example:

- Developers: "Can you figure it out earlier! How can we start working without a final draft?" or "The requirements review has passed, and the requirements are frozen and cannot be changed!"
- Testers: "P0 test case fails, we will stop testing" or "As soon as entering the system testing phase, the requirements cannot be changed!"

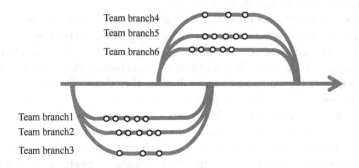

FIGURE 14.6   Dual-version branch-based release after architecture decoupling.

- Ops staff: "Can you notify us in advance for the next deployment" or "The deployment steps must be reviewed by us and filled in according to the operation standards, and there should be no omissions."
- Project managers: "Requirement changes must be strictly controlled, otherwise the project progress may be out of control".

In order to avoid errors, in large product teams, strict processes are often used to control risks. Among various functional departments, this kind of process often forms a kind of self-protection in upstream and downstream delivery. For example, even if the developer promises "a minor change", testers must do a complete regression, because they are responsible for the quality of the software that is finally released, and the past experience of testers shows that "developers' words are untrustworthy". However, product managers may say to himself, "What are these hundreds of people doing every day? The features were discussed a long time ago, why they are not released?"

As described earlier in this chapter, the entire product team was divided into disciplines by responsibility. It is hoped that each functional discipline will perform its duties and work together to achieve the common business goals of the product. This kind of division is a good organizational structure when the team is small, and it is easier for them to concentrate and complete known tasks efficiently. However, once the team is large, or the way to achieve the goal is not clear, this structure may lead to inefficiency.

Although everyone is aware of the overall goal of the product line, each discipline cannot be fully responsible for this goal. All of them will unconsciously pay more attention to their own work goals and standpoint. Every release needs to coordinate the resources between these disciplines, which requires a lot of communication and coordination.

How to motivate teams to break the barriers between disciplines? How to promote the awareness of overall interests? How to make the collaboration process not only look good but also really helpful to pursue the same goals?

Through discussions, the Change Committee finally decided to change the organizational structure by business orientation. This idea originated from the "feature team" advocated by agile software development. The difference is that each sub-team is not only responsible for multiple roles to deliver some software features end-to-end but also for achieving clear business goals. In fact, each sub-team is a mini-business unit, which is solely responsible for a certain range of sub-businesses, that is, a team with relatively complete domain is responsible for the business goals and performance results of the business area.

For this kind of business-oriented feature team, its goal is no longer to "deliver a set of features quickly" mentioned in some agile solution, but to take charge of the delivery of business value, that is, sub-teams shall be "business goal-oriented" to ensure the realization of the business strategic goals of the product.

We take sub-domains as a mini-business unit, and each unit has a responsible person who will lead the multi-role feature team. This team has its own business goal, which is something like, "In the next six months, the team's business performance will surpass other competitors, and the monthly average DAU in this sub-business domain will increase by 40%".

The organization structure at this point showed the post-improvement state of the team: a business-oriented feature team (six business centers and five supporting sub-departments). The personnel seats of the entire product line were adjusted, and the original seating area arranged by disciplines is changed to one by business domains. At the same time, for the staff in supporting departments (such as QAs in test center), if they participate in the work of a business domain, they should sit by the side of the staff of this center and hold responsibility for its business goals.

In this adjustment, a relatively big challenge was the selection and appointment of the person in charge of the business center. Since the person in charge of each business center can be regarded as a business leader instead of a R&D leader, he (she) needs to have an in-depth understanding of the annual strategy of the entire product line, and at the same time formulate a strategic landing plan for his team to achieve the business goals for which he is responsible, not just design and implementation of features.

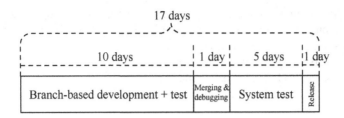

FIGURE 14.7 Version development cycle after the FT transformation.

Through this transformation, each business center has its own definite business goals to strive for, and the working atmosphere has also undergone great changes. When you walk to the working space of a business center, you will often hear conversations like the following:

- Developers: "Put this button is on the right, will it be better? This user experience seems to be not good enough, you'd better modify this design. I'll work late today and make some improvements".
- "I can help you trigger several scenarios to verify this feature", said a tester to a developer.
- "After you've fixed it, tell me right away, let me experience it first", said a product manager to a developer.
- "Is there a new version that can be verified?", aid a tester to a developer.
- "Everyone should verify it…it will be merged into the trunk soon…", aid a project manager to the team.

This change has led to unprecedented enthusiasm and initiative of all business teams, the internal closed loop of the business center becomes more prominent, and the communication efficiency has been improved. In the stage of branch R&D, the obvious boundary between the original development stage and the test stage has disappeared, and the delivery cycle was shortened from 15 days to 10 days, without any decrease in the output, as shown in Figure 14.7.

"Business FT (Feature Team)" effectively improves efficiency and solves the issue that disciplines strive for their own interests. However, after two releases, new voices emerged in business centers:

"Our feature has been done, but we have to wait to merge until the other two centers to complete their work. They are too slow; they are wasting our time!"

"We want a canary release to verify the requirements, and we don't want to wait for the product-level release to be scheduled".

The appearance of this sound was expected. After the adjustment of the organizational architecture, the morale and enthusiasm of each business center was mobilized. It had its own business goals, and the cooperation of all roles was the first priority.

However, the entire product R&D workflow has not changed, which is still a dual-version parallel mode (see Figure 14.6), which makes at least three business centers advance and retreat together to jointly release a large version. Each center wanted to have greater freedom, instead of being constrained by other centers.

14.3.3 R&D Workflow Reengineering

How about reducing the constraints from other business centers immediately and allowing them to release with freedom? The project management group held discussions and listed the following issues to be resolved:

1. Under what circumstances can each business center release their version externally? What is the quality standard for an outgoing version? How to ensure quality?

2. What is the relationship between the unified version of the entire product line and the separate version of each business center? When should they be merged into the unified version? How to merge the versions of different centers together?

3. Will too many version fragments harm the user experience? How can we protect user experience and receive feedback as soon as possible?

4. Who has the authority to approve outgoing versions? What is the strategy for the outgoing versions?

5. Do the outgoing versions of a business center contain the features of other business centers? Which features are contained?

6. If business center A has just released version A1, and business center B has completed a new version B1, will version B1 be merged with version A1 immediately?

7. If version A1 has to be rolled back due to a serious issue, how to deal with the subsequent version B1 or even C1?

8. Multiple centers want to release a new version at the same point. Do they need to merge them into one before releasing?

9. After the release of this new version, what should they do if a serious quality issue is found in the code of a branch version developed by one of the centers?

In order for each business center to operate according to its own R&D rhythm without affecting other centers, and to ensure the smooth running of all versions of the product, the above problems must be resolved.

14.3.3.1 The purpose and principles of multi-version release

They shall first resolve the most critical item. But which is the most critical item? After in-depth discussion, they found that the most critical problem was not in the list above which are all around "how to solve the conflictions in outgoing versions", while the most critical item for outgoing versions is that "What are the purpose and principle of the fast release of outgoing versions?" Only by answering this question can we figure out the solutions to the previous bunch of items on this basis.

The purpose is, of course, for quick verification. There are two aspects to be verified:

1. **Code quality.** Because it is an Internet product facing a large number of users, and its form is a Windows application not deployed at server side. Therefore, it can be considered that the environment for each installation is different, including the operating system and patch version, and other installed software. By releasing an outgoing version, code quality defects can be found as early as possible with the least impact.

2. **Business performance.** For this kind of consumer products, we cannot directly ask end users "What are your requirements?", because there are so many users and requirements, they cannot be exhaustive, and nobody could represent anyone else. As such, product manager needs to improve the product based on the real user feedback on the product. After the improvement is made, it is necessary to verify whether the changes meet the user requirements as soon as possible. The best way to quick verification is to let real users use it earlier and get early feedback such as issue reporting, experience feedback, and data collection.

There are two principles for releasing:

1. **Don't make users feel harassed.** If a user is frequently harassed by product upgrade, it is a kind of harm to the user. How to prevent users from having this trouble? Our principle is to "try to send no more than one upgrade reminder to each user within a month.

2. **Outgoing versions must be qualified so as not to make early users have any unpleasant experience.** The quality standards must be defined for releasing and rollback of the Beta

version. The standard for releasing is the same as the quality standard for large release. The standard for rollback means that if the quality feedback on an outgoing version reaches a specified level, it should be defined as "inferior quality and must be withdrawn". This principle is not easy to follow, because it requires support from both historical and new coming data.

Now that everyone has reached an agreement on the principles, the next step is to figure out how to do it.

14.3.3.2 Hybrid branch of virtual trunk

The team expected to achieve high-frequency release of multiple versions of the product line. The first solution was "Trunk-based Development & Branch-based Release". To achieve high release frequency, the original long-period branch mode would not work. Higher-frequency release relies on Trunk-based Development (see Figure 14.8), just like Paul Hammant had pointed out in an article on Facebook's Trunk-based Development in 2013. However, the team only had a few end-to-end automated regression testcases which were so flaky that they could not play the role as a safety net. It is unrealistic to build an automated safety net in a short time. In addition, it is unlikely for developers and testers to change their work habits in a short period of time while coping with the delivery pressure at the same time. Therefore, when dozens of people develop on the same trunk, it is impossible to guarantee the quality of the trunk.

Since this solution was unworkable, we decided not to make big changes on the original workflow, but only made some improvements. The original branching strategy was the team branch, that is, each FT had an exclusive branch (see Chapter 8 for details). The costs of merging and verification are high, the integration frequency is low, and the quality risk is uncontrollable. If we could achieve "no merging", would it be solved? We split the codebase by business domain. In this way, each business center had its own independent codebase and no longer modified the code in the codebase of other teams, as shown in Figure 14.9.

So, how could the six teams work together based on a separate codebase?

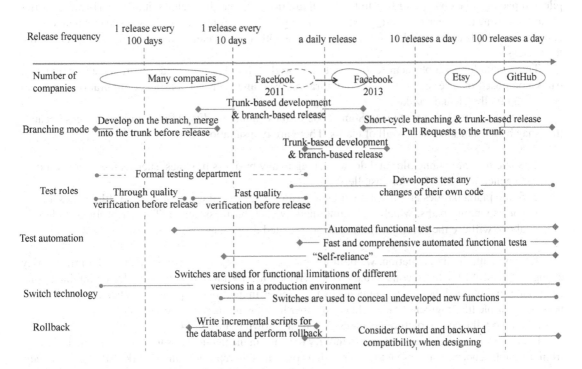

FIGURE 14.8   Mapping branching models to release frequency.

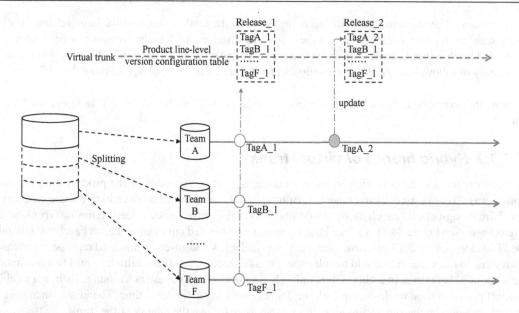

FIGURE 14.9   Multi-codebase development mode centered on version configuration table.

Assuming that the product line has just released a quality-compliant version, that is, the version "Release_1" in Figure 14.9, the source code of this version corresponds to different tags (TagA_1, TagB_1,..., TagF_1) in the codebase of each business center. These six tags form a configuration tuple, which is known as "version configuration list", that is, the latest qualified version tag (last_good_version_tag).

When team A wants to release with new features, it only needs to combine its version tag "TagA_2" with the "last_good_vesion_tag" of other teams to form a new version configuration list, and then compile and package the code according to this configuration list, and then release it after verification. After release, it is time to change the "last_good_version_tag" of Team A to "TagA_2", and use this new version configuration tuple as the baseline for the next release. Other teams can do the similar steps when asking for a release.

There is no longer a physical repository at the product line level, instead, it is replaced by a virtual trunk composed of a series of version configuration lists, and each version tag configuration tuple is a version tag on the virtual trunk.

However, reality is not that ideal. Some code or files cannot be divided into multiple pieces because they may be used or modified by all of teams. There are two situations here:

1. Some files are public files and do not belong to any business modules, such as the scripts used to generate the application installers.
2. Some plaintext files are maintained by all teams, such as a file with a series of file names and corresponding paths, which are maintained by each business center. The script for installers above will use the list in the file to perform related operations.

To cope with the first situation, we built a separate repository to store these public and infrequently changed codes. As for the second situation, we divided it into multiple fragments by maintainers, and each center maintained their own fragments by themselves in their own repository. When this file list was needed, multiple file fragments were spliced together by tools in the public repository.

As a result, the code structure becomes the one as shown in Figure 14.10.

In Figure 14.10, when team A needs to modify the code in the public repository, it needs to cut a branch from the public codebase and use it together with its own domain repository in its work. After team A's current version passes the quality verification, the changes on the branch of the public repository can be merged

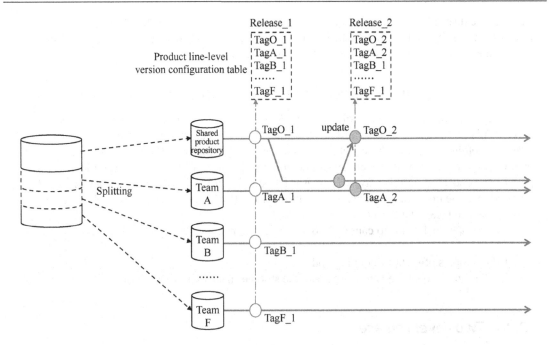

FIGURE 14.10   Hybrid branch release with public codebase branches.

back into the trunk of the public repository and tagged with "TagO_2". In this way, the latest product version configuration list consists of the following tag collection {TagO_2, TagA_2, TagB_1,…, TagF_1}.

14.3.3.3 Create a unified product library

Certain detailed problems need to be solved too. Developers will face a basic problem after splitting codebase: How to debug code locally? Each developer needs the code of the other five teams to debug the application. Since the source code of the other five teams is not provided, each team must offer others with qualified binary components built by themselves.

In order to do it, we split the solution file of the project (the solution file of the project "Visual Studio") so that the respective components can be generated independently. The splitting principles are as follows:

- Each team has its own project build files for its own repository.
- Each team's own code should be linked to create binary components.
- Each team should only depend on the binary components offered by other teams.
- Developers should get the qualified binaries of other teams easily when they need.
- Every binary from all teams should be traceable in the official artifact repository. "Traceable" means that the source code, revision and author can be easily found (see Chapter 11 about SCM (Software Configuration Management)).
- The caller can only invoke the service provided by other teams by public API.

According to the above principles, we have sorted out the tasks to be completed:

- Refactor the existing project solution files to create corresponding project files for each module.
- Provide a way to automatically put the binary components created and verified by each team into a unified artifact repository under unified management.
- Provide tools for developers to fetch binaries from the artifact repository above with one click, so as to facilitate debugging.

During the discussions with the team, an issue in the legacy codebase is that the large PDB files were committed into SVN (Subversion), which seriously violates SCM principles shown in Chapter 11. Therefore, the PDB files were also taken out from the codebase.

WHY DID THE TEAM PUT THE BINARY FILES IN SVN

Why did the team put the binary files in SVN? The reason couldn't be simpler – they were too "lazy". This product uses lots of third-party library files. For easier access to these files, the team directly submitted them to the codebase. Moreover, every time the official release package was built before release, PDB files were generated at the same time. These large binary files were also put into the codebase. In this way, when a user found a defect in the software package, it would be reported to the team, then developers would look for the PDB files of the corresponding version in the codebase to locate the defect.

But this approach tends to cause the following problems:

1. Developers often fail in pulling code.
2. The source codebase is too large, and the storage space expands too fast.

14.3.3.4 Two-level release

We wanted each business center to release its own candidate features and verify their quality and performance as soon as possible by collecting the user feedback. However, the candidate features have to pass the verification before being promoted. So, we setup a two-level release: one is for business center level, meaning that each center can release trial versions with an exclusive version config list to small groups. The other is for product level, meaning that the unified version has a single unified version config list for the product, as shown in Figure 14.11.

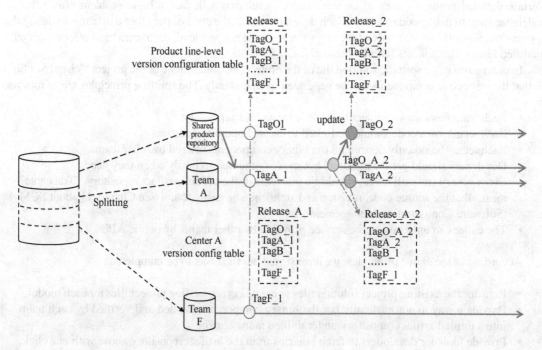

FIGURE 14.11   Schematic diagram of two-level release.

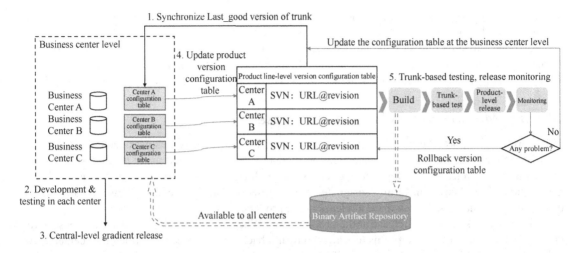

FIGURE 14.12   Update process of two-level version configuration table.

When Team A modifies code and adds new features, they shall first release at the business center level: use Release_A_2 (see Figure 14.11) – a version configuration list for Team A – to build, verify, and take a canary release at the business center level. If it is good enough, the branch of the public repository owned by Team A would be merged into the trunk of the public repository as TagO_2. After that, Team A can use Release_2, the version config list at the product level to build, verify, and take a release at the product level, which means more broad users.

Once the product-level release is successful, the Continuous Delivery Platform will automatically push the code with the tag "TagO_2" in the public repository down to the other branches of the public repository, and update the content of Last_good_version in all of the version configuration list at the business center level. At this point, all business centers have to use Last_good_version as the baseline for any coming release.

When the latest release of the product level has to be rollbacked due to a serious quality issue, developers just need to reset the version configuration list with the previous list. The platform will send notification to others. The workflow of the entire product is shown in Figure 14.12.

14.3.3.5 Quality assurance mechanism

The challenges for quality management of Windows application with Internet access come from the version fragments and the uncontrolled operating environment. Different users may get a variety of versions from different channels. The operating systems are constantly patched or upgraded, especially Windows that has patch packages almost every week. In addition, in order to provide a better user experience, almost all customer software avoid forcing users to upgrade. To ensure the quality of outgoing versions, we have established a gradient release mechanism at both the business center level and the product level.

As compared with the unified major-version release before the transformation starts, the later multi-branch based minor-version release has a prominent difference, that is, it has increased the number of outgoing versions. There must be a proper mechanism for controlling external release, quality monitoring, and recall of each minor version, as well as a strategy for merging branch code with trunk code after successful quality verification, otherwise there will be chaotic versions or even situations out of control.

Therefore, we specified quality standards for each team's branch-based and trunk-based outgoing versions and monitored them accordingly. Different gradients correspond to different standards. For example, the branch-based outgoing versions have four gradients as 1x, 5x, 10x, and 20x to verify the stability of the release from any business center. The trunk-based outgoing versions have eight levels of gradients, including 1y, 2y, 10y, 50y, 100y, and 200y. Each gradient has stability baseline with multiple indicators, one of which is crash rate. Once the release does not meet the baseline of the daily crash rate, it is not allowed to be merged into the trunk, but fixed immediately and locally.

Such mechanism stimulates the business leaders to pay equal attention to business indicators and basic quality. If the basic quality is not good enough, their new features cannot be released in time before fixing the quality issues even though the new features is ready and has nothing to do with the blocker bugs.

14.3.3.6 Multipartite collaborative release

This workflow supports the parallel development and release for multiple business centers at any time. Well, how to manage the release frequency at the product level? We've tried many mechanisms to coordinate the unified release of multiple business centers, and finally proved that the effective mechanism is not a "planned economy" (uniformly designated release time), but a "free economy" (as long as the code of any center is qualified, he can drive a release at the product level).

There is a "token" for the release at the product level. When a center is about to drive a release at the product level, it shall first acquire this token and return it back after the release, while other centers have to keep waiting until this token is returned. If a business center holding the token fails to conduct a quality verification in a timely manner, then other centers will be forced to queue up for release. This is a typical style of six-step check-in dance.

A Continuous Delivery platform supports two or more business centers to release a version together, they can simply update their latest code tags in the version configuration list at the product level. As shown in Figure 14.13, only one business center plays a leading role in a certain release, with other centers acting as "free riders".

After a period of operation, two or more business centers releasing versions together have become less and less. Why? It is because we have a rule: when there is a "free riders" release with serious bugs, both the driver and riders have to rollback. So, each center prefers to release its own code independently, so as not to be implicated by others. Of course, the version configuration list managed by a genuine Continuous Delivery platform is fairly complicated, because each center has multiple repositories (an entire product had altogether 12 repositories at that time), and configuration management and version compilation need to support variables such as @latest, @last_good, etc.

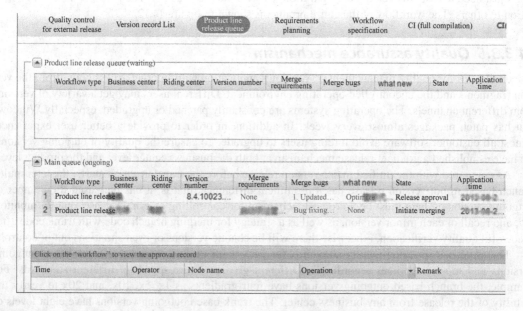

FIGURE 14.13 Customed Continuous Delivery management platform.

14.3.3.7 A build cloud for compilation

Before the workflow was changed, each center managed its own powerful machine for compilation and build. In case of compilation and building at the product level, unexpected failures occurred from time to time. Many failures were caused by the inconsistent and chaotic compilation environment of each center. Therefore, we established a unified cloud platform for compilation and building at the product level to be used by all centers. Even the center-level release is compiled on this cloud. In order to speed up compilation, commercial tools with the capability of incremental compilation were also purchased.

14.3.4 Optimization for Automation Efficiency

Now we have created a feasible R&D management model and it works in the context. The next step is to optimize the speed of the workflow as a whole, and further improve software quality.

For example, when any defect is found in an outgoing version, the manual modification of the version configuration list is error-prone. Whenever the version number Last_good is updated, the code synchronization to the branches of each team is also done manually, but some teams may forget about it. As the number of releases is on the rise, testing efficiency needs to be improved.

It is a key to eliminate manual operations as much as possible by automation to avoid human errors, and improve quality assurance efficiency. We built a visual Continuous Delivery platform, a testing automation system, and a testcase conflict analysis system, and also introduce distributed compilation with a cloud platform. Consequently, as for a release at the product level, the time span from code merging to release is shortened from seven days (two-level version release) to four hours, as shown in Figure 14.14.

The crash rate was relatively high, so we setup a special force to press down to a specified level. However, there are many long-tail crashes that were not easy to reproduce or repair, we had to disband this workgroup, dispatch all crashed cases to each center, and ask them to fix their own cases. Since the

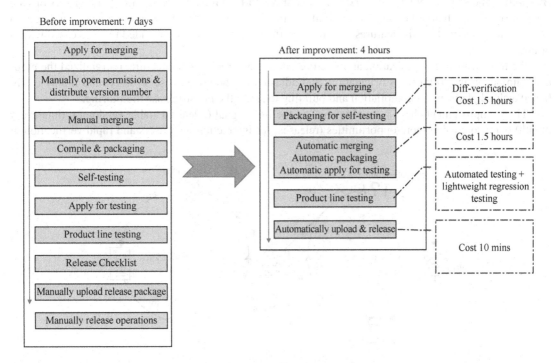

FIGURE 14.14 Comparison of time span from merging to release before and after the improvement.

code had been decoupled, most crashes could be located to domain modules that a center was accountable for. Besides, an overall quality platform was built to monitor, analyze, and verify for further optimization.

Two Beta versions can be released every day. In order to make the version configuration list at both levels remain consistent, we've also developed an automatic synchronization mechanism. Once the version configuration list at the product level is updated, there will be automatic synchronization to each business center, so that they can update their code baseline as soon as possible, quickly integrate with the features of other centers, and finally achieve the effect of continuous integration (CI) among the six business centers.

In order to verify the effect of the newly built mechanism in rapid release, monitoring and alarm, one-click hemostasis, and one-click rollback, we also organized "fire drills": some problematic code was deliberately designed and randomly released to the designated machines within a given period of time, in an aim to verify whether the team has a valid workflow in response to emergencies and to improve it continuously.

These automated monitoring means can minimize the impact on users and improve emergency response capability of the team.

14.4 SUMMARY

Thanks to a series of continuous improvements, the team is capable of twice releases every day at the product level, and every week there will be a qualified candidate version for a large-scale release. There are more releases at the business-center level. In addition, users do not receive many notifications of upgrading, because the versions for fast verification of features at the business-center level are released to users who are isolated.

This improvement is to build the double-flywheels of Continuous Delivery, as shown in Figure 14.15. By splitting the features of a major version into multiple parallel minor versions, these minor versions are verified right away before being released to all users to obtain user feedback as soon as possible. Based on the real feedback data, the features contained in the minor versions are decided to be released widely or not.

We transformed the application architecture into the Microcore Architecture, reorganized the product team according to business orientation, and adjusted the branch-release strategy, and finally established a cloud platform for compilation and building to strengthen post-release monitoring.

These improvements have not only achieved the initial goal (release a stable version on time every month) but also created more opportunities (releases) for interaction with users and rapid verification of

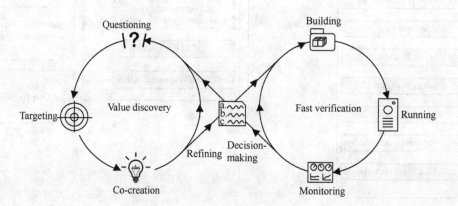

FIGURE 14.15 Double-flywheels of Continuous Delivery.

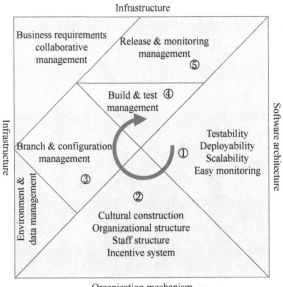

FIGURE 14.16   Tangram of Continuous Delivery.

the product. The construction of a tool platform is able to solidify workflow. And clearly defined rules can reduce the costs of communications for releases.

After mapping these improvements to the Tangram of Continuous Delivery (see Figure 14.16), you may find that in the entire improvement process we made more efforts in improving the five plates in the order shown in the figure, but not all of the practices in Continuous Delivery 2.0 were fully implemented. For example, we didn't mention automated unit testing, functional testing, practices such as iteration management, retrospective, and story wall management, and we didn't stress the six-step check-in dance for CI.

In fact, we didn't spend too much time on these small-team level practices, but concentrated on the overall optimization of the entire team.

Of course, this is not to say that practices in small-team level are not important. It is to say that in the implementation process, we must flexibly formulate plans according to the team status, product stage, and specific goals. The goal is not to introduce many so-called best practices, but to solve the top-priority issue faced by the team within a limited time.

The foremost thing for large dot-com companies to make continuous improvement is that the leadership team must have the determination to do so. Especially, when short-term improvements have yielded no significant effect, they need to be confident enough to overcome the resistance of organizational inertia to transformation.

How Can Small Teams Implement a "Counter Attack"?

15

This chapter talks about how can a small team (less than ten people) walk out of the shadow of "death march" to achieve "zero-defect delivery" through continuous improvement (CI). The product delivered by this team is an embedded software in mobile devices distributed to users. It is characterized by a high distribution cost, and a high reparation cost in case of defects. The Shift-right Testing strategy as described in Chapter 13 could not work, and we could only use the Shift-left Testing strategy.

This team is a cross-function feature team with members playing different roles. The key to this improvement was to challenge the team's original way of working and change their work habits. This improvement ran through the entire project development cycle about 24 weeks, and finally fixed their way of working by guiding them to discover and improve themselves.

15.1 BACKGROUND

Company N was once a world's leading mobile device manufacturer, and started an all-round agile transformation as early as 2009. This case occurred in the company's subsidiary in mainland China. With a research and development (R&D) department made up of about 500 people, this subsidiary had an organizational structure at that time illustrated in Figure 15.1. This subsidiary had several R&D lines and product planning lines. Each R&D line lead by a Line Manager served as a functional module of mobile devices (such as system kernel, audio/video, and so on). Each line was staffed with its own developers and testers. However, the Line Manager didn't report work to the R&D department, but to the Product Management Team (PMT) of the product planning line. This is partly because the company produces mobile devices, rather than Customer Apps. The overall roadmap of mobile devices is uniformly formulated by the company, which is oriented to different markets around the world. The team of each R&D line was responsible for developing and maintaining all modules of products, and the R&D cycle of each new type of product was more than ten months.

When the R&D of a new product was initiated, the subsidiary would dispatch personnel from various service lines to form a new project team and divide them into sub-teams according to their respective modules. The technical leader (see Figure 15.1) was the Scrum Master of sub-teams, and the PMT would assign a product owner to serve as the product owner of sub-teams. This new project would be run with the Scrum of Scrums mode, that is, the operating mode of each sub-team was to comply with the Scrum framework, and this project had communication channels between Scrums (see Figure 15.2). In addition, there was a full-time CI team responsible for the maintenance of the CI practices of the new product, such as building the product regularly every day, maintaining, and running a set of automated functional test cases.

However, even with "agile" mode, when entering the stage of system integration, previous products would have many defects, and the schedule and quality were still risky. Also, the team collaboration

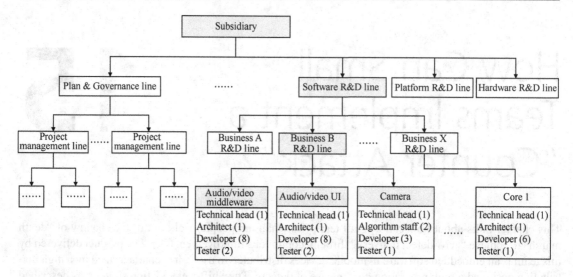

FIGURE 15.1   Organization structure of company N after agile transformation.

facilitated by Scrum mode had not become smoother. It is evidenced by a chat about the "retrospective meeting" in the elevator room:

A: "Are you going to a meeting?"
B (a Scrum Master): "Yes. We're going to discuss about the development of new features".
A: "But your team is about to have a retrospective meeting? You'll miss it!"
B: "Oh, I must thank this technical discussion, I just can't bear the retrospective".
A: "You're right. The retrospective is of no use in solving problems, but to blame".

Company N's agile transformation had lasted for three years. All teams had built the Scrum framework, but it seemed like a copycat instead of a veritable Scrum framework. At first glance, they could coherently finish all the routines of Scrum, but in fact, they made every movement feebly and paradoxically.

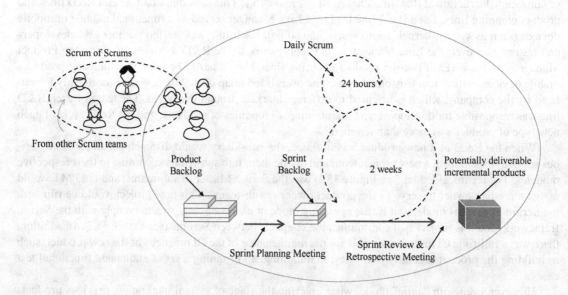

FIGURE 15.2   Scrum framework.

Under this circumstance, it was hard to make in-depth improvements by publicity and education, but refer to the real improvement cases of typical teams within the company, and made it as a cornerstone for making a wider range of organizational improvements. So, the R&D department decided to select a pilot team to receive in-depth coaching.

15.1.1 A "Death March" before Improvement

It was the R&D team responsible for audio/video UI module that was selected as the pilot team. They had just completed a Death March in a project.

DEATH MARCH

The term Death March was derived from the book *Death March* (1997) of Ed. Yourdon. It usually refers to the software projects with a development cycle more than twice as long as expected. It is used to describe projects that are almost impossible to complete in accordance with the schedule, indicating that an unbearable atmosphere of potential failure is permeated around project participants.

This pilot team consisted of a product owner from the PMT and the original team members developing audio/video UI, as shown in Figure 15.1.

1. Inexperienced team members. Most of the developers and testers had been in the company for less than half a year, and some team members were just recruited three months ago.
2. Low morale. In the previous project that was just delivered, the development took only one month, but one and a half months were spent in fixing bugs, and working overtime even became a routine.

15.1.2 Zero-Defect Delivery after Improvement

The selected project was to adapt mobile operating system for a new mobile device, which required the participation of three large R&D teams (hardware team, platform R&D team, and software R&D team). The project had a total of more than 200 people, and the entire development cycle was expected to be ten months. Among them, the software R&D team had about 100 people; they were divided into multiple Scrum teams according to different feature modules. As a R&D project for a mobile device-oriented product, it was remarkably different from the Internet products in the following aspects:

- A long development cycle (more than six months) for one-shot release.
- A large number of participants (about 200 people).
- High quality requirements (if a defect is found after the feature phones are sold, the recall and repair costs are quite high, so comprehensive and thorough quality control is required, and a defect-free delivery should be achieved as far as possible).
- A large legacy software. The software had a history of ten years with a codebase storing more than 15 million lines of code.

After months of hard work, the audio/video UI R&D team had achieved the goal of defect-free and punctual delivery – no other team had done so in the past.

- Time and scope: Even if optimization requirements are added in the later stage, R&D tasks can still be completed on time.

- Product quality: All features are verified to be defect free after delivery.
- Collaboration process: The team abandoned many original workflows and created a new development practice. For example:
  - Requirements decomposition (user story) and relative estimation.
  - Establish a Kanban practice based on the flow of small requirements (user stories), and no longer track individual activities and tasks.
  - Use the Trunk-based Development mode.
  - Developers write automated unit tests.
  - Each small requirement is split into multiple tasks.
  - Submit the code to the trunk once a task is completed.
  - Once each small requirement is completed, the feature acceptance test is carried out.

15.2 IMPROVEMENT METHODOLOGY

The transformation path of large teams is utterly different from that of small teams. It is more effective for a large team to start transformation with the overall optimization (see Chapter 14). However, for a small team with fewer resources and less decision-making influence, it should pay more attention to CI within the team.

15.2.1 Guiding Ideology

The guiding ideology of "goal-driven, starting from simple issue, and continuous improvement" remains unchanged. After discussing with the team's manager (the head of the R&D line), the audio/video UI R&D team should fulfill the following goals in this pilot project:

- Time and scope: Within the planned timetable, complete feature development.
- Quality: The quality of the deliverables reaches the standard at one time.
- Process: Establish a good workflow and a set of good work habits, and the team experiences can be solidified.

15.2.2 Selection of the Pilot Team

Choosing a pilot team usually considers the following four points:

1. Moderate pressure and slack time. After all, everyone in the team needs to improve themselves, not just to improve the process itself. If the project has a tight schedule and the R&D team is "exhausted", then members will tend to reject any change, because any change at this time has great uncertainties and risks. However, the existence of delivery pressure is reasonable, or else the pilot effect can hardly be achieved, and the "pilot project" itself will be meaningless.
2. Team leader should be open-minded enough to be able to withstand pressure and dare to try. This transformation is a challenge to everyone in the team, especially to the team leader, because he (she) bears the main responsibility for the final delivery. Without an open mind, he (she) is likely to deal with problems and challenges in an old-fashioned manner. If so, he (she) will fall into a self-enclosed protection state.
3. Team members are enthusiastic. If team members are not eager for the upcoming changes, they will lack positive thinking, interaction, and feedback in the improvement process. After the end

of the pilot, they will not have a strong sense of pride and accomplishment. This is inconsistent with the meaning and original intention of the pilot team.
4. The business side has a strong demand for frequent and rapid delivery. If the business side is not demanding in this regard, even if the team has mastered various skills, its deliverables will be overshadowed by the lack of positive feedback from the business side.

Through a thorough communication with a R&D line manager, we had reached a consensus. According to the requirements status of the new project, as well as the ability of team leader and the enthusiasm of team members, we could select a pilot team from the several sub-business teams under his management.

15.3 STAGE 1: PREPARATION

When the pilot started, this project had entered the R&D preparation period. The product owner and technical leader had received the product backlog that they were responsible for, and the technical leader had made a preliminary estimate (the estimation unit is "human week" as shown in Figure 15.3). Other developers and a tester (only one) in the team had no idea of the specific feature contents. Careful readers may find that this product backlog has the following characteristics in Figure 15.3:

1. There are two epic stories in Figure 15.3 (① and ②), and each epic story contains multiple user stories (requirements).
2. Each user story is written in the format of "As a user, I'd like to do xxxx".
3. Each user story has a business priority (the first column of numbers in Figure 15.3).

This shows that the team had received Scrum training and had a better understanding of the Scrum operation process.

Priority	Epic	User story	Estimate (person/week)	UX estimate
①	(Easy Editing-Video Editing mode UI)			3
116		As an user, I'd like to enter the edit mode by choose "Replace voice"	2	
113		As an user, I want to see the progress bar in the editing mode.	0.5	
117		As an user, I want to see the current playing time and length of the progress	0.5	
120		As an user, I'm able to adjust the volumn in the editing mode.	0.5	
114		—Depends on video MO design, current effort based on simple design	1	
111		As an user, After I choose "Replace voice" in opthon menu, current video should start to play from the top	1	
119		As an user, After I choose "Replace voice" in opthon menu, MSK	1	
118		As an user, After I choose "Replace voice" in opthon menu, play icon	1	
②	(Easy Editing-Video Editing mode UI)			
90		As an user, I'd like to record voice while playing video and replace the original sound in video clip.		0.3
93		As an user, I'd like to choose the start point of recording through	2	1
91		As an user, I'd like to start recording by press MSK ("select" key) —Depends on video MO design, current effort based on average design	4	

FIGURE 15.3   Schematic diagram of the original product backlog.

15.3.1 Feature Introduction and Requirements Decomposition

The team held a meeting to introduce product features where the product owner explained the feature requirements (see Figure 15.4), and further split and reorganized the product backlog.

Compared with senior engineers, the estimation from a less experienced engineer would be longer, and the accuracy would be lower. Compared with a small and simple requirement, the larger one would be harder for team members to understand and communicate. So, it is prone to cause ambiguity and have a negative impact on the quality and efficiency of implementation.

Facts have proved that in the process of requirements splitting, the team discovered and clarified some inconsistent understandings of requirements that had already existed, as well as some business scenarios missed by the product manager in advance. The final product backlog is shown in Figure 15.4. For details about requirements decomposition, see Section 6.3.

Careful readers may notice the details in Figure 15.4. The estimation was not done at this point but added after the following activities. Moreover, some items in the product backlog were not the same as the requirements for user stories in the textbook.

- Technical note: Entry UI_014 also indicates how to implement it (see the underlined text in Figure 15.4).
- The title format is not that important: UI_017 is not written in the standard format for user stories.
- Special user story: The name of the entry UI_024 is "Spike on US_014" ("spike" is a metaphor for quick learning and trying). Because the team thought that the implementation of US_014 was uncertain and required a little research in advance.

No.	External dependency	User story	Estimated points
UI_001		As an user, I'd like to see an option to clip my music/voice file	0
UI_002		Building UT framework for Audio clipping Delegate and run locally	2
UI_003		Create the skeleton for the Audio Clipping Delegate	3
UI_004		Make the Audio Clippintg Delegade unit test run automatically	2
UI_005		As an user, I'd like to enter the edit mode by choose "Clip" from opton menu. —Launch the Audio Clipping Delegate when selecting the Clip option from the	5
UI_006	Core_005	If Core_005 CAN be done before UI_006, user story is: —User Edit Delegate interface with delayed feedback. If Core_005 CAN NOT be done before UI_006, user story is: —Fake functionlity in UI layer（copy file in FS)	2
UI_007		As an user, I'd like to have a visual indicator while saving file. —Stqrt the Audio Clipping controller and make htat clip the predefined file	5
UI_008		Handle end key pressed on the wait note（Saving process)	5
UI_009		Current track in NPS as input to the Audio Clipping Delegate	1
UI_024		Spike on US_014	5
UI_014	Core_005	As an user, After I choose "Clip" in option menu, current music should start to play from the top: —Create a new MO MO clip which inherit from MO Sound —Make the Audio Clipping Controller create it —Make the MO Clip have the interface to the Tone Server	8
UI_012		As an user, After I choose "Clip" in option menu, MSK change to "Select"	1
UI_013		As an user, I'd like to see a progress bar which can indicate: —Music playing progress	2
UI_015		As an user, I'd like to use MSK to mark the start point	2
UI_016		As an user, After start point marked, I'd like to use MSK to mark the end point	2
UI_017		Display FF button in the Audio Clipping UI Delegate	1

FIGURE 15.4 Product backlog after decomposition and estimated points.

15.3.2 Architecture Design and Requirements Dependency Identification

At the time of requirements splitting, the team also had some design discussions. For example, since the new feature was not available in previous products at all, engineers intended to isolate it from the old codebase and implement a new module interacted with old one by an anticorrosive layer. This is like a Facade Pattern in design. Through this isolation, the independence of new feature could be guaranteed, and it was easy to maintain and enhance the feature later. Its schematic diagram is shown in Figure 15.5.

This was in fact a small step for architecture decoupling, and the team had to take on extra work. In addition, some requirements dependencies were also identified in the discussion. These dependencies included not only those within the team but also on other teams. For example, entries UI_006 and UI_014 depended on the interface provided by the No. 005 Requirement of the audio/video middleware team (Core team).

After splitting, the team immediately arranged a meeting to discuss what they should do to guarantee the project quality and schedule once entering the development stage. The team decided to introduce three new practices, namely, automated unit testing, code review before check-in, and automated code-style check. This is why there are entries UI_002 and UI_004 in Figure 15.5. They were not user stories, but two tasks that must be completed in order to improve quality and efficiency.

15.3.3 Workload Estimation and Scheduling

After the requirements were split, it was time to estimate and schedule their work. A team member raised questions as follows:

"If we write unit tests, will the workload be doubled?"

"We've not written unit tests before, so can we add the learning time into the schedule?"

"How much time to be added for code review?"

"Does the test time need to be estimated separately?"

Finally, the team adopted a new estimation by "Story Points", which is a relative size estimation without a time unit. This method is based on the following assumptions:

1. Development activities should always be the bottleneck in the entire process (this is also the ideal state of value flow). In other words, testing for a certain requirement can be completed quickly after it is dev-completed. So, the test exclusive cycle can be ignored, as shown in Figure 15.6.

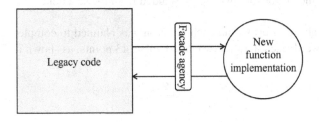

FIGURE 15.5 Schematic diagram of architecture decoupling.

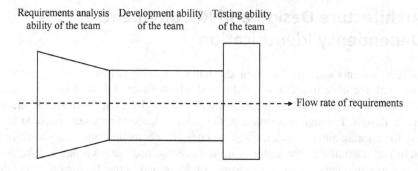

Requirements analysis ability of the team Development ability of the team Testing ability of the team

Flow rate of requirements

FIGURE 15.6 Flow speed is limited by the minimum bottleneck of the entire pipeline.

2. Regarding the total workload for developing, we can approximate that greater workload of development will lead to greater workload of unit testing and code review. That is to say, for the two requirements i and k, the ratio of workload for coding and debugging is similar to that for unit testing and for code review, as shown in Figure 15.7. In the figure, Vc is the workload for coding adjustment of a piece of requirement; Vt is the automation testing workload of it; Vr is the code review workload of this requirement. Therefore, when doing estimation, we can only consider the workload of coding and debugging.

The specific estimation method can be found in Appendix B. It should be noted that deviations are unavoidable for any estimate. The size of a deviation is related to many factors, but as long as the requirements have similar size and the workload is less than one person-week, the deviation is usually acceptable for a long-cycle project.

After splitting and estimating, the team had obtained a new user story list and workload, as shown in Figure 15.4. In this list, there are a total of 39 user stories, with a total scale of 120 points.

Now the next step was to estimate the duration to complete the project. When discussing the amount of work that can be done in each iteration, the following four factors need to be considered:

1. Learning space: The output of the first three iterations is usually low. After the project is started, the team still needs some preparations, for example, team-level CI server and automation build scripts, learning to write automation unit tests, and getting accustomed to new workflow.
2. Readiness: After going through three iterations, the work speed will increase, because the preparation of basic tools has been completed at that time, team members are familiar with the workflow, and the automation unit testing will provide a "safety net" for the team to modify the code and discover problems in time.
3. Buffer: Although being confident in the results, the technical leader still added a buffer time of 1.5 iterations in order to have greater certainty.
4. Composition of working hours: Normal working hours (no extra work at night), excluding weekends, and holidays. Due to a large time span, team members reported their vacation arrangements, so the time on vacation was also excluded from the schedule.

According to the above information, each iteration was planned to complete nine points at the first three iterations. Afterward, each iteration would complete 13 points, as shown in Figure 15.8. It is worth

$$\frac{V_{c\,(i)}}{V_{c\,(k)}} \approx \frac{V_{t\,(i)}}{V_{t\,(k)}} \approx \frac{V_{r\,(i)}}{V_{r\,(k)}}$$

FIGURE 15.7 The workload of development, unit testing, and code review is proportional.

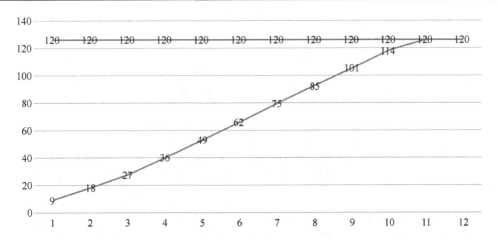

FIGURE 15.8 Burn-up chart of original project plan.

noting that the "complete" here is not mean to complete the development activities of developers, but to pass the testers' acceptance.

15.4 STAGE 2: DELIVERY

This period was of great significance for the team to achieve true transformation. Before the final result (software delivery) was obtained, all the activities done in the preparation stage couldn't make the team fully confident in software delivery. In delivery stage, the team was guided to identify problems, seek CI, and encourage team members to participate in process improvement and construction, in order to be capable of self-driven.

15.4.1 Improve Workflow with Kanban

The Kanban method is, first of all, an effective method for discovering process problems. By visualizing the current process status, identifying existing problems, and quickly formulating and implementing countermeasures, the Kanban method is favorable for CI and fulfillment of the goal of increasing efficiency. Now, I'd like to introduce how did the team identify and solve problems by visualizing the process.

15.4.1.1 Identify bad smells

In previous project, the entire team could only deliver two requirements per iteration. Owing to large granularity, these two requirements had been posted on the left side of the whiteboard and remained motionless until the end of the iteration. The names of the team members were written on the right side of the whit board, and there were only three columns respectively showing "To Do", "Doing", and "Done". The specific tasks of the team members were filled in each column, and each member had a corridor, as shown in Figure 15.9.

This story wall layout has two bad smells: one is a two-week iteration (a team only does Story 1 and Story 2 with heavy workload). The other is to templatize task decomposition of developers and testers (see Table 15.1), which is in line with the task decomposition in the waterfall development method described in Chapter 6.

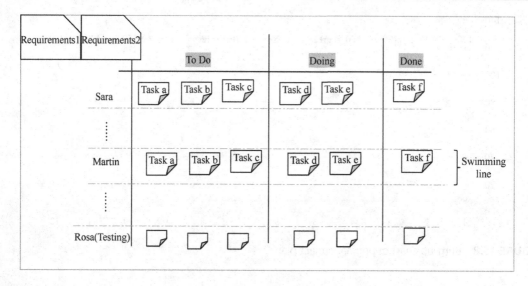

FIGURE 15.9 Original task wall (used to track members' work).

These two bad smells may cause three problems:

1. Late integration. Only at the end of this iteration can developers' code for the two requirements be integrated for testing. Since the integration is too late, the quality may be uncontrollable in the process.
2. The quality of tasks cannot be verified. In the work process, there is no specific standard for task-completed (same as Definition of Done [DoD]), and it is only decomposed according to the type of work itself.
3. The test cases written by testers are only used at the end of an iteration for integration.

15.4.1.2 Let the value flow

In this pilot project, we took the tasks like templates as the "columns" of the story wall and put them at the top of the column, and then put the split user stories (fine-grained requirements) as work items in the corresponding status bar on the wall. As the project progresses, these fine-grained requirements flow from the left to the right of the whiteboard. Whenever a user story goes to the last column ("Done"), it means that it has passed the acceptance test, and its story points can be counted as "iteration speed". In this way, the team can see the real project progress at all times, as shown in Figure 15.10.

You may have noticed that in the "Development" column, there is a small note in the upper right corner of the first requirement saying "bug". On the real story wall, that is a red note attached to the requirement. This status indicates that it has been developed, but a bug is found during testing. Testers abbreviate the defect on a red note, paste it on the requirement card, put it back into the "Development" column, and notice developers to fix.

TABLE 15.1 Task decomposition by developers and testers

DEVELOPER	TESTER
a. Design <X> module	a. Write testcases for Story
b. Modify <X> module	b. Test Story <A>
c. Code review of modified <X> module	

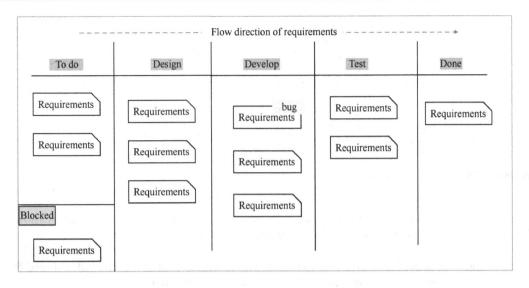

FIGURE 15.10   Story wall centered on value flow.

In the "Blocking" column, there are requirements that are under development but unable to proceed for the time being due to external reasons (such as external dependencies or unavailable external environments) in the process. The Scrum Master shall pay special attention to this column and urge the proposition of a solution.

CONFUSION OF TESTERS

1. How can we display the testing-related work (such as writing testcases) on the story wall? On the story wall, we only track changes in the requirement status, not to record the workload of each team member. The requirements placed in the "To Do status bar" should be those for writing acceptance conditions or testcases.
2. When to write testcases?
    We hope to prepare enough test cases for each requirement in the iteration before entering an iteration. What needs to be ensured is that before developers start the development of this requirement, we've finished writing test cases and have them passed the review. The form of review is not limited, sending emails or face-to-face communication is both available.

15.4.1.3 Standard definition of done in explicit declaration

Many developers were "novices". In order to help them quickly understand the system architecture, use the readymade system development framework proficiently and correctly, so as to ensure code quality and avoid rework due to too many defects in the later stage, the team made two commitments at the launch of the project: (1) Module design documents must be written and reviewed before coding. (2) Code review is required after coding. However, in the actual operation, developers failed to do so, they did not write design documents until finishing coding.

At an iteration retrospective meeting, we re-emphasized these two commitments and clarified the activities that must be completed each time the Story was moved. In order to remind everyone at all times,

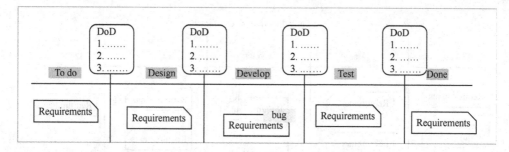

FIGURE 15.11   User story wall with DoD.

we printed them out and pasted them between each column, as shown in Figure 15.11. This is known as "Definition of Done", and its state transition conditions are as follows:

- To Do → Design: The acceptance conditions (or test cases) must be written and reviewed by product personnel, developers, and testers, and there is no objection.
- Design → Development: Complete the update of design documents and complete the design review.
- Development → Test: Write corresponding automated unit test cases, ensure that all test cases can pass, and code review is completed.
- Test → Done: All testcases passed and all bugs are fixed.

15.4.1.4 Graffiti design, eliminate waste

We use letters to indicate the state of requirements, "D" stands for "design" for a day, "C" stands for "coding", "T" stands for "testing", and "B" stands for "blocked". At the same time, these four capital letters are used to record the stay time of each requirement in a state at the daily stand-up (not accurate to the hour but only to the day). As shown in Figure 15.12, the requirement US_009 lasts for two days in "Design" state, three days in "development state", one day in "blocked" state, and also one day in "testing" state.

The technical leader discovered a strange phenomenon: there was no significant difference in the duration of "design state" of both simple and complex requirements. Why was that? By observing developers' behavers, he found the reason. When a developer took a new requirement, his habitual behaviors were as follows:

1. Write down the relevant module design in Word document at first.
2. Email his design to other developers for review.
3. Wait for other developers to reply to his email.
4. Modify the Word document according to the comments in their replies.
5. The design is done after the modification is completed.

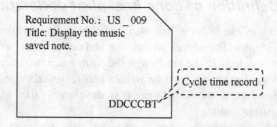

FIGURE 15.12   Card with cycle time.

There is no problem with the work steps, the problem lies in their way of working. When writing a Word document, people will spend time beautifying the document (this is understandable, we all want to make our design drawing look nice). However, this kind of document beautification is a waste of time before the design is recognized. So, we made some adjustment to ask everyone to "design on the whiteboard", that is, the workflow is divided into the following steps:

1. The developer Sara takes a requirement to do the preliminary design by herself. Instead of writing on a Word document, she just draws a blueprint on paper with a pen.
2. Sara invites her colleagues to the whiteboard, drawing the blueprint on the whiteboard while explaining to them (it usually takes about five minutes).
3. Listeners directly give feedback.
4. Sara writes a design document based on the feedback.
5. Sara submits the document to complete the design.

Although there are also five steps, two wastes are eliminated: one is unnecessary beautification of Word documents. The other is waiting for an email reply. The team does not need to go to the conference room to find the whiteboard, there is one close to team members' desks. No team member likes to discuss matters by walking a long distance to a conference room, they may give up opportunities for discussion because of inertia. Moreover, going far away from one place to another is an unnecessary waste.

After this improvement, the duration of requirements in "Design" state was significantly shortened.

15.4.1.5 Clarify state and care about rapid flow of requirements

In the "Development" column of the story wall, requirements cards were often piled up. Through observation, we found that each developer, after finishing the work in their hands, would email it to code reviewers and prompt them. Then, he would immediately take another requirement to start.

Code reviewers themselves are also developers in the team and may be coding on their own requirements. At this time, the usual behaviors of code reviewers are to complete their own work first before reviewing the code of others. Since everyone has this tendency, cards will accumulate on the "Development" column. Many requirements have been implemented, but remain in that column to wait for code review.

So, the team added the column "Code Review" to the story wall. After developers complete their own development task and send the email for code review, the requirements can be moved to the "Code Review" column. In this way, we can clearly know which requirements are under development and which ones are under code review, as shown in Figure 15.13.

The team also agreed that when a code review application was issued, the code reviewer must be notified. If the reviewer didn't reply within two hours, the developer would remind him again. This refers to the flow principle in lean theory, that is, to allow WIP (Work In Progress) to flow quickly in the entire value flow, otherwise it will have an adverse effect on downstream work. For example, the backlog of large volumes of work unevenly burdens downstream sector.

15.4.1.6 Avoid unnecessary task switching

In an iterative retrospective meeting, Rosa (tester) put forward two bad phenomena: one was that some requirements had obvious defects, but they would enter the testing phase; the other was that simple bugs wait longer to be fixed.

In the past, developers would fix bug until they finished all of their work. But there were "bad smells": one was that developers had insufficient self-testing of requirements, and there was a suspicion that testers were treated as "assistants". The other was that bugs could not be fixed immediately. According to the team's agreement, developers should conduct development self-tests based on the acceptance conditions of each requirement to ensure that there were no obvious bugs. To emphasize this agreement, we added a

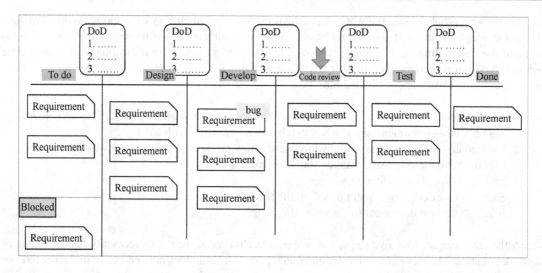

FIGURE 15.13   Add "code review" to clarify the state.

"Development Self-Test" column on the whiteboard, as shown in Figure 15.14. At the same time, we also defined the DoD from "Development" to "Development Self-test", that is, re-read the requirements cards to ensure that no content is omitted. Another item was added to the DoD from "Development Self-test" to "Test", that is, check the acceptance conditions of the requirements one by one to confirm that they have been met.

In addition, due to the previous adjustment about the code review, it could be done within two hours. Therefore, we removed it from the story wall, as shown in Figure 15.14.

15.4.1.7 No feedback is a "risk"

If the coding time of a requirement is too long, a lot of code will be cumulated. It also leads to more work of one-time code review which would be hard to guarantee the code quality. However, certain requirements cannot be split (forcibly split requirements may not be accepted or cost too much to pass the acceptance). Therefore, the team agreed on a weak feedback, that is, each major requirement can be split into

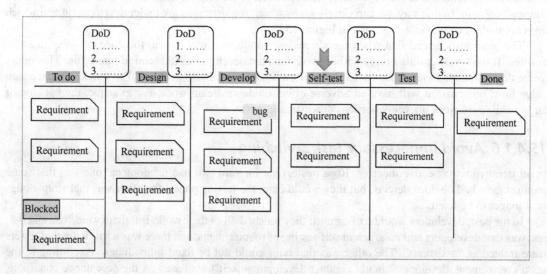

FIGURE 15.14   Replace "code review" with "development self-test".

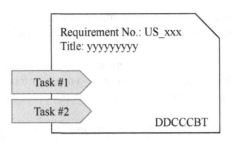

FIGURE 15.15   A user story card with multiple tasks

multiple development tasks; although each development task cannot be checked and accepted by testers, it can be verified in code review. Such a requirement will have multiple tasks written on a note and attached to the requirements, as shown in Figure 15.15.

15.4.1.8 Limit the quantity of WIP

As the project progressed, the symptom of "requirements accumulation" appeared on the story wall. This time the "accumulation" occurred in the "Test" state. More and more features were added to the system, and more regression contents needed to be tested than in the early stage. In addition, after the development was done, the number of bugs was also on the rise. Although the team could fix these bugs in a relatively short period of time, there was only one tester, and it was too late to verify these bugs.

What should they do? In addition to emphasizing the self-test of developers and enhancing the completeness of test cases, the team also adopted the strategy of "limiting the quantity of WIP" in the lean theory. The concept of "WIP" comes from the theory of lean production management, which refers to the semi-finished products that are still not delivered in the production process. In the lean production system, inventory is divided into three types: raw material inventory, WIP inventory, and finished product inventory. It holds that inventory does not increase value, but only increases cost.

At the daily stand-up, the testers would evaluate whether they could finish the tests and acceptance of all requirements in the "Test" state before 4:00 pm that day. If he could do so, then all work would proceed normally; otherwise, the technical leader would assign developers who would finish their requirements on the same day without taking new requirements to assist testers in accomplishing the requirements acceptance, as shown in Figure 15.16.

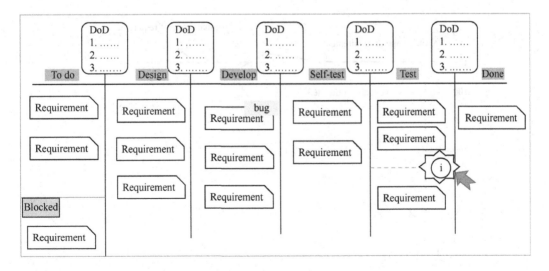

FIGURE 15.16   Limit the quantity of WIP, stop the line to expand test capacity.

It seems that the "test" stage is limited by a maximum bandwidth. Once testers' productivity is exceeded, the development activities in the previous stage will be halted to wait for expansion of testing capacity. See the four working principles in Chapter 3.

So far, the team's agreement could basically ensure that all user requirements could flow smoothly, the workload at all stages would be free from becoming too much or too little.

Finally, some lean theories and quality management techniques are summarized and listed as follows:

1. Value Stream Mapping (story wall is the embodiment of "value-centric workflow").
2. Reduce the batch size of unit work (split a large requirement into smaller ones).
3. CI (continuously observe the workflow, find problems, and improve working mode).
4. Limit the quantity of WIP (testers evaluate production capacity every day).
5. Built-in quality (each link has its DoD to avoid unnecessary task switching).

15.4.2 Bug-Free Delivery

The project did not proceed normally according to the team's initial plan. Instead, all features were successfully delivered in the 10th iteration ahead of time, and the two reserved buffer iterations were not used at all, as shown in Figure 15.17. It can be seen from the figure that in the actual project execution process, the scope of requirements is constantly changing (iteration 6, 7, 8, and 10). In the 9th iteration, the team has completed all the original features. At the time of product review, the general product owner expressed to add some features of experience optimization, so additional 13 points were done in the 10th iteration.

After the delivery of the 10th iteration, the team began to work on other projects. For the entire program of this new mobile device, the work was not over yet, there were still several important stages, which were integration testing, system testing, and field testing. The delivery quality of the team was really good, and no bugs were found in the subsequent stages. This was due to a lot of meticulous improvements in the pilot journey.

15.4.3 Trunk-Based Development and CI

The development speed of the first three iterations in Figure 15.17 was far below the team's expectations, because the team had taken more time in setup team CI, changing branch strategies, and migrating code version management systems.

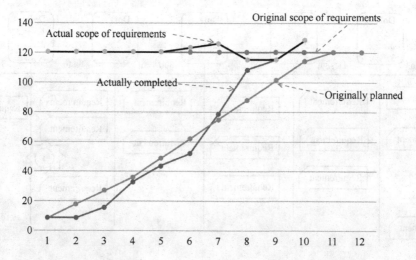

FIGURE 15.17 Project burn-up chart.

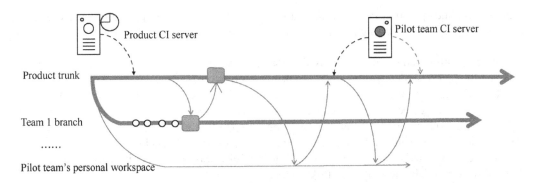

FIGURE 15.18 Company N's branch strategy and pilot team's branch strategy for a new product project.

For any software project involving more than 100 people, the branch strategy of codebase has always been an annoying issue. How to coordinate the code merging operations of so many people for one product in such a long release cycle? Company N adopted the team branch model (see Figure 15.18), that is, the entire new product has a trunk, and each Scrum team will cut a branch from this trunk. The opportunity of merging those branches into the trunk is after each team has finished a large and complete feature set.

The resulting problem is that although a product-level CI server is setup on the product trunk, the low-frequency merging will limit the effect of daily CI. Before merging back into the trunk, each team usually synchronizes the trunk code to its own branch after its own features are done; therefore, each time the code change set will be quite large, coupled with a heavy workload for one-time merging. Once a team finishes merging, it takes a long time to stabilize the trunk code quality.

The pilot team did the same in the first two iterations. It once planned to build a CI server for its own team branch, so that the code of its own members could be continuously integrated on the team branch. However, the developers responsible for setting up the team's CI server had tried for a long time, but still failed to make the server run functional tests. It was difficult to run functional tests which were written and maintained by a dedicated automated testing team. The team had no idea where the test code was placed and what environment was required, it had to seek help from that dedicated team.

During this period, we had features to be merged into the product trunk, and the responsible developers took a long time to get it done. In addition, in these two first iterations, Company N as a whole switched from Synergy (a code version control system) to Git, which also had a certain impact on the pilot team. The combination of these factors lowered our delivery volume in the first three iterations.

Developers proposed to abandon the team branch and directly check into the product trunk. Because of architecture isolation, automated unit testing, and fine granularity of requirements, the code quality was controllable. Moreover, it also reduced a centralized merging operation from the team branch to the product trunk, as shown in Figure 15.18. Developers would automatically run unit tests and code scans every time they submitted code to the product trunk, so that the team could comply with the six-step check-in dance for CI (see Section 9.2) and get quality feedback in time.

It is worth mentioning that during the preparation period, all team members read through the code specifications of Company N, and they were asked to raise questions about the specifications and discuss them together. The goal was to make team members understand and abide by the specifications, so as to keep scanning code specifications in the CI practice.

15.4.4 Shift-Left Testing

Chapter 13 briefly discusses the flattening trend of testing activities and points out that for those products with high fixing costs after distribution, the testing activities usually cannot be shifted to the right, but to the left. The mobile operating system in this case happens to this type of application. Therefore, during the delivery period, a lot of testing activities were "shifted to the left".

- When splitting requirements, we used "capable of verification" as one of the splitting criteria. See Chapter 6 for detailed methods and principles of requirements decomposition.
- Before coding, testcases of each requirement were prepared in advance, and all roles would be reviewed together to reach an agreement, so that test cases went ahead of the rest to clarify software requirements and quality requirements in the first place.
- Developers wrote automated unit tests to ensure their own code quality.
- The tester verified each user story immediately after it was developed, instead of waiting until a feature was fully developed just like before.

The product was written in C/C++. Before the start of the project, the team spent an afternoon to train all developers to use the CppUnit framework and write unit tests in a Code Dojo to let them try TDD. In actual work, TDD is not forced, only unit test code must be written.

According to the final statistical results of the project code, the ratio of product code to test code was 1:1.2, meaning that every 100 lines of product code had 120 lines of test code. The test code included automated test fixture. See Chapter 10 for details about automated test management and test fixture.

15.4.5 Code Review

When Company N switched the code VCS from IBM's Rational Synergy to Git, and provided GitFlow and code review tool, code review workflow was much smoother, and its graphical interface is shown in Figure 15.19. The tool execution process was as follows:

1. When someone submitted code, the system platform would automatically create a temporary branch.
2. There were a series of tests on this branch, and only after these tests were passed would it be truly merged into the product trunk. These tests are as follows:
   - The automatically created automated test task (ROBOT_task) must be executed successfully (we had asked the team responsible for configuring this automated test to include

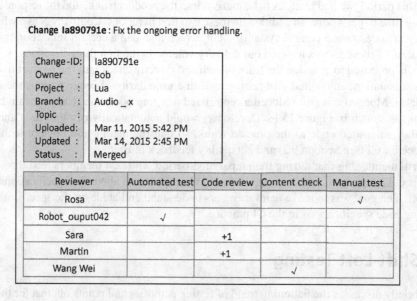

Change Ia890791e : Fix the ongoing error handling.

Change-ID:	Ia890791e
Owner :	Bob
Project :	Lua
Branch :	Audio _ x
Topic :	
Uploaded:	Mar 11, 2015 5:42 PM
Updated :	Mar 14, 2015 2:45 PM
Status. :	Merged

Reviewer	Automated test	Code review	Content check	Manual test
Rosa				√
Robot_ouput042	√			
Sara		+1		
Martin		+1		
Wang Wei			√	

FIGURE 15.19   State of code submission.

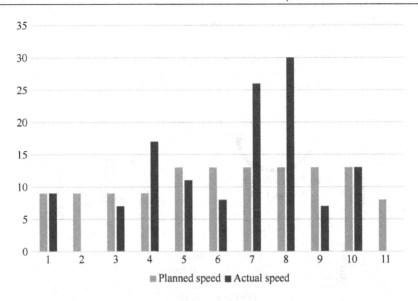

FIGURE 15.20 Comparison between planned and actual iteration speed.

the pilot team's unit test cases), which was equivalent to the mandatory implementation of Step 4 in six-step check-in dance for CI, namely, second personal build verification.
- The code review score for each submission must be two points or more.
- Pass content check (an internal term).
- Pass manual test.

15.4.6 Care More about Process in Addition to Results

After Company N brought in the Scrum framework, it has paid great attention to Sprint Success. At the iteration summary meetings, some Scrum Masters who used the Scrum framework often said that "This iteration failed". There were even statistics about the proportion of failed iterations. Such practice would make immature agile teams pay more attention to iteration speed and forget to make improvement during the progress.

Our pilot team deliberately downplayed the concept of "Sprint Success" and paid more attention to the improvement of working mode. As shown in Figure 15.20, we did not complete each iteration according to the iteration plan velocity in the early stage, but this did not hold back our successful delivery in the end. The result is always determined by the process, let the team pay more attention to the process and spend more time on process improvement.

15.5 SUMMARY

Since Company N's product line for the mobile device-based software had been organized and operated in accordance with the Scrum framework, and its software architecture did not need overhaul, our improvement work centralized on the "infrastructure" of the continuous delivery tangram. Through the pilot team's "business requirements collaborative management", the improvement of "branch and configuration management" and "build and test management" was respectively promoted, as shown in Figure 15.21.

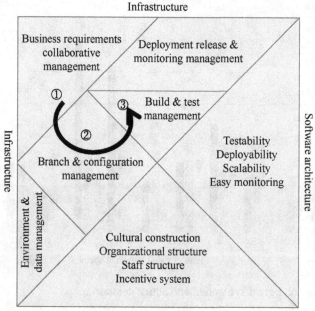

FIGURE 15.21   Continuous delivery tangram.

As for the characteristics of the project itself, although the product R&D and improvement was done in a large team of more than 100 people, the focus of this case is greatly different from the Internet products as introduced in Chapter 14. After the mobile operating system is released, once its quality is found defective, the recall and repair costs are very high. Therefore, Shift-left Testing is more helpful for improving the code quality before release and for reducing overall costs. In short, in this case, a lot of improvements were made to the team's internal development process to ensure the quality of software delivery. The result of improvement is shown in Figure 15.22.

Before improvement		After improvement
• Task splitting	→	Story splitting
• Estimate by Man-day	→	Ranking-based estimate
• Improvised plan	→	Explicit PRAD-based release plan
• Track personal task walls	→	Focus on the story wall of flowing requirements
• focus on success of Sprint	→	Downplay the concept of Sprint success
• Branch-based development	→	Trunk-based development
• Story-based code submission	→	Daily submission by each person based on development tasks
• Patched development	→	Separation of concerns through design
• Coding specifications like "white elephant"	→	Coding specifications recognized and strictly followed by the team
• Final integration test	→	Testing on time
• Synergy	→	GIT
	→	Unit-level integration testing
	→	Unit testing

FIGURE 15.22   Comparison of the items before and after improvement.

From the perspective of organizational culture, the characteristic of this case is to establish a small and self-driven environment for a team inside the company and establish a quality culture different from other teams. The advantage is that the number of people involved is limited, the impact is controllable, and it is easy to produce a more systematic improvement effect. At the same time, the small team is one of the sub-teams of a large project team, which can form a sharp contrast with others to be a large demonstration significance. It can be chosen as the first pilot team for the company's agile and lean transformation project, and for providing more experience and confidence for subsequent improvement.

DevOps Driven by Developers

16

Now whenever people talk about DevOps, some of them will think of microservice, Docker technology, Kubernetes service orchestration, and deployment pipeline. According to James Coplien, author of the book *Lean Architecture: For Agile Software Development*, overemphasis and focus on tools such as Docker, Jenkins, test frameworks, Mock framework, or continuous improvement (CI) server is contrary to the top value highlighted by the Agile Manifesto: "individuals and interactions over processes and tools". Tools make repetitive work simple, but they are not panacea to everything. Collaboration between people is more important. Smooth collaboration between different roles can increase efficiency even more.

This case happened before the concept of microservices was born, and Docker technology was not mature as well. However, the team applied the idea of Continuous Delivery 2.0 to strengthen the collaboration between developers and DevOps personnel. After four months of improvement, on the premise of ensuring the delivery quality, the team increased delivery frequency by nearly six times, greatly accelerated its response speed to requirements, and performed better in satisfying business requests; moreover, it reduced the investment in testing manpower by about 30%, and successfully transformed to the DevOps mode.

16.1 BACKGROUND

Around 2010, the domestic Internet industry developed rapidly, and agile methods were also expanded in the domestic software industry. The organizational structure of Company B at that time is shown in Figure 16.1. All testers belong to a single quality assurance department, and the Ops engineers belong to a single operation department. Product managers and developers belong to each business line. Each business line is composed of multiple business departments, and each business department has product personnel and developers for the product. The company also has a Project Management Office (PMO), whose work mainly includes the following three parts.

1. Tools and platforms: There are project management platform and corporate codebase and version management platform, as well as requirement management tools and CI tools.
2. Process improvement team: It researches and brings in world's leading project management ideas in software industry, pilots them in the company, and improves project efficiency.
3. Knowledge management: Build a supporting platform for knowledge accumulation.

This case, happened in 2011, was associated with a team under a certain business line of Company B. This team was providing back-end service (hereinafter referred to as Service S) for web search products. It was a relatively independent subsystem (see its architecture in Figure 16.2). Service S received requests from other services and offered its own results to downstream services. It consisted of seven modules, with total code size of about 100,000 lines and all written in C/C++ language. Each module was a separate process (or considered as a microservice) running on nearly 300 servers, starting from the front-end data stream acquisition, to the analysis, classification, and storage of data stream.

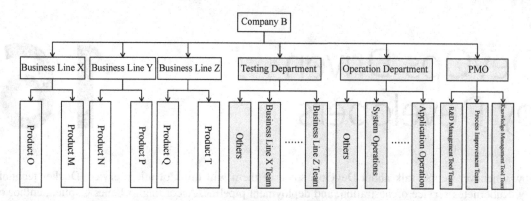

FIGURE 16.1　Schematic diagram of Company B's organizational structure.

16.2 ORIGINAL WORKING MODE

All software development of Company B was implemented through the project responsibility system. A project might be a large feature point or architecture transformation, or it might be a collection of multiple small features. According to the scale and importance of requirements, the project was divided into four levels, namely A, B, C, and D levels. A D-level project might be completed by a developer in a few days, while an A-level project might take half a year or even longer with more people. A D-level project is usually directly handled by technical personnel. For large-scale projects, they might have designated product owners and test leaders.

The project mode was "branch-based development, centralized joint debugging, and centralized testing". In the stage of branch-based development and centralized joint debugging, testers were less involved but focused on understanding requirements. The branching mode is shown in Figure 16.3; it was a typical "Branch-based Development & Trunk-based Release" mode (see details about this mode in Chapter 8).

Considering the stability of the production environment, the operation department specified that the deployment could only be done on Tuesday and Thursday, and only one project is allowed to launch at a time. Due to many project branches, there were often cases where multiple projects were verified on the development branch concurrently and queued to be merged into the release branch.

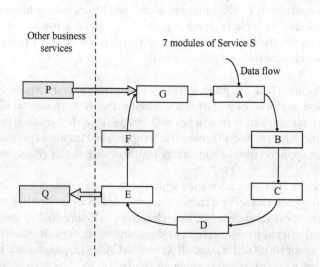

FIGURE 16.2　Architectural diagram of Service S developed by the team.

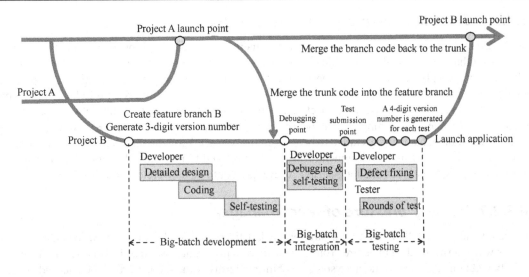

FIGURE 16.3 Company B's project code branch management method.

In order to upgrade the new architecture of Service S, an A-level project was established, which was expected to take three months. In addition to the existing four developers, two testers were assigned to this project. Service S was a back-end service without front-end UI, so no product owner was needed, and the requirements collection and other related tasks were undertaken by developers themselves.

16.3 KEY POINTS OF IMPROVEMENT

This section mainly explains the key points of improvement.

16.3.1 Improvement Methodology

"Goal-driven, starting from simple problems, and continuous improvement" is the guiding ideology of the entire improvement process. Since the team originally implemented the project-based mode (see Chapter 8) that at the stages of development, debugging and integration testing, problems, or bugs in software were in concentrated outbreak. These bugs were not only associated with software quality, but also related to unclear requirements and inconsistent understanding, which resulted in an uncertain project deadline. At the same time, unexpected issues on the production line might disrupt the development pace of the project, adding uncertainties to the delivery time.

The reasons for the abovementioned problems are related to their project management philosophy and development methods, and changes need to be made in terms of project management methods, code branch management, research and development (R&D) infrastructure and team members' work awareness.

16.3.2 Define Goals of Improvement

Each role has some pain points. Only by understanding these pain points can we comprehensively evaluate the current situation of the team and formulate reasonable periodic improvement goals. At the same time, we could also find an improvement path.

16.3.2.1 Expectations of department director

The department director said, "As for project management, one of the big problems we face is poor planning. It's not that we don't make plans, but that different circumstances always make some projects uncontrollable. For example, the projects of the architecture group are usually important and large projects, and the development cycle is relatively long, usually three months. Two months for development and one month for testing. But for a particular project, it may be greatly uncontrollable with a delivery date changing from time to time. For example, just in the week before, we cancelled the Project K. It was staffed with 30 people per month, but it always failed to be merged into the trunk for one reason or another. Eventually, because changed timing and environment, it was called off and to no avail. Therefore, I don't have any high expectations. I just want this long-period A-level project to be delivered in time".

16.3.2.2 Delivery pressure of team manager

The team manager said, "First of all, I desire for quick delivery, but we don't know how to deal with these projects with transformed architecture. You are an expert in this regard, we must fully cooperate with your work. In addition, although we do have some flexibility in terms of the scope of requirements and delivery time for this project, some requirements must be completed by the given date in a specified month".

16.3.2.3 Annoyances of project leaders

After communicating with the responsible persons respectively for development and testing, I've learned the things that make them feel bored:

- Inaccurate estimates, many temporary insertions, and project plans hard to be carried out.
- By the specified test time point, developers have not completed the joint debugging, and there is no package to be tested.
- When packages are ready to be tested, testers had been assigned to other projects.
- After testers come back to work on the original project, they may find too many low-level problems in the code that block testing.
- The testing has to be on hold to waiting for fixing by developers.
- It takes a long time to prepare the testing environment and test data.
- Some configurations in production need to be synchronized to testing environment for testing.
- The packages are handed over to testers over and over again, making repeated manual testing totally unbearable.
- When it is time for releasing, they still need wait in line.
- When it's my turn to release my code, I have to pull the latest code from release branch to merge with mine, and then have them tested again.
- If the previously released code contains certain defect to be rolled back for fixing, we have to strip it out, build and test again.
- We've written a lot of release documents and handed them to the Ops engineer, but he says that the documents do not meet the operation specifications and need to be revised.
- The Ops engineer eventually finishes deployment, but a problem exposes shortly afterwards, and it turns out that the configuration files are mistaken.

Through investigation and discussion, leadership at all levels of the team defined the improvement goals of this project, and explained them to all stakeholders at the project kick-off meeting. The goals included short-term and mid-term ones. The short-term goals are listed as follows with priority from high to low:

1. The project is to be delivered within the expected time.
2. Create a new effective way of working.
3. Establish the necessary infrastructure to support the Continuous Delivery mode.

The mid-term goals are as follows:

1. Shorten the release cycle and go live quickly.
2. Do not lower the quality in production.
3. Reduce the total investment in testing resources.

These two goals correspond to two stages, respectively. The first stage is "Agile 101" driven by CI, which successfully completes one release and lays the foundation in terms of process and tools for subsequent releases. The second stage is to create Continuous Delivery mode with DevOps culture.

16.4 STAGE 1: AGILE 101

The Agile 101 model, which is also known as the Water-Scrum-fall model here, refers to the division of the iteration time box within each stage under the waterfall development framework. Its iteration cycle is usually one to four weeks. Each iteration cycle in the phase involves requirements analysis, code development, and tests. And there is demonstration and acceptance at the end of each iteration. However, before entering the development phase, there are also phases for requirements collection, analysis, and planning; after the development phase is over, one or two iterations will be arranged for the final system testing. In the end, the system may be scheduled for staging and then launched in production, as shown in Figure 16.4.

The characteristics of the Agile 101 mode are as follows: the major phase in the waterfall mode have not changed, and only the internal activities in each phase are appropriately adjusted. This mode is usually applied to teams that do not have a deep understanding of Continuous Delivery and complete R&D infrastructure but want to make improvements.

This team used the Agile 101 mode for two purposes: one is to do capacity reserve for implementing the Intercity Express Mode (see Chapter 8) in the future. The other is to cultivate the quality awareness and good collaboration of team members.

16.4.1 Make a Trustable Plan

First of all, we needed to answer this question: "When will this project be completed and launched?" Now the tech lead had already obtained the requirements of this project, and done some requirements analysis and outline design based on previous work experience. However, this was a project with a heavy R&D workload and a long delivery cycle. Therefore, we decided to adopt a new way of requirements analysis, estimation, and planning to further improve the project plan.

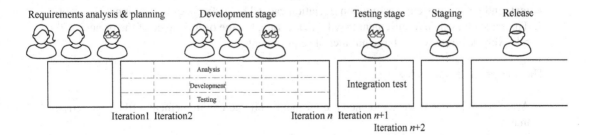

FIGURE 16.4 Agile 101 mode.

16.4.1.1 Requirements decomposition

If the team had followed the previous convention, they would have already started code development. However, I insisted that the requirements should be further broken down and that testers should be involved. This work didn't have to take place in a conference room. In this project, the development leader himself did a round of requirements splitting according to the following three points and presented them to the test leader for review. The test leader reviewed and supplemented the split requirements offline, and then discussed with the development leader to form a consensus.

1. Each requirement was implemented in less than three days. In this pilot, in order to learn about the quality of the code we wrote and find the bugs in the code as soon as possible, we split all requirements into fine-grained ones. The implementation of each smaller requirement was estimated to take half a day to two days. In this way, once a requirement was developed, tester would test it. So, if there was any problem, they could find it quickly.
2. The requirements decomposition followed the INVEST principle, namely, Independent, Negotiable, Valuable, Estimable, Small, and Testable (see Chapter 6 for more details).
3. Trade-offs during the decomposition. When learning about requirement decomposition, the team encountered a problem, that is, it felt that these six principles could not be met at the same time after splitting. The development lead asked that some relatively large requirements must exist. If they were split into small ones, demand side or testers seem to be unable to do acceptance testing, so how to deal with that.

It is true that individual requirements cannot be accepted in the UI before they are fully completed. However, if we can break them down into small requirements, and testers can find some way to verify the correctness of their operation, it is also feasible, such as directly viewing the results in a log file or database. Although from the user perspective, the feature cannot be delivered yet, we can test every small requirement as early as possible to get earlier feedback to ensure their correctness implementation. But it must be remembered that such big requirement should not be too many.

If these six principles must be prioritized, the latter three principles (EST) should take precedence over the first three ones (INV) when splitting requirements into smaller ones.

16.4.1.2 Relative estimation

We got a list of requirements that both developers and testers understood and agreed on the acceptance criteria. The next step was to estimate the workload. We used the ranking method to estimate the requirements (see Appendix B for the detailed operation method). This ranking method has two claims and four premises.

The two claims are as follows:

1. Compared with the traditional relative estimation method, this method puts lots of requirements together and compares them; it is easier to estimate the workload in combination with the context, and it can reduce the estimation deviation caused by differences in personnel capabilities.
2. The scale of a single requirement may be inaccurate, but the overall scale of the project will be relatively accurate with a large number of requirements.

The four premises are as follows:

1. At least two people understand each requirement well and can implement it (the time required may vary).
2. There is no need to evaluate the workload of testing activities, because we assume that testing is not a bottleneck, and that testing can be completed in time, while implementation is the

bottleneck of the entire process. If testing becomes a bottleneck, we can even doubt there is "excessive investment of development resources".

3. All requirements have been broken down, and their scales do not differ too much.
4. The number of requirements is relatively large.

After estimation, the overall workload of our entire project was 66 points. Sometimes, the estimation showed that the relative workload was "0", because its workload was relatively small. The way to deal with this situation was to add up several "0" points to 1 point. Note that it was not a combination of requirements, but just the addition of workload, that is, "0+0+0+...+0=1".

16.4.1.3 Initial plan

Although we knew the scale of workload, we still didn't know when the project would be completed. We needed to know the capacity of the team to make plana. In order to know the capacity, we must answer the following questions:

16.4.1.3.1 Ideally, what is the weekly working hours of the team?
Assuming that everyone works eight hours a day, subtract one hour for the weekly meeting of the architecture group, subtract the ten minutes for daily stand-up of our team, and subtract the daily non-working hours (it is estimated as two hours per day since all of us work eight hours per day), then the actual production time of each developer in a week is 28 hours, that is, each developer has about 5.5 hours per day.

16.4.1.3.2 Ideally, how many requirements can be fulfilled each week?
Then we guided developers to estimate their weekly development speed. I printed all the requirements on paper, and each piece of paper was printed with a requirement. The rule was like this: I take out some requirements to show to everyone. If the team as a whole believes they can be done, they will say "Yes"; otherwise, they will say "No". Before starting the estimation, I reminded team members that each developer only had 5.5 hours of production time every day.

I took out the first requirement, and everyone nodded to show "Yes". I took out the second requirement and asked: "If added with this requirement, can you finish within a week?" They nodded again. When I took out the fifth requirement, everyone shake their heads. So I took a requirement back from the desktop, replaced it with another one and asked, "What about now?" Everyone nodded again. Then I added another requirement, and everyone still nodded. So, I kept adding one more requirement, and everyone shook their heads. I marked all the requirements on the desktop except the last one and collected them as a group. After that, I repeated the practice with another set of requirements to collect the second group.

At this point, I summed up the points of each group of requirements and compared their results which turned out to be little different, and the average number of points was 22. Well then, excluding the later stage of integration test, in theory, the team could develop and complete the project in only three weeks.

16.4.1.3.3 Actually, how many requirements are most likely to be developed each week
Many issues take place every day (online abnormal monitoring and diagnosis, emergency hotfix, temporary communication with other teams), so it takes time to have these issues addressed. How long will it take the team on average to deal with matters that are not part of the project scope? Two senior engineers have to spend about 50% of their day working hours, and other two developers need about 30%. So, it is estimated that the entire team spends 40% of working hours handling other tasks.

In addition, it is impossible for us to implement requirements all the time; we also spend some time in communication, for example, discussing requirements details with testers and confirming testcases for acceptance. This may take up 10% of our time. Based on this estimation, developers still have 50% of available time. Therefore, 11 points of requirements can be completed every week ($22 \times 50\% = 11$), so iterative development requires six weeks ($66 \div 11 = 6$).

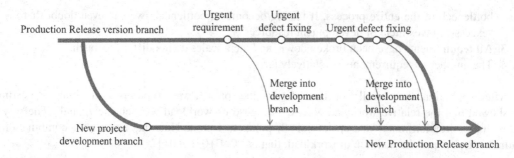

FIGURE 16.5   The trunk-based development strategy adopted in Agile 101.

In the iterative development, testers will do incremental testing: once the implementation of a requirement is completed, it will be tested immediately. If a bug is found during testing, developers are asked to fix it right away. So, the development velocity may be slower a little than the estimated one. Therefore, we set a development period as 6.5 weeks.

16.4.1.3.4 How to support feature requests in production during the entire project development process?

This was the first time that the team used this iterative method, and it had not yet reached the state of Continuous Delivery. Therefore, the branching mode had not changed (see Figure 16.5) that a development branch was cut from the release trunk for new project development. Any temporarily urgent requirements or serious bugs will be implemented on a separate branch which was cut from the release branch separately and quickly merge it into the trunk.

All these new requirements or bugfixes should be recorded in the requirements list of this project and merged into the new project development branches according to the actual situation. Due to architectural changes, some code for urgent requirements couldn't be merged and only be re-implemented on the development branch. Therefore, we reserved three days to fulfill this part of the legacy release requirements.

So far, the total time of development was expected to be seven weeks.

16.4.1.3.5 What's time for system testing?

Testers raised a question: "Seven weeks is the time for completing requirements' implementation. The requirements implemented at the last day of the last iteration also needs time to be tested. After that, a complete test of the entire system is required. Previously the system test took one month. How long will this system integration test take?"

As of the traditional process, the testing phase was relatively late, and more contents needed to be tested. In addition to functional testing, there were also performance testing, stress testing, and stability testing. The longest time was spent in the "Big Ring Test", which is a special test environment most similar with production. It run tests with actual and real-time data, but the processing results are not stored in production. By convention, the Big Ring Test takes at least one week, normally two weeks. There will be some minor fixes during this period. The Big Ring Test is mainly to perform partial drainage of actual data to observe whether any abnormalities occur. If there is an abnormality, it needs to be analyzed and resolved.

Now the team employs "Agile 101", which greatly reduces the quantity of bugs found in the later testing phase. In addition, as long as the requirements are tested immediately after they are implemented. So, at the end of the last iteration, the number of requirements that have not tested should not be too many, and the testing time for these requirements will be fairly short. Therefore, we tentatively set two weeks for the integration test.

16.4.1.3.6 How about other tests (such as performance test and stress test)?

For performance testing, we do it once a week to get the result data. If there is an issue with the package, we will diagnose and fix it immediately. In doing so, the quality feedback will be quick.

According to the current logic, the entire project is expected to take seven weeks for development phase, and the system testing is expected to take two weeks, so the entire project will cost about nine weeks to complete.

16.4.1.3.7 Do we need to consider dependencies when planning?
In terms of business and technology, is there any dependency between our project and other teams? Yes, there are indeed some business dependencies. Our project cannot go online until another project does so. The progress of the dependent project is faster than our own, so it should not be a blocker.

In this estimated plan, we have not thought about people's casual leave and sick leave, team activities and statutory holidays. If all of these factors are counted, the entire project might cost 9.5 weeks to complete.

16.4.1.3.8 Is it more realistic to add buffer time to the overall project plan?
After the plan was made, I communicated with the team manager. This project plan didn't involve any abnormal situations but contained multiple assumptions. For example, the full development velocity is 22 points/week; 40% of time is spent in dealing with non-project affairs; three days in total are occupied by non-work affairs (statutory holidays, team activities, and temporary vacations).

These three assumptions may not be true and need to keep eyes on it. In the overall project, it may be more appropriate to include a "two-week" buffer. In the process of the project, this buffer time may help avoid potential risks.

PARID factors need to be considered when formulating a plan, namely Priority, Assumption, Risk, Issue, and Dependency.

16.4.2 Start the Development Stage

After the project plan was formulated, the team would start development. The first step was to determine the iteration cycle and agree on the team's collaboration process.

16.4.2.1 Selection of iteration interval

Before determining the iteration interval, let's first learn about a metaphor. As shown in Figure 16.6, when the lake surface is high, the rocks in the lake are covered by water. Even if there are large rocks, people cannot see them. But when the lake level falls, some big rocks are exposed. As the lake level further decreases, smaller rocks will gradually be discovered. If the height of the water surface is regarded as the time of each iteration, then the rocks can be regarded as issues in daily work.

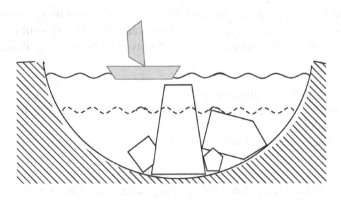

FIGURE 16.6 Lake and rocks.

If we use the traditional mode with the cycle of three months, the water level is high, and the issues (that is, rocks) in daily work are difficult to expose. When we use the iterative mode, the time becomes shorter, which is equivalent to a drop in the water level, and the problem is easily exposed.

What is an appropriate water level? It depends on the specific situation of the team. The lower the water level, the stronger the discomfort it brings to the team and the easier it is to feel frustrated. But if the water level is too high, the problem is not easy to expose, the team will be less motivated to make improvement, and its behavioral inertia will lead to slow improvement, thus making problems hard to be discovered.

For the sake of safety, this team chose two weeks as interaction interval which was only used for periodic workload planning and retrospective meeting, because we demanded that each code submission should generate workable software, which presented higher requirements for team collaboration.

16.4.2.2 Team collaboration process

Since each code submission should generate workable software, it poses higher requirements for team collaboration, and for quality of each activity and deliverables in the process.

16.4.2.2.1 Working conventions for each iteration

A friendly atmosphere does not necessarily produce an efficient team, but a consensus must be the cornerstone of a combative team. In an iteration, how can team members cooperate with each other? After project estimation and planning, I introduced the development process of each iteration, discussed with team members, and worked out an iterative workflow with team. Some rules are as follows:

- Morning meeting at 10:00 am every day.
- On the last Friday afternoon of each iteration, spend one hour doing team review and making a development plan for the next iteration.
- Each iteration plan includes a development plan and a test plan (that is, how many requirements can be developed and how many requirements can be tested).
- Plan at the speed of development and test our iteration plan at the speed of verification without defects.
- Do not re-estimate.
- Estimate newly added requirements.

16.4.2.2.2 The agreement on a single requirement implementation

The traditional mode was to develop and test in big batch, but in the new iterative mode, a unit to be implemented is a single requirement, which is about to be tested immediately after implementation, as shown in Figure 16.7.

"Implemented in big batch" means that a developer does not start debugging with others until all or most features are implemented. Testers will not perform integration testing until the debugging is done. Developers and testers in the team also raise some doubts from "single case development, immediate testing":

- Why should I finish coding all in one go?
- I'd like to write a rough framework first, and then add more features. It is more efficient in development, isn't it?
- If a big feature is implemented separately, does that mean there is lots of repetitive work?

These three questions reflect people's different focal points in the two methods of "big batch delivery" and "small batch delivery". Big batch delivery emphasizes the efficiency of each processing phase, and its assumption is that the rate of genuine products in each phase is very high, and there is few or no

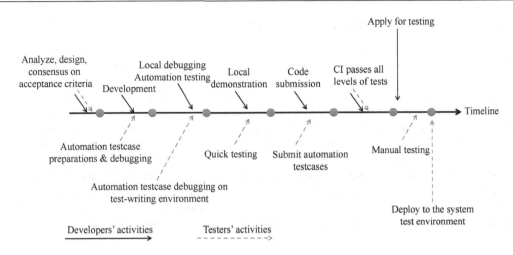

FIGURE 16.7 The life cycle of a requirement (user story).

error at all. However, this assumption is basically invalid for software development. Testing, as a follow-up phase with large-scale verification, often leads to three consequences:

1. Requirements are not fully considered.
2. A large quantity of bugs found in later integration testing.
3. Bugs are not fixed in time, resulting in unpredictable delivery time.

Iterative development is for small-batch delivery, and it follows the quality principle like this: "Cease dependence on inspection to achieve quality. Eliminate the need for inspection on a mass basis by building quality into the product in the first place". It comes from the "built quality in" principle – the third quality management principle proposed by Dr. Deming. So, how can we constrain the process quality of each activity?

16.4.3 Constraints on Process Quality

Owing to the fine granularity of requirements (usually within two days), it is necessary to find an effective way to detect the problem as early as possible at the lowest possible cost. So, we introduced the CI practice in the team. Before the start of this project, Company B had begun to introduce the idea of "continuous integration", but the team took it as an automatic packaging and uploading tool in the final test stage, which had nothing to do with its own development activities. The genuine CI practice is a collaborative activity that developers and testers have to participate in every day, requiring them to abide by the six-step check-in dance for CI (see details about the six-step check-in dance in Chapter 7). This way of working posed a big challenge to the working habits of this team. Therefore, we specially organized a two-hour learning and discussion session to figure out some work improvement items.

16.4.3.1 How to consciously abide by CI discipline?

Developers did not have such a habit yet, although they had reached an agreement on it. How to supervise them to perform this agreement more efficiently? We placed a lava lamp at a prominent location in the team's work area and linked it with the status on the CI server. When a CI build failed, the lamp turned red. This became a way for public monitoring. I have seen a variety of similar practices. For example, some teams use big monitor to display the build status, while others play music (although a bit noisy). In short, it is a rule of quality that reminds every member not to destroy the teamwork spirit, just like traffic lights.

16.4.3.2 How to shorten the build time?

A full build of the project took 40 minutes. If it was done in the style of check-in dance, it would take too long every day, so this problem must be solved. Developers must be able to complete the build and tests within 15 minutes.

Developers were free from such trouble previously. Why was that? Because developers could build code at any time they wanted before system testing without any tension. It is not big deal in daily work because of relatively less check-in, and nobody even care about the build result for the submitted code before testing phase. The role of the SVN (Subverion) at that time was only to prevent the loss of code, not a tool for team collaboration.

Presently, in the iterative mode, all developers have to build code every day. So, it came to be a problem needs to be solved. We located dedicated force to build the first version of a distributed build cluster using open-source software (this was the prototype of the company-level C/C++ compilation cluster) in three weeks. So, both developers and Jenkins (a tool for CI) can execute their own builds on it.

CLOUD BUILD PLATFORM

In Company B, most of the back-end services under the Business Line A are C/C++ programs on the Linux platform. Many developers share the same physical Linux machine for coding, and each is assigned an account and password. Every developer performs daily compilation work on this machine. The performance of the machine is not bad, and its stutter is usually ignored by other developers when the frequency of compilation and build is not high. However, after using the CI model with higher build frequency, the operations of other developers may be frozen.

In this context, the company's PMO created a "build cloud" to support parallel builds by multiple people. At the same time, multiple compilation tasks can be parallelized to shorten the time of single compilation. Its working method is similar to the building management service as discussed in Section 7.4 (see Figure 7.9). Its solution is "open-source tools + customization", and its structure diagram is shown in Figure 16.8.

When developers finish writing the code and are ready to submit, they may run a command script "localbuild.sh" on his machine. The system will submit the current version number of SVN together with the patch file to the server, and the server will put it in the queue. Once there are free

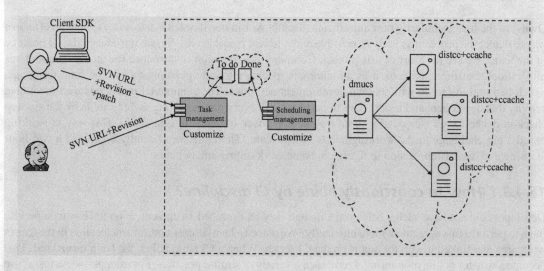

FIGURE 16.8 Schematic diagram of a cloud build platform.

resources, it can be automatically compiled and packaged. If something goes wrong, programmer can get immediate feedback. If there is no problem, developer can submit the code.

The platform is based on a series of open-source solutions, coupled with some custom development, and able to provide incremental compilation and full compilation. Its compilation cluster initially contains 30 compilers, and the unified management of the environment ensures that anyone that modifies the code will access to consistent dependent libraries and compiler versions, and eliminates failed build arising from all inconsistencies.

With this distributed compilation mechanism, the overall compilation time is shortened. Developers usually use incremental compilation, and switch to full compilation before submission, while the CI platform always uses full compilation. In this way, a balance between feedback speed and quality is guaranteed.

16.4.3.3 Developers cannot run automated tests

The product had a batch of automation testcases which were stored in the Quality Assurance (QA) department's own codebase. There are some drawbacks (see more Chapter 10). Only those with permission (QAs) could run them. This approach was quite natural under the traditional model, because test cases were usually written by testers for regression test or serving as a gate to start testing, in order to improve the efficiency of testers. The code was usually written by dedicated persons after a certain version of the product was basically stable. Moreover, the provisioning cost for testing was relatively high, including machine application, system installation, and data preparation. However, the frequency of the test execution was relatively low (possibly once a quarter) in traditional mode, so the cost of these factors was not a big deal.

In iterative development, the first users of automated tests are developers, and they should use these tests to check whether his code destroys the original features at the first time before submitting the code. It will increase the frequency of the test running, and lead to the request for optimization.

QAs are fond of this way of working (more use of testcases), so they immediately applied for machine resources for it. Due to the tight binding between the testcase and the testcase management system, the codebase failed to be quickly moved in a short period of time (in fact, it took time to negotiate with the head of the QA department). Therefore, we made an expedient decision, that is, QAs temporarily provide a script to developers to call these testcases to run automatically. QAs will configure the scripts for developers. The data required for the test are also prepared by QAs with one-click. It is not the best for self-help, but it is good enough at that time.

16.4.3.4 Automation testing strategy

Iterative development requires rapid testing. Now that we already have some testcases, we'd better make a good use of them. But when will new testcases be written? When can we run them? Who should write them? Which case should be written? All these issues must be agreed before the team starts. According to the Test Pyramid (see Chapter 10), and the current state of the team, we made a test agreement as shown in Figure 16.9.

1. Unit test: The team had never written unit tests. Without enough exercises in this regard, everyone felt uneasy to write. And the quality of the unit testcases was relatively low. Implementing bad testcases would incur a high cost. Therefore, unit testing was abandoned in the first stage of the pilot.
2. Module automation test: It refers to the test of a certain module which consists of multiple internal classes. Such test is determined according to different requirements. Generally speaking, if the feature is not directly manifested in the external interface, a feature automation test will be run here.

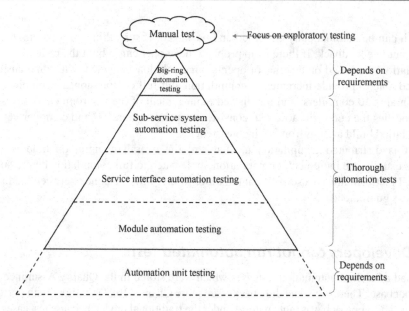

FIGURE 16.9   Distribution of automation tests.

3. Interface automation test: It refers to the testcases of the interface called by outside. At this layer, the team runs comprehensive tests on it and strives to achieve full automation coverage. Since the entire subsystem basically has the characteristics of "high cohesion and low coupling", and the boundaries of each sub-module are basically clear, automation tests at this layer will have the most cost-effective ROI.

4. Subsystem-level automation test: It refers to the overall end-to-end automation test of Service S (covering seven modules) undertaken by the team. This level of automation test covers the main process of the service to ensure the correct operation of each service module. Due to the high cost and the more complex environment, the team will determine whether to implement testcases based on specific circumstances before coding.

5. Big Ring automation test: It refers to the interactive test between Service S and external system. Due to the highest cost, the most complex environment, and more dependent factors, the testcases in this regard are of the minimum quantity. Before coding the requirements, the team will determine whether to implement this part of testcases according to the specific situation.

Before starting implementation of a new requirement, developers and testers will discuss together to determine which verification points need to be covered by automation testcases or by manual at the levels of module automation and Big Ring automation.

All the above-mentioned automation testcases are written by testers. Each developer can execute a command on his own development machine to call a script provided by a tester. It would trigger all the automation tests he wants to run. As early mentioned, before submitting a code change every time, developers should run all automation testcases. When the code changes are submitted to the team branch, all automation testcases will be automatically triggered.

16.4.3.5 What to do in case of insufficient environments for automation tests?

In the traditional mode, the test environment required for tests running is not demanding, that is, one project has one environment, multiple projects share the same environment, or manual testing and automation test share the same environment.

However, when the iterative mode is employed, all developers need to run automation testcases, and each code submission will trigger automation testcases. Therefore, developers become the first users of automation tests, and there are far more developers than testers. Therefore, we need more test environments.

The old automation tests needed to deploy seven modules to three physical machines. But we cannot apply for so many machines to run multiple sets of automation testcases. After discussion, the reason for why three physical machines were needed: some config information in the seven modules is hard-coded, and such code cannot be modified after build. If the seven modules are installed on the same machine, they will be unworkable due to the conflict of config information (such as the log input directory, the port number used for communication between modules). We modified such code to make it configurable, so that seven modules can be deployed on the same machine.

After the change, three independent environments can be deployed on the same physical machine. In this way, developers have enough environments to run automation tests.

16.4.3.6 How to determine a requirement can be tested?

When a developer thinks that he has implemented a requirement, he must satisfy two conditions:

1. A tester has done the quick check on the developer's machine.
2. All automation tests have passed (including new and revised automation testcases for this requirement).

After these two conditions are met, the developer will notify the tester of the build number, and the tester can download the package corresponding to the build number from the CI system for more comprehensive testing.

16.4.3.7 How to do performance and stress testing?

We need to feedback the quality of the software under development as early as possible. How can we forget performance and stress tests? But these tests are to be done in the later stage of testing, usually with a long preparation time, a long running time, and a high cost. In order to achieve a balance between rapid feedback and high-cost comprehensive quality monitoring, our response strategy is to use some key use cases, select specific indicator dimensions, run these tests in a short time, and then judge performance and stress risks based on performance and stress curves.

Due to limited time, we cannot develop an automation program for curve comparison in a short period of time. Only thresholds are given for a few indicators, and the alarm will sound if there is an abnormality. In addition, manual comparison will be performed regularly. In this way, in each iteration there will be one or two performance and stress tests of on a latest build. If a performance hazard is found, the team will immediately designate a person to analyze and determine a schedule to fix if it was a bug.

Although it cannot fully reflect the real situation, it can reduce some quality risks in the middle of the development.

16.4.3.7.1 Job requirements for developers

In the traditional mode, the development cycle is long, and each developer is solely responsible for one or two modules. After everyone has completed the code, they will conduct debugging together. In the iterative mode, all requirements are included into the iterative plan and prioritized according to the PARID factors. This requires each developer to touch as many different modules as possible so as not to delay the project progress.

For this project, all members' programming skills were not a crucial blocker. So, we think that everyone should be able to modify several modules.

16.4.3.7.2 Self-improvement of the team

In each iteration the team will hold a retrospective meeting, which is different from the project meeting. This meeting is to discuss the challenges in team members' collaboration and daily work to figure out countermeasures, so that the team can continuously improve their work happily and efficiently. It is the most important Agile practice. Even if other practices cannot be implemented, the team should stick to this kind of meeting.

Many teams that use the agile development method may ignore iteration review, or turn it into a venue of complaining, which is detrimental to the team. The former will reduce the long-term combat effectiveness of the team, the latter is even worse since it may destroy the cohesion of the team.

After the retrospective meeting, the team spends a little time making a simple plan, that is, based on the completed tasks of the previous iteration and the time estimation of the next iteration, developers will evaluate and select the high-priority requirements from the product backlog as the goals of the next iteration. There is not any specific showcase for completed features, because everyone can see the real project progress every day.

16.4.3.7.3 Initial estimate can't be modified

Any new requirement can be estimated, but for an estimated one, there is no need to estimate it again. The reasons are fairly simple:

- For new requirement: Since it is not estimated before, a quick discussion and estimation should be done to include it into the project development plan.
- For estimated requirement: The estimate of a single requirement is inherently inaccurate. The previous estimation is based on a total of requirements as a whole, so the estimated result will not deviate greatly due to the estimation deviation of individual requirements. While the project is progressing, some developers may reflect that the actual workload of a certain requirement is much greater than its estimated value, therefore asking for re-estimation.

16.4.3.7.4 Secret in the burn-up chart

Figure 16.10 is a burn-up chart of the first stage of the project, its horizontal axis is time (in weeks) and its vertical axis is workload (points); from top to bottom, the three curves represent the scope of requirements, the number of developed requirements, and the number of accepted requirements. This burn-up chart reflects the problems that many teams encounter when they've just adopted this iterative method.

1. Code coupling and old development habits will affect iterative delivery. In the first three weeks of this project, no requirements were delivered. Why was that? At the project planning stage, the requirements had been split into smaller ones, and developers had confirmed that these requirements could be implemented independently in business level. However, several high-priority requirements crossed and interfered with each other at code level. When implementing the first requirement, developers found that they needed to modify the code blocks involved in the second requirement. The software modularization was not good enough as they had imagined when they were drawing up the plan.

    In addition, this was also related to their old habits, that is to say, when developers were working on a requirement, they couldn't help but want to implement the next requirement together, they thought they would save time and effort since they would not have to go back to change the code again. Despite of varied reasons, the results were the same, that is, no requirements implemented and about to be tested until three iterations came to an end.

2. The estimates of developers are always optimistic. Attentive readers may find that there is a problem with the project plan: the original plan was to complete the project in nine iterations, but the project was still going on by the 14th week on the burn-up chart. Why was that?

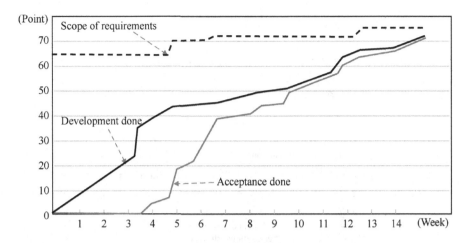

FIGURE 16.10   Project burn-up chart for Agile 101 mode.

On the one hand, when estimating the requirement at the beginning, developers had no idea of the challenges brought by iterative delivery to high-quality code. In the past, developers had been accustomed to fully implementing all features (basically run through), and fixing problems and bugs afterwards. In other words, code was not good enough to deliver, as long as developers themselves were confident in their code, then their "development work" was over. Therefore, the estimation was also based on such low-quality standards.

On the other hand, non-project matters took more time than the team imaged. The team estimated that the non-project matters would take up 40% of their time. But the fact was not like this. We noticed this phenomenon in the first iteration, because everyone would talk about these matters at the daily stand-up. Therefore, in the second iteration, team members would record the time spending on these non-project matters. At that time, we were not concerned about what these emergencies were, but about how much time they took up team members every day.

The recording was very simple. Next to the story wall (whiteboard), there was another whiteboard on which we drew a table for each person to leave their records about the time they spent on non-project matters, such as communication with other teams, and online monitoring and bug fixing. The filling rules were also very simple: Each person fills it after daily stand-up; the recording accuracy only needs to be around half an hour; fill in the actual working hours (less than eight hours a day is allowed); overtime is also included (work more than eight hours a day), as listed in Table 16.1 (the information in the table is only indicative, not real data).

The team made two agreements: the specific data that they've collected will not be disclosed to the public. Individual performance assessment is free being affected and everyone's effort is recognized.

Based on statistics, we found that in the column "project time", the investment of senior staff was only 30%, and that of junior staff was 50%. This was one-third less than our estimate (60%). Therefore, in the fourth week of the project, we knew that one of the assumptions in the initial plan (personnel time investment) was untenable. We communicated with the relevant stakeholders of the team to let them know the specific conditions and risks of the project, and made corresponding adjustments to the delivery expectations.

TABLE 16.1   Team members' distribution time sheet.

TIME	ZHANG XX	LI XX	YANG XX	WU XX
YY/DD	2/3/1	2/2/1	1/1/2	1/1/2
YY/DD	0.5/2/3	1/2/3	2/2/1	3/2/0.5
YY/DD	2/2/1	2/2/1	2/2/1	2/2/1

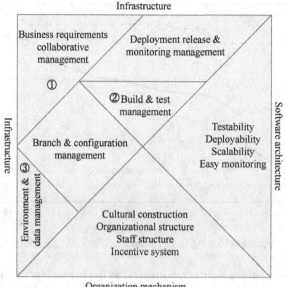

FIGURE 16.11 Improved layout of Continuous Delivery tangram.

In the end, the development iteration of this project was completed at the end of June, went through an overall acceptance test in mid-July, and was about to be launched. This was also the starting point of the second stage of the journey – the journey of continuous through DevOps transformation.

16.4.4 Summary of Stage One

We mainly took changes in three aspects (see Figure 16.11) which are business requirements collaborative management, build and test management, and environment and data management. Among them, the transformation of requirements collaboration management and build & test management is the biggest, which basically subverts the entire workflow, which also changes the work face of the team. The main improvement includes the following seven points:

1. Reasonable business goal.
2. Transparency in project plan, progress, and result.
3. The workflow with high-quality delivery defined and observed by themselves.
4. Periodic proactive retrospective instead of incident-driven review.
5. Organize workflow by fine-grained requirements.
6. Six-step check-in dance for CI.
7. Appropriate use of automation testing to improve quality feedback efficiency.

16.5 STAGE 2: DevOps TRANSFORMATION

The team was very confident about the quality of the first stage. Moreover, by the exercises of the first stage, the team had become familiar with the entire process and infrastructure, and they were more open to "small-batch" approach. Therefore, the goal of our second stage was put on the agenda which was that the release interval should be every three weeks, and every two weeks in two months later.

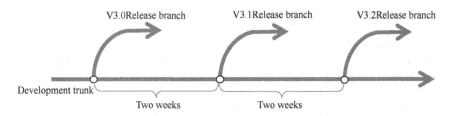

FIGURE 16.12 Intercity Express Mode and Trunk-based Development & Branch-based Release.

Instead of using the concept of "project", the team planed its work in an "Intercity Express" high-frequency release mode, and changed its branching mode to "Trunk-based Development and Branch-based Release" (see Chapter 8), as shown in Figure 16.12.

16.5.1 "Conflict" with Ops Engineers

Based on several months of teamwork, I thought that the team was fully capable of releasing once every two weeks. However, after discussion, team members decided not to be too aggressive, and adjusted the release once every three weeks. This was much faster than the original release every three months.

When explaining the upcoming "Intercity Express" mode to the customer who was using Service S, team members were greatly affirmed, expressing that this mode could solve the old problem of "delayed requirements response", and agreeing to schedule and manage requirements in the following way:

1. Publish the time point and the corresponding product backlog on wiki.
2. Customers present requirements at any time.
3. In the product backlog, there are not only customer requirements but also self-optimization requirements.
4. A brief meeting on requirements is held every Monday to negotiate and adjust the requirements schedule.

However, at hearing this agreement, the Ops engineer was against it immediately for two reasons:

1. Ops are worried about the inability to product quality, which may lead to production accidents. While the testing phase is so long before this change, we have to deal with problems one after another. Now that three weeks is so short for testing, bugs can hardly be avoided.
2. We will be exhausted. Every time a product was released, it needed to be deployed on more than 300 machines. In the traditional way, it was deployed only once every three months; now it is deployed once every three weeks. The workload has increased by four times!

Concerns about product quality are inevitable and normal. Their past experience has told them so. To dispel their worry, we must work two aspects:

One is to let the Ops engineer see how the team's daily workflow increases transparency.

1. The team explained in detail the current workflow to the Ops engineer, and let him learn about the current quality assurance means.
2. Invite the Ops engineer to join team activities and discussions. For example, he is invited to attend the standup at least twice a week and the retrospective meeting.
3. Involve the Ops engineer into the team's IM channel so that he is aware of the progress at any time. By doing so, the team is no longer a black box to Ops engineer.

The other is to optimize the deployment process of Service S to minimize the workload. The team promised to adjust the system architecture to make operation work easier and more efficient in response to the rapid release. In the old days, the team was "too busy" to care about what the Ops engineer had put forward. However, once the release frequency is increased, things that were not problems in the past have now become problems that need to be solved. If a deployment operation is to be performed on more than 300 machines every two or three weeks, it is necessary to structure and improve the operation of rapid release, so as to turn many manual operations into automated ones.

16.5.2 Specific Obstacles in High-Frequency Deployment and Release

The whole team (including the Ops) sat down together to discuss existing and possible problems. Regarding deployment and operation, there are some specific issues to be resolved. For example:

- Due to historical reasons, the deployment patterns of the modules are inconsistent. Although the log of each module supports flexible configuration now, the real config items in production have not changed yet, which is not conducive to unified operation and maintenance.
- When two modules are deployed, the Ops need to manually create a temporary directory to back up the data generated by the program.
- The deployment location of the same module on each machine is different.
- The ports configured on each machine for the same module is also inconsistent.
- Some ports and file paths in two modules are "hard-coded".
- The deployment document is written by the developer every time, and the Ops completes the actual execution operation according to the document.
- The deployment process in production is different from both test environment and staging environment.

These practices or phenomena violate many principles of infrastructure management. In addition, there are some remaining issues that need to be resolved. For example:

- The test code is still in the independent test codebase.
- The debugging environment for developers is still shared, there is only one set, which interferes with each other.
- At present, test coverage is still insufficient, and QAs still have a lot of manual regression.

16.5.3 Overall Solution Design

Now managers and team have accepted the iterative mode, and become eager for further improvement. In order to achieve high-frequency release as soon as possible, we designed a total solution to the series of problems mentioned above by transforming the R&D infrastructure from all dimensions.

16.5.3.1 Adjustment of automation testing strategy

By practicing automation testing before, the team has basically mastered the principles of testcase writing. We decided to extend the test scope to both ends, as shown in Figure 16.13. We trained all developers on unit test framework.

It is a waste to test the same logic with testcases at multiple levels, including waste in writing and maintenance costs, as well as waste in data preparation and running time. How can we reduce or eliminate

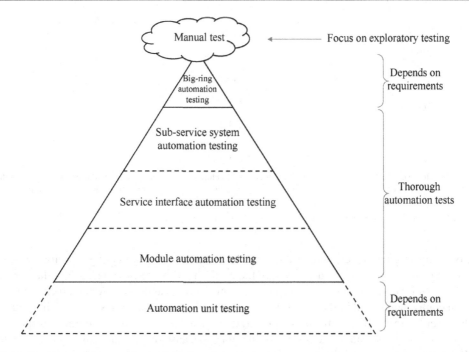

FIGURE 16.13 Expand the coverage of automation test layers.

such waste? The only way is to further strengthen the communication between developers and testers, that is, testers can do white box (gray box) analysis and gray box (black box) testing. The testers have coding skills and also accept the idea of "the cases hard to verify at high-level can be done by low-level tests".

16.5.3.2 Convenience of running tests

Since the rapid release has a higher requirement for testing, this "higher" is not only reflected in writing tests, but also in the execution efficiency and feedback speed of the tests.

In order to improve the efficiency of test to let developers not bother each other, we have established a tests cluster. By the optimization of SCM (Software Configuration Management), every two people have a dedicated environment for running tests at any time. Meanwhile, we have established multiple sets of test environments to ensure that multiple functional testcases can be executed in parallel at the same time so as to shorten the feedback time. Of course, all this is done in one click, thanks to the perfection of two clusters-the compilation cluster and the test cluster. For the design of these two clusters, see Chapter 7.

16.5.3.3 Put test code with product code

We also put the test code as close as the code under tests. So, both developers and testers can easily fetch the code with tests to run. For the entire team, the communication cost and the management cost of test-cases are greatly reduced.

16.5.3.4 SCM optimization

1. Codebase structure. Create a new product directory (xxService), and port all the code origi-nally scattered in different directories to it. At the same time, a directory of tests is added to it to store the integration tests for modules, as shown in Figure 16.14a.

   In addition, under each module, some directories have been added, as shown in Figure 16.14b. Careful readers will find that under the test directory, a unit test directory has been added to

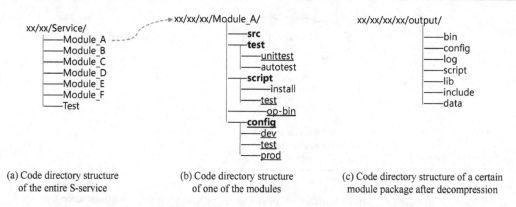

(a) Code directory structure of the entire S-service

(b) Code directory structure of one of the modules

(c) Code directory structure of a certain module package after decompression

FIGURE 16.14   Unified standardization of configuration management.

store unit tests for corresponding modules. In addition, there is a config directory under the root of the module, which is used to store the config items of the module, such as the ports that need to be used, the directory of swap files during runtime, and so on. Among them, the key of each config item stored in the dev, test, and prod subdirectories are the same, but the values are different, corresponding to the development, testing, and production environment, respectively. Some scripts are stored in the script subdirectory. Because the product has some config items that need to be dynamically generated by certain rules, the rules and scripts are also placed in the codebase for version control.

By this way, binary packages can be separated from config items, so that the deployment of different environments can be done by "same package and different config files". At the same time, there is an 'install' directory under the script directory at the same level as "src". The module installation and deployment script are in this directory. The installation and deployment scripts of each module of the S service are all written by the Ops engineer. In addition, the same deployment script is used for different environments with different deployment config.

2. Standardization and version management for output. We have used the CI previously, and all the tested packages to be tested are built by CI server, rather than by the testers manually. Therefore, we use the build number (build_id) as a unique identifier to identify different versions of the packages.

According to the Ops requirements, we standardized the installers, such as the location and directory structure after installation, as shown in Figure 16.14c. The output of each module package is uniform. Also, there is a text file in the installation package which holds the URL of the corresponding code repository in this build, and the revision id of the source code. Once you want to find the source code by the binary package, you could unzip the package to get it from this text file.

16.5.3.5 Package management

There are more than 300 machines online, and there are also many test machines (including development, manual testing, and automation testing). We hope that the software stack on these machines is controlled and can be prepared with one-click (that is, all the preparations for any of the above environments can be completed by running one command). In this way, no matter what the role is, you can easily accomplish such things without the help of others, making it no longer "something that only experts can do". As shown in Figure 16.15, after the package automatically built by the CI server is placed in the temporary artifact repository (see Chapter 11). Once it passed a series of automation tests and manual verification by testers, it would be marked as "meets quality standards". Only those (version 9 in Figure 16.5) marked as "meets quality standards" in temporary artifact repository can be further deployed by moving

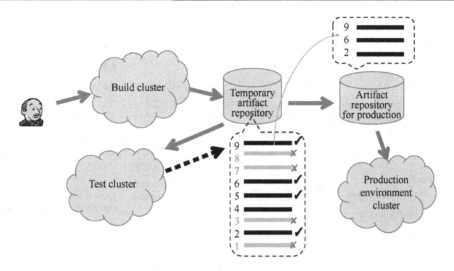

FIGURE 16.15 Package management.

to production artifacts repository, and then the Ops engineer click the deployment button to check and deploy it automatically.

16.5.3.6 Optimization of deployment and monitoring

We plan to deploy production environments by automation. So, who knows the production and Ops requirements best? Of course, it is the Ops engineer. So, the Ops engineer volunteered to write deployment scripts.

How can we ensure the correctness of these script logic before production deployment? If these same scripts can be used in all test environments for developers and testers, it could be more confident to use on production. Since there are many deployment operations for this version with the same deployment scripts, when the production is officially deployed, these scripts have been tested many times, thus greatly reducing the probability of errors. It has truly achieved "one-click deployment to different types of environments in the same way".

In addition, we setup some scripts to monitor the deployment process and some key indicators after deployment. Therefore, there is not too much to manually check as before.

After that, the manual workload of the Ops engineer dropped by nine-tenth, and the cycle time for deployment to 300 units is also reduced to one-fourth of the original.

16.5.4 Team Changes in the DevOps Stage

After the second transformation, the team's workflow is shown in Figure 16.16. The main changes include the following four aspects:

1. A complete cross-functional team, the Ops engineer actively participate in the team's daily work and iterative meetings.
2. All content is version controlled, including source code, test code, configuration item information of various environments, related packaging and installation scripts, and data.
3. All environments are standardized and managed, and the test environment can be prepared with one click.
4. Establish a complete deployment pipeline, which can be released to multiple deployment environments with one click.

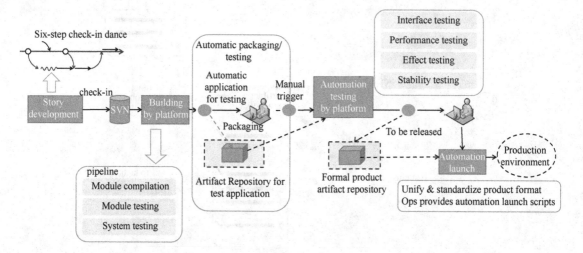

FIGURE 16.16   Team collaboration process under Continuous Delivery mode.

16.6 SUMMARY

This case is a typical case of achieving Continuous Delivery for a small team without changing the original company's organizational structure. It is a successful case of the transformation into the DevOps mode leading by R&D side. Of course, the team has a good CI foundation, naturally transitioned to the Continuous Delivery model, and formed the DevOps culture within the team.

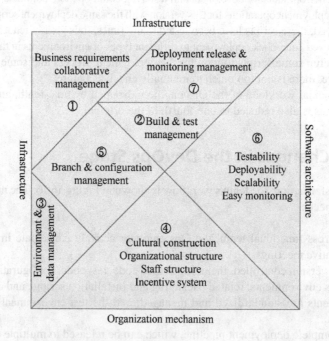

FIGURE 16.17   All-round transition to Continuous Delivery.

This case involves all the pieces in the Continuous Delivery tangram. Although some pieces have large changes, some sections have small changes, as shown in Figure 16.17.

All improvements had similar steps, that is, "clear goals – diagnose problems – solutions –continuous operation (optimization)". In these steps, as long as you have a mindset of continuous learning, master the thinking principles of Continuous Delivery value loops, and understand the working principles and good practices in various fields of Continuous Delivery tangram, you can find the current best solution through continuous experimentation.

Appendix A: Three Evolutions of Software Engineering

In the 1950s, computers could only be used by professionals. Today, smartphones and portable devices are everywhere, and even pre-school children can operate tablet computers flexibly. Sixty years ago, files could not be easily exchanged between two computers, the exchange between two different applications on the same computer was also difficult; but today, the network provides lossless file transfer between two platforms and applications. Thirty years ago, multiple applications could not easily share the same data; but today is the era of "big data", in business, economic, and other areas, decisions will increasingly be made on basis of data and analysis, rather than based on experience and intuition. The development of software engineering models, concepts, and methods is shown in Figure A.1.

The various methods in Figure A.1 are based on the time when they were found in official reports, books, or software products. "DSDM" refers to Dynamic System Development Method; "XP" refers to eXtreme Programming; "FDD" refers to Feature-Driven Development; "RUP" refers to Rational Unified Process; "ASD" refers to Adaptive Software Development; "SAFe" refers to Scaled Agile Framework; "LeSS" refers to Large-Scale Scrum; and "Nexus" refers to scaled Scrum framework.

Software technology is rapidly applied to all walks of life, which has also kept the number of software-related practitioners in a state of shortage, especially those with experience. In order to cope with the problems of strong software demand, shortage of employees, and rapid expansion of the software itself, a variety of engineering methods have also emerged in the software engineering discipline, as shown in Figure A.1.

A.1 BIRTH OF SOFTWARE ENGINEERING

When the computer was born, the threshold for using a computer was very high (including the cost of using it, as well as the requirements for computer knowledge and skills), and only a few people could master it. This kind of expensive equipment is naturally used for scientific calculations, and the process from requirements generation to software delivery usually did not require many people to complete.

A.1.1 Software Crisis

With the widespread application of small and medium-sized integrated circuits, minicomputers flourished in the 1950s and 1960s, and many high-level programming languages continued to appear. Demand for software applications is growing rapidly. However, the software delivery capacity in the industry is low, leading to the following serious problems:

1. Software development costs and progress are out of control. Expenses overruns and schedule delays frequently occur. Sometimes, we have to take some expedient measures in order to catch up with the schedule or reduce the cost, which often seriously damages the quality of the software product.

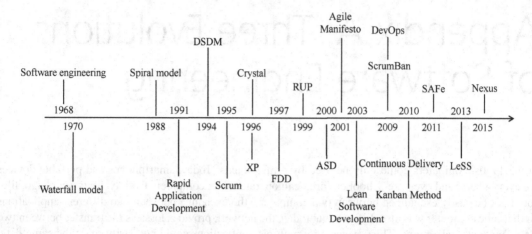

FIGURE A.1 Evolution of software engineering models, concepts, and methods.

2. The reliability of software is poor. Although it consumes a lot of manpower and material resources, the correctness of the system is becoming more and more difficult to guarantee, the error rate has greatly increased, and the losses caused by software errors are very alarming.

3. The software is difficult to maintain. The lack of corresponding documentation makes it difficult to locate and correct program errors. Sometimes, existing errors are corrected, and new errors are introduced. Maintenance takes up a lot of manpower, material resources and financial resources.

In 1968, computer scientists from all over the world held an international conference in Garmisch, a beautiful town in southern Germany, to discuss the aforementioned crisis in the software industry for the first time. At the conference, F. L. Bauer proposed the notion of "software crisis" to describe the problems at the time. Everyone hopes to learn from the best practices in the field of construction engineering (because the field has applied the method to complete large-scale engineering projects on time, with quality, and within budget in a systematic, rigorous and measurable manner), and find out the way of multi-person collaborative development of high-quality large-scale software. At the conference, the term "software engineering" was formally put forward. A new engineering discipline – Software Engineering – was born for researching and overcoming software crises.

A.1.2 Waterfall Model

In the late 1960s, as the project manager, Dr. Winston W. Royce led the completion of the development of a large software project, and in 1970 published an article entitled *Managing the Development of Large Software Systems* in IEEE. In this article, he described a software development model, as shown in Figure A.2. The entire software development process is similar to a waterfall, which is the famous "waterfall model".

The software demander expects to use the waterfall model only once to get the final version of the software. This model quickly became a de facto standard for the entire software industry and was widely used. It appeared in a way of "valuing process and document", with clear organizational structure and responsibilities of software team, as shown in Figure A.3.

However, everyone did not pay attention to the reminder Royce gave in the article: "I believe in this concept, but the implementation described above is risky and invites failure....... Do it twice. If a computer program is being developed for the first time, arrange matters so that the version finally delivered to the customer for operational deployment is actually the second version insofar as critical design/

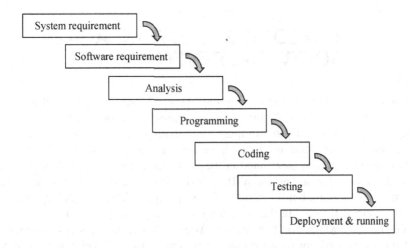

FIGURE A.2   Waterfall software development model.

operations are concerned. Note that this is simply the entire process done in miniature, to a time scale that is relatively small with respect to the overall effort". In other words, the purpose of using the waterfall model for the first time in a software project was not to develop an entire software system that could be directly delivery, but to quickly understand the real software requirements and solution feasibility.

The waterfall model must meet three prerequisites for a one-time success, that is, during the software development process, the following three preconditions can be guaranteed:

1. The business problem that is being solved is known and fixed.
2. The software solution to the business problem is predictable and fixed.
3. The technical solution for building the software is clear and there are no unknowns.

Unfortunately, these three preconditions are all uncertain. Since there are relatively limited general-purpose talents who have not only mastered computer software development but also have a good understanding of business domain knowledge, it is a difficult problem to be able to describe business problems clearly and translate them into software requirements documents. In addition, there are relatively few well-trained and experienced software developers, and it is impossible to ensure the establishment of the second and third premises. The "Chaos Report" of Standish Group proves that the one-time success rate of software projects is much lower than that of construction projects.

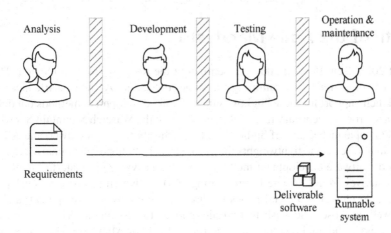

FIGURE A.3   Teamwork with clear boundaries.

A.2 SECOND EVOLUTION: AGILE SOFTWARE DEVELOPMENT

With the development of hardware and the popularization of microcomputers, the demand for software has exploded after the 1980s. At this time, a large-scale software often consists of millions of lines of code, with hundreds of programmers participating. How to construct and maintain such large-scale software efficiently and reliably has become a new problem. Brooks, the author of the book *The Myth of Human Moon*, mentioned in the book that the OS/360 system developed by IBM has more than 4,000 modules, about one million instructions, invested 5,000 man-years, and cost hundreds of millions of dollars, but the result was still postponed. deliver. A large number of errors (more than 2,000) were still found in the system after delivery. Many software engineers have questioned "waterfall model", which has become a software engineering model that emphasizes documentation and processes, and put forward many different software development methods based on their own experience. These methods are all based on the basic idea of "Iterative & Incremental Development" (IID), which can be traced back to the 1950s. As mentioned in the book *Iterative and Incremental Development: A Brief History* published by Craig Larman and Victor R. Basili, Gerald M. Weinberg once said that as early as 1957, under the leadership of Bernie Dimsdale of IBM's Service Bureau Corporation, we were using incremental development methods. He was a colleague of von Neumann, perhaps learned from him, or natural occurring.

A.2.1 Prelude-Spiral Model

In 1988, Barry Boehm officially came up with the "Spiral Model". It combines the waterfall model and the rapid prototyping model, and emphasizes the risk analysis that other models ignore. It takes into account the iterative characteristics of rapid prototyping and the systematic and strict monitoring of the waterfall model. The biggest feature of the spiral model is the introduction of risk analysis that other models do not have, so that the software has the opportunity to stop when major risks cannot be ruled out to reduce losses. At the same time, building a prototype at each iteration is a way to reduce the risk of the spiral model. The spiral model is more suitable for large and expensive system-level software applications.

In the 1990s, a variety of lightweight software development methods have emerged (see Figure A.4). The term "lightweight" is compared with "waterfall model" (also called "traditional model").

A.2.2 Birth of the Agile Manifesto

In the spring of 2000, Kent Beck organized a seminar at the Rograve Hotel in Oregon. The participants included supporters of Extreme Programming and some "outsiders". At the Rogriffe meeting, the participants expressed their support for these "lightweight" software development methods but did not make any official statements. From 11 February to 13 February 2001, at the Wasatch Mountain Snowbird Ski Resort in Utah, USA, 17 people including Jeff Sutherland, Ken Schwaber, Martin Folwer, and Alistair Cockburn got together again to discuss the lightweights they proposed. They hope to summarize the commonalities and differences of software development methods from the heavyweight waterfall method. Participants included representatives from Extreme Programming, Scrum, dynamic software development methods, adaptive software development, crystal series methods, feature-driven development, and practical programming, as well as those who wish to find alternatives to "document-driven, heavy-duty software development process". The final result of the meeting is the Agile Manifesto, as shown in Figure A.5. It also summarizes the 12 principles of Agile software development. They include:

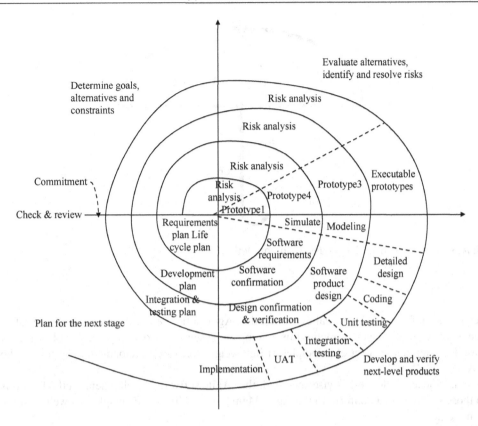

FIGURE A.4 Spiral model for software development.

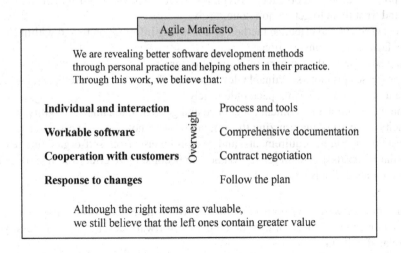

FIGURE A.5 Agile Manifesto.

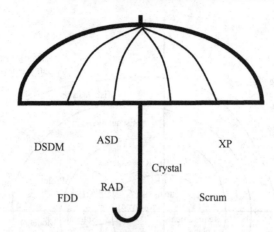

FIGURE A.6   Umbrella-shaped agile development method.

It can be seen from this historical event that the "Agile software development" we often refer to has not been a software development method or a complete system methodology since its birth. It satisfies the above declaration and A set of principles of lightweight software development methods, as shown in Figure A.6.

For convenience, unless otherwise specified, the "Agile software development method" in this book refer to those methods that conform to the Agile Manifesto and Twelve Principles, as well as subsequent evolution methods.

1. Our highest priority is to satisfy the customer through early and Continuous Delivery of valuable software.
2. Welcome changing requirements, even late in development. Agile processes harness change for the customer's competitive advantage.
3. Deliver working software frequently, from a couple of weeks to a couple of months, with a preference to the shorter timescale.
4. Business people and developers must work together daily throughout the project.
5. Build projects around motivated individuals. Give them the environment and support they need, and trust them to get the job done.
6. The most efficient and effective method of conveying information to and within a development team is face-to-face conversation.
7. Working software is the primary measure of progress.
8. Agile processes promote sustainable development. The sponsors, developers, and users should be able to maintain a constant pace indefinitely.
9. Continuous attention to technical excellence and good design enhances agility.
10. Simplicity – the art of maximizing the amount of work not done – is essential.
11. The best architectures, requirements, and designs emerge from self-organizing teams.
12. At regular intervals, the team reflects on how to become more effective, then tunes and adjusts its behavior accordingly.

In this cluster of software development methods, two methods are worth noting. They are Scrum and eXtreming Programming. Because in the contemporary software development process, you can always see practices related to them.

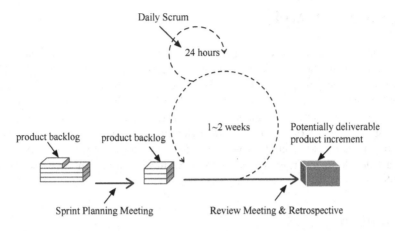

FIGURE A.7   Scrum framework.

A.2.2.1 Scrum framework

In 1993, Jeff Sutherland and Ken Schwaber formally proposed Scrum, which is an Agile framework, not a complete process for developing a complete product. The framework is shown in Figure A.7. Its core idea first appeared in an article entitled *The New New Product Development* in the Harvard Business Review in 1986. The article pointed out that Nonaka and Takeuchi used the analogy of rugby to emphasize the importance of the team and how to perform better in the development of new complex projects. Their research results provide some basic concepts for Scrum, including small self-organizing teams, common goals, autonomy, and cross-functionality. The values of Scrum include commitment, courage, focus, openness, and respect.

A.2.2.2 Extreme programming

In 1999, the first edition of the book *Extreme Programming Explained* written by Kent Back was published, marking the official appearance of this method. Its values include communication, simplicity, feedback, and courage. It is known for software engineering practices such as continuous integration, test-driven development, pair programming, and simple design. Originally, it contains a total of 12 major practices, namely:

1. The Planning Game
2. Small Releases
3. Metaphor
4. Simple Design
5. Testing
6. Refactoring
7. Pair Programming
8. Collective Ownership
9. Continuous Integration
10. 40-hour week
11. On-site Customer
12. Coding Standard.

Among these 12 practices, technology-related engineering practices accounted for half. It can be seen from them that there is a high degree of attention to software code quality.

A.2.3 Evolution of Agile

Under the umbrella of "Agile", the community has continued to prosper and develop. These methods absorb and learn from each other and continue to evolve themselves. For example, since 2008, Scrum has incorporated several engineering practices in the eXtreme Programming into Scrum practices.

The Scrum framework has received widespread attention because of its simple and easy-to-understand management framework and a good commercial ecosystem (authorization and certification system). At the same time, in order to adapt to different organizational environments and software characteristics in different fields, many software development methodology researchers have developed different software development frameworks based on Scrum, the representative ones being Scrumban, SAFe, and LeSS.

A.2.3.1 Scrumban

In 2009, Corey Ladas proposed the Scrumban software management framework in the book *Scrumban*. It is an agile management methodology, a hybrid framework of Scrum and Kanban methods. It was originally a way to transition from Scrum to Kanban methods. The current suggestion is that when the team uses Scrum as their working method of choice, they can use the Kanban method as a transparent method of team work to observe, understand, and continuously improve their working methods.

A.2.3.2 SAFe

In 2011, Dean Leffingwell officially released the first version of the SAFe on his website. It aims to promote coordination, cooperation, and delivery between multiple agile teams, and try to solve some of the difficulties and problems encountered after expanding the agile working method to the entire enterprise. It is often regarded as Scrum at the enterprise level. Its main knowledge system inputs are Agile software development, lean product development, and system thinking.

Currently, the latest version is called "SAFe 4.0 for Lean Software and Systems Engineering", and its main changes include:

- Support software development and system development (software and hardware development).
- The new value flow level includes new roles, activities and artifacts for building large-scale systems.
- The overall blueprint is more concise and lightweight, and available to be expanded to meet the needs of large-scale value flow and complex system development.
- Enterprise-level Kanban system to manage the flow of work at all levels.
- New project portfolio and portfolio-level elements, including the association with corporate strategy, and coordination of value flow within the portfolio.
- Enterprise value flow is managed by the interconnected Kanban system, which helps visualize work and limit WIP, and accelerate the continuous flow of value delivery.
- Updated SAFe requirements model to better reflect additional backlog items.
- Updated built-in quality practices (previously knowns as "code quality") to adapt to software and system development.
- A new layer – Foundation Layer – is provided.

A.2.3.3 LeSS

In 2013, LeSS was formally established. It is a software product development framework that extends Scrum by extending rules and guidelines without losing the original purpose of Scrum. Its creators Craig Larman and Bas Vodde said that since 2005, they have summarized and put forward this framework based on their own experience to help some companies carry out agile transformation, especially in the telecommunications and financial industries.

The goal of LeSS is to "reduce" the complexity of the organization, that is, eliminate unnecessary complex organizational solutions and solve them in a simpler way, such as fewer roles, fewer management levels, and fewer organizations structure.

This framework is divided into two levels: the first level is designed for up to eight teams; the second level is called "Less Huge", which introduces some additional expansion elements for hundreds of developers.

A.2.3.4 Nexus

Nexus is a framework for developing and maintaining large-scale software development projects. It was released in 2015. The Nexus Guide already contains more than 40 practices, which can be used with the Scrum Guide to extend Scrum and support the integration of multiple software development teams. Nexus Ken Schwaber is the author of the Nexus Guide and one of the original authors and signatories of the Agile Manifesto. He is also the creator of the Scrum Alliance. In a public interview, he pointed out:

> The Nexus guide is a companion to the Scrum guide. It is available to everyone for free and online. It describes a clip-on extension framework that can promote the work integration of 3–9 Scrum teams (usually) for software development.
> Nexus differs from other extension methods (such as SAFe, DAD, and LeSS) in scope, method, and cost. Nexus is just to solve the problem of expanding software development, involving the product to-do list, budget, goals, and scope.
> Nexus is also just a framework… Nexus cannot guarantee success, but it is not a formula. To succeed, people need to implement software development in the most appropriate way. Individuals and interactions are more important than processes and tools.

A.2.4 Summary of Agile Software Development

Most of the Agile software development methods are derived from past actual combat experience, a set of patterns are found from practice, and then summarized and refined. Agile software development methods emphasize cross-functional small team collaboration and close cooperation with customers to deliver usable software as soon as possible. Each method defines some of its own implementation practices or working methods at the implementation level, and more emphasis is placed on teamwork, iterative development, and continuous learning, rather than a one-shot approach in the field of construction engineering management borrowed by "heavy methodology", as shown in Figure A.8.

Of course, some Agile software development methods have disappeared from people's sight (such as crystal method, DSDM, and Rapid Application Development (RAD), which is Rapid Application Development) or are gradually disappearing (such as extreme programming). But its core values have been widely accepted, and there has been a fusion of multiple methods.

A.2.5 Software development inspired by TPS

Taiichi Ohno applied the Ford system as the basis of the Toyota Production System (TPS), and defined the system as "absolute elimination of waste". This system and the ideas it contains have won widespread credibility for the Japanese manufacturing industry, especially Toyota. In any working method based on lean manufacturing and TPS, lean has begun to be used as a covering

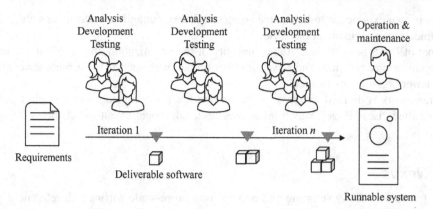

FIGURE A.8   Underlined agility of short-term iteration and cross-departmental collaboration.

term, including lean construction and lean laboratory. Lean principles are being successfully applied to product design, engineering, supply chain management, and other fields, and are now being applied to software development.

The historical roots of Lean thinking can be traced back to the early 20th century. At that time, Ford Motor Company introduced "Just In Time" (JIT). As described in the book "Lean Thinking" by Womack and Jones in 1996, all the basic principles of lean manufacturing are in Ford's *My Life and Work* (1922), *Today and Tomorrow* (1926), and *Moving Forward* (1930) appeared.

A.2.5.1 Lean software development method

In 2003, the Mary Poppendieck and Tom Poppendieck published the book *Lean Software Development: An Agile Toolkit* by studying the TPS and lean thinking and applying lean thinking to the software development process, marking the official birth of the "lean software development".

Strictly speaking, the lean software development method does not include a clear development process and practice. Instead, it is guided by lean thinking and puts forward seven principles in software development. They are: (1) eliminate waste; (2) build quality; (3) create knowledge; (4) delay decision-making; (5) fast delivery; (6) respect for people; and (7) overall optimization.

At the same time, It speaks about Wastes in software development present in seven ways. These are as follows: (1) software defects; (2) unused features; (3) avoiding task transfer; (4) delayed feedback; (5) semi-finished products (including unrealized requirements, untested code, unrepaired errors); (6) task switching; and (7) unnecessary processes (such as no output reviews, writing documents that no one can read, original simple but complicated processes).

A.2.5.2 Kanban

David Anderson was influenced by the author of the book *The Principles of Product Development Flow: Second Generation Lean Product Development*, applied the ideas in information technology (IT) projects, combined with the Kanban practice and constraint theory in TPS, and proposed the "Kanban Method". In 2010, David Anderson published the book *Kanban*. He also described the evolution of this method in the book, from the use of Theory of Constraints in a Microsoft project in 2004 to the official use of the Kanban method in a Corbis project in 2006.

The Kanban method treats the software development process as a value stream, and believes that pull management can produce better results. Strictly speaking, it is not a software development method, but a methodology that guides enterprise change in a gradual manner. The wonderful thing is that it seamlessly integrates with the original development process of the enterprise and restricts the number of products in progress. A series of simple and feasible techniques to find and relieve the pressure and bottlenecks in the software development process and improve production efficiency.

A.3 THIRD EVOLUTION: DevOps

The various agile development methods mentioned above are mostly based on customized software projects for enterprise applications. Due to enterprise-related audits or other reasons, the release of this type of software is characterized by a relatively long-time release interval. Therefore, the functional differences between the two releases will be huge. In this case, software delivery often encounters the "last mile" problem. In other words, there is a high degree of uncertainty and uncontrollability in the process from the completion of function development to the official launch (i.e., integration testing and online deployment phase). It often appears that "the project progress begins to stagnate after 90%. It will take a long time and a lot of cost (even more than the first 90% of the working hours and construction period) to complete the last 10%".

Although Agile software development method emphasizes the iterative mode, it is mostly applied in the early stage of the entire software development project. The focus of its problem solving is more on the software product requirements analysis and code development phase. Therefore, we often see a phenomenon, that is, software companies claiming to have been agile transformation still maintain the original development rhythm. In fact, they are in waterfall model with only iteration management and few agile engineering practices in the development phase. In the final integration test stage, they still often face the "last mile" problem, resulting in an uncontrollable project progress. When the software is released, it is still facing the big challenge, and even requires all staff to be on standby at any time. Nevertheless, they are often messed up by various unexpected problems.

A.3.1 The Rise of the DevOps Movement

With the vigorous development of the Internet, the rise of entrepreneurship, and web startup companies, this has also brought new challenges to software development. The challenge of enterprise-customed software lies in the fact that the software deliverer does not understand the business domain. However, for customer-facing web services, the difficulty is that their services offer a large number of users to use, and there is no clear demand representative, so it is more difficult to capture user needs. Therefore, the rapid deployment of software and the collection of real feedback from users have become a major demand for Web products.

In 2008, the Agile wave that advocated "short iterations, fast feedback" as the main form of software delivery has not been fully absorbed by the industry, and the third evolution "DevOps" has quietly arrived. Patrick Debois proposed "Agile Operations and Infrastructure" at the Agile 2008 Conference held in Toronto. It was John Allspaw's 2009 Velocity Talk with Paul Hammond, "10+ Deploys Per Day: Dev and Ops Cooperation", helped start the DevOps movement, and shed a new light on the entire software industry. In this speech, John and Paul first put the deployment and release link to a more important position in the entire software life cycle.

At the end of 2009, Patrick Debois held a seminar called "DevOpsDays" and coined the term "DevOps". It is formed by splicing some letters of the two English words "development" and "operation". It is not difficult to imagine that it was originally a campaign to promote the close collaboration between "development" and "operation", and it was precisely the hope that the deployment bottleneck caused by departmental barriers would be eliminated.

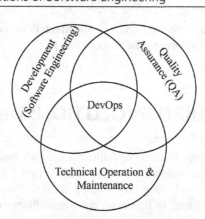

FIGURE A.9   DevOps collaboration within the IT department.

In 2011, it was defined on Wikipedia as "DevOps is a series of processes, methods, and systems used to strengthen communication, collaboration, and integration between the development, operation, and quality assurance. It emphasizes the relationship between development and operation. Interdependence to achieve timely release of software and achieve corporate business goals", as shown in Figure A.9. In 2017, it was defined on Wikipedia as: "DevOps is a software engineering culture and practice that aims to unify software development and software operation and maintenance".

Just like "Agile" ten years ago, "DevOps" is now a very popular buzzword, and its definition is constantly changing, and there is no completely unified definition. It seems that everyone has a different understanding of it. To a set of methods and practices, to the culture and management of the entire software organization. This also fully illustrates the expectations that people place on it, and the ideas and concepts it advocates are also rapidly heating up.

A.3.2 Birth of Continuous Delivery

The book *Continuous Delivery* (2010) describes in detail how to shorten the time from code submission to production deployment with lower cost and risk, and become a real starting point for DevOps. The publication of this book also marked the birth of the term "Continuous Delivery". The book described a series of principles and many practices to achieve the above goals. One of the authors of the book, Jez Humble, was leading the product GoCD (named "Cruise" from 2008 to 2010) that we mentioned many times in early chapters. Many practices in the book came from the team.

In the book "Continuous Delivery", Continuous Delivery is described as "a capability that can safely and quickly deliver all types of changes to customers or deployment them in production in a sustainable manner, regardless of whether these changes are new features, configuration changes, fixed defects, or new experiments. Its goal is to quickly release software value with high quality and low risk". The core model is the deployment pipeline, and the core principles include:

- Built quality in.
- Work in small batches.
- Automate everything as much as possible, which means that computers perform repetitive tasks, people solve real problems.
- Relentlessly pursue continuous improvement.
- Everyone is responsible.

Jez Humble believes that the three pillars of Continuous Delivery are configuration management, continuous integration, and continuous testing.

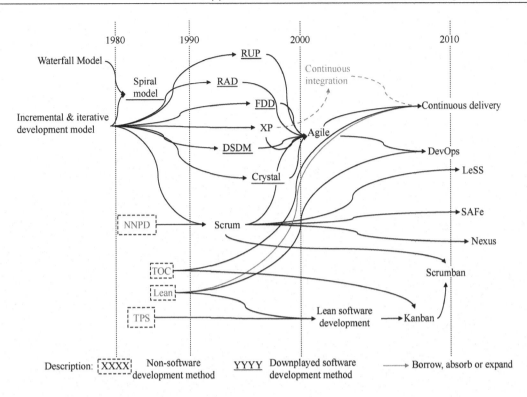

FIGURE A.10   Chronicle of software engineering methods.

A.4 SUMMARY

So many concepts and methodologies are inextricably linked (as shown in Figure A.10), and they have witnessed the evolution of the software engineering field. The wheels of the times are still moving forward, and we look forward to the revolution in the field of software engineering brought about by artificial intelligence.

Appendix B: User Story Estimation by Relative Size

This method is my own creation based on my personal work experience and was published on InfoQ China – a well-known tech news website in mainland China – in 2011. Since this method was used in the two cases in Chapters 15 and 16, I think it's better to have it explained in detail in a separate appendix. Readers that are interested in it may search the original text on https://www.infoq.cn/.

B.1 HOW TO DO ESTIMATION BASED ON THE RELATIVE SIZE OF USER STORIES?

The estimation of software projects has always been a difficult problem. They cannot be estimated with a budgeting quick checkbook like in civil engineering. However, in order to maximize resource utilization, coordinate the work of multiple teams, and make contractual commitments to customers, it is necessary to estimate the workload of software projects. This appendix mainly discusses user story estimation in projects under agile development. The prerequisite of this estimation is requirements decomposition, that is, a requirement document has been split into multiple fine-grained requirement descriptions (see Chapter 6 for details about requirements decomposition).

There are multiple methods for workload estimation, and they can be roughly divided into absolute estimation and relative estimation. In this book, "absolute estimation" refers to the estimation in absolute time such as hours or days; the "relative estimation" is an estimate made by comparing the size of user stories, and the estimated result has no time unit (the difference between them is beyond the scope of this book). Relative estimation method can be implemented in different ways.

B.1.1 The Difficulty of Relative Estimation

The following phenomena often appear in the process of relative estimation, especially for those teams that use relative estimation for the first time:

- When determining the benchmark unit "1" for relative estimation, it is difficult for developers to find a suitable user story as a benchmark.
- Developers pay more attention to discussing the points of a single user story, rather than the relative size compared with other user stories.
- The total time spent in estimating is relatively long (usually an entire afternoon or even a day).

B.1.2 Goals

When a software project has a large workload, make a release plan before starting software development.

B.1.3 Prerequisite

The project scale is large (1 to 3 months period), and a user story list has been obtained according to the principle of splitting user stories (INVEST principle). The list has been discussed by each role and the content of each user story has been discussed. Reach a consensus. At the same time, the team can basically guarantee:

- Each card will have two or more developers to understand and have the ability to implement.
- Developers basically understand the work content of each user story.

B.1.4 Assumptions

The assumptions of this method are as follows:

- The objective workload of user stories will not be different due to the differences of specific developers (although the time spent may be different for different personnel).
- Due to the large number of existing user stories, the estimated objective scale will not deviate too much.
- Developers are the bottleneck, so only the developers estimate their development scale, excluding the test effort of user stories.

B.2 STEPS

Let's introduce the steps of the relative ordering.

B.2.1 Step 1: Prepare

- A large conference room.
- All developers are present.
- Write all user stories to be estimated on the card (write each requirement in one sentence and make sure everyone can understand it).
- Sellotape (attach cards to a whiteboard or wall).

B.2.2 Step 2: Preliminary Sorting

1. Distribute the cards equally to every developer participating in the project according to the number.
2. Let a developer take a card A and paste it on the wall (any one is fine).
3. Let each developer compare the card in his hand with all the cards that have been pasted on the wall, then paste it at the corresponding position on the wall according to the following rules.
   - If the card in hand is equivalent to the workload of wall A, stick it under the card A.
   - If the card in hand has more workload than card A, stick it on the right side of A.
   - If the card in hand has less workload than card A, stick it on the left side of A.
   - If C's workload is between A and B, put it between A and B.

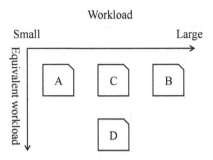

FIGURE B.1   Cards are arranged according to workload.

By analogy, as shown in Figure B.1, the workload relationship of the four cards is A<C≈D<B.

In this step, all developers can post cards at the same time, as long as they do not interfere with each other to disturb their judgments.

After all the cards are pasted, developers start to double-check whether the position of each card is appropriate, as shown in Figure B.2.

B.2.3 Step 3: Discuss Differences

If you have objections to the location of a card, please discuss it with others. This may be caused by the inconsistent understanding about the content. So, it needs to be discussed in depth until it is agreed in which column it should be. It's important to note that don't try to discuss precise workloads, just be relatively accurate.

B.2.4 Step 4: Determine the Workload Scale

Use the numbers 1, 2, 3, 5, 8, 13 or 1, 2, 4, 8, 16 to place them on the columns that have a contrast relationship in order. In Figure B.3, each story card listed under 2 should have about twice the workload of that listed under 1.

B.2.5 Step 5: Merge Adjustment

For those columns that do not yet have digital identifications on the column headers (columns "K", "C", and "L" in Figure B.3), developers should put them in the appropriate position according to the closeness

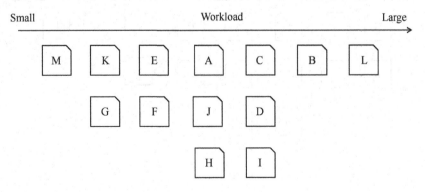

FIGURE B.2   Results of preliminary sorting.

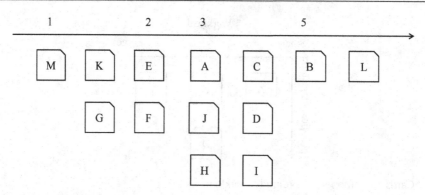

FIGURE B.3 Determine the workload scale.

of their workload. In the adjacent column, it may move to the left or right, as shown in Figure B.4. At this time, team members will also discuss the workload of some cards and possibly adjust their positions.

Finally, multiply the number of user stories in each column by the number at the head of the column, and then add the numbers to get the overall scale of the project.

B.2.6 Precautions for Use

There are several precautions for the operation process of using the relative ordering method.

1. Before estimating, you should ensure that the size difference between all user stories is not too large. For example, one user story takes about an hour to complete, while another user story takes two weeks. At this point, it shows that the granularity of user stories is unreasonable and does not conform to the S principle in the INVEST principle (see Chapter 6). Small requirements may need to be merged with other requirements, and large requirements must be split.
2. If the number of cards in each column does not conform to the normal distribution, but there are more cards at both ends and fewer cards in the middle, which also indicates that there may be a problem with the granularity of the user story and need to be reviewed.
3. If there are several related stories of the same size in a column (such as supporting UnionPay card, supporting MasterCard, supporting VISA card), and finishing a card first, the workload of the other two will be reduced, you can put any one of them in the current column, the other

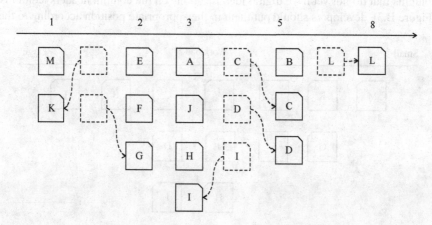

FIGURE B.4 Ranking of adjusted workload.

two can be considered in a smaller column. However, the specific situation still needs to be analyzed in detail, because the actual situation is more complicated. However, this type of analysis and verification work is indispensable in the overall review process.

4. When discussing and moving cards, you should compare them more with other cards instead of directly saying which number column a card belongs to. Because the numbers at the head of the column are relative values, and there is no comparison with other cards, these numbers are meaningless.

5. During the discussion, some problems or information that have not been discovered before will be captured. At this time, it must be recorded in time. For unclear questions, business personnel should give a conclusion on the spot.

6. When this method is used for the first time in a team that did not try relative estimation before, it is best to be guided by someone with some experience to properly verify the scheduled order.

B.3 SUMMARY

This method of scale estimation and planning is indeed not easy to accept by those teams that are new to Agile software development, especially in those teams that are accustomed to using WBS decomposition methods for planning. They will struggle with "1" How long does it represent? Is it a day for senior developers or a day for novices?

As mentioned earlier, this sorting method has its preconditions and assumptions. When splitting user stories, full discussion is needed to let team members understand each user story. This is the prerequisite for the success of this method (see Chapter 6 for the principles and methods of requirement splitting). Of course, adequate communication is also a prerequisite for the success of Agile software development methods.

Index

Printed in the United States
by Baker & Taylor Publisher Services